Emerging Trends in Computational Intelligence and Disruptive Technologies

(Volume 5)

Embracing the Digital Horizon: Pioneering Commerce and Management Strategies for a Transformative Future

Edited by

D. Arul Pon Daniel

Department of Computer Science & Applications
Loyola College of Arts and Science, Mettala
Rasipuram Taluk 637408, Tamil Nadu
India

T. Rajasanthosh Kumar

Department of Mechanical Engineering
Oriental Institute of Science and Technology
Bhopal 462022, Madhya Pradesh
India

&

Satya Prakash Yadav
School of Computer Science Engineering and Technology (SCSET)
Bennett University
Greater Noida 201310, Uttar Pradesh
India

Emerging Trends in Computational Intelligence and Disruptive Technologies

(Volume 5)

Embracing the Digital Horizon: Pioneering Commerce and Management Strategies for a Transformative Future

Editors: D. Arul Pon Daniel, T. Rajasanthosh Kumar and Satya Prakash Yadav

ISBN (Online): 978-981-5324-96-9

ISBN (Print): 978-981-5324-97-6

ISBN (Paperback): 978-981-5324-98-3

First published in 2026.

Bentham Science Publishers Pte. Ltd.
No. 9 Raffles Place
Office No. 26-01
Singapore 048619
Singapore
Email: subscriptions@benthamscience.net

CONTENTS

Preface

This book explores a wide range of current subjects and advanced technologies that are shaping the world we live in today. The book explores various contemporary subjects and advanced technologies that are shaping today's world. Each topic represents a crucial area of research or practice with substantial implications for enhancing efficiency, effectiveness, and progress in their respective professions. This book aims to provide insights into significant commercial and technological breakthroughs, ranging from innovative pricing tactics and enhanced HR management to the application of AI in construction and advanced E-commerce monitoring systems. The underlying topic discusses supply chain networks, sentiment analysis, LED cubes, media pipelines, and the profound influence of AI, deep learning, and quantum machine learning. This comprehensive book explores practical applications in various industries, including healthcare, finance, manufacturing, and education. It analyses technologies such as 3D printing, digitalized HR, and generative AI. The manuscript addresses pressing issues such as disease detection, environmental challenges, and digital addiction, providing a comprehensive perspective on the modern world for both professionals and academics.

This preface encompasses a diverse range of current subjects, all of which contribute to the larger story of technological advancement and its influence on society. As these sectors evolve, they offer the potential to address complex problems and unlock new opportunities for innovation and growth.

This inclusive guide explores and discusses practical applications in healthcare, finance, manufacturing, and education. It also provides insights to professionals and researchers by exploring important advances in healthcare, finance, manufacturing, and education. The outcome is a comprehensive examination of the impact of these technologies and strategies on various firms and their ability to address critical issues.

D. Arul Pon Daniel
Department of Computer Science & Applications
Loyola College of Arts and Science, Mettala
Rasipuram Taluk 637408, Tamil Nadu
India

T. Rajasanthosh Kumar
Department of Mechanical Engineering
Oriental Institute of Science and Technology
Bhopal 462022, Madhya Pradesh
India

&

Satya Prakash Yadav
School of Computer Science Engineering
and Technology (SCSET)
Bennett University
Greater Noida 201310, Uttar Pradesh
India

List of Contributors

A. Swathi Department of IT, QIS College of Engineering & Technology, Ongole 523272, Andhra Pradesh, India

A.K. Sharma Department of CSE, School of Engineering & Technology, Career Point University, Kota 325003, Rajasthan, India

A.L. Parvathi Department of CSE, QIS College of Engineering & Technology, Ongole 523272, Andhra Pradesh, India

Abhishek Jain Department of Computer Science and Engineering, Uttaranchal University, Dehradun 248007, Uttarakhand, India

Aditya Sai Srinivas Department of AIML, Jayaprakash Narayan College of Engineering, Mahabubnagar 509001, Telangana, India

Aiman Peerzade Department of Management Studies, Rizvi College of Arts, Science and Commerce, Mumbai 400050, Maharashtra, India

Ajit Prasad Mahato Department of commerce, NERIM Commerce College, Guwahati 781022, Assam, India

Alekh Alekh Department of Computer Applications, SRM Institute of Science and Technology, NCR Campus, Modinagar, Ghaziabad 201204, Uttar Pradesh, India

Anil Kumar N. Department of Electronics and Communication Engineering, School of Engineering, Mohan Babu University, Tirupati 517102, Andhra Pradesh, India

Anzar Ahmad Department of Electronics & Communication, Graphic Era Deemed to be University, Dehradun 248002, Uttarakhand, India

Arpit Jain Department of Computer Science Engineering, KLEF (Deemed to be University), Guntur 522302, Andhra Pradesh, India

Arpitha Devangavi Department of Artificial Intelligence and Machine Learning, BNM Institute of Technology, Bangalore 560070, Karnataka, India

Ayain John Department of IoT, School of Computer Science and Engineering, Vellore Institute of Technology, Vellore 632014, Tamil Nadu, India

B. Amrutha Raju Department of CSE (Data Science), CMR College of Engineering & Technology, Hyderabad 501401, Telangana, India

B. Chaitanya Department of IT, Andhra Loyola Institute of Engineering and Technology, Vijayawada 520008, Andhra Pradesh, India

B. Lakshmi Department of Computer Applications, Velagapudi RamaKrishna Siddhartha Engineering College, Siddhartha Academy of Higher Education (Deemed to be University), Vijayawada 520007, Andhra Pradesh, India

B. Sravani Department of IT, Andhra Loyola Institute of Engineering and Technology, Vijayawada 520008, Andhra Pradesh, India

Basi Reddy A. Department of Computer Science and Engineering, School of Computing, Mohan Babu University, Tirupati 517102, Andhra Pradesh, India

Bilal Asghar School of Business, Al Fayha College, Al Jubail 31961, Saudi Arabia, AL Jubail Kingdom of Saudi Arabia, Saudi Arabia

Boppudi Lingarao	Department of S&H, QIS College of Engineering & Technology, Ongole 523272, Andhra Pradesh, India
Bramah Hazela	Amity School of Engineering & Technology, Amity University Lucknow Campus, Lucknow 226028, Uttar Pradesh, India
C Barna A Naidu	School of Business & Management, Christ University, Pune 412112, Maharashtra, India
Ch. Silpa	Department of IT, QIS College of Engineering & Technology, Ongole 523272, Andhra Pradesh, India
D. Divya Kalpana	Department of CSE, QIS College of Engineering & Technology, Ongole 523272, Andhra Pradesh, India
D. Joseph Reethika	Department of IT, Andhra Loyola Institute of Engineering and Technology, Vijayawada 520008, Andhra Pradesh, India
D. Karunamma	Department of CSE, QIS College of Engineering and Technology, Ongole 523272, Andhra Pradesh, India
D.K. Girija	Department of Computer Science, Government First Grade College, Tumkur 572102, Karnataka, India
DA. V.L. Narayana Rao	Department of ECE, QIS College of Engineering & Technology, Ongole 523272, Andhra Pradesh, India
David Asirvatham	Faculty of Innovation and Technology, Taylor's University, Subang Jaya 47500, Selangor, Malaysia
Deepika Verma	Department of Computer Science and Engineering, School of Engg. & Technology, Om Sterling Global University, Hisar 125001, Haryana, India
Dolores L Montesines	College of Computer Studies, University of Perpetual Help Systems DALTA, City of Bacoor 4102, Cavite, Philippines
E. Pradeepthi	Department of IT, Andhra Loyola Institute of Engineering and Technology, Vijayawada 520008, Andhra Pradesh, India
Edmar G. Tan	College of Information and Communication Technology, Taguig City University, Taguig City 1630, Philippines
Edward N. Cruz	College of Computer Studies, University of Perpetual Help Systems DALTA Molino, City of Bacoor 4102, Cavite, Philippines
G. Durvasi	Department of IT, Andhra Loyola Institute of Engineering and Technology, Vijayawada 520008, Andhra Pradesh, India
G. Maheswara Rao	Department of ECE, QIS College of Engineering & Technology, Ongole 523272, Andhra Pradesh, India
G. N. R. Prasad	Department of MCA, Chaitanya Bharati Institute of Technology, Hyderabad 500075, Telangana, India
G. Silpa	Department of Management, School of Commerce and Management, Mohan Babu University, Tirupati 517102, Andhra Pradesh, India
G. Siva Prasad	Department of CSE, QIS College of Engineering & Technology, Ongole 523272, Andhra Pradesh, India
G. Uday Kishore	Department of CSE (Data Science), CMR College of Engineering & Technology, Hyderabad 501401, Telangana, India

G. Venkata Lakshmi	Department of CSE (Data Science), CMR College of Engineering & Technology, Hyderabad 501401, Telangana, India
Gaikar Vilas B.	Department of Economics, Smt. CHM. College, University of Mumbai, Mumbai 421003, Maharashtra, India
Gundraju Yamuna	School of Commerce and Management, Mohan Babu University, Tirupati 517102, Andhra Pradesh, India
H Swaraj Bharath	Department of CSE (Data Science), CMR College of Engineering & Technology, Hyderabad 501401, Telangana, India
J Siva Ram Prasad	Department of Mathematics, Velagapudi RamaKrishna Siddhartha Engineering College, Siddhartha Academy of Higher Education (Deemed to be University), Vijayawada 520007, Andhra Pradesh, India
J. Divyashree	Department of Chemistry, PES PU College, Bangalore 560050, Karnataka, India
J. Rameshkumar	Department of Electronics and Communication Engineering, K.S.R. College of Engineering, Namakkal 637215, Tamil Nadu, India
J. Ramya	Department of Business Administration, SRM Institute of Science and Technology (Vadapalani Campus), Chennai 600026, Tamil Nadu, India
Jafar Ali Ibrahim Syed Masood	Department of IoT, School of Computer Science and Engineering, Vellore Institute of Technology, Vellore 632014, Tamil Nadu, India
Janardhana Rao	Department of MBA, QIS College of Engineering & Technology, Ongole 523272, Andhra Pradesh, India
Jayashree Jayashree	Department of Artificial Intelligence and Machine Learning, BNM Institute of Technology, Bangalore 560070, Karnataka, India
K Parish Venkata Kumar	Department of Computer Applications, Velagapudi RamaKrishna Siddhartha Engineering College, Siddhartha Academy of Higher Education (Deemed to be University), Vijayawada 520007, Andhra Pradesh, India
K. Ankababu	Department of MCA, QIS College of Engineering & Technology, Ongole 523272, Andhra Pradesh, India
K. Bhanu Sree	Department of IT, Andhra Loyola Institute of Engineering and Technology, Vijayawada 520008, Andhra Pradesh, India
K. Gideon	Department of IT, Andhra Loyola Institute of Engineering and Technology, Vijayawada 520008, Andhra Pradesh, India
K. Guru Surya Bharat Kumar	Department of Computer Applications, Velagapudi RamaKrishna Siddhartha Engineering College, Siddhartha Academy of Higher Education (Deemed to be University), Vijayawada 520007, Andhra Pradesh, India
K. Jaya Krishna	Department of MCA, QIS College of Engineering & Technology, Ongole 523272, Andhra Pradesh, India
K. Maharajan	Department of Computer Science and Engineering, School of Computing, Kalasalingam Academy of Research and Education, Krishnankoil 626126, Tamil Nadu, India
K. Sahithi	Department of IT, Andhra Loyola Institute of Engineering and Technology, Vijayawada 520008, Andhra Pradesh, India

K. Sai Charitha Department of IT, Andhra Loyola Institute of Engineering and Technology, Vijayawada 520008, Andhra Pradesh, India

K. Satya Sai Bhuvanesh Department of IT, Andhra Loyola Institute of Engineering and Technology, Vijayawada 520008, Andhra Pradesh, India

K. Sreenath Department of IT, QIS College of Engineering & Technology, Ongole 523272, Andhra Pradesh, India

K. Sunila Jasmin Department of IT, Andhra Loyola Institute of Engineering and Technology, Vijayawada 520008, Andhra Pradesh, India

K. Vivek Department of CSE, QIS College of Engineering and Technology, Ongole 523272, Andhra Pradesh, India

K. Om Sathvik Department of IT, Andhra Loyola Institute of Engineering and Technology, Vijayawada 520008, Andhra Pradesh, India

Kamal Dhanda Department of Computer Science and Engineering, School of Engg. & Technology, Om Sterling Global University, Hisar 125001, Haryana, India

Kodavalla Jeevan Krishna Department of IT, Andhra Loyola Institute of Engineering and Technology, Vijayawada 520008, Andhra Pradesh, India

Kuchikar Aneeque Ahmed Department of IT, Andhra Loyola Institute of Engineering and Technology, Vijayawada 520008, Andhra Pradesh, India

Kuheli Mondal Department of ECE, QIS College of Engineering & Technology, Ongole 523272, Andhra Pradesh, India

Kunal Gaurav Department of WPU School of Business, Dr. Vishwanath Karad MIT World Peace University, Pune 411038, Maharashtra, India

Kundan Kumar Department of Technical Services (Tata Project Limited), Department of Technical Services (Tata Project Limited), Hyderabad 500016, Telangana, India

KVJ. Bhargav Department of ECE, QIS College of Engineering & Technology, Ongole 523272, Andhra Pradesh, India

L. Bharathi Department of IT, QIS College of Engineering & Technology, Ongole 523272, Andhra Pradesh, India

L. Kanya Kumari Department of IT, Andhra Loyola Institute of Engineering and Technology, Vijayawada 520008, Andhra Pradesh, India

L.S. Geeta Department of Computer Science & Engineering, BNM Institute of Technology, Bangalore 560070, Karnataka, India

Lakshmi Prasad Department of IT, Andhra Loyola Institute of Engineering and Technology, Vijayawada 520008, Andhra Pradesh, India

Leena Jain Department of Computer Applications, Global Group of Institutes, Amritsar 143501, Punjab, India

M Nirmala Department of Computer Science and Engineering, New Horizon College of Engineering, Marathalli, Bangalore, 560103, India

M S Ramesha Department of Mathematics, Government College for Women, Mandya 571401, Karnataka, India

M. Bhavya	Department of CSE, QIS College of Engineering and Technology, Ongole 523272, Andhra Pradesh, India
M. Narendra	Department of MCA, QIS College of Engineering & Technology, Ongole 523272, Andhra Pradesh, India
M. Parameswar	Department of CSE (Data Science), CMR College of Engineering & Technology, Hyderabad 501401, Telangana, India
M. Rama	Department of IT, QIS College of Engineering & Technology, Ongole 523272, Andhra Pradesh, India
M. Rashmi	Faculty in Computer Science, Government First Grade College, Bangalore 560057, Karnataka, India
M. Ravichand	Department of English, V. R. Siddhartha Engineering College, Siddhartha Academy of Higher Education, Vijayawada 520007, Andhra Pradesh, India
M. Sandra Carmel Sophia	Department of English, KLEF (Deemed to be University), Guntur 522302, Andhra Pradesh, India
M. Sathya	Department of IT, Nadar Saraswathi College of Engineering and Technology, Theni 625 531, Tamil Nadu, India
Martha Tri Lestari	Department of Digital Public Relations, School of Communication & Business, Telkom University, Bandung 40257, West Java, Indonesia
Md. Imran	Department of IT, Andhra Loyola Institute of Engineering and Technology, Vijayawada 520008, Andhra Pradesh, India
Mohammad Shukur	Department of IT, Andhra Loyola Institute of Engineering and Technology, Vijayawada 520008, Andhra Pradesh, India
Monica Bhutani	Department of Electronics and Communication, Bharati Vidyapeeth's College of Engineering, New Delhi 110063, India
Monica Gupta	Department of ECE, Bharati Vidyapeeth's College of Engineering, New Delhi 110063, India
Mulugu Prudhvi Sriram	Department of IT, Andhra Loyola Institute of Engineering and Technology, Vijayawada 520008, Andhra Pradesh, India
Munish Kumar	Department of Computer Science and Engineering, KLEF (Deemed to be University), Guntur 522302, Andhra Pradesh, India
N Kirubasankar	Department of Business Studies, Sri Manakula Vingayagar Engineering College, Madagadipet 605107, Puducherry, India
N. Hariharan	Department of Mechanical Engineering, QIS College of Engineering & Technology, Ongole 523272, Andhra Pradesh, India
N. S. Kalyan Chakravarthy	Center for Data Science, School of Computer Science and Engineering, QIS College of Engineering & Technology, Ongole 523272, Andhra Pradesh, India
N. Srinu	Department of CSE, QIS College of Engineering & Technology, Ongole 523272, Andhra Pradesh, India
Neelam Raut	Department of WPU School of Business, Dr. Vishwanath Karad MIT World Peace University, Pune 411038, Maharashtra, India

P. Adi Lakshmi	Department of CSE, QIS College of Engineering & Technology, Ongole 523272, Andhra Pradesh, India
P. Bhaskar	Department of IT, QIS College of Engineering & Technology, Ongole 523272, Andhra Pradesh, India
P. Narendra	Department of EEE, QIS College of Engineering & Technology, Ongole 523272, Andhra Pradesh, India
P. Sudheer	Department of CSE (AI&ML), CVR College of Engineering, Ibrahimpatnam 501510, Telangana, India
P. William	Department of Information Technology, Sanjivani College of Engineering, Savitribai Phule Pune University, Pune 411007, Maharashtra, India
Pastor R Arguelles, JR	College of Computer Studies, University of Perpetual Help Systems Dalta, City of Bacoor 4102, Cavite, Philippines
Pramoda Patro	Department of Mathematics, KLEF (Deemed to be University), Hyderabad 500045, Telangana, India
R. Amutha	Department of ISE, AMC Engineering College, Bengaluru 560083, Karnataka, India
R. Deepika	Department of IT, Andhra Loyola Institute of Engineering and Technology, Vijayawada 520008, Andhra Pradesh, India
R. Senthamil Selvan	Department of Electronics and Communication Engineering, Annamacharya Institute of Technology and Sciences, Tirupati 517520, Andhra Pradesh, India
R. Shankar	Department of CSE, QIS College of Engineering and Technology, Ongole 523272, Andhra Pradesh, India
Raja Kumar Murugesan	School of Computer Science, Taylor's University, Subang Jaya 47500, Selangor, Malaysia
Rama Devi P.	Department of English, KLEF (Deemed to be University), Guntur 522302, Andhra Pradesh, India
Rashi Rashi	GL Bajaj Institute of Management and Research. PGDM Institute, GL Bajaj Institute of Management and Research. PGDM Institute, Greater Noida 201310, Uttar Pradesh, India
Renu Vij	University School of Business, Department of AIT Management, Chandigarh University, Mohali 140413, Punjab, India
Rodelio Dela Fuente	College of Information and Communication Technology, Taguig City University, Taguig City 1630, Philippines
Rupak Sharma	Department of Computer Applications, SRM Institute of Science and Technology, NCR Campus, Modinagar, Ghaziabad 201204, Uttar Pradesh, India
S Shivananda	Department of ISE, M S Ramaiah Institute of Technology, Bangalore 560054, Karnataka, India
S. Sivakumar	Department of Electrical and Electronics Engineering, Vel Tech Rangarajan Dr. Sagunthala R & D Institute of Science and Technology, Avadi, Chennai 600062, Tamil Nadu, India

Sanjay Sharma	Department of Applied Sciences and Humanities, Ajay Kumar Garg Engineering College, Ghaziabad 201009, Uttar Pradesh, India
Sankara Mahalingam M.	Department of Computer Science and Engineering, School of Computing, Kalasalingam Academy of Research and Education, Krishnankoil 626126, Tamil Nadu, India
Santosh Reddy P.	Department of Computer Science & Engineering, BNM Institute of Technology, Bangalore 560070, Karnataka, India
Saurav Das	Department of Mechanical Engineering, QIS College of Engineering & Technology, Ongole 523272, Andhra Pradesh, India
Shabnam Siddiqui	Department of Commerce and Management, Faculty of Management Studies (FMS-WISDOM), Banasthali Vidyapith, Tonk 304022, Rajasthan, India
Sk. Heena	Department of CSE, QIS College of Engineering & Technology, Ongole 523272, Andhra Pradesh, India
Sk. Sheema	Department of CSE, QIS College of Engineering & Technology, Ongole 523272, Andhra Pradesh, India
Somesubhra Panda	Department of Electrical Engineering, Global Institute of Science & Technology, Medinipur 721657, West Bengal, India
Suresh Babu Chandolu	Department of CSE (AI & ML), Dhanekula Institute of Engineering and Technology, Vijayawada 521139, Andhra Pradesh, India
T. Jayasri	Department of CSE, QIS College of Engineering & Technology, Ongole 523272, Andhra Pradesh, India
T. Nikitha	Department of IT, Andhra Loyola Institute of Engineering and Technology, Vijayawada 520008, Andhra Pradesh, India
T. Suresh	Department of Computer Applications, Velagapudi RamaKrishna Siddhartha Engineering College, Siddhartha Academy of Higher Education (Deemed to be University), Vijayawada 520007, Andhra Pradesh, India
Tanwir Alam	Department of Mechanical Engineering, Maulana Mukhtar Ahmad Nadvi Technical Campus, Malegaon 423203, Maharashtra, India
Thanapal Pandi	School of Computer Science and Engineering and Information Systems, Vellore Institute of Technology, Vellore 632007, Tamil Nadu, India
Thiruma Valavan A	Training Department, Indian Institute of Banking & Finance, Mumbai 400005, Maharashtra, India
U. Prasad	Department of CSE, QIS College of Engineering & Technology, Ongole 523272, Andhra Pradesh, India
U. Sireesha	Department of Computer Applications, Velagapudi RamaKrishna Siddhartha Engineering College, Siddhartha Academy of Higher Education (Deemed to be University), Vijayawada 520007, Andhra Pradesh, India
Ujwal Dhokania CA	Swayam Siddhi College of Mgmt and Research, Swayam Siddhi College of Mgmt and Research, University of Mumbai, Mumbai 421003, Maharashtra, India

Uppada Bhaskar Department of IT, Andhra Loyola Institute of Engineering and Technology, Vijayawada 520008, Andhra Pradesh, India

V. Gopinath Department of Mechanical Engineering, QIS College of Engineering & Technology, Ongole 523272, Andhra Pradesh, India

Vijay Kumar Rayabharapu Department of Civil Engineering, B V Raju Institute of Technology, Hyderabad 502313, Telangana, India

Vijay Singh Thakur Department of Computer Science and Engineering, Hindustan College of Science and Technology, Mathura 281122, Uttar Pradesh, India

Vikas Roshan Department of Applied Sciences and Humanities, Ajay Kumar Garg Engineering College, Ghaziabad 201009, Uttar Pradesh, India

Vishwa Priya V Department of Computer Science, Vels Institute of Science, Technology and Advanced Studies, Chennai 600117, Tamil Nadu, India

Y. Kalyana Krishna Department of ME, QIS College of Engineering & Technology, Ongole 523272, Andhra Pradesh, India

Y. Yaswanth Kalyan Department of IT, Andhra Loyola Institute of Engineering and Technology, Vijayawada 520008, Andhra Pradesh, India

Yogeesh N Department of Mathematics, Government First Grade College, Tumkur 572102, Karnataka, India

CHAPTER 1

Pricing Strategy of Electric Vehicle Charging Station Behaviour on Charging Station

Kundan Kumar[1,*], **S. Sivakumar**[2], **Neelam Raut**[3], **Kunal Gaurav**[3], **G. Silpa**[4] and **Somesubhra Panda**[5]

[1] *Department of Technical Services (Tata Project Limited), Hyderabad 500016, Telangana, India*

[2] *Department of Electrical and Electronics Engineering, Vel Tech Rangarajan Dr. Sagunthala R & D Institute of Science and Technology, Avadi, Chennai 600062, Tamil Nadu, India*

[3] *Department of WPU School of Business, Dr. Vishwanath Karad MIT World Peace University, Pune 411038, Maharashtra, India*

[4] *Department of Management, School of Commerce and Management, Mohan Babu University, Tirupati 517102, Andhra Pradesh, India*

[5] *Department of Electrical Engineering, Global Institute of Science & Technology, Medinipur 721657, West Bengal, India*

Abstract: Congestion at Electric Vehicle (EV) Charging Stations (CS) is influenced by the activity of EV owners and their choice of charging stations. With a set price plan, certain charging stations become overcrowded with EVs waiting to charge, while others have available electric plugs. This situation negatively impacts the income of Charging Station Operators (CSOs) and the welfare of EV users.

This study proposes a dynamic pricing method to move EVs from crowded to uncongested CSs by adjusting charging fees at various periods. The issue involves scenario-based stochastic optimization to maximize CSO revenue. Furthermore, an attraction functional method is created to measure EV owners' charging choices, taking into account the effective characteristics of CSs. A genuine method for CS sites and EV routes is created using Quantum Geographic Information System (QGIS) software to compute distances between EVs and CSs. The suggested framework is evaluated in three stages and compared to the fixed-price strategy. The proposed dynamic pricing method reduces congestion in CSs, increases EV charging by up to 49%, and boosts CSO income.

Keywords: Charging stations, CSO, Electric vehicle, Price strategy, QGIS.

[*] **Corresponding author Kundan Kumar:** Department of Technical Services (Tata Project Limited), Hyderabad 500016, Telangana, India; E-mail: getkundan.singh1987@gmail.com

D. Arul Pon Daniel, T. Rajasanthosh Kumar & Satya Prakash Yadav (Eds.)

INTRODUCTION

Recently, consumers and governments have been integrating transportation electrification to achieve lower fuel costs and cleaner energy. EVs are gaining popularity due to advancements in manufacturing technology [1]. EVs can activate in both Vehicle-to-Grid (V2G) and Grid-to-Vehicle (G2V) methods, making them versatile resources for power networks. Excessive EV adoption may disrupt power grid operations and pose significant issues for Distribution System Operators (DSOs) [2]. Managing EV charging at charging stations and on the grid is a challenging issue in power system research. Study a situation where certain CSs are clogged using EV customers waiting for charging, but others have enough charging outlets, depending on location, number, and time slot [3]. This negatively influences the grid load profile and reduces CSO earnings from selling power to EV customers. Electricity prices are the primary factor attracting EVs to uncongested CSs. Multiple dynamic charge strategies are suggested for this purpose [4].

The paper investigates charging price strategy rivalry among CSOs using game theory frameworks. The Stackelberg game approach is used to study price rivalry among CSs with renewable power sources [5]. This study examines the cost adaptability of EVs, the impact of distance among CSs and EVs, and the effect of charging outlets. However, it does not use a realistic EV route model and calculates distances using a simple geometric model, which lowers the precision of the outcomes [6]. The article proposes a non-cooperative Stackelberg game-based CSO strategic charge pricing mechanism. The Stackelberg optimal framework, which considers price competition among numerous CSOs and privacy-conservation requirements, is solved by a soft actor-critic-based multi-agent deep reinforcement learning system [7]. This study does not provide a closed-form explanation for vehicle attraction to distinct CSs. The authors examine competition for prices among CSs with limited-service capacity using a normal potential game framework [8]. They also suggest a decentralized algorithm for efficient cost collaboration to achieve balance and maximize societal welfare, but their cost competition method does not account for the impact of plugged capacity and charger types, which affect CS competition.This study mathematically models EV charging choices based on key criteria, including EV and CS location, charging outlet number, and CS average charging power. QGIS is used to accurately predict distances for the billing process and dynamic pricing scheme [9]. The authors propose a dynamic pricing strategy to eliminate residential-CS load overlaps by promoting PEV load shifting during nighttime peak hours. This approach aims to dynamically adjust pricing incentives to encourage PEVs to shift into less underutilized CSs. While steering EVs towards uncongested CSs improves the daily load profile, it may not optimize income [10]. The study examines electric car travel patterns to forecast their controlled capacity. The study examines the charging preferences of various customers and develops a pricing model that addresses microgrid dispatching and electric vehicle charging demand according to price signals. Analysing the EV charging issue from the viewpoint of EV types and status, rather than power system factors, might lead to inaccurate answers due to numerous variables and uncertainties [11].

This paper's main contributions are: Created an attraction function to describe EV charging choices based on CS charging price, distance, number of charging ports, and average charging power. Proposed dynamic pricing method formulating probabilistic optimization issues based on scenarios to guide EV owners from crowded to uncongested CSs, maximizing gross profit for all CSs. QGIS software and tools were used to create an accurate geographical representation of locations on CS, as well as to calculate the shortest paths from EVs to CSs for the charging process and the dynamic rating method [12].

The structure of the paper follows: the system methods are explained in section 2, including the attraction function depicting user selection of charging CS, EV charging method, and important assumptions. In section 3, the dynamic pricing method is introduced using a stochastic optimization issue based on the scenario. Next, section 4 discusses the performance assessment and simulation findings of the created pricing plan. Finally, section 5 presents key findings.

ELECTRIC VEHICLE CHARGING SYSTEMS

This section describes the modelling of the EV charging system in this study. EV charging CS selection assumptions are outlined. The CS coverage zone and attraction to EVs are specified. Modelling EV charging and CS distribution follows.

Presumptions

Studying various types of behavioural traits of people has shown that many EV charging habits were influenced. Generally, these aspects are socio-demographic and alternative. Behavioural studies use socio-demographic characteristics to represent passengers' shifts in charge preferences. Sociodemographic, activity participation, and travel behaviour are linked. Income, gender, age, education level, and driving experience considerably impact the travel habits of higher-income and lower-income individuals. The approach also takes into account individual variation and uses latent characteristics such as risk aversion & positive vehicle maintenance attitudes as unique influencing factors.

Case considerations include battery SOC, charging cost, anxiety about range, *etc.* Among the most crucial parameters, SOC indicates the vehicle's remaining energy. Electric vehicle tourists also worry about the price. Many consumers favour inexpensive prices; however, some electric vehicle drivers are time-conscious and will pay extra to visit uncongested CSs. In this study, an empirical charging behavior model that incorporates the real characteristics of CSs in EV charging decisions is recommended, as socio-demographic factors are qualitatively random variables.

Coverage Zone and CS Attraction Function

Understanding how EV drivers choose Charging Stations (CSs) is crucial to encourage the use of less busy ones and increase Charging Station Operator (CSO) revenue. Based on the law of sales prices magnitude, two stations bring in business in retail from any city or town near the breaking point in proportion to their populations and inversely to the square of their distances. Quantifying this notion is possible using the following function:

$$\frac{T_A}{T_B} = \frac{POP_A}{POP_B}\left(\frac{l_B}{l_A}\right) \tag{1}$$

Where T_A and T_B reflect commerce from the intermediary site drawn via centres A as well as B, respectively, POP_A as well as POP_B centre populations, I_A and I_B are centre distances.

Charging Station (CS) coverage zones are defined by boundary points. CS can attract more EVs with a larger coverage zone. Equation (2) shows that CS coverage relies on the energy price given the set number of outlets charging and the grade power charge for CSs. In Section IV, the CSs are assumed to include an online crowd meter, allowing EV owners to check plug availability at various CSs and make judgements. This modification modifies the suggested attraction function:

$$ATT_{ij}^{t} = \frac{S_i P_i N_{av,i}^{t}}{Pr_i^{t}(d_{ij}^{t})^2} \tag{2}$$

The number of CS_i charging connectors at time t is $N^{t}_{av,i}$.

Model of EV Charging

This section proposes a model for the EV charging process during the research period (Fig. **1**). The CSs' data, plug status, maximum allowed waiting time, and study time horizon are initialized in the model.

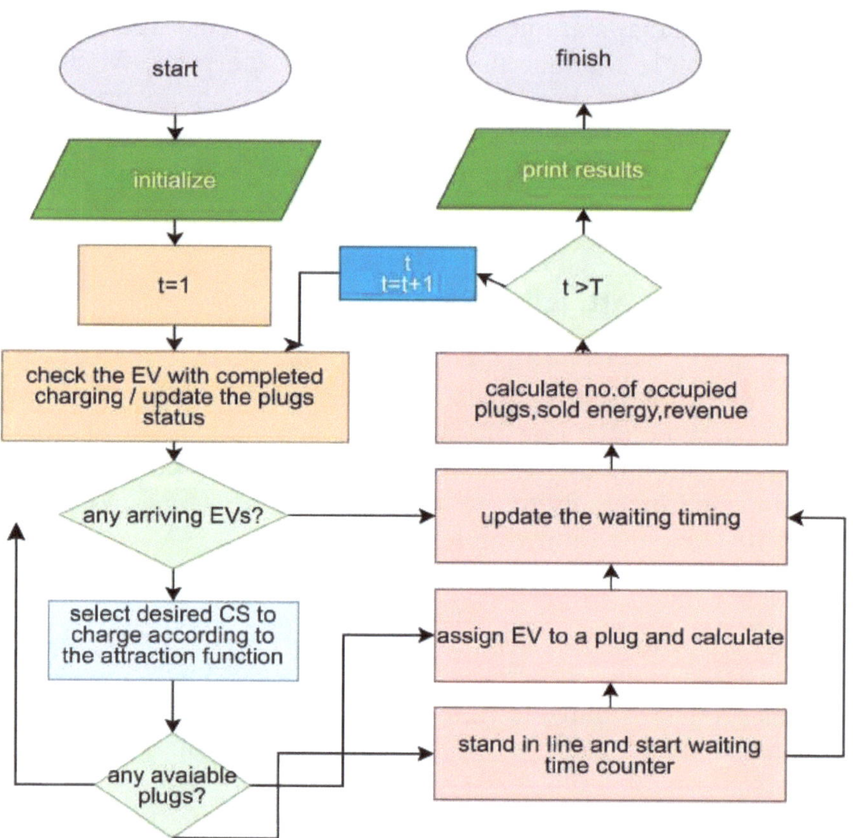

Fig. (1). EV charging process.

MAXIMIZING TOTAL CSO REVENUE WITH DYNAMIC PRICING STRATEGY

This section proposes a dynamic pricing strategy, objective function, optimization approach, and restrictions to address the flexibility of charging prices for CSs. Properly regulating CS charging costs encourages EV owners to use uncongested CSs, which optimizes the energy provided overall and EV consumers' welfare by decreasing the waiting time. A situation-based stochastic optimization technique takes into account the unpredictability of EV plans, beginning and ending SOC, the time of departure, and EVs' locations when determining the target CS to charge, making a worst-case scenario always conservative. A rigorous scenario-based analysis compares the worst-case dynamic pricing plan versus the fixed pricing strategy. A probability distribution may be used for scenario selection; however, great uncertainty about EV time of arrival, beginning and conclusion

SOC, and EV batteries makes it difficult to develop an accurate distribution. This study uses a comprehensive scenario-based methodology.

Dynamics Pricing Strategy: Situation-based Stochastic Optimization

The attraction function of (3) and the charging EV method in Section 2. The goal is to find the optimal CS charging costs (Pr_i^t) that allow CSs to accommodate the most EVs during the research.

Changes in CS attractiveness may help the CSO sell more electricity and maximize profits by encouraging EVs to pick cheaper, less crowded CSs. (4) calculates profits CS_i at time t using energy price, utilized plugs, and charging power. Equation (5) defines the scenario-based randomized optimum problem's objective function for all time-slotted CSs.

$$f_i^t = Pr_i^t N_{occ,i}^t P_i \tag{3}$$

$$\frac{max}{Pr_i^t} \; f = \sum_{t=1}^{T} \sum_{i=1}^{M} Pr_i^{t,\omega_r} N_{occ,i}^{t,\omega_r} P_i \; \forall \omega_r \epsilon W \tag{4}$$

Where ω_r represents the poor case situation in vagueness established by W. The goal line purpose is to section 2. C's EV charging procedure model and charging price constraints.

$$Pr \leq Pr_i^t \leq \underline{Pr} \;\; \forall i, t \tag{5}$$

Minimum charge price usually covers: Electricity, infrastructure, maintenance, taxes, and earnings. However, power market competition and customer demand set the maximum charge price. Market authorities may regulate prices to prevent price gouging.

Method for Optimization

Replace Pr_i^t with x to express (6)'s restricted optimization problem.

$$min - f(x), \qquad h(x) = 0, \qquad g(x) \leq 0 \tag{6}$$

With twice constantly differentiable functions f, h, and g. An inner technique may replace (7)'s non-linear program with barrier subproblems.

$$h(x) = 0, \qquad g(x) + s = 0 \tag{7}$$

The equation includes slack variables (s > 0), z = (x, s), as well as the barrier parameter (μ > 0).

DEVELOPING DYNAMIC PRICING STRATEGY PERFORMANCE EVALUATION

The section includes situation studies to demonstrate the effectiveness of the suggested active pricing method. Additionally, an accurate CS location and EV routing model is shown utilizing geographic tools. Additionally, pertinent discussions and results are provided.

Simulations and Scenarios

This study examines three scenarios (Table **1**) to assess the results of the suggested CS dynamic pricing method. Scenario 1 uses fixed pricing, with power prices matching the normal charge rate of scenario 2. The active pricing approach in Case 2 aims to maximize overall income for the CSO by adjusting the billing price of CSs over time. CSs are furnished with a web-based crowd meter. Case III alters the attractions task of the CS. The CS with an average recharging capacity of 8.3 kilowatts and Level 2 chargers is analyzed, along with the quantity of charging ports. Additionally, this research includes 4 DC quick CSs using a normal power charging of 51 kW to examine the influence of charging level. A geographical tool is essential for a meaningful knowledge of CS sites and EV routes. High-capability QGIS software was employed for this purpose. The actual EV demand profile pattern in Fig. (**2**) was employed in this investigation.

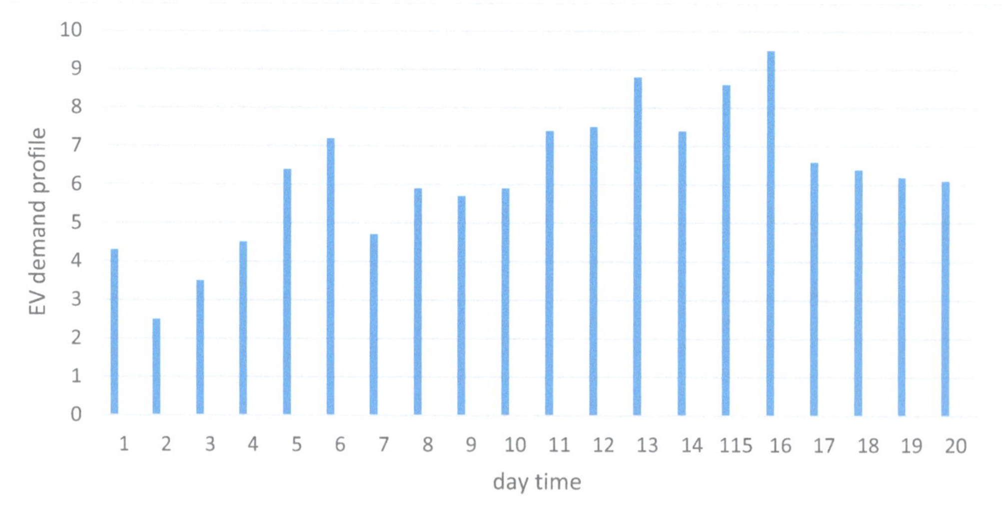

Fig. (2). EV demand profile pattern.

Table 1. Scenarios

Number of Cases	Description
I	Fixed-price approach
II	Framework for dynamic pricing
III	Framework for dynamic pricing + Crowd meter-equipped CSs

Discussion and Results

This part presents extensive findings and discussion to assess the suggested dynamic pricing method. In a fixed price (situation 1), 759 EVs are assessed throughout all period slots, resulting in total income. Case 1 charge pricing is consistent across all CSs and periods. The suggested dynamic pricing strategy in scenario 2 may expand EV charging to 1047 by adjusting charging prices and managing consumer attractiveness to CSs that are uncongested. Total wholesale energy grew from 21.62 MWh in case 1 to 29.65 MWh in case 2, reflecting the entire income. Case III involves CSs sharing information with EV customers *via* a crowd meter, which is online and displays the number of accessible electrical plugs at every CS. This knowledge leads to more EVs visiting uncongested CSs, resulting in 1129 charged EVs. The suggested dynamic pricing model helps reduce average waiting time by dispersing congestion in CSs, as seen in Fig. (**3**). EV owners may charge at home or elsewhere after accounting for a maximum waiting time in EV charging process modelling. Consumer dissatisfaction with charging infrastructure is demonstrated when EV drivers abandon stations after prolonged waiting times. Example II's dynamic pricing approach influences CSs' rivalry to attract EVs through contrasting boundary positions and cover zones (Fig. **4**). For clarity, Fig. (**4a**) depicts hourly boundary point movements between CS5 and nearby CSs, whereas Fig. (**4b**) shows dynamic charging costs. For instance, CS6's charge price decreases at h=4, increasing appeal and expanding its coverage zone. During h=4, more EVs in the routes between CS5 and CS6 choose to charge at CS6 owing to the higher pricing of CS5. Similar findings are observed for CS5 and CS12 interactions at h=4. The CS12 charging fee is lower during this hour to encourage EVs. Fig. (**4a**) shows that the price decrease affects the distance between CS5 and CS12, as per the boundary point. EVs between CS5 and CS12 are more drawn to CS12 during the fourth hour owing to its lower charging price compared to the preceding time slot.

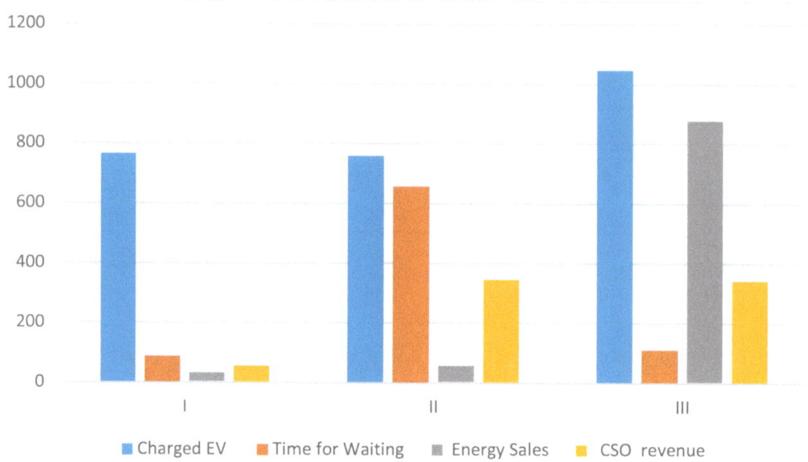

Fig. (3). Suggested dynamic pricing model.

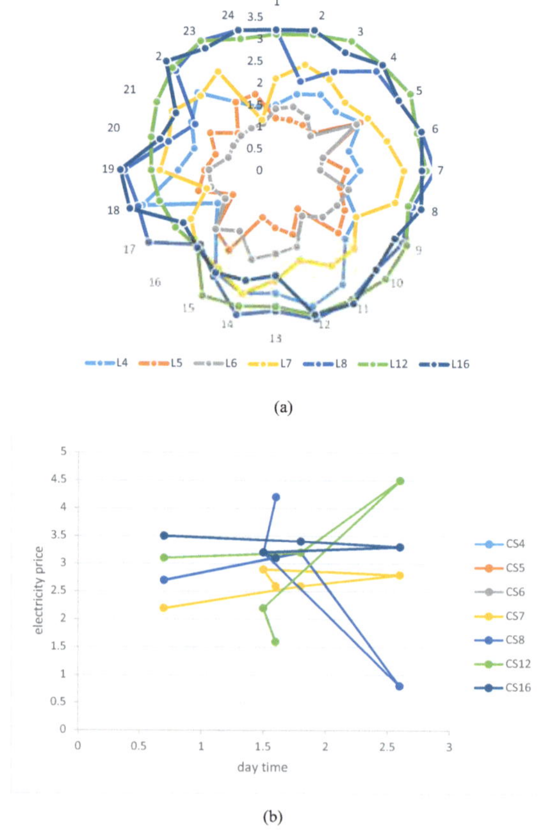

Fig. (4). (a) Hourly boundary point movements, (b) Dynamic charging costs.

CONCLUSION

This study examines how dynamic EV charging cost affects EV distribution among CSs. This research presents a mathematical model illustrating how electric plug configuration, charger type, distance from CS, and recharging fees affect EV charging choices. To maximize CSO revenue, a dynamic pricing strategy uses context-aware stochastic optimization to determine optimal charging rates for all CSs across every time slot in the period. QGIS software methods routes of EVs and locations of CS to determine accurate distances between CSs and EVs. Total CSO revenue, customer satisfaction, and CS congestion are evaluated under fixed, simple variable, and dynamic pricing conditions using crowd meters in online pricing scenarios. Results show that the suggested dynamic pricing mechanism may boost EV charging by 37.10% and CSO income by 41.6% compared to fixed pricing. The case study found that EV owners use the online crowd meter to make varied selections, resulting in a 3.3% increase in energy sales and CSO income. The suggested dynamic pricing technique enhances customer satisfaction by decreasing waiting times at busy CSs. Research indicates that DC quick chargers are more appealing to EV proprietors, leading to 78% higher CSO income and 7 times faster charging times.

REFERENCES

[1] A. S. Thakur, T. L. Alex, and A. Nighojkar, "Artificial intelligence in maritime anomaly detection: A decadal bibliometric analysis (2014–2024)", *Journal of The Institution of Engineers (India): Series C,* pp. 1-25, 2025. [http://dx.doi.org/10.1007/s40032-025-01169-w]

[2] U. Yokkampon, A. Mowshowitz, S. Chumkamon, and E. Hayashi, "Robust unsupervised anomaly detection with variational autoencoder in multivariate time series data", *IEEE Access,* vol. 10, pp. 57835-57849, 2022. [http://dx.doi.org/10.1109/ACCESS.2022.3178592]

[3] N. Dhieb, H. Ghazzai, H. Besbes, and Y. Massoud, "A secure AI-driven architecture for automated insurance systems: Fraud detection and risk measurement", *IEEE Access,* vol. 8, pp. 58546-58558, 2020. [http://dx.doi.org/10.1109/ACCESS.2020.2983300]

[4] S. Devaguptam, S.S. Gorti, T.L. Akshaya, and S.S. Kamath, "Automated health insurance processing framework with intelligent fraud detection, risk classification and premium prediction", *SN Comput. Sci.,* vol. 5, no. 5, p. 450, 2024. [http://dx.doi.org/10.1007/s42979-024-02801-9]

[5] Y. Supriya, N. Victor, G. Srivastava, and T.R. Gadekallu, "A hybrid federated learning model for insurance fraud detection", *International Conference on Communications Workshops: Sustainable Communications for Renaissance, ICC Workshops,* pp. 1516-1522, 2023. [http://dx.doi.org/10.1109/ICCWorkshops57953.2023.10283682]

[6] Vishakha D. Akhare and L. K. Vishwamitra, "Machine learning models for fraud detection: A comprehensive review and empirical analysis", *Journal of Electrical Systems,* vol. 20, no. 3s, pp. 1138-1149, 2024. [http://dx.doi.org/10.52783/jes.1427]

[7] S.H. Mousavi Anijdan, D. Sadeghi-Nezhad, H. Lee, W. Shin, N. Park, M.J. Nayyeri, H.R. Jafarian, and A.R. Eivani, "TEM study of S′ hardening precipitates in the cold rolled and aged AA2024 aluminum alloy: influence on the microstructural evolution, tensile properties & electrical conductivity", *J. Mater. Res. Technol.,* vol. 13, pp. 798-807, 2021. [http://dx.doi.org/10.1016/j.jmrt.2021.05.003]

[8] K. Zhu, J. Wang, W. Zhang, X. Zhu, and X. Lu, "Effect of deposition strategies on microstructures, defects and mechanical properties of 5356 aluminum alloy by wire arc additive manufacturing", *Trans. Nonferrous Met. Soc. China,* vol. 34, no. 2, pp. 423-434, 2024. [http://dx.doi.org/10.1016/S1003-6326(23)66408-8]

[9] K.K. Jha, and M. Imam, "Microstructure evolution and local mechanical properties of friction stir additively manufactured (FSAM) AA5083/AA6061/AA7075 gradient composite", *Mater. Sci. Eng. A,* vol. 903, p. 146668, 2024. [http://dx.doi.org/10.1016/j.msea.2024.146668]

[10] G. Shin, M. Ebrahimian, N.K. Adomako, H. Choi, D.J. Lee, J-H. Yoon, D.W. Kim, J-Y. Kang, M.Y. Na, H.J. Chang, and J.H. Kim, "Microstructural evolution and mechanical properties of functionally graded austenitic–low-carbon steel produced via directed energy deposition", *Mater. Des.,* vol. 227, p. 111681, 2023. [http://dx.doi.org/10.1016/j.matdes.2023.111681]

[11] P. Patro, "A hybrid approach estimates the real-time health state of a bearing by accelerated degradation tests, Machine learning," 2021, Accessed: Apr. 11, 2025. [Online]. Available from: https://ieeexplore.ieee.org/abstract/document/9708591/ [http://dx.doi.org/10.1109/ICSTCEE54422.2021.9708591]

[12] Kishor, K., Agrawal, K.K., Yadav, S.P. *et al.* SPAM: An Enhanced Performance of Security and Privacy-Aware Model over Split Learning in Consumer Electronics. Program Comput Soft 50, 875–899, 2024. [http://dx.doi.org/10.1134/S0361768824700816]

CHAPTER 2

Optimization of HR Management System based on IoT

Rama Devi P.[1,*], **C. Barna A. Naidu**[2], **Gundraju Yamuna**[3], **Anzar Ahmad**[4], **Tanwir Alam**[5] and **M. Sandra Carmel Sophia**[1]

[1] *Department of English, KLEF (Deemed to be University), Guntur 522302, Andhra Pradesh, India*

[2] *Department of School of Business & Management, Christ University, Pune 412112, Maharashtra, India*

[3] *School of Commerce and Management, Mohan Babu University, Tirupati 517102, Andhra Pradesh, India*

[4] *Department of Electronics & Communication, Graphic Era Deemed to be University, Dehradun 248002, Uttarakhand, India*

[5] *Department of Mechanical Engineering, Maulana Mukhtar Ahmad Nadvi Technical Campus, Malegaon 423203, Maharashtra, India*

Abstract: This research develops and implements an edge management system, optimizes the corporate HR system using IoT-first technology, and examines the demand phase. After installing the software, hardware, and edge node management platform, the edge layer's possible interactions with the sensor, boundary, and cloud layers must be analyzed. Then, to ensure reliable communication between the various layers of the system, the organization's type-driven hyperlink selection method and the northbound multi-link transitioning method are developed and executed, respectively. The edge management system may fulfill the expansion, intelligence, and safety needs of IoT applications by implementing the aforementioned functionalities. Conducting thorough research is essential for identifying corporate functional and performance needs, creating a logical framework, and designing the system's architecture and other components. Individuals can adapt the system to their needs by utilizing its three pre-built modules: organizational change management, remuneration and benefits, and people transformation. System components include staff change management, organizational management, benefits and pay management, and personnel data management. HR management is covered in these modules. The system meets design goals utilizing advanced tools and software.

Keywords: Edge management system, Hyperlink selection, Internet of things, Optimization of HR, System components.

* **Corresponding author Rama Devi P.:** Department of English, KLEF (Deemed to be University), Guntur 522302, Andhra Pradesh, India; E-mail: ramadevinaresh@gmail.com

D. Arul Pon Daniel, T. Rajasanthosh Kumar & Satya Prakash Yadav (Eds.)

INTRODUCTION

Many businesses have come to realize that they need to maximize the importance of their human resources and utilize them as a key factor in this new market environment. However, to achieve this, they must implement a robust human resource management strategy and utilize a range of techniques [1]. This realization is a direct result of the material age and the fast expansion of financial globalization. Effective human resource management requires both a solid strategy and technology tools to accomplish it [2]. As computer and network technology advances, the integration of objects into the internet blurs the line between the virtual and real worlds, resulting in the IoT. This search arrangement is crucial for processors to obtain data regarding the physical environment and is essential for a successful IoT system [3]. IoT search involves gathering, storing, and organizing spatial-temporal data for user searchability [4]. As big data and 5G technologies mature, IoT corporate data has grown exponentially, requiring significant computational power [5]. Cloud computing's fixed architecture makes it challenging to complete tasks efficiently, even with improved hardware performance. To address this, an effective computing architecture and optimization scheme are needed to address the root cause [6]. Due to the fixed cloud computing architecture, the IoT network architecture (Fig. **1**) lacks flexibility [7]. Future networks should be adaptable to changing business needs and environments, requiring intelligence [8]. Enhancing HRM Information Technology (IT) may enhance resource integration and lower management expenses. Numerous HRM software systems are homogenous, utilized for statistical data, and may waste resources due to limited interaction, compatibility, and repetitive procedures [9]. Integrating HRMS allows for the integration of management resources, enabling the development of new activities [10].

Rapid advancements in science and technology have ushered in a new era. The advancement of science and technology has not only improved everyday lives but also opened up opportunities for business growth [11]. Technological advancements, including big data, IoT, and others, have led to the integration of new technologies into enterprise management. This trend is expected to continue in the future [12]. Enterprises must address key issues such as maximizing human resources value, meeting employee needs, maximizing economic benefits, and developing in complex markets. Due to intense market competition and advancements in electronic technology and information systems, human resource management is becoming increasingly important in today's society. Human resource management information systems are widely recognized and utilized throughout all areas of society [13]. Future company growth relies on HR management systems to respond to market changes and drive reform. The method enhances staff management efficiency and fosters task development. The safety of user information is a growing concern for industries such as the internet and communications. The data handled by HR management systems cannot be changed at will. To prevent theft and protect individuals, strict controls should be implemented to protect data resources.

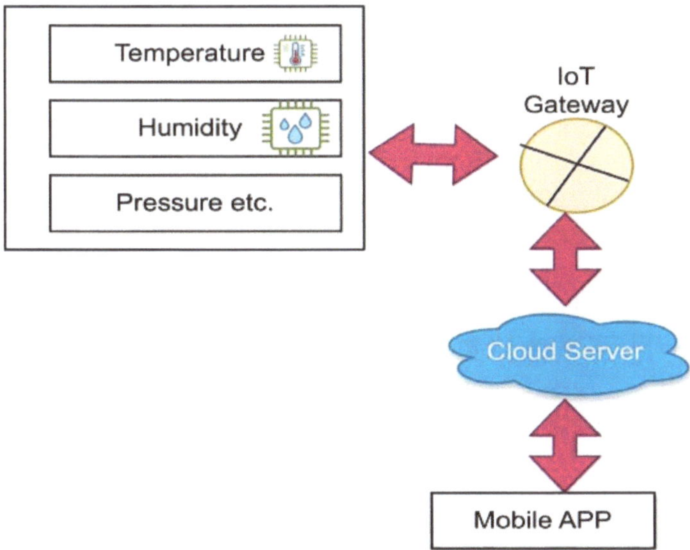

Fig. (1). IoT network architecture.

INFORMATION SYSTEM DESIGN ANALYSIS WITHOUT IOT

HR-IoT Design

IoT systems are crucial for creating spatial-temporal data in our data-driven culture. The IoT is crucial to several industries, including environmental monitoring and smart manufacturing. Building a complete IoT system requires addressing the issue of large data volumes and spatial-temporal data categorization. The basic architecture for cloud computing involves the Sensing Terminal (SE) or User Terminal (UE) uploading IoT data directly to the cloud, which then feeds back the data once the activity is completed. However, the postponement of the round-trip period due to information transmission is significant. Excessive data concentration strains bandwidth, leading to network congestion, jitter, and a worse user experience in IoT applications. Incorporating edge computing architecture into IoT systems may successfully address this issue. The edge management paradigm integrates edge cloud components into the core of computing on the edge, which is built of edge nodes. Located at the user side of the access network, the edge cloud is between the consumer layer and the network. Edge control systems provide reduced task processing latency and more adjustable functionalities due to their geographically dispersed deployment. The scenario method layout of the edge management system is presented in this work.

The static-priority scheduling method assigns distinct business processes varying priorities, which remain constant throughout system operation, ensuring the highest-priority execution. The system executes the low-priority monitoring procedure more frequently in a real-world context. High-priority services, including emergency alerts, are prioritized above other services and get CPU processing power when they occur. With pre-emptive scheduling, the system prioritizes business operations accordingly. The system starts with the highest-priority task in higher-priority scenarios. To determine the best offloading strategy, the method requires information on the compute and storage needs of all subtasks in the assignment group. Additionally, during periods of high task production, NEN may lack sufficient computational or storage capabilities. Subtasks that require time to accomplish may be prioritized when added to the task queue and offloaded. This method aims to minimize the execution duration of task T during peak generation. When considering multi-edge node computing cooperation, subtask elements should comprise Predicted Execution Time (PT), Computational Resource Needs (PC), and Storage Resource Requirements (PS). As NEN has limited CPU cores and PC is connected to PT, subtasks may have 1 or 2 cores, depending on the connection between PT and the standard predicted time to execution age of the subtasks in TS.

$$m_i = \frac{1}{n} \sum_{N=1}^{n} \sum_{J=1}^{n} m_J^t m_i^2(t_n) \tag{1}$$

$$m_i^2(t_n) = \sum_{N=1}^{n} \sum_{i,J=1}^{n} t_i^J i_I^2 \tag{2}$$

System Design Information

Organization management provides personnel, employment, and organization information to subordinate divisions in the HR system. It enables HR managers to conduct complete management and gives employment and staffing statistics to help the CEO understand the firm. The primary function of the personnel management change module is to track information on changes to staff categories, jobs, and tasks. In addition to handling conversions, redeployments, and separations, it also handles resignations, dismissals, terminations, negotiated terminations, layoffs, retirements, leaves of absence, death, and prolonged retirements, among other types of changes. There are two ways to apply for staff transfers: *via* the permission process or directly. For staff deployments and separations, there are four ways: no approval, directly, through the approval procedure, or directly recorded in the deployment or separation record. Once the conversion procedures are complete, personnel information will be updated with the conversion date and the decision made. After implementing the redeployment process, personnel's job status, including starting date, category, and type, is updated. A transfer request form may also be generated immediately. Following separation, personnel information, including date and type, will be recorded in the separation process. Employees will be reminded of their contract validity and the terms of their employee agreement during the separation process.

Optimization System Design

This article focuses on data categorization and anomalous processing techniques for IoT spatial-temporal data. To improve the speed and accuracy of IoT search, real-time classification and storage of collected information *via* a temporal database can be used to search various kinds of data simultaneously. Additionally, a study of the objective tracking algorithm for spatial-temporal data can enhance efficiency and accuracy. This report focuses on four key research points: examining current deep learning algorithms, combining them with IoT real-time search systems, addressing diverse search data, and applying them to data cleaning, dimension reduction, feature extraction, and the semantic classification of transmitted information. To improve indexing performance, a deep learning system classifies actual IoT transmission information and creates a suitable storage structure for the data chunks.

Target tracking techniques using IoT spatial-temporal information are built, current methods and convolution neural networks are analyzed, actual time dynamical target tracking is employed, and deep learning algorithms increase target identification and accuracy. The IoT search platform, cloud architecture, information storage structure, real-time search efficiency, and implementation are presented.

RESULTS ANALYSIS

System Performance

The departmental file node is used to compile comprehensive departmental information, support human resource management, and communicate data to associated management, thereby reducing input volume. Job administration aims to efficiently maintain and update work information in the system, including deletion, addition, editing, and modification. This node allows units to access their organization chart based on their management scope and viewing patterns. Users can customize the organization chart by selecting the desired roles or departments, as well as background color, orientation, connecting lines, display items, typefaces, and boundaries. Along with the firm hierarchy, users can view staff details, including names and photographs, by clicking on their respective positions. Employee cards may be printed directly. The role of post management involves creating and maintaining group posts, selecting successors, and analyzing the appointment scenario for the position or department see Fig. **2**). Managing job information involves setting basic information, quality indicators, qualifications, and work authority. Attachments can be browsed, downloaded, and uploaded, supporting job descriptions and list output. Job browsing evaluates posted positions, browses current and previous candidates, and queries posting history.

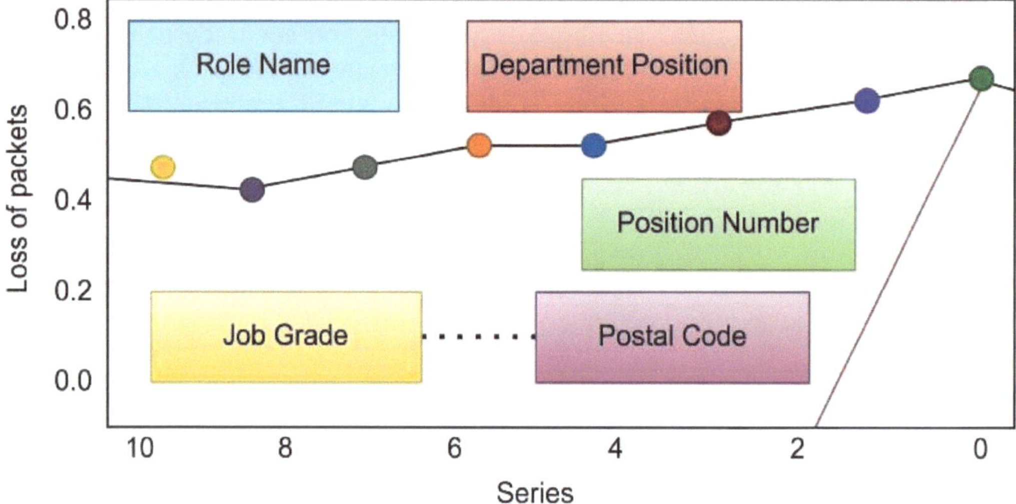

Fig. (2). Appointment scenario.

The major types of personnel information are personal, subset, and job. Add operators, personnel cards, and rosters for joint assessment, batch image export, and quality management module support. This may help workers assess their job abilities through ability matching. Enabling the competence management module allows the ability to match personnel and roles, as shown in Fig. (**3**).

Statistics are often used to analyze employee data, including work, personal, and transfer information, including present, dismissed, and retired workers. Flexible statistical assessments of personnel data can be performed and visualized using various graphical representations. Utilizing deployment records enables customizable statistical analysis of personnel deployment, providing statistics and graphs. Salary systems should be based on performance, fairness, and efficiency, as well as jobs or postings. The e-HR system's salary system construction involves establishing an organization's salary system, including multi-payroll category settings, salary rule table configuration, salary item settings, salary periods, rate of tax structure, substitute bank setup, and statistical report. This interface allows managing payroll item properties, such as number rules, inclusion in the system for payroll, carryover to the following period, and tax item counting. The ability (payroll) for lower-level units to make direct references to designated objects is seen in Fig. (**4**).

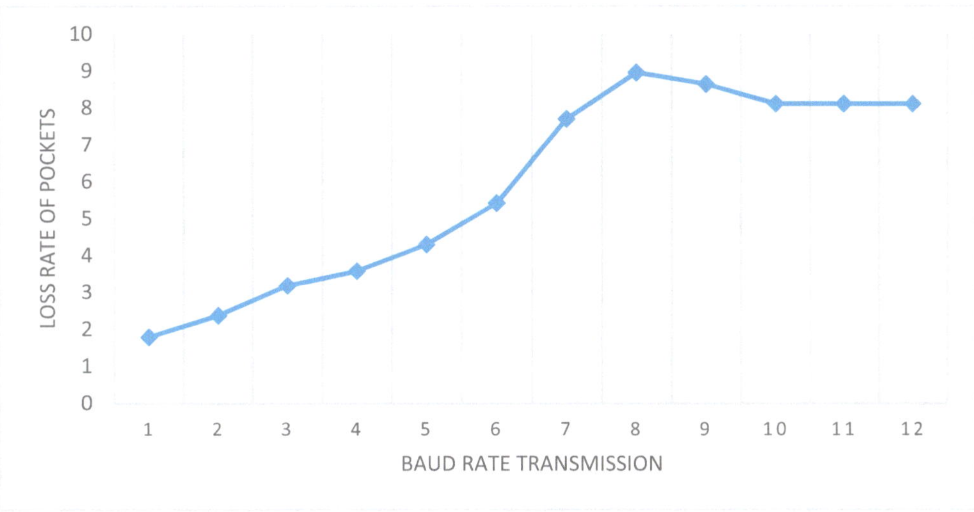

Fig. (3). Ability matching analysis.

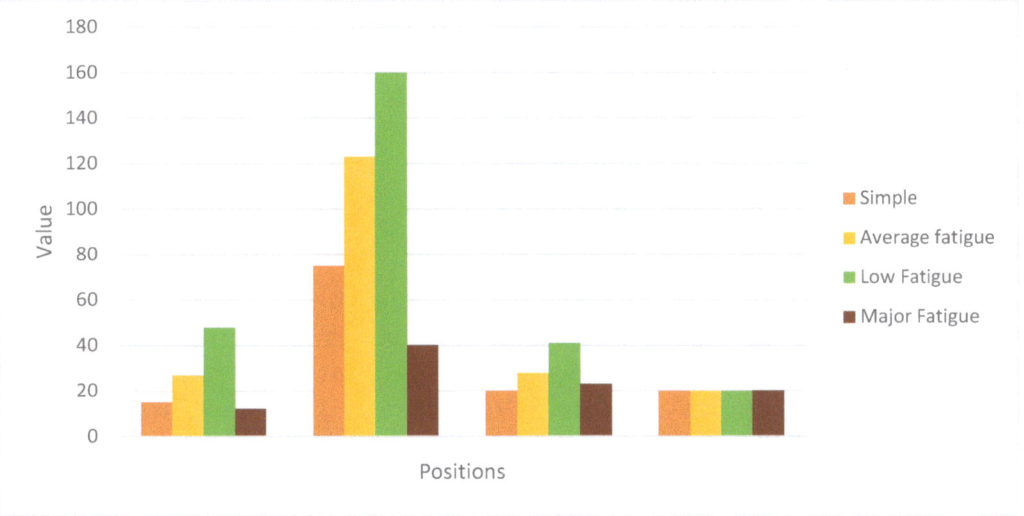

Fig. (4). Ability (payroll) for lower-level units.

This interface allows users to set payroll periods, refer to accounting periods, configure issuance categories, and import payroll accounting data from outside the system. The evaluated system yielded positive results, particularly the flexible query engine and statistical output, which revolutionized manual statistics. Organization, personnel information, employee change, and salary management modules provide exact facts for scientific decision-making. Following the system's environment and installation criteria, a black-box evaluation of system functioning is conducted. The results suggest that the information system meets the needs of HR management.

Optimization Results Analysis

Service firms must plan their IT systems to support financial, administrative, and commercial processes, just like those in other industries. The corporation could consider optimizing business quality management through the use of information systems, improving human resource scheduling to minimize expenses, and enhancing customer engagement. Consider effective facility and equipment management for project customers to maximize property value and extend service life. Additionally, strengthen parking management to maintain public revenue and customer interests. The business management department manager held seminars and discussed the optimization of the IT system with IT professionals and business personnel, resulting in a comprehensive plan from various perspectives and business modules, including upgrades to the OA office system. The approval process has been simplified to better communicate the company's control authority. Additionally, material management has been strengthened to track and manage material usage, reducing waste and improving cost control. The organization is contemplating implementing payroll, asset, and warehouse management systems over time, while also conducting demand data and market research. Integrating payroll, assets, and warehouse management into the OA office system allows accurate attendance data capture, reference-based asset depreciation, and joint control of resources and low-value consumables to reduce waste and streamline processes (overall cost analysis) as shown in Fig. (**5**).

There are modules in the service system that help manage client relationships, schedule maintenance, inspect facilities and equipment, and verify quality on-site. Fig. (**6**) illustrates that a creative dispatching system streamlines and statistically dispatches employees, and statistical reports and dispatch records directly correlate workload to wages.

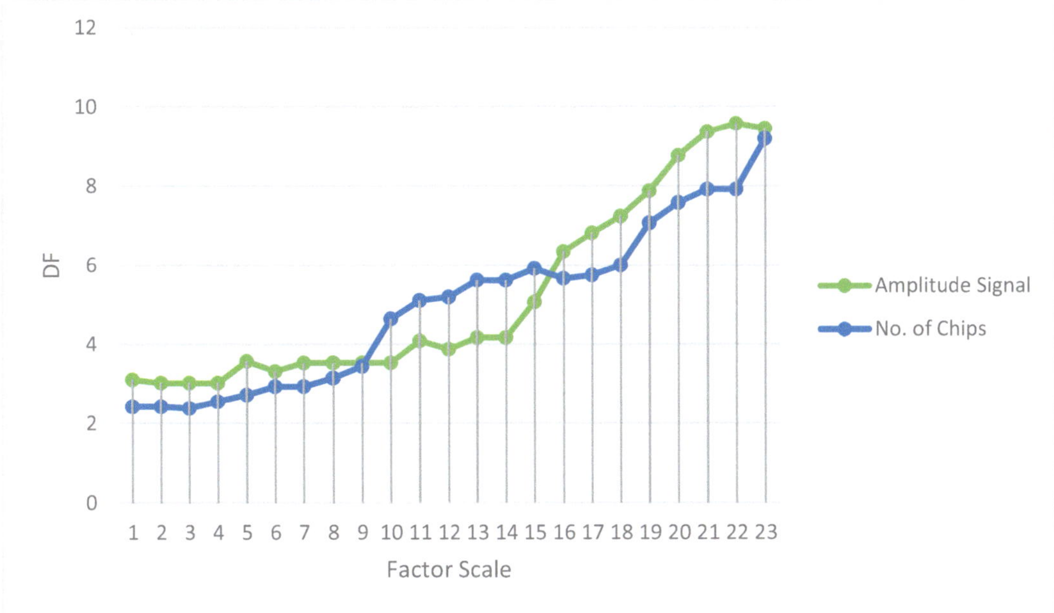

Fig. (5). Overall cost analysis.

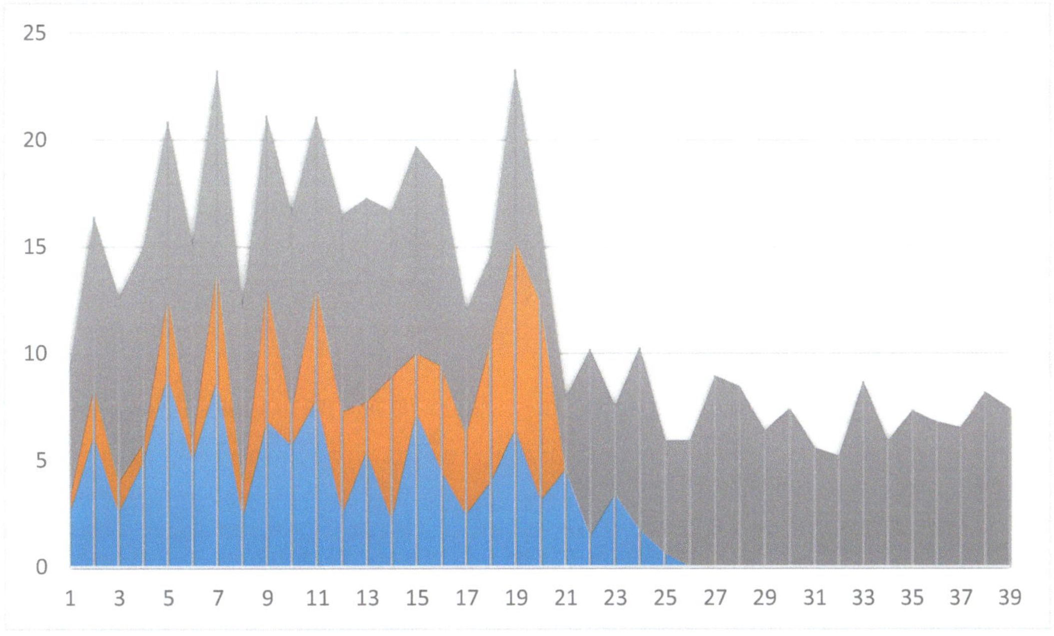

Fig. (6). Creative dispatching system streamlines and statistically dispatches.

This enables the collection of quantitative indicators for use in performance evaluations. IT professionals must negotiate and communicate with system suppliers to optimize the implementation of IT systems in various areas. Communication port diversity and integration with system providers must be prioritized to ensure seamless operation. To exchange information and resources between functional systems, relevant data must be synchronized with charging data in the Suyuan management system, attendance management information imported into the salary management system for salary calculation, and CRM information. The system should be consistent and closed-loop. Different information systems are more professional; thus, management priorities should determine the promotion rate of each system. Integrating information technology management through data platforms and data mining can enhance market competitiveness by facilitating the integration and sharing resources across service processes.

CONCLUSION

The proposed central multitasking programming solution with a distinct edge node aims to minimize processing delays for small activities in IoT settings. The approach involves creating a multilayer scheduling framework that combines process and thread scheduling, using a preempt static priority algorithm for various services. This study introduces a dynamic priority-based scheduling approach for threads in high-concurrency enterprises, utilizing a task execution urgency factor determined by residual computations within the job time limit. Findings indicate that the suggested multilayer setup strategy greatly improves task processing efficiency and reduces processing delays for minor workloads. The system enhances efficiency, collaboration, employee motivation, performance management, decision support, real-time monitoring, risk mitigation, competitiveness, and HRM strategy technical support. The platform supports corporate HR management, strategic enhancement, and competitiveness, ensuring successful operations.

REFERENCES

[1] A. S. Thakur, T. L. Alex, and A. Nighojkar, "Artificial intelligence in maritime anomaly detection: A decadal bibliometric analysis (2014–2024)", *Journal of The Institution of Engineers (India): Series C,* pp. 1-25, 2025. [http://dx.doi.org/10.1007/s40032-025-01169-w]

[2] Y. Chen, C. Zhao, Y. Xu, and C. Nie, “Year-over-year developments in financial fraud detection via deep learning: A systematic literature review,” Jan. 2025, Accessed: Mar. 09, 2025. [http://dx.doi.org/10.48550/arXiv.2502.00201]

[3] E. Altulaihan, M. A. Almaiah, and A. Aljughaiman, "Anomaly detection IDS for detecting DoS attacks in IoT networks based on machine learning algorithms", *Sensors,* vol. 24, no. 2, p. 713, 2024. [http://dx.doi.org/10.3390/s24020713]

[4] U. Yokkampon, A. Mowshowitz, S. Chumkamon, and E. Hayashi, "Robust unsupervised anomaly detection with variational autoencoder in multivariate time series data", *IEEE Access,* vol. 10, pp. 57835-57849, 2022.

[http://dx.doi.org/10.1109/ACCESS.2022.3178592]

[5] F.K. Alarfaj, and S. Shahzadi, "Enhancing fraud detection in banking with deep learning: Graph neural networks and autoencoders for real-time credit card fraud prevention", *IEEE Access,* 2024. [http://dx.doi.org/10.1109/ACCESS.2024.3466288]

[6] Li, H., & Wang, W. Optimization of the enterprise human resource management information system based on the internet of things, Complexity, vol. 2021, Article ID 5592850, 12 pages, 2021. [http://dx.doi.org/10.1155/2021/5592850]

[7] H. Palivela, V. Rishiwal, S. Bhushan, A. Alotaibi, U. Agarwal, P. Kumar, and M. Yadav, "Optimization of deep learning-based model for identification of credit card frauds", *IEEE Access,* vol. 12, pp. 125629-125642, 2024. [http://dx.doi.org/10.1109/ACCESS.2024.3440637]

[8] M. Monshizadeh, V. Khatri, M. Gamdou, R. Kantola, and Z. Yan, "Improving data generalization with variational autoencoders for network traffic anomaly detection", *IEEE Access,* vol. 9, pp. 56893-56907, 2021. [http://dx.doi.org/10.1109/ACCESS.2021.3072126]

[9] C. Huot, S. Heng, T.K. Kim, and Y. Han, "Quantum autoencoder for enhanced fraud detection in imbalanced credit card dataset", *IEEE Access,* vol. 12, pp. 169671-169682, 2024. [http://dx.doi.org/10.1109/ACCESS.2024.3496901]

[10] A. Iqbal, and R. Amin, "Time series forecasting and anomaly detection using deep learning", *Comput. Chem. Eng.,* vol. 182, p. 108560, 2024. [http://dx.doi.org/10.1016/j.compchemeng.2023.108560]

[11] C. Farkostteknik, "Credit card transaction fraud detection using neural network classifiers," 2023, Accessed: Mar. 09, 2025. [Online]. Available from: https://urn.kb.se/resolve?urn=urn:nbn:se:kth:diva-325808

[12] N. Dhieb, H. Ghazzai, H. Besbes, and Y. Massoud, "A secure AI-driven architecture for automated insurance systems: Fraud detection and risk measurement", *IEEE Access,* vol. 8, pp. 58546-58558, 2020. [http://dx.doi.org/10.1109/ACCESS.2020.2983300]

[13] K. S. N. V. K. Gangadhar, B. A. Kumar, Y. Vivek, and V. Ravi, "Chaotic variational auto encoder based one class classifier for insurance fraud detection," Dec. 2022, Accessed: Mar. 09, 2025. [Online]. Available from: https://arxiv.org/abs/2212.07802v1

CHAPTER 3

Evaluation of HR Management System Based on the IOT

J. Ramya[1,*], **G. Venkata Lakshmi**[2], **Anzar Ahmad**[3] and **G. N. R. Prasad**[4]

[1] *Department of Business Administration, SRM Institute of Science and Technology (Vadapalani Campus), Chennai 600026, Tamil Nadu, India*

[2] *Department of CSE (Data Science), CMR College of Engineering & Technology, Hyderabad 501401, Telangana, India*

[3] *Department of Electronics & Communication, Graphic Era Deemed to be University, Dehradun 248002, Uttarakhand, India*

[4] *Department of MCA, Chaitanya Bharati Institute of Technology, Hyderabad 500075, Telangana, India*

Abstract: The Internet is one of the new market economic innovations of the 21st century. The Internet of Things (IoT) is a new technology that integrates processors, the net, and portable phone networks. It has large potential applications and is considered one of the five key developing sectors. The IoT sector faces tremendous competition due to the fast growth of digital technology and the evolving market economy. The strength of an enterprise's market competitiveness is, to some degree, determined by the consequences of Human Resources (HR) management. This chapter analyzes the fundamental features of the Internet industry and examines the competitiveness of Internet enterprises to study industry HR management. It directly relates to several factors of HR and uses the AHP process to develop the Internet initiative hierarchy. Finally, this chapter investigates an IoT company's human resources organization quality assessment model, strategy, and optimization, which supports their market competitiveness with theory.

Keywords: AHP, Digital technology, Human resource management, IoT, Internet enterprise hierarchy.

INTRODUCTION

The Internet of Things (IoT) connects computers, the Internet, and mobile networks after the third data industry revolution. Large application potential is one of the five emerging calculated productions [1]. Forrester forecasted that the IoT market will be the next trillion-dollar communication service, bringing 30

* **Corresponding author J. Ramya:** Department of Business Administration, SRM Institute of Science and Technology (Vadapalani Campus), Chennai 600026, Tamil Nadu, India; E-mail: ramya.jayaram80@gmail.com

D. Arul Pon Daniel, T. Rajasanthosh Kumar & Satya Prakash Yadav (Eds.)

times more value than the Internet. Computers, the Internet, and mobile networks collectively constitute the Internet of Things (IoT) after the third wave of information technology [2]. One of the five emerging key sectors is big application development. According to Forrester, the IoT industry is expected to become the next trillion-dollar communication service, 30 times larger than the Internet [3]. IoT refers to the installation of information-sensing devices that can all connect to the network for simple identification and administration. The Basic IoT information diagram in Fig. (**1**) shows that the IoT industry is:

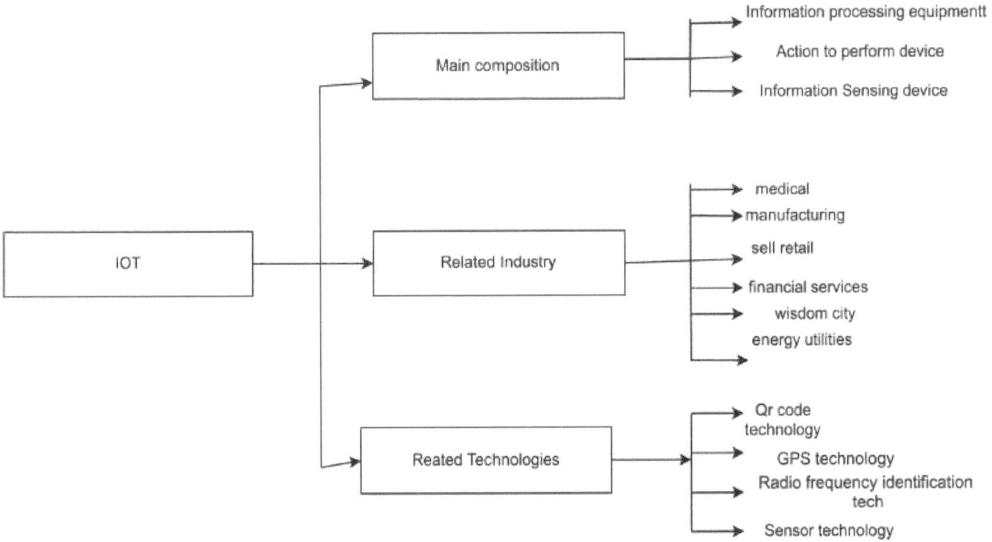

Fig. (1). Basic IoT data diagram.

- Knowledge sensing and networking devices that perceive the external environment, process information, and implement actions.
- Industries IoT generally comprises.

IoT-driven manufacturing: The next industrial revolution has started

Using IoT technology, industrial enterprises can leverage feedback data from products and equipment to evaluate risk, preserve assets, and enhance employee safety [4]. A better understanding of consumer preferences and behaviour may enhance product development, dependability, performance, and service. In the medical field, IoT enables patients to receive therapy at home. IoT technology enables medical professionals and equipment to monitor patients, improving conditions and enabling faster action. Appreciation of health tracking and condition will be faster than previously [5]. The use of IoT technology in the medical field can automate and speed up logistical processes. Additionally, Unicom Internet information may enhance the quality and variety. For example, baby monitor markets capture data *via* continuous video and audio technology; however, false alarms are common. Using IoT technology, parents may get timely alerts on their phones if their infant stops breathing unexpectedly. Energy and utilities: IoT technology can augment energy sources and requests, enabling the clean utilization of renewable energy for power generation [6]. People can access equipment information online in real-time, thereby decreasing the impact of power outages. All smart cities are called Wisdom cities, since city building requires knowledge; therefore, they cannot be built instantly. IoT technology can enhance energy efficiency, improve traffic management, and boost citizen security. With IoT, half of the world's population and urban inhabitants may enjoy a simpler, cleaner, safer, and more enjoyable existence. In data-driven global financial services, IoT enhances intelligence, reduces risk, and enhances the digital experience. It calculates insurance costs, analyzes credit for precise and individualized retail banking, and creates bespoke new products [7]. The furniture market is very active, and demand is strong due to the importance of home items in everyone's life [8]. According to recent data, 80% of the domestic market has been involved in making intelligent appliances. Some examples of devices that can be linked to the Internet include vacuum cleaners, televisions, washing machines, air conditioners, bicycles, locks, and even blood pressure monitors [9]. The Internet of Things (IoT) is expected to generate a trillion-dollar technology economy in the next decade *via* its use in transference, conservational, protection, governance, public security, and health [10 - 12].

IoT Technology Generally Includes

Computer, statement, and sensor technology make up information technology's three main technologies. According to bionics, the processor is a “brain” that processes and classifies information, its statement system is a “nervous system” that passes material, and sensors are “sense organs”. The Internet of Things (IoT) consists of tiny wireless sensor technologies and a sensor network, which acts as a perception. Radio-Frequency Identification (RFID) technology identifies targets and reads/writes data wirelessly *via* radio waves. RFID Technology is used in several sectors, including ID cards, electronic toll collection, logistics management, and others. Although RFID technology is established and has low-cost labels, it lacks data gathering functions such as product identification and storage quality. It has limited applications in metal and liquid environments. It is part of the IoT information acquisition technology. QR Code technology, a mobile intelligent gadget, has become more widespread due to its ability to store more information and complicated data forms, expanding its application area. The Global Positioning System (GPS) is a next-generation satellite-based navigation and positioning system that enables air, marine, and land users to navigate in three dimensions in real-time. IoT applications rely on Global Positioning Systems (GPS) as a mobile sensing approach for intelligent transportation, data collection, and item tracking. Sensor systems, ad hoc networks, LAN, and WAN technologies comprise the basic technology of the data convergence layer. According to the introduction, IoT technology involves utilizing Internet technology in everyday life to connect intelligent devices and better meet people's needs. The IoT industry is crucial for future development, and optimizing Human Resources (HR) management strategies in banking and manufacturing can enhance enterprise market competitiveness and advance potential. This article analyzes IoT industry human resources management strategies, evaluating them using the AHP method and a multi-objective genetic algorithm. Our study focuses on an IoT firm and applies theory to optimize human resources management strategy.

A HUMAN RESOURCE MANAGEMENT STRATEGY OPTIMIZATION EXAMPLE FOR THE IOT INDUSTRY

IoT Industry Introduction

IoT's goal is to "use knowledge and knowledge to generate high-quality life." With expertise in smart homes, intelligent buildings, intelligent security, green logistics, and intelligent management information platforms, they serve the city. These systems cooperatively maximize resource advantage.

The State of Human Resources in the Internet of Things Sector

There is a lack of emphasis on people's priorities, work flexibility, and initiative in today's Internet company workforce management practices, with the main focus being on staff allocation. High stability is the defining feature of people management models, although this is not the case in contemporary HRM. Human resource management in the modern era is founded on the idea of giving equal weight to development and utilization, emphasizing people-centeredness, recognizing that HR is both reproducible and adaptable, placing a premium on achieving organizational goals, and unlocking individuals' full potential. Inspiring individuals, helping them reach their full potential, and motivating them to work constructively, actively, and creatively are the most important factors. Combining human resources management strategy with company characteristics may impact the value of the firm, as measured by key indicators. f_{hr} is the IoT enterprise's HR management strategy score, given as:

$$f_{hr=}\sum_{i=1}^{k} k_i \times f_i \tag{1}$$

K is crucial to assessing firm HR management, whereas ki and fi indicate weight and the I-score function. Section 2.1 shows the enterprise's HR management strategy, and important indicators, including completion, innovation, research and Development (R&D), stability, and company growth in. Market research and consulting firms agree that obtaining a degree in innovation R&D is critical to growing a stable business. Stability and capacity growth within a corporation are dependent on innovative R&D. Innovation in R&D is crucial for firm stability and capacity expansion. Stability aids corporate growth. The Internet of Enterprise judgment matrix evaluates human resources management strategies. A_{hr} of major goal weights:

$$A_{hr=}\left[1\ 3\ 7\ \frac{1}{3}\ 1\ 5\ \frac{1}{9}\ \frac{1}{7}\ \frac{1}{5}\right] \tag{2}$$

Optimizing Human Resources Management Strategy in IoT Enterprises

Previously, the Enterprise-related HR organization's policy defined the key features and weights for the assessment index. To compute the scores of an IoT firm's human resources management plan, analyze the organization and draw conclusions from almost 10 years of important indicators. Fig. (**2**) displays the 10-year target score for the corporate HR management approach. While the IoT has enhanced business human resources management over the last decade, the overall level remains low and requires optimization. Formula for f_i is:

Fig. (2). Target score of the company's HRM strategy in about 10 years.

$$f_i = f(x_1 x_2 \dots \dots x_{j\dots\dots}) \tag{3}$$

The first factor impacting the human resources assessment indicator is Xj.

A 10-year analysis of human resource management and company operations reveals that factors such as material rewards, performance bonuses, employee capacity-building training, and promotion systems have a significant impact on HRM scores.

According to Figs. (**3** and **4**), the company's human resources management strategy optimization process involves four major components. Figs. (**3** and **4**) illustrate the optimization method for providing material incentives and performance bonuses, as well as expanding training and staff advancement opportunities for workers.

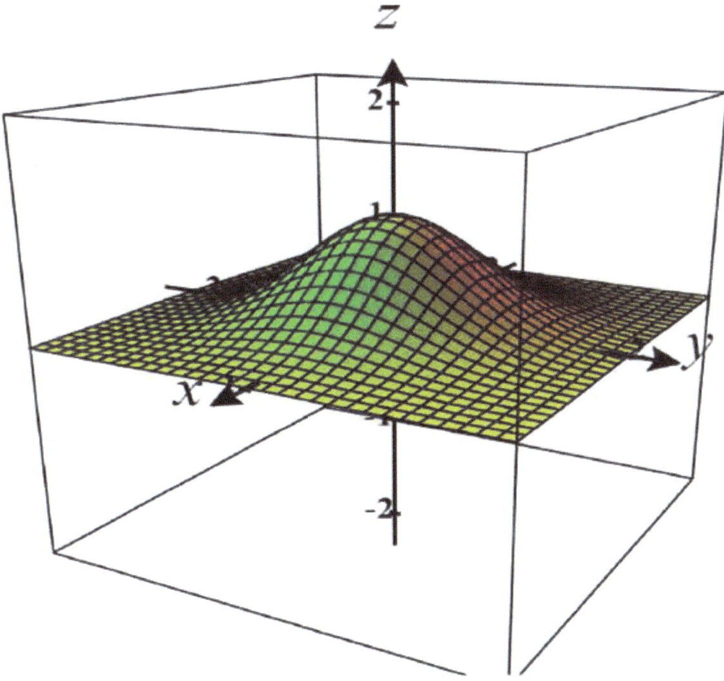

Fig. (3). To optimize human resources management strategy, consider material incentives and performance bonuses.

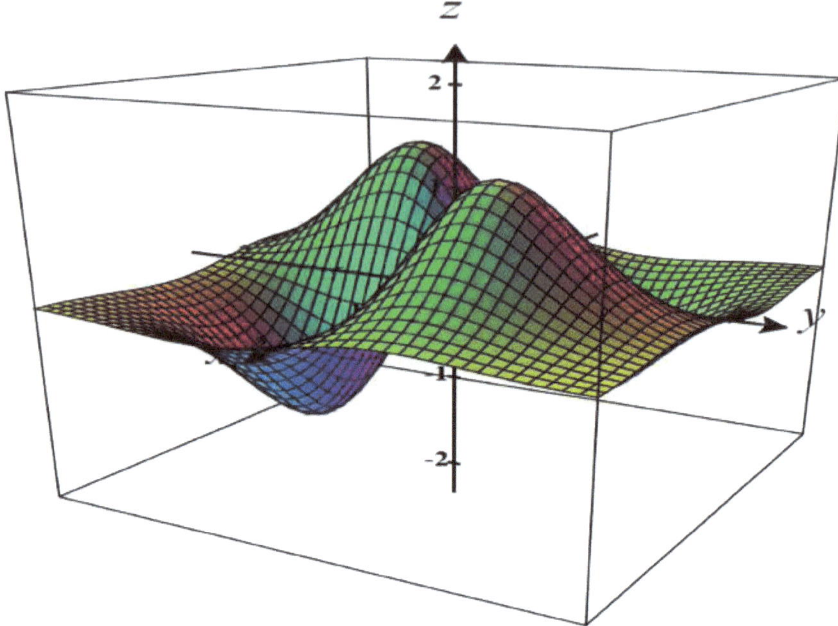

Fig. (4). To optimize human resources management, consider expanding training and staff advancement systems.

Figs. (**3** and **4**) demonstrate that nonlinear factors affect the evaluation of enterprise HR management strategies, but rules exist for determining them. To improve competitiveness, enterprises should optimize their HR management strategy by considering key factors.

Results in Fig. (**5**) show the relationship between business HR management strategy ratings and tangible rewards, performance bonus plans, training for capacity development, and a system for job promotions. (1) As shown in Fig. (**5**), the evaluation of a company's HRM strategy is affected differently by material reward, performance incentive plans, staff size, development training, and job advancement systems; (2) improving presentation is not always a crucial factor, and (3) other factors to be considered comprise:

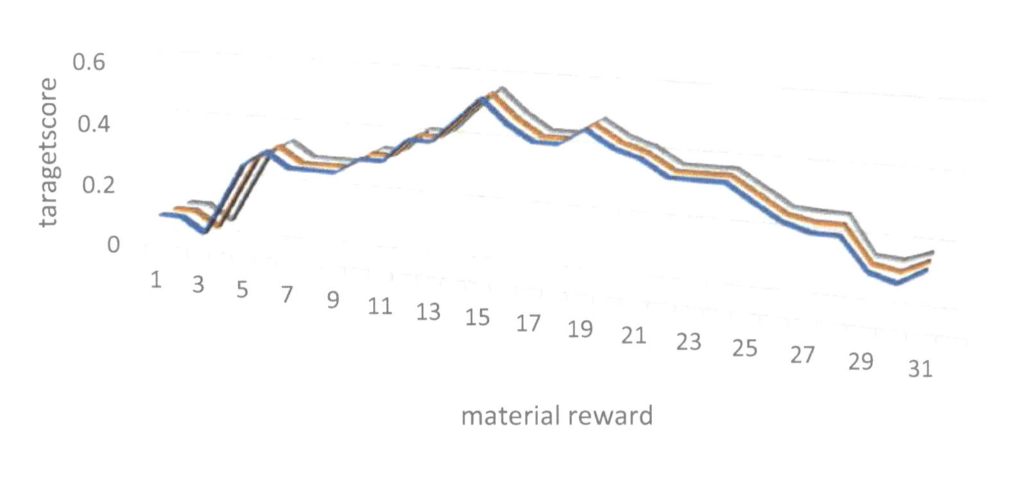

Fig. (5). HRM score and monetary reward.

CONCLUSION

In this article, we will explore the Internet of Things (IoT), the Analytical Hierarchy Process (AHP) in human resources, and other related concepts, properties, and principles. We will also examine the current development of the IoT market and how HR is currently managed. According to research, human resource management in the Internet of Things (IoT) sector is primarily concerned with how to distribute workers' time and energy; however, this approach places too much emphasis on work as the centre of an organization's operations, discourages employees from taking initiative, and generally fails to meet the needs of the Internet industry. The article analyzes the internal development of IoT manufacturing, focusing on the enterprise. By enhancing transportation, environmental protection, governance, public security, and health, the Internet of Things (IoT) is projected to create a trillion-dollar technological economy over the next decade. The findings can contribute to effective operations of Internet enterprises.

REFERENCES

[1] R. Devi et al., "Optimization of HR Management System based on IoT."

[2] Kishor, K., Agrawal, K.K., Yadav, S.P. *et al.* SPAM: An enhanced performance of security and privacy-aware model over split learning in consumer electronics. Program Comput Soft, vol. 50 pp. 875–899, 2024.
[http://dx.doi.org/10.1134/S0361768824700816]

[3] Y. Chen, C. Zhao, Y. Xu, and C. Nie, Year-over-year developments in fnancial fraud detection *via* deep learning: A systematic literature review, Jan. 2025, Accessed: Mar. 09, 2025.
[http://dx.doi.org/10.48550/arXiv.2502.00201]

[4] E. Altulaihan, M. A. Almaiah, and A. Aljughaiman, "Anomaly detection IDS for detecting DoS attacks in IoT networks based on machine learning algorithms", *Sensors,* vol. 24, no. 2, p. 713, 2024. [http://dx.doi.org/10.3390/s24020713]

[5] Y. Yang, K. Zheng, B. Wu, Y. Yang, and X. Wang, "Network intrusion detection based on supervised adversarial variational auto-encoder with regularization", *IEEE Access,* vol. 8, pp. 42169-42184, 2020. [http://dx.doi.org/10.1109/ACCESS.2020.2977007]

[6] B.M. Naman, B. Mardan, and A. Mohsin Abdulazeez, "Credit card fraud detection based on machine learning classification algorithm", *Indonesian Journal of Computer Science,* vol. 13, no. 3, 2024. [http://dx.doi.org/10.33022/ijcs.v13i3.3996]

[7] H. Palivela, V. Rishiwal, S. Bhushan, A. Alotaibi, U. Agarwal, P. Kumar, and M. Yadav, "Optimization of deep learning-based model for identification of credit card frauds", *IEEE Access,* vol. 12, pp. 125629-125642, 2024. [http://dx.doi.org/10.1109/ACCESS.2024.3440637]

[8] H. Fathy, The Evaluation of Electronic Human Resources (eHR) Management based Internet of Things using Machine Learning Techniques, ALRCIT Journal (Business & Information Systems), vol. 1, no. 1, pp. 65□85, Dec. 2024. [http://dx.doi.org/10.21608/ajcit.2025.312947.1003]

[9] C. Farkostteknik, “Credit Card Transaction Fraud Detection Using Neural Network Classifiers,” 2023, Accessed: Mar. 09, 2025. [Online]. Available from: https://urn.kb.se/resolve?urn=urn:nbn:se:kth:diva-325808

[10] S. Devaguptam, S.S. Gorti, T.L. Akshaya, and S.S. Kamath, "Automated health insurance processing framework with intelligent fraud detection, risk classification and premium prediction", *SN Comput. Sci.,* vol. 5, no. 5, p. 450, 2024. [http://dx.doi.org/10.1007/s42979-024-02801-9]

[11] S. Mewada, “Smart diagnostic expert system for defect in forging process by using machine learning process.,” 2022. [http://dx.doi.org/10.1155/2022/2567194]

[12] H. Yadav, S. Singh, K. K. Mishra, S. Srivastava, M. S. Naruka and S. P. Yadav, Brain tumor detection with MRI images. *International Conference on Computational Intelligence and Sustainable Engineering Solutions (CISES)*, pp. 519-527, 2022. [http://dx.doi.org/10.1109/CISES54857.2022.9844387]

CHAPTER 4

Integration of AI and Construction Projects for Cost Simulation

Vijay Kumar Rayabharapu[1,*], **G. Uday Kishore**[2], **Leena Jain**[3], **Monica Gupta**[4] and **Bramah Hazela**[5]

[1] *Department of Civil Engineering, B V Raju Institute of Technology, Hyderabad 502313, Telangana, India*

[2] *Department of CSE (Data Science), CMR College of Engineering & Technology, Hyderabad 501401, Telangana, India*

[3] *Department of Computer Applications, Global Group of Institutes, Amritsar 143501, Punjab, India*

[4] *Department of ECE, Bharati Vidyapeeth's College of Engineering, New Delhi 110063, India*

[5] *Amity School of Engineering & Technology, Amity University Lucknow Campus, Lucknow 226028, Uttar Pradesh, India*

Abstract: It is helpful for management to have a clear understanding of the project's scope and trajectory early on, so they can make informed estimates about the project's primary engineering quantity and cost. Furthermore, it may aid managers in avoiding risks, making appropriate construction deployments, and preventing the introduction of adverse project elements; it can also play a significant guiding role in the project's ongoing construction management. In this research, we build a system to simulate the costs of building projects using artificial intelligence. The primary use of Building Information Modelling (BIM) in this system is to model the cost of construction engineering, which is then combined with the price file for analysis and evaluation. The chapter's intelligent model has the potential to impact building project costs significantly, according to experimental studies.

Keywords: Artificial intelligence, Building information modeling, Construction management, Intelligent model, Project's scope.

INTRODUCTION

The development of manufacturing cost management is a lengthy process. Devise a modern engineering cost organization. Project cost management approaches have evolved as nations and regions have blended their features [1]. Although the

* **Corresponding author Vijay Kumar Rayabharapu:** Department of Civil Engineering, B V Raju Institute of Technology, Hyderabad 502313, Telangana, India; E-mail: vkraya@gmail.com

D. Arul Pon Daniel, T. Rajasanthosh Kumar & Satya Prakash Yadav (Eds.)

theory of contemporary engineering management of costs began relatively late, it has rapidly developed based on several management models, including those from India [2]. After the Republic of India was founded, the country adopted the former Soviet Union's engineering building management model to create a limited system of management compatible with a planned economy, which helped the economy recover and grow [3]. Marketization has experienced an upward trajectory since the establishment of the reform, and the initial approach to leadership has been unable to meet the needs of contemporary and rapid market growth. India's engineering cost sector has also entered a golden era. Project pricing continues to evolve, cost management has improved, and the consulting business has grown significantly [4]. The country's engineering cost structure likewise switched from fixed-rate to list-based pricing. In India, project cost control is internationalizing, becoming more specialized, and utilizing information technology.

Traditional quota or list measuring and pricing are precise, but they require lengthy working hours, a huge labor input, an enormous workload, and accurate drawings [5]. Today's building business requires bidders to provide quotes rapidly. Bidding firms sometimes limit bid quotes to personal experience [6]. This unconvincing offer relies on personal engineering experience. Rapid engineering of quantity and cost estimates eliminates time-consuming and laborious quota or list procedures, meeting contemporary market efficiency demands [7]. The model foundation of this method is based on data samples from numerous completed market projects, making the indicators credible and providing crucial data and theoretical guidance for bidding and quote decision-making [8].

Effective project cost management is crucial for achieving economic success. Extreme managerial and cost control wastes societal resources and keeps the project in a state of uncertainty, which hurts the company's long-term growth [9]. By comparing the project's cost estimates with those of the actual finished project, management can rapidly grasp the project's evolution and examine its deviations [10]. Meanwhile, they may track project issues and adjust the plan [11]. This chapter explores the development of an AI-powered construction project cost modeling system. BIM is typically used to model building projects, aiming to increase cost accuracy in this system [13-15].

AI-BASED BUILDING STRUCTURE SIMULATION

In computational geometry, Voronoi diagrams are of significant importance. Voronoi diagrams divide the plane into distinct regions. It's defined:

Give p_i (i =1, 2, 3… n) as a station a set P = $\{p_1, p_2, p_3,..., p_n\}$ of n distinct ideas at distinct plane locations. The equation below shows how to classify all plane points by Euclidean distance and get the point set VR (p_i) nearest to each p_i:

$$VR(p_i) = \{q|qp_i| \leq |qp_j|, \ \forall j \neq \ i, \ p_i, p_j \ \in P\} \quad (1)$$

|qp| is the Euclidean distance between p and q. The Voronoi area of point pi is VR (p_i). As illustrated in the equation, p_i The Voronoi diagram is the blending of all stations' Voronoi regions:

$$V\,D(P) = U_{i=1}^{n} VR(p_i) \quad (2)$$

The plane has non-overlapping subregions, each representing a site. |qp_i |≤|qp_j |, for each idea q in the pi subarea at the place, wherep_j ƐP-$\{p_i\}$. The Voronoi grid, consisting of 8 discrete points, is shown in Fig. (**1**).

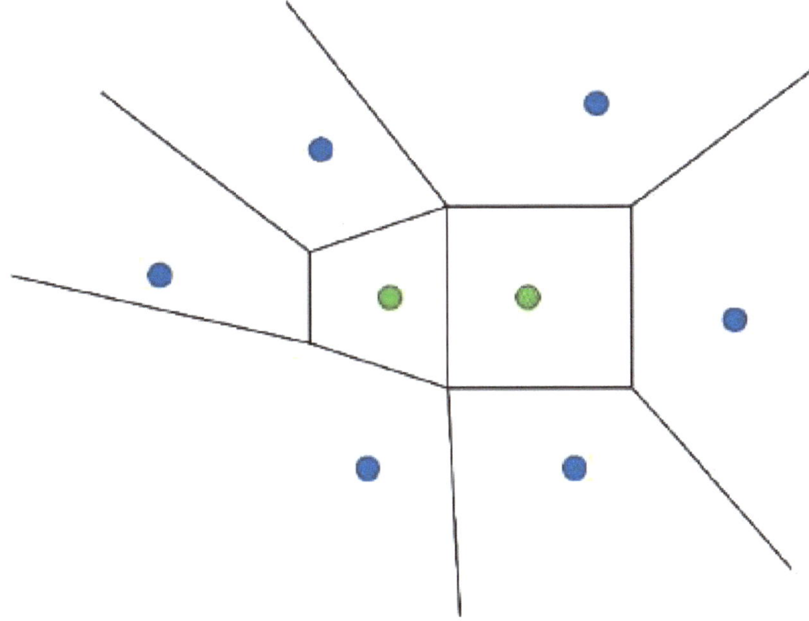

Fig. (1). 8 discrete points of the Voronoi diagram.

A vertex pi in a multi-boundary polygon P is considered concave if an angle α > 180° between it and the two related sides in the Voronoi diagram's drafting region. Sites are P's concave vertices or edges. Voronoi diagrams of polygon P are formed by the union of Voronoi regions at each site. This yields a Voronoi diagram of polygon P:

Different sites list three bisector types:

- Fig. (**2a**) depicts the vertical bisector of the link between the vertices.

- Fig. (**2b**) illustrates the parabola bisector between the vertices and edges.
- Fig. (**2c**) represents the bisector of an angle created by two sides.

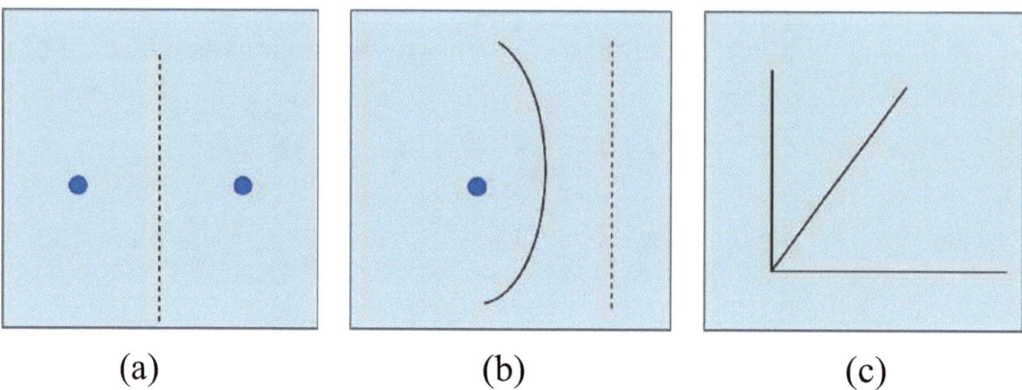

Fig. (2). The three intersections

Next, partition all stations' Voronoi areas using the three bisectors. Importantly, each concave vertex represents the termination point of the Voronoi diagram created by the polygon to split its Voronoi area with the two sides' Voronoi areas. Next, join the two edge vertical bisectors. The three bisectors shown above, in addition to the vertical bisectors of the convex vertices, split the Voronoi diagram for the polygon. A Voronoi edge is the common edge connecting the Voronoi regions of two sites, and a Voronoi vertex is their intersection. Voronoi edges and vertices form the polygon's Voronoi skeleton route. Fig. (**3**) illustrates a multi-boundary polygon Voronoi diagram. The polygon Voronoi skeleton route is the dotted line.

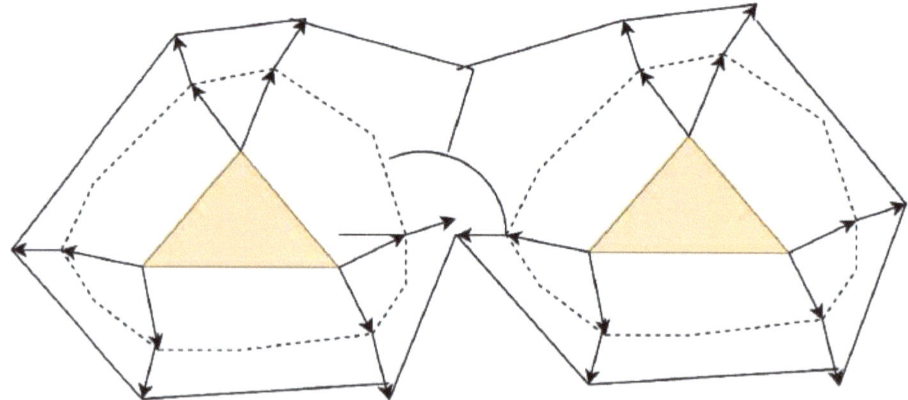

Fig. (3). Multi-boundary polygon Voronoi diagram.

This chapter introduces the concept of poor visibility in the context of polygonal regions. Q is an area of polygon P. S is faintly observable relative to Q if a point in Q can see s in P. You can see the point p1 in Q at the points s in Fig. (**4a**), and Q is close to p1p2. Accordingly, s is a point that is just marginally observable about Q. Point s is poorly visible about Q in the polygon P if station s can view a given point in Q. Fig. (**4b**) shows the feebly visible region of Q in the polygons P, which is the collection of all points of Q that are weakly visible.

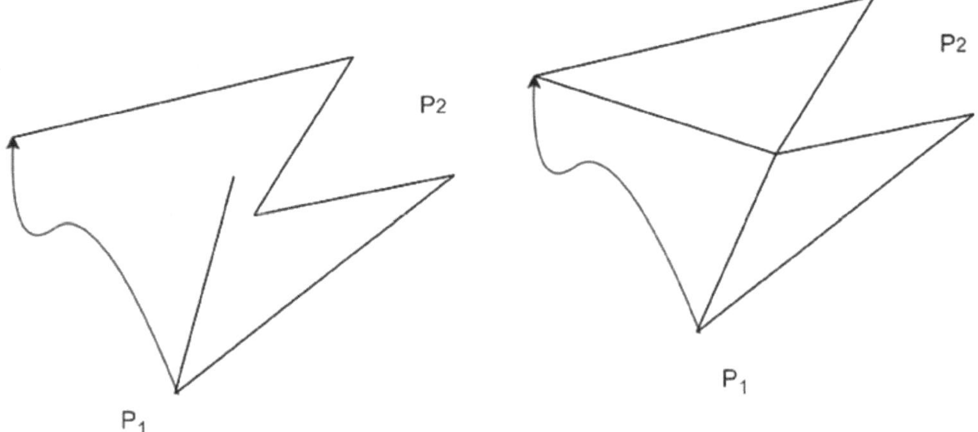

Fig. (4). Visibility is low.

Below is a method for easily creating an MR environment in big interior areas like museums and art galleries. The building approach suggested in this study has four steps:

- Create the virtual scene.
- Map the virtual scene to the actual world.
- Set the wall transparency value.
- Correcting offset errors

First, build the scene, then create the virtual scene to match the actual one. In HoloLens, Multiview geometric reconstruction is used to scan and build scenes. In many interior environments, scanning is unsuitable for MR applications. There are two reasons: scanning is time-consuming and difficult, and saving the full area at once is impossible. This article replaces the tedious scanning procedure with a prebuilt virtual wall model, storing the actual environment's structural information for reuse. Method details:

- A two-dimensional wall diagram of the real world is derived from three data sources in this article. (1) The user may create walls using multitouch or cursor operation in this article's 2D structure diagram, which matches the actual environment's structural specifications (Fig. **5a**). The user may alter the wall by entering its length in the text field after sketching. (2) Fig. (**5b**) shows how the edge detection method extracts the 2D building structure diagram from the plane structure diagram. (3) The article presents the 2D structural diagram after importing the preexisting spatial 3D model.
- After obtaining a 2D structural diagram in step 1, the technique transfers it to the surface-running design end. A virtual wall model is then constructed as the program iteratively processes the data associated with every node in the structural diagram.

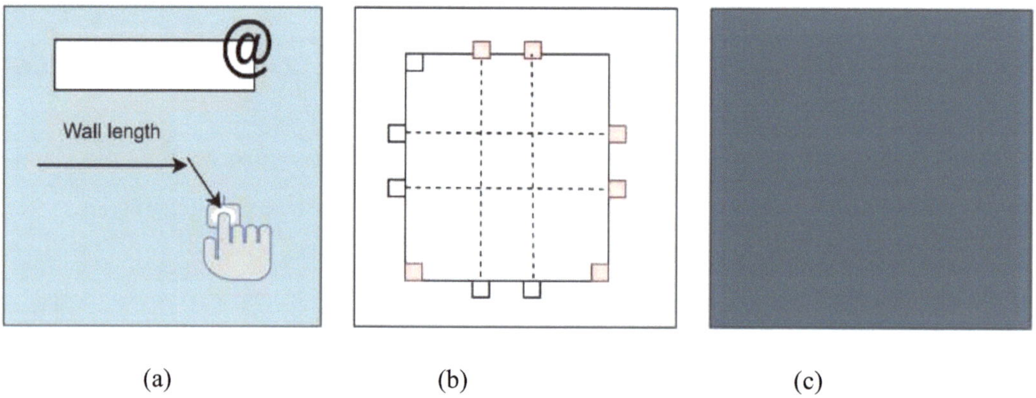

Fig. (5). A 2D building technique structure diagram. a) Parameterized 2D structural drawing. b) Input plane structure. (c) Processed 2D structural figure.

Fig. (**5a** and **5b**) show a two-dimensional structure drawing based on parameters, whereas Fig. (**5c**) shows the input smooth structural figure, and the correct side shows the processed construction figure.

For the experience to be authentic, the virtual scene and real environment must be accurately mapped, transformed into an integrated coordinate system, and the scene registered. A design-side digital coordinate system is created in this article. The actual world and HoloLens may be aligned 1:1. This article represents real-world locations using this coordinate system.

CONSTRUCTION COST SIMULATION USING AI AND BIM

The feasibility study, project design, bidding, implementation, conclusion, approval, delivery, use, and project post-evaluation are all part of the whole-process project cost management, which follows engineering project construction procedures. Each of these steps is mapped out in Fig. (**6**), which shows the relevant project cost valuation documentation. Before applying BIM software to the building engineering price file control, it is necessary to clarify the information trade structure of the model (Fig. **7**) and its use for the improved control of the project's cost (Fig. **8**). This will lay the groundwork for further refined applications. The model is examined and validated after construction, primarily to assess its impact on BIM simulation and project cost assessment. You can see the outcomes in Fig. (**9**). Experimental evidence from the sources cited above supports the validity of the approach put forth in this article.

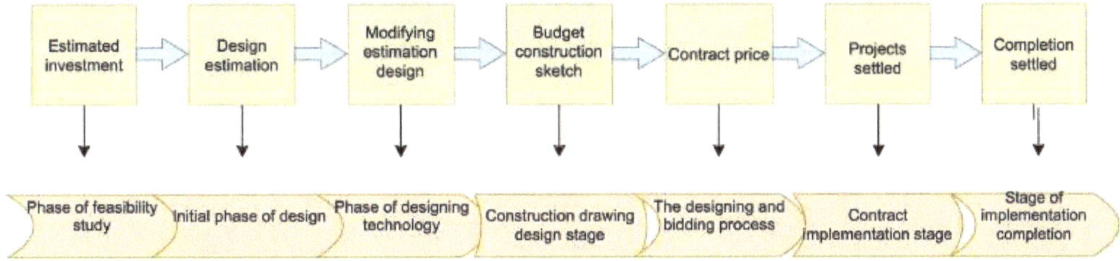

Fig. (6). File for valuation.

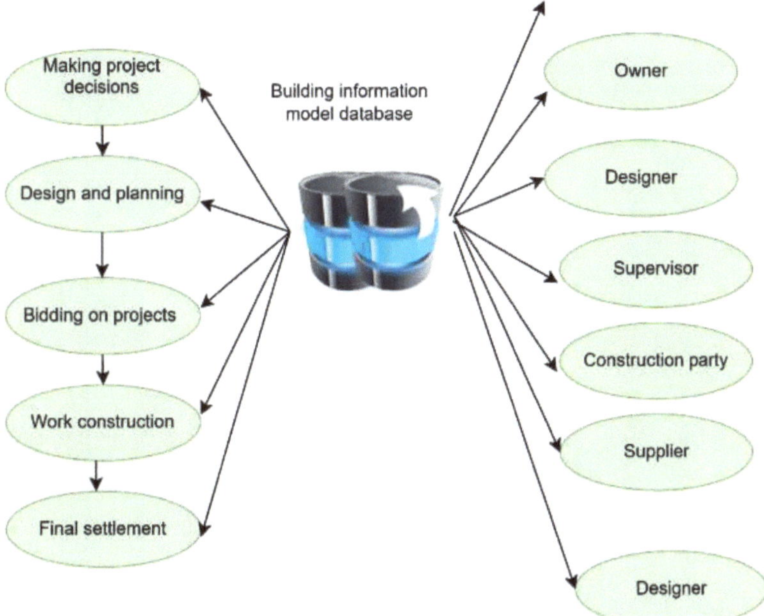

Fig. (7). Information model interchange diagram.

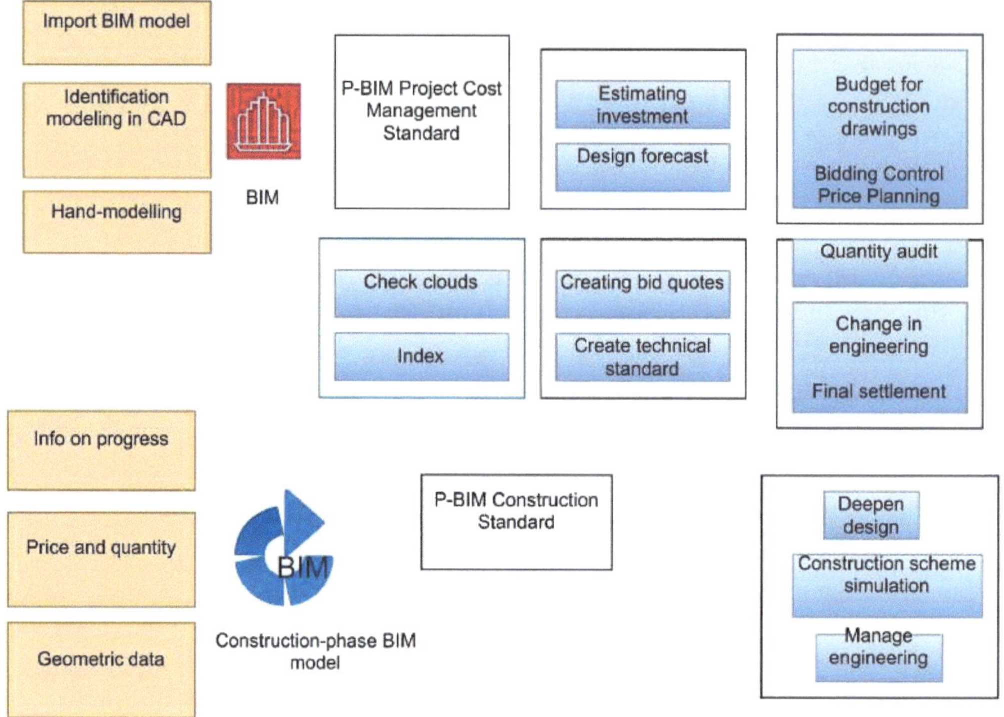

Fig. (8). Enhanced project cost management BIM model.

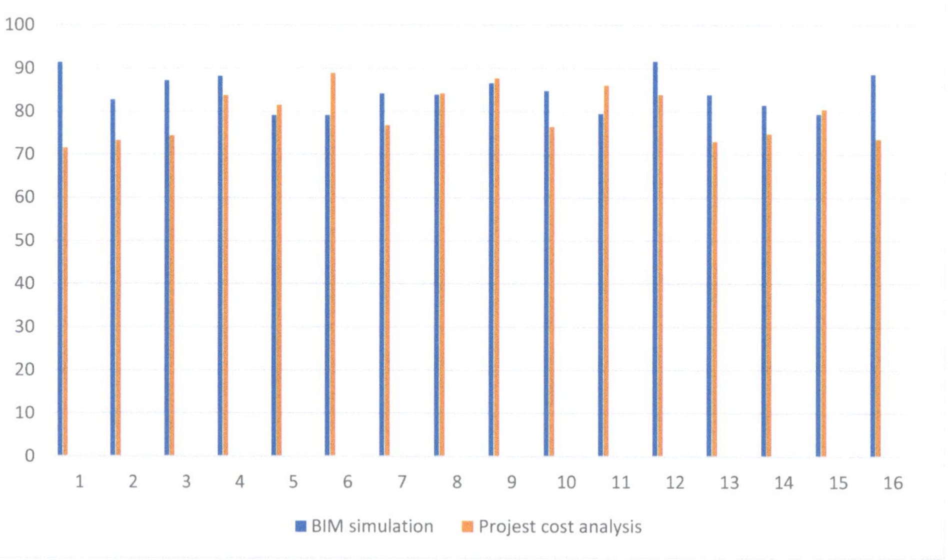

Fig. (9). Using AI for BIM simulation and project cost assessment.

CONCLUSION

Projects incorporate design, structure, materials, and installation, and they undergo numerous phases from decision-making to completion. Different parties in different professions or phases may use other strategies to present and handle the same information, leading to duplication and difficulty in sharing. Information underpins BIM. BIM models start with a single element or item and use parameters to communicate its physical properties, geometry data, price data, and construction requirements. It then organizes and stores this data in a database using 3D Boolean calculations and spatial topological connections to create a numerical model. Furthermore, the BIM-based project method allows for the alteration of important data at any moment to reflect project changes, thereby eliminating information duplication and facilitating easier stakeholder information exchange.

REFERENCES

[1] Singh, Chaitanya & Subrahmanya Srinivasa Rao, Motukuri & Mahaboobjohn, Y. & Bonthu, Kotaiah & Kumar, T. Applied machine tool data condition to predictive smart maintenance by using artificial intelligence 2022.
[http://dx.doi.org/10.1007/s40032-025-01169-w]

[2] Serugga, Joas. "Digital Twins and AI Decision Models: Advancing Cost Modelling in Off-Site Construction" *Eng* 6, no. 2: 22, 2025.
[http://dx.doi.org/10.3390/eng6020022]

[3] S. Yilmaz, D. Kumar, S. Hada, S. Demirkesen, C. Zhang, and H. Li, A PMBOK-based construction cost management framework for BIM integration in construction projects. *Int. J. Constr. Manag.,* vol. 25, no. 8, pp. 861–875, June 2025.

[4] A. S. Thakur, T. L. Alex, and A. Nighojkar, "Artificial intelligence in maritime anomaly detection: A decadal bibliometric analysis (2014–2024)," *Journal of The Institution of Engineers (India)*: Series C, pp. 1–25,
[http://dx.doi.org/10.1007/s40032-025-01169-w]

[5] A. Iqbal, and R. Amin, "Time series forecasting and anomaly detection using deep learning", *Comput. Chem. Eng.,* vol. 182, p. 108560, 2024.
[http://dx.doi.org/10.1016/j.compchemeng.2023.108560]

[6] N. Dhieb, H. Ghazzai, H. Besbes, and Y. Massoud, "A secure AI-driven architecture for automated insurance systems: Fraud detection and risk measurement", *IEEE Access,* vol. 8, pp. 58546-58558, 2020.
[http://dx.doi.org/10.1109/ACCESS.2020.2983300]

[7] A. Kanksha, A. Bhaskar, S. Pande, R. Malik, and A. Khamparia, "An intelligent unsupervised technique for fraud detection in health care systems", *Intell. Decision Technol.,* vol. 15, no. 1, pp. 127-139, 2021.
[http://dx.doi.org/10.3233/IDT-200052]

[8] S. Devaguptam, S.S. Gorti, T.L. Akshaya, and S.S. Kamath, "Automated health insurance processing framework with intelligent fraud detection, risk classification and premium prediction", *SN Comput. Sci.,* vol. 5, no. 5, p. 450, 2024.
[http://dx.doi.org/10.1007/s42979-024-02801-9]

[9] F. Louati, F.B. Ktata, and I. Amous, "Enhancing intrusion detection systems with reinforcement

learning: A comprehensive survey of RL-based approaches and techniques", *SN Comput. Sci.,* vol. 5, no. 6, p. 665, 2024.
[http://dx.doi.org/10.1007/s42979-024-03001-1]

[10] F. Aslam, A.I. Hunjra, Z. Ftiti, W. Louhichi, and T. Shams, "Insurance fraud detection: Evidence from artificial intelligence and machine learning", *Res. Int. Bus. Finance,* vol. 62, p. 101744, 2022.
[http://dx.doi.org/10.1016/j.ribaf.2022.101744]

[11] B.N. Muthura, and A. Matheka, "A hybrid model for detecting insurance fraud using K-means and support vector machine algorithms", *Open Journal for Information Technology,* vol. 6, no. 2, pp. 143-156, 2023.
[http://dx.doi.org/10.32591/coas.ojit.0602.05143m]

[12] T. Walczyna, D. Jankowski, and Z. Piotrowski, Enhancing anomaly detection through latent space manipulation in autoencoders: A comparative analysis, *Applied Sciences 2025*, Vol. 15, Page 286, vol. 15, no. 1, p. 286, Dec. 2024.
[http://dx.doi.org/10.3390/app15010286]

[13] K. , A. Kishor, An enhanced performance of security and privacy-aware model over split learning in consumer electronics, *Programming and Computer Software*. vol. 50, pp 875-899, 2025.
[http://dx.doi.org/10.1134/S0361768824700816]

[14] S. Mewada, “Smart diagnostic expert system for defect in forging process by using machine learning process.,” 2022.
[http://dx.doi.org/10.1155/2022/2567194]

[15] D. Goel, D. Singh, A. Gupta, S. P. Yadav and M. Sharma, "An efficient approach for to predict the quality of apple through its appearance", *International Conference on Computer, Electronics & Electrical Engineering & their Applications* (IC2E3), pp. 1-6, 2023.
[http://dx.doi.org/10.1109/IC2E357697.2023.10262569]

CHAPTER 5

E-Commerce Order Management System by GPST Tracking System

Santosh Reddy P.[1,*], **Jayashree**[2], **Arpitha Devangavi**[2] and **L.S. Geeta**[1]

[1] *Department of Computer Science & Engineering, BNM Institute of Technology, Bangalore 560070, Karnataka, India*

[2] *Department of Artificial Intelligence and Machine Learning, BNM Institute of Technology, Bangalore 560070, Karnataka, India*

Abstract: Supply chain management systems, such as order management systems, impact customer satisfaction and corporate profits. Order management software helps hardware stores keep sales and purchase data. Faulty records lead to unhappy customers, less money in storerooms, and slower sales. Customers submit orders, visit hotels or cafeterias to learn about the cuisine, and then pay; this requires time and human labor. E-commerce sites make it easier to purchase all our everyday necessities thanks to technology. In this sophisticated technological age, we have no app or website to acquire recipe ingredients. This document reduces ingredient waste, time, and cost. Provide recipes and quantities within 1–2 hours. This mechanism will enable us to deliver orders quickly to our customers.

Keywords: E-commerce, GPST, Supply chain management, Tracking system.

INTRODUCTION

Order management takes place in order to obtain the right inventory at the right place at the right time, in the right numbers, in the right structure, and at the right price [1]. Inspired by this approach, inventory includes materials and extras that enhance the creation and gathering process but don't shape the end item or raw resources [2]. Having inadequate stock structures will result in a company suffering huge losses; therefore, the role of Stock Executives is of the utmost importance. The company's appearance can be enhanced with a robust stock management system [3]. Thus, it requires intentional stock management, controlled by a team of professionals [4]. Most emphasis is on creating a division for Western businesses since Western executives are aware of efficient stock. Thus, this study examines a material chain shop to increase topography [5]. Stock

[*] **Corresponding author Santosh Reddy P.:** Department of Computer Science & Engineering, BNM Institute of Technology, Bangalore 560070, Karnataka, India; E-mail: santoshreddy@bnmit.in

D. Arul Pon Daniel, T. Rajasanthosh Kumar & Satya Prakash Yadav (Eds.)

and creativity work together to achieve one goal. Failure to produce stock will result in stoppages and subsequent production problems. The Consumable Store Stock Count and Adjustment Policy and Procedure states that Rustenburg Warehouse reduces inventory holding and costs [6].

Stock and creativity work together to achieve one goal. The Consumable Store Stock Count and Adjustment Policy and Procedure states that Rustenburg Warehouse reduces inventory holding and costs [7]. Smaller companies may send goods to the stock area rather than an accepting area, and if they are discount wholesalers, they may sell finished goods rather than raw materials or parts [8]. From inventories, merchandise is transported to generating offices for completion. An enterprise's stock receives 60% of the money. Material management involves organizing, confirming, maintaining, and providing the proper material, quantity, and location at the right time to coordinate and plan mechanical project development in an integrative course [9]. Extraordinary or scarce stock can lead to company failure. A recommendation that stocks out a simple inventory item may cause group endings [10]. Stock management and stock casing are seen on the board. The stock management process helps determine the optimal stock level and address issues related to good stock and lead time. Stock inventory is a significant advantage in this particular area; executives have been deeply invested in ramping up production to meet growing business demands. [11]. Due to global rivalry, several governments have adopted Just-In-Time (JIT) inventory systems. Many organizations have used JIT to manage their inventory management systems and reduce inventory expenditures. Stock management using the Just in Time Technique. This gadget reduces costs, a JIT advantage [12]. This mechanism will enable us to deliver orders quickly to our customers. Ingredient quantities classify many recipes under this approach. Users can register for the app by signing up. Each user has a separate app login account [13]. Customers can add recipes to our app for a unique service [14]. Users with a valid login ID and admin approval can upload recipes to our app. Customers may also watch video lessons on our app to create recipes. Order tracking is available through the app, and updates on order delivery allow users to monitor their orders. Personalized recipes are also available, and users may edit recipe components to their desired quantities.

METHODOLOGY

Paper should be used to visualize page components before computer construction. Using cartoons and storyboards, arrange the site's look and navigational structure like a site map. The current approach requires individuals to buy items at the market to prepare recipes. Because not all the necessary items are in one place and some are even unavailable in local marketplaces, a lot of time is spent. After one usage, certain goods in large quantities expire since they are no longer needed in subsequent recipes, resulting in wasted money and resources (Figs. **1** and **2**).

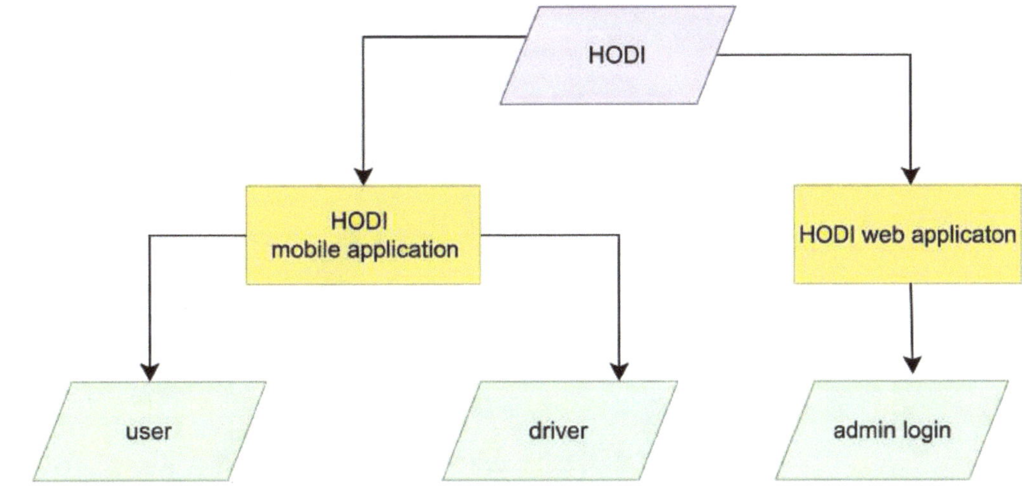

Fig. (1). System specification.

Site Map-Hodi

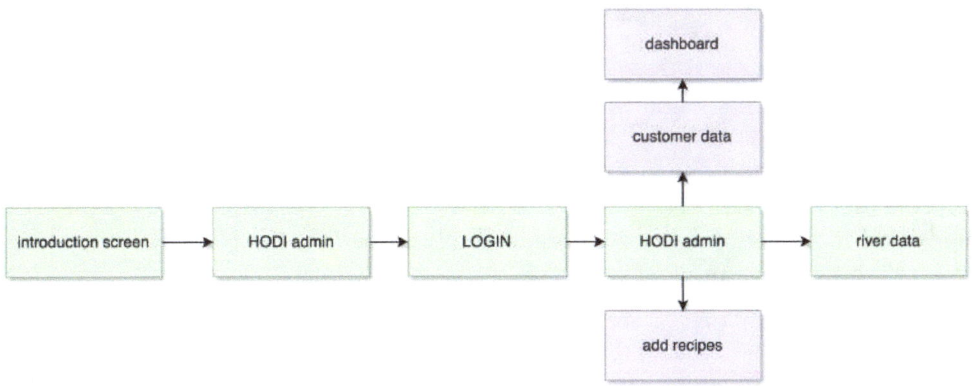

Fig. (2). Website maps for HODI.

IMPLEMENTATION

Register/Login

End-users may register and log in using HODI. Individuals must register and log in to use the HODI system. The system supplier provides login and registration functionalities for all users.

Home Customer

Customers may access their home pages by signing in (Fig. **3**).

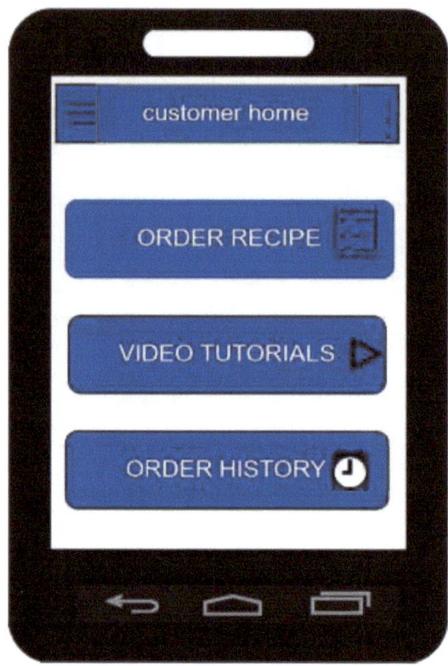

Fig. (3). Customer home android app.

Click the "Order Recipes" link to view and order recipes. It takes the user to the recipe screen. To see how-to videos for the recipes, click the Video Tutorials icon. Redirects the visitor to a new screen with video links. To view previously ordered recipes and those that were not delivered, click the "Order History" button, which redirects the user to a new screen with the order history.

Driver Home

Logging in as an employee will take you to the customer's location. By clicking "My Profile," users may access and change their profile information. Click the "Order Area" button to display the delivery location. Click on the "Order History" icon to examine previous orders and incomplete recipes.

Customer-Side Navigation

Customers can perform several tasks through site navigation (Fig. **4**).

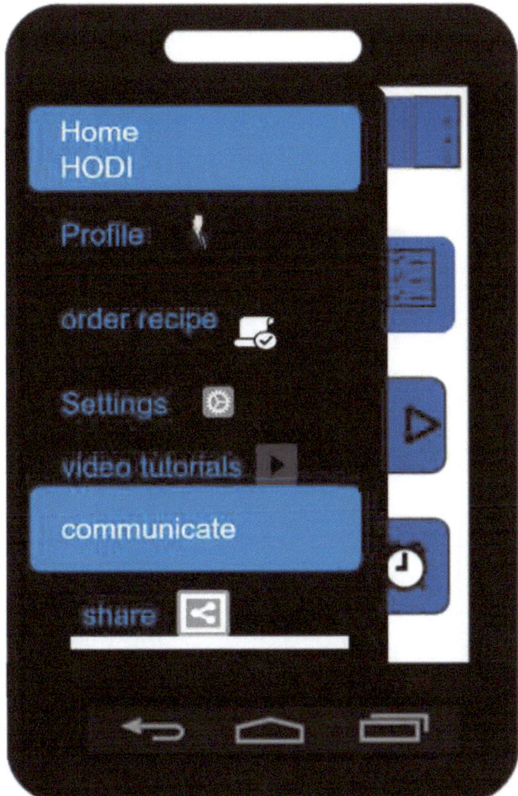

Fig. (4). Customer-side android app navigation.

TEST CASE

The software testing standard IEEE software test documentation Std 829-1998 is the basis for this test. This standard defines the basic test papers for dynamic software testing and dictates the purpose, outline, and content of these documents. Some of the papers in the standard, such as the test plan and incident report, can be utilized for development and code reviews, despite their primary focus on dynamic testing. This standard is also applicable to any digital computer used in commercial, scientific, or military systems. Applications are not limited by system size, complexity, or criticality.

Recipe Category Search

Table **1** depicts the Recipe category search.

Table 1. Recipe category search.

Engineer Test	ARTHI
Test case ID	TC2.
UC/FR/NFR	11/11/2023.
Purpose	This test aims to ensure the appropriate functioning of Recipe Searching.
Pre-req	To utilize the HODI Android app, log in as a customer.
Test data	The system will supply the necessary recipe by category.
Steps:	There are stages to complete this exam. These steps follow. 1. Sign in to the "Customer Portal" 2. Hit the search bar. 3. Choose the desired search category. 4. Click the "Search Recipe" button.
Status	Pass.

DISCUSSION

Eliminating ingredient waste saves both money and quantity. Packets of materials used in small amounts are not valuable. Since Ingredients are scarce in the local market, provide the required components and alternatives. Our recipes and ingredients are affordable; however, when purchasing ingredients for recipes, they may not be readily available locally due to their limited packaging options. Many moderate quantities of materials are provided in packets that expire after use. An Android app is used for ordering, and a web-based admin site and Firebase database are utilized for data storage. Our program offers classified recipes, order monitoring, and the ability to contribute your recipes. We also provide video services to demonstrate how to prepare a specific meal. Users can view their search history, connect via direct chat, and rate recipes. User data and orders will be managed on the website.

CONCLUSION

Every test case is positive, which proves that the whole System works and runs perfectly. Test cases thoroughly evaluate HODI in every area, ensuring it is bug-free, crash-tested, and demonstrates that the overall system functionalitymeets expectations.

REFERENCES

[1] Mewada, Shivlal & Saroliya et al. Smart Diagnostic Expert System for Defect in Forging Process by Using Machine Learning Process. Journal of Nanomaterials. pp. 1-8, 2022. [http://dx.doi.org/10.1155/2022/2567194]

[2] S. M. Ilyas, Asghar Ali Shah, and Ali Sohail, "Order management system for time and quantity saving

of recipes ingredients using GPS tracking systems," *IEEE Access*, 2021.
[http://dx.doi.org/10.1109/ACCESS.2021.3090808]

[3] Jingjie Wang, Wei Bai, and Yongbin Liu, "Optimization for the human resources management strategy of the IoT industry based on AHP," Computational Intelligence and Neuroscience, vol. 2022, Article ID 3514285, 2022.
[http://dx.doi.org/10.1155/2022/3514285]

[4] R.A. Alzahrani, M. Aljabri, and R.A. Mustafa Mohammad, "Ad click fraud detection using machine learning and deep learning algorithms", *IEEE Access,* vol. 13, pp. 12746-12763, 2025.
[http://dx.doi.org/10.1109/ACCESS.2025.3532200]

[5] B.M. Naman, B. Mardan, and A. Mohsin Abdulazeez, "Credit card fraud detection based on machine learning classification algorithm", *Indonesian Journal of Computer Science,* vol. 13, no. 3, 2024.
[http://dx.doi.org/10.33022/ijcs.v13i3.3996]

[6] R.A. Bauder, and T.M. Khoshgoftaar, "Medicare fraud detection using machine learning methods", *Proceedings - 16th IEEE International Conference on Machine Learning and Applications, ICMLA,* pp. 858-865, 2017.
[http://dx.doi.org/10.1109/ICMLA.2017.00-48]

[7] F. Louati, F.B. Ktata, and I. Amous, "Enhancing itrusion detection systems with reinforcement learning: A comprehensive survey of RL-based approaches and techniques", *SN Comput. Sci.,* vol. 5, no. 6, p. 665, 2024.
[http://dx.doi.org/10.1007/s42979-024-03001-1]

[8] X. Zhao, Q. Zhang, and C. Zhang, "Enhancing transaction fraud detection with a hybrid machine learning model", *4th International Conference on Electronic Technology, Communication and Information, ICETCI,* pp. 427-432, 2024.
[http://dx.doi.org/10.1109/ICETCI61221.2024.10594463]

[9] P. Kamuangu, "A review on financial fraud detection using AI and machine learning", *Journal of Economics, Finance and Accounting Studies,* vol. 6, no. 1, pp. 67-77, 2024.
[http://dx.doi.org/10.32996/jefas.2024.6.1.7]

[10] Akinbusola Olushola and Joseph Mart. Fraud detection using machine learning. *ScienceOpen Preprints*. 2024.
[http://dx.doi.org/10.14293/PR2199.000647.v1]

[11] N. Cristianini, and J. Shawe-Taylor, "An introduction to support vector machines and other kernel-based learning methods", *An Introduction to Support Vector Machines and Other Kernel-based Learning Methods,* no. Mar, 2000.
[http://dx.doi.org/10.1017/CBO9780511801389]

[12] G. Kotlarski, "Electron-Beam Welding of Titanium and Ti6Al4V Alloy", *Metals,* vol. 13, no. 6, p. 1065, 2023.
[http://dx.doi.org/10.3390/met13061065]

[13] Z. Dong, M. Xu, H. Guo, X. Fei, Y. Liu, B. Gong, and G. Ju, "Microstructural evolution and characterization of AlSi10Mg alloy manufactured by selective laser melting", *J. Mater. Res. Technol.,* vol. 17, pp. 2343-2354, 2022.
[http://dx.doi.org/10.1016/j.jmrt.2022.01.129]

[14] H. Yadav, S. Singh, K. K. Mishra, S. Srivastava, M. S. Naruka and S. P. Yadav. Brain tumor detection with MRI images, *International Conference on Computational Intelligence and Sustainable Engineering Solutions (CISES),* pp. 519-527, 2022.
[http://dx.doi.org/10.1109/CISES54857.2022.9844387]

CHAPTER 6

Inline Sentimental Analysis Using Social Voice Messages

Sankara Mahalingam M.[1,*], K. Maharajan[1], N. Srinu[2], T. Jayasri[2], V. Gopinath[3], Martha Tri Lestari[4] and **Kuheli Mondal[5]**

[1] *Department of Computer Science and Engineering, School of Computing, Kalasalingam Academy of Research and Education, Krishnankoil 626126, Tamil Nadu, India*

[2] *Department of CSE, QIS College of Engineering & Technology, Ongole 523272, Andhra Pradesh, India*

[3] *Department of Mechanical Engineering, QIS College of Engineering & Technology, Ongole 523272, Andhra Pradesh, India*

[4] *Department of Digital Public Relations, School of Communication & Business, Telkom University, Bandung 40257, West Java, Indonesia*

[5] *Department of ECE, QIS College of Engineering & Technology, Ongole 523272, Andhra Pradesh, India*

Abstract: In the present world, it is challenging to study sentiment and emotion in human multimodal language. However, in specific cases, such as calls, only sound information is available. In this work, we examined sentiment analysis and feeling identity freely. Current self-supervised learning models, especially speaker-mindful pre-preparation models, were used to prepare discourse, particularly in widespread discourse portrayals. For three sentiment tasks and an emotion test, three distinct sizes of universal models were examined. The study found that two types of sentiment analysis produced the best results, based on weighted and unweighted accuracy scores of 81% and 73%, respectively. When compared to previous methods that utilized multimodal fusion, our binary classification of unimodal audio data performed competitively. The models failed to make accurate predictions during an experiment, as evidenced by their inability to make precise predictions on tasks involving sentiment analysis and emotion detection. As the number of courses available increases, the reported performance decreases in the six-class emotion, three-class sentiment, and seven-class sentiment tasks may also be attributed to the inconsistent nature of the datasets.

Keywords: Feature extraction, NLP, Recurrent neural networks, Sentiment analysis.

[*] **Corresponding author Sankara Mahalingam M.:** Department of Computer Science and Engineering, School of Computing, Kalasalingam Academy of Research and Education, Krishnankoil 626126, Tamil Nadu, India; E-mail: sankaramahalingam@gmail.com

D. Arul Pon Daniel, T. Rajasanthosh Kumar & Satya Prakash Yadav (Eds.)

INTRODUCTION

Using machine learning and natural language processing, an inline sentiment analysis system analyzes spoken language to identify emotions and feelings [1]. This method has several potential applications, such as providing emergency services with real-time information about the caller's emotional state and analyzing phone conversations and audio messages to determine the speaker's emotional state [2]. The system utilizes acoustic analysis, prosodic aspects, and lexical analysis to identify patterns in speech that may reflect emotions, enabling the analysis of voice messages or calls [4]. For instance, if you want to express excitement, you may use a high-pitched voice and babble; however, a low-pitched voice and agitated speech pace would imply sadness or despair [5, 6]. When used in customer service interactions, sentiment analysis can reveal how customers feel, enabling businesses to cater to their needs more effectively [8]. Textual communication, such as social media feeds and online reviews, may also indicate popular opinion [9]. During emergency calls, in-line sentiment analysis may identify distress and warn authorities [10]. Consider a hypothetical emergency hotline contact from a visibly concerned or frightened person. Here, the sentiment analysis system may notify appropriate parties of the caller's current emotional condition. Last, integrated sentiment analysis may improve communication, customer service, and emergency response times.

ALGORITHM

This approach utilizes lexical or dictionary-based emotional word grading to assess the tone of a text. Our opinions assign a positive, negative, or neutral value to every word, adding all ratings to determine the text's cumulative tone. Recurrent neural networks provide real-time sentiment analysis. With additional data and expertise, these computers can learn complex word associations. RNNs process input sequences sequentially, using earlier sequence knowledge to influence the current sequence. Voice-based sentiment analysis uses syllable order to determine the speaker's mood. RNNs must be trained to recognize voice inflection by converting speech into characteristics. Mel Frequency Cepstral Coefficients (MFCCs) are used to describe the spectral features and evolution of speech signals. To train a Recurrent Neural Network (RNN) to identify speech mood, convert the audio stream into attributes. Supervised learning trains the RNN using sound samples and sentiment labels. After learning from past sequences, the RNN changes its internal state to assess MFCC features. It understands the speaker's mood and timing between speech portions.

Real-time emotion classification is possible with RNNs after training. According to its internal state, an RNN successively classifies speech emotion. People describe speech signal spectral properties and variations using MFCCs, which converts audio into attributes, starting RNN speech mood training. Using audio data and sentiment labels, supervised learning trains RNNs, whichadjust their internal state to analyze MFCC qualities after learning from previous sequences, enabling RNNs to recognize spoken emotions and temporal relationships. Following training, RNNs can classify emotions in real-time audio samples, as it analyzes voice input, an RNN identifies sentiment using speech internals, as shown in Fig. (**1**). RNN identifies sentiment using speech internals.

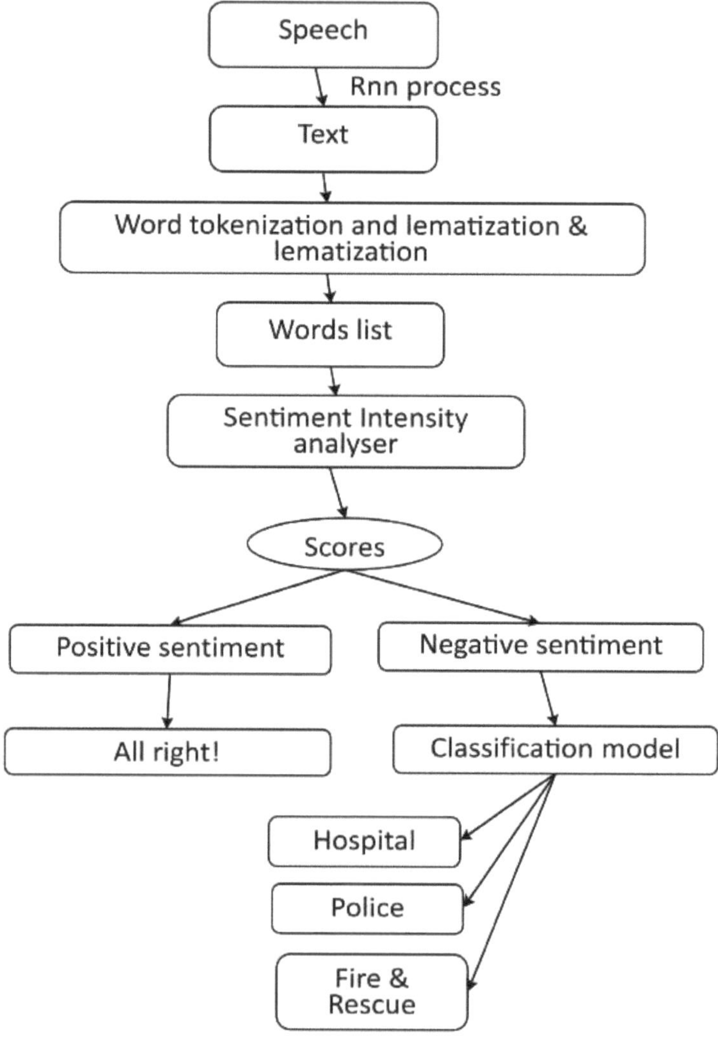

Fig. (1). RNN identifies sentiment using speech internals.

MODEL DESCRIPTION

This method determines if a word is negated by searching for negation terms in the input text. A class called "Vader Constants" is defined in the code, which holds various constants related to the VADER algorithm. This class outlines the variables and methods it encompasses:

Words and phrases that convey a positive or negative feeling may have their sentiment ratings increased or decreased using these constants.

- A set of negation words that can be used to change the meaning of phrases that follow them.
- A specialized idiomatic dictionary with sentiment scores.
- A regular expression that is used to remove punctuation from text.
- A list of punctuation characters.

The Senti Text class appears to tokenize and preprocess the input text, which includes eliminating punctuation, handling emoticons and contractions, and recognizing words in all capital letters.

The Google Translate API is used in conjunction with the Google library to translate text from a user-specific language to English. The language codes are picked from a pre-defined list of supported languages in the library's "LANGUAGES" dictionary. The detect() function detects the language of the input text, which is then translated to English using the translate() method. We did text preparation tasks, including eliminating punctuation, stop words, and lemmatization. This code looks to be preparing text for a given input text. The string and Counter modules from the Python standard library, as well as three modules from the Natural Language Toolkit (NLTK) library, including stop words, WordNet Lemmatizer, and word tokenizer, will be imported. The text will then be processed by converting it to lowercase and removing any punctuation marks using the translate function. It is then tokenized into individual words using the tokenize function, which is subsequently filtered using the stop words, ('English') to eliminate common English stop words. Lastly, the WordNet Lemmatizer is used to lemmatize each word, transforming it into its basic form. After the code has been pre-processed, we will perform sentiment analysis using the (Valence Aware Dictionary and Sentiment Reasoner) VADER tool from the Natural Language Toolkit (NLTK) package.

The function accepts a text string as input and returns the positive and negative VADER scores as output. It then calculates the proportion of positive and negative sentiment in the text and presents a graphical representation of the findings using a pie chart generated with the Matplotlib tool. When we perform sentiment analysis on the statement, we will determine if the sentiment of the input text is negative and then identify terms related to emergency services, such as police, hospital, and fire. If any of these terms are found in the input text, we will display a picture corresponding to the applicable emergency service. We are showing the photos using the Matplotlib package, which appears to be operating correctly, assuming the image files are available in the working directory. After completing the sentiment analysis of text-based data, we will utilize a speech recognition algorithm that leverages the Google Translate API to translate spoken text into English. Speech recognition begins with importing the required libraries: Playground, Google Translate, requests, (Operating System) OS, string, collections, Matplotlib, (Natural Language Toolkit) NLTK, and WordNetLemmatizer. Following the first pre-processing of the voice, the user is invited to select a language from a list. If the language chosen is legitimate, the matching language code is used to set the translation destination to English. The "Take Command" function captures audio from the microphone and recognizes spoken text using the speech recognition library. The identified text is then translated into English for additional examination using the Google Library. Once we have finished analyzing the speech, we will convert it to text and apply all the preprocessing procedures we have done for text, such as lemmatization, stopword removal, stemming, and tokenization, to obtain our output. This output will indicate the organization we need to contact in case of an emergency.

RESULTS

We conducted sentiment analysis on both text and voice to ensure our model's applicability. The graph below depicts the outcome of sentiment analysis on textual data when we provided a negative sentiment assertion shown in Fig. (**2**).

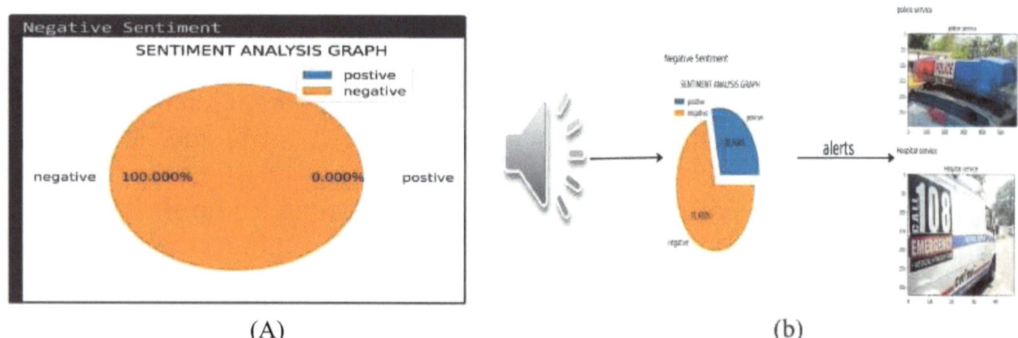

(A) (b)

Fig. (2). Negative sentiment.

In this case, we have specified a statement with a term that signals the necessity for hospital services. Hence, by analysing the sentiment analysis shown in Fig. (**2**) and suggesting the essential service for that specific situation, our machine accurately identified the comment.

For the voice analysis, we provided a remark that is difficult to discern whether it is positive or negative, and the sentiment analysis for the sentence is shown in Fig. (**3**).

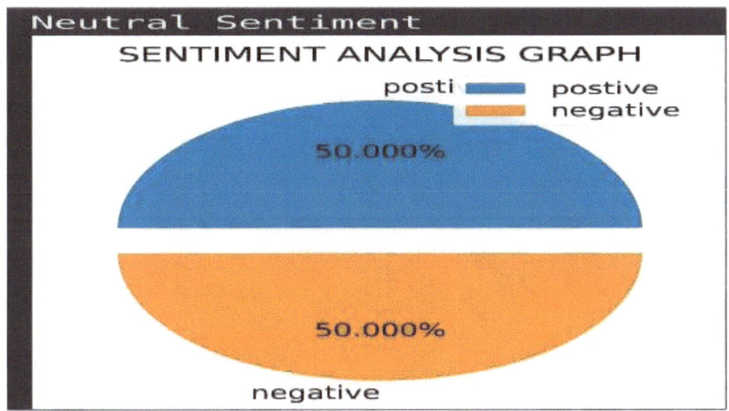

Fig. (3). Sentiment analysis graph.

Our model has also categorized this, and because it did not detect any negative sentences, it provided the outcome as shown in Fig. (**4**) and rejected the assertion.

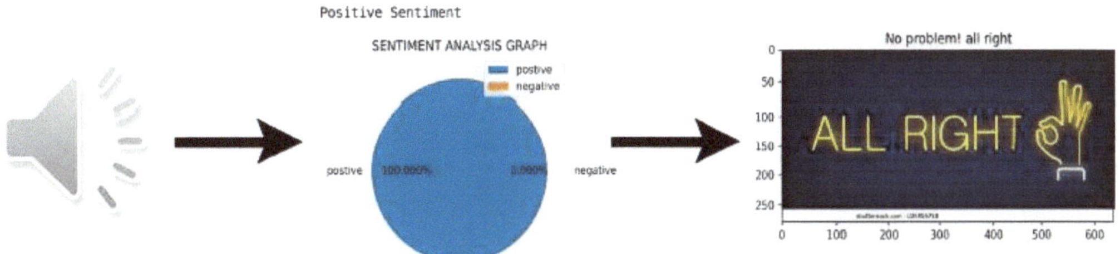

Fig. (4). Positive sentiment.

CONCLUSION

It can be challenging, yet also interesting, to conduct emotional research on social voice notes. There is a lot we can learn about the speaker's mood and the general tone of the talk by listening to voice messages and studying their tone, pitch, and content. Advanced Natural Language Processing (NLP) algorithms, such as speech recognition and emotion detection algorithms, can detect tone nuances like sarcasm, excitement, and sadness, which are essential for vocal sentiment analysis. Speech fluctuations, background noise, accents, and speech difficulties may render sentiment analysis algorithms inaccurate when analyzing social voice messaging. Voice messages often contain personal or sensitive information; therefore, privacy issues must be handled discreetly.

Sentiment analysis of social voice communications may benefit organizations, academics, and people despite these obstacles. It may assess consumer satisfaction, social media sentiment, and mental health trends by analyzing spoken interactions. Despite the hurdles of sentiment analysis in social voice messaging, the insights collected may help us comprehend human emotions and behaviour in the digital era. Future advancements in NLP and machine learning will enhance voice message sentiment analysis.

REFERENCES

[1] C Singh, R Chaitanya, S Rao *et al.* “Applied machine tool data condition to predictive smart maintenance by using artificial intelligence,” 2022. [http://dx.doi.org/10.1007/978-3-031-07012-9_49]

[2] S. Mewada, A. Saroliya, N. Chandramouli, T. R. Rajasanthosh Kumar, M. Lakshmi, S. S. Christal Mary and M. Jayakumar, “Smart diagnostic expert system for defect in forging process by using machine learning process,” *Journal of Nanomaterials*, vol. 2022, pp. 1–8, 2022. [http://dx.doi.org/10.1155/2022/2567194]

[3] Jingjie Wang, Wei Bai, and Yongbin Liu, “Optimization for the human resources management strategy of the IoT industry based on AHP,” *Computational Intelligence and Neuroscience*, vol. 2022, Article ID 3514285, 2022. [http://dx.doi.org/10.1155/2022/3514285]

[4] A. S. Thakur, T. L. Alex, and A. Nighojkar, “Artificial intelligence in maritime anomaly detection: A decadal bibliometric analysis (2014–2024),” *Journal of The Institution of Engineers*: Series C, pp. 1–25, Jan. 2025 [http://dx.doi.org/10.1007/s40032-025-01169-w]

[5] F. Aslam, A.I. Hunjra, Z. Ftiti, W. Louhichi, and T. Shams, "Insurance fraud detection: Evidence from artificial intelligence and machine learning", *Res. Int. Bus. Finance,* vol. 62, p. 101744, 2022. [http://dx.doi.org/10.1016/j.ribaf.2022.101744]

[6] X. Kewei, B. Peng, Y. Jiang, and T. Lu, "A hybrid deep learning model for online fraud detection", *2021 IEEE International Conference on Consumer Electronics and Computer Engineering, ICCECE 2021,* pp. 431-434, 2021. [http://dx.doi.org/10.1109/ICCECE51280.2021.9342110]

[7] A.V. Panin, M.S. Kazachenok, K.V. Krukovsky, L.A. Kazantseva, and S.A. Martynov, "Comparative analysis of weld microstructure in Ti-6Al-4V samples produced by rolling and wire-feed electron beam additive manufacturing", *Phys. Mesomech.,* vol. 26, no. 6, pp. 643-655, 2023. [http://dx.doi.org/10.1134/S1029959923060048]

[8] M. Sam, R. Jojith, and N. Radhika, "Progression in manufacturing of functionally graded materials and impact of thermal treatment—A critical review", *J. Manuf. Process.,* vol. 68, pp. 1339-1377, 2021. [http://dx.doi.org/10.1016/j.jmapro.2021.06.062]

[9] BramahHazela, “Machine Learning: Supervised Algorithms to Determine the Defect in High-Precision Foundry Operatio,” 2022.

[10] K. P. S. V. V. S. R. Saklani, "Multicore Implementation of K-Means Clustering Algorithm," 2023. [http://dx.doi.org/10.1109/ICAAIC56838.2023.10140800]

Emerging Trends in Computational Intelligence, Vol. 5, 2026, 57-66

CHAPTER 7

LED Cube Using Arduino to Support Dyslexic Children

Sankara Mahalingam M.[1,*], **P. Bhaskar**[2], **A. Swathi**[2], **K. Jaya Krishna**[3], **G. Siva Prasad**[4], **Edmar G. Tan**[5] and **DA. V.L. Narayana Rao**[6]

[1] *Department of Computer Science and Engineering, School of Computing, Kalasalingam Academy of Research and Education, Krishnankoil 626126, Tamil Nadu, India*

[2] *Department of IT, QIS College of Engineering & Technology Ongole 523272, Andhra Pradesh, India*

[3] *Department of MCA, QIS College of Engineering & Technology, Ongole 523272, Andhra Pradesh, India*

[4] *Department of CSE, QIS College of Engineering & Technology, Ongole 523272, Andhra Pradesh, India*

[5] *College of Information and Communication Technology, Taguig City University, Taguig City 1630, Philippines*

[6] *Department of ECE, QIS College of Engineering & Technology, Ongole 523272, Andhra Pradesh, India*

Abstract: Dyslexia is a condition that normally occurs in children with average or above-average intelligence. Children with dyslexia show symptoms of slow reading, writing problems, lack of communication, and also suffer from short-term memory. Studies show that education can have a significant impact on a child's life and influence their future job opportunities. Literacy is affected significantly when there is no clear understanding of the structure of the language and its phonological components. Dyslexic children especially face obstacles in reading and writing proficiency due to the linguistic component of language. To nurture children affected by dyslexia, various projects and programs are introduced to increase phonological awareness in children. Game-based learning is an effective method for enhancing children with dyslexia's interest in learning. The game-based learning model is interactive, attractive, user-friendly, and easily understandable by children. A Game-based learning model must address language-based learning difficulties that are considered both cognitive and emotional. In this prototype model, a 5x5x5 LED cube has been developed and is being tested for its performance.

Keywords: Arduino, Dyslexia, Game-based learning.

* **Corresponding author Sankara Mahalingam M.:** Department of Computer Science and Engineering, School of Computing, Kalasalingam Academy of Research and Education, Krishnankoil 626126, Tamil Nadu, India; E-mail: Sankaramahalingam@gmail.com

D. Arul Pon Daniel, T. Rajasanthosh Kumar & Satya Prakash Yadav (Eds.)

INTRODUCTION

Dyslexia is a condition that normally occurs in children who possess normal qualities and intelligence [1]. Children with dyslexia show symptoms of slow reading, writing problems, lack of communication, and also suffer from short-term memory [2]. Studies show that education can influence a child's life and also affect their future job opportunities [3]. Literacy is affected significantly when there is no clear understanding of the structure of the language and its phonological components [4]. Dyslexic children face obstacles due to the linguistic component of the language [5]. To nurture the children affected by dyslexia, various projects and programs are introduced to increase phonological awareness in children [6].

Game-based learning is the best method that can enhance the interest in learning in children with dyslexia [7]. The game-based learning model is interactive, attractive, user-friendly, and easily understandable by the children [8]. A Game-based learning model must address language-based learning difficulties that are considered both cognitive and emotional [9]. In this prototype model, a 5x5x5 LED cube is designed and tested for kids to start to learn the phonological components by acknowledging the whole words and later realizing the relationship between the letters displayed and sounds being presented [10]. The countless approaches available for developing literacy skills in children with dyslexia include repeated reading practice, frequently used word drills, improving the glossary and connotation, and developing the rate at which they process words and their syllable patterns [11].

Apace with this entrenched analogue apprenticeship, a preview of game-based learning in digital has come up with a reassuring new technique to address a child’s inspirational barriers, considering games can overturn a socially significant form the latest research by Holmes (2011) set in the context of children family houses revealed that a preview of game-based learning improved the children's participation in reading and writing activities [12], encouraged skill reinforcement, and enhancedtheir learning progress. However, challenges come with the usage of games [13]. The need to choose suitable games in the kids' zone to support adjacent development, alongside the importance of ensuring that reading and writing activities are well-defined, highlights the requirement for a perfect balance between a child's independence and parental guidance.

In this modern technological world, devices like mobile phones, tablets, and other smart devices have become an integral part of our lifestyle [14]. Accordingly, in recent years, smart-device-based game applications have been developed for kids affected by dyslexia, which will assist them in boosting their learning. With the help of mobile devices, children can easily learn lessons and review them at any time and place they choose [15]. Interactive media components have been integrated into the game application to attract the kids and grab their attention.

Many software-based applications have been developed to boost these children. However, to achieve a perfect balance between attraction and innovation, the need for physical models to help visualize 3D structures is inevitable. Game-Based Learning (GBL) explains how the principles of gaming are integrated into the educational sector to encourage participation, inspiration, and the learning. Surveys show that GBL integrations can boost the learning process of children affected by dyslexia. One out of ten children of the population in developed countries are dyslexic, with 4% of them severely affected by dyslexia.

Children tend to have a high interest in digital and game literacy as games are an essential part of their lives. Children often tend to avoid reading activities; thus, GBL helps in digital education games by incorporating motivational components. This game includes rewards (*i.e.*, money, prizes, *etc*.), levels (*i.e.*, easy to difficult), achievements (*i.e.*, task completion), feedback, and strike rate.

LED cubes are ideal learning models for kids. LED cubes, which resemble toys, would engage kids and help them learn in a fun and engaging manner. Dyslexia affects children differently. Over 40 dyslexia-related traits exist. Cognitive or logical dysfunction makes it hard for kids to examine closely. The 3-dimensional LED cube helps youngsters understand various topics starting at age 4 and may be readily modelled. The chosen age group or topics should inform the LED cube's design. Based on the given criteria, cube size and complexity will vary.

When building an LED cube with the microcontroller, the number of patterns increases as the model grows, which may lead to insufficient physical I/O ports or higher processing costsBecause of this, an Arduino Mega is preferable for such applications. Arduino switches logic states quicker than microcontrollers. The 5x5x5 LED Cube is a child dyslexia visual aid. The cube has 125 LEDs in a matrix configuration, 5 levels stacked with 25 LEDs each.

MOTIVATION

Dyslexia is a neurological learning disorder that is often observed among children between the ages of 5 and 6. It makes it hard for the children to use and recognize sounds in language. Children with dyslexia sometimes show slower language development than other children their age, and they tend to learn more slowly than other children.

They often struggle to distinguish between new and familiar terms. A dyslexic youngster may not always lack intelligence. These children may thrive in school and in society if they get the proper assistance.

To support these children, they need a more innovative and attractive way of learning to capture their attention. Additionally, education and entertainment are mutually dependent. Even normal children love to learn entertainingly. There are many Game-based learning tools available in the market. Thus, the proposed system is motivated to help children with dyslexia improve their learning process through the means of education and entertainment. The suggested learning paradigm, which is intended to help kids with dyslexia, makes use of an Arduino Mega 2560, an LED cube, and a Bluetooth module and microphone sensor. Children's learning is aided by the visual patterns shown by the Arduino Mega-controlled LED cube.

Bluetooth is used by the guardian or parent of the children to provide patterns as inputs to the LED cube and a mic sensor is used to get the speech input from the children. An LED cube is mainly used to get a three-dimensional view of the patterns where the LEDs are placed on the x-axis, y-axis, and z-axis to provide a cube shape. The types of LED cubes present in the market such as 3x3x3, 4x4x4, 5x5x5 and 8x8x8.The proposed system uses a 5x5x5 LED cube. A 5x5x5 LED cube is used because it provides the overall best size for the cube. This LED cube consists of 125 LEDs in total. The LED present in the cube is divided into five layers, which will be named L1, L2, L3, L4, and L5, each consisting of twenty-five LEDs. These five layers are further divided into a matrix form, where there will be five LEDs in each row and column of the matrix.

The above Fig. (**1**) is a visual representation of the LED cube, which comprises five layers of LEDs arranged in a 5x5 matrix. These layers are connected to form the cube by placing one layer over the other. This matrix is better understood in Fig. (**2**).

The working of the LED cube is based on the principle of optical phenomenon known as persistence of vision. The LEDs used in this model are a monochromatic LED matrix. To display the patterns, an LED is flashed rapidly so that the image remains in memory for some time after the LED is turned off. To give a three-dimensional view, each layer of the LED cube is flashed fast, one after another. The process of flashing LEDs is known as multiplexing. Multiplexing is defined as the process of combining multiple signals into a single signal using a shared medium.

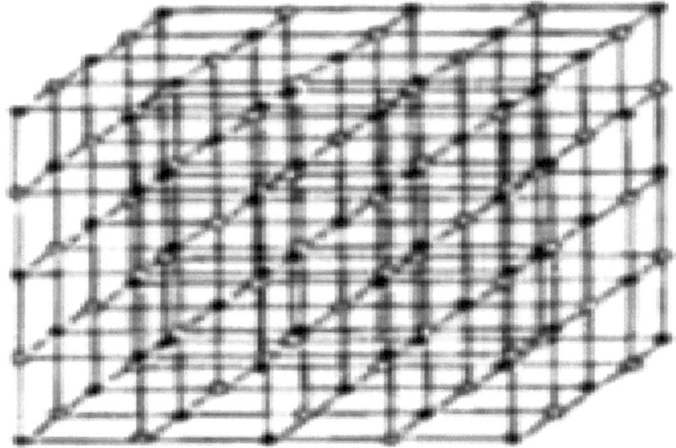

Fig. (1). 5x5x5 LED cube.

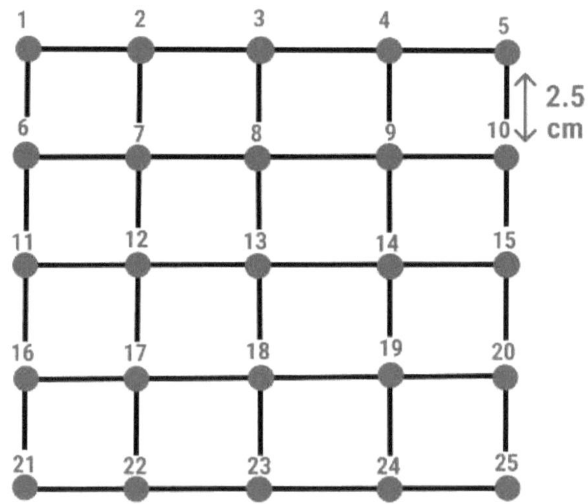

Fig. (2). 5x5 arrangement.

The LED cube can be controlled either by using Arduino or without Arduino. But when compared to an LED cube without Arduino, the usage of an Arduino-based LED cube is a better choice because of the number of pins available in the connection. In the proposed model, Arduino Mega 2560 is used to provide a power supply and control the LED cube. It assists children with dyslexia in learning through its hypnotic effect, as light dazzles in patterns controlled by Bluetooth.

In the LED cube, the positive pins present in the LEDs are connected from different layers. The connected positive pins of the cube act as columns, consisting of twenty-five columns in a 5x5x5 LED cube. The columns connected by the positive pins will feed up the positive supply from the Arduino. The five layers connected will be used for the number of LEDs present in a 5x5x5 LED cube is 125 LEDs. The Arduino doesn't have enough digital pins to support 125 LEDs and Arduino Mega has only 54 digital pins. So, instead of 125 connections, the cube only requires thirty connections by multiplexing.

The purpose of Bluetooth in the proposed model is to provide an input pattern to the LED cube which is controlled by the parent or guardian of the children affected with dyslexia. Bluetooth is a communication device in IoT devices of short range between devices the peers as well as a device to the peripherals. It acts as a Personal Area Network (PAN) for communication purposes. The patterns displayed in the LED cube are listed in below in Table **1**.

The number of patterns displayed is based on the size of the cube. As the LED cube's dimension increases, the number of patterns displayed can also be increased.

Table 1. Patterns displayed in the LED cube

Alphabets	**A, B, C, D, E, F, G, H, I, J, K, L, M, N, O, P, Q, R, S, T, U, V, W, X, Y, Z**
Integers	0,1,2,3,4,5,6,7,8,9
Expressions	+, -, x, %

Bluetooth operates between the frequencies of 2402 and 2480 MHz. It divides the data being transmitted into packets, which are then transmitted on any one of the designated Bluetooth channels. The Bluetooth is connected to the HC-05 module, which will be a better option to use for the serial port type of protocol module. This module is specially designated for wireless connection, which is serial.

Bluetooth enables informed decisions between two devices with minimal configuration requirements. The transfer of data in an IOT device using Bluetooth happens with the help of a mesh network.

The mic sensor is a module that is used to detect sound. In the prototype, the mic sensor is used as an input device when it detects the sound of the child while they pronounce the pattern. The sensor employs a microphone that acts as the input to the buffer, a peak connecting the ground. Similarly, all the negative terminals of LEDs are connected.

The ATmega2560 microcontroller was used in the project because it provides 54 digital I/O pins. The main feature of ATmega2560 is the ability to communicate with a computer, another Arduino, or other the microcontrollers. It consists of four hardware *i.e.*, a UART to communicate in serial mode. A detector and an amplifier. When the mic sensor detects, it processes the output voltage signal to the microcontroller. The sensor is connected to an analogue pin in the board.

An I2C LCD Adaptor is attached to the board. It displays the sound detected by the microphone sensor when the child pronounces the pattern displayed by the parent, using Bluetooth, and matches the predefined frequency. If the sound matches the predefined frequency, it displays the frequency successfully matched and moves to the next character in automatic mode. If the frequency is not matched & it displays the same character.

Arduino Mega microcontrollers act as the brain of our system, where the entire system program is stored. Microcontrollers, such as PIC, are a better option for the development process of LED cubes. However, as the cube's size increases the number of pins required to build the cube also increases. Thus, Arduino Mega is the best choice.

IMPLEMENTATION

The LED cube in the proposed model is constructed using 125 LEDs. It is arranged in five layers from top to bottom, consisting of twenty-five LEDs measuring 5x5. The LEDs present in the horizontal layer are connected by their cathode, while all five horizontal layers are connected by the LEDs present in the vertical layer. The recommended gap between two LEDs is 2.5 cm. The 125 LEDs are controlled by 30 pins of the Arduino Mega 2560. The display of the LED cube is multiplexed in a way such that there is one to each of the five layers in the cube and 25 to each LED in a layer, making a total of 30 connections. The cube is refreshed at a regular time interval for software interrupts. In the cube, each layer will be active for 2 ms, whereas the entire cube will be refreshed every 10 ms to result in a display with no flickering. The 5x5 matrix will be connected to and controlled by the transistor, which is connected to the anodes of the LED. The transistor is held at +5V. Each LED will have a distinct position in the LED cube, which can be named by layer and the column number. For example, the first LED of the cube is named as (layer 1, c1), the second LED is named as (layer 2, c2), and so on. Therefore, to turn on the image below in Fig. (**3**) best represents the connection of the LED cube.

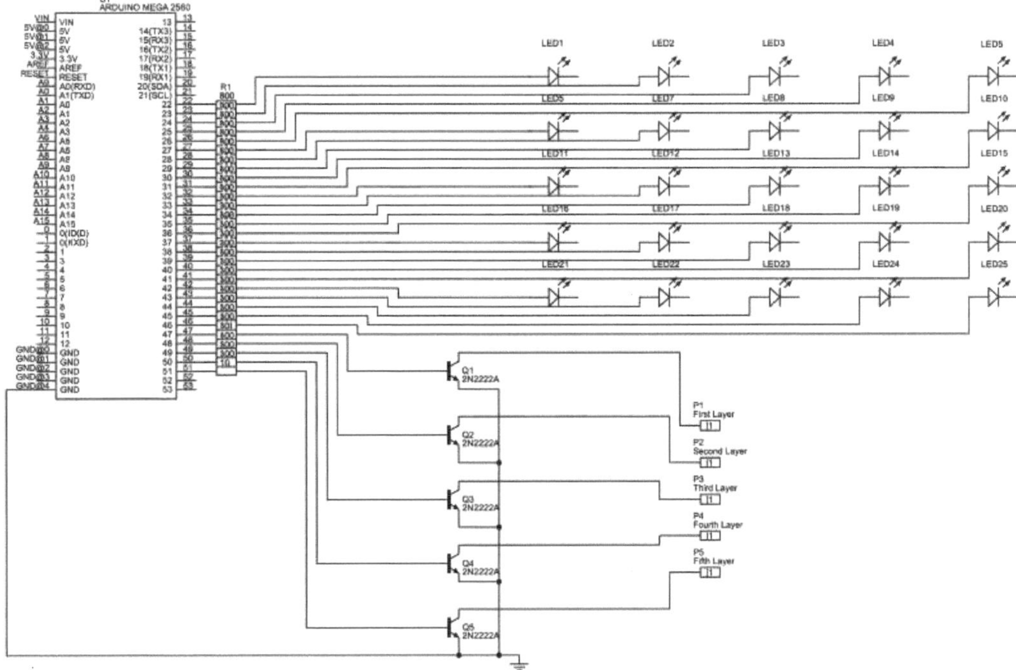

Fig. (3). LED cube connection.

Next, the Bluetooth (Fig. **4**) connected to Arduino Mega is interfaced with the Bluetooth device. The baud rate is set to 9600. To turn on/off the LEDs in a particular pattern "Bluetooth terminal app is downloaded" from the Play Store. The Arduino requires a 4 4-pin connection and the Bluetooth can be interfaced easily with the default serial communication of the Arduino.

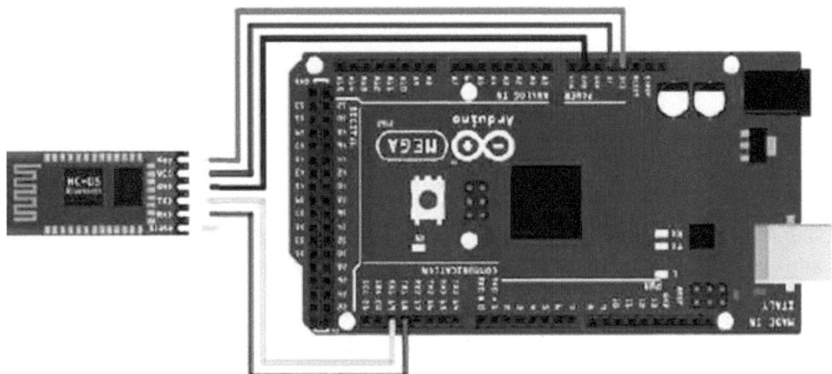

Fig. (4). Interfacing bluetooth HC-05 module.

The sound sensor is utilized to detect the sound of the environment easily. The standard mic sensor consists of three pins, *i.e.*, GND, VCC, and Vin. The ground pin is united to the Vcc pin present in the Arduino mega. The Vin is connected to the analogue input pin AI of the Arduino Mega 2560. This sensor converts vibration into an audio signal using a microphone built into the sensor. The microphone present in the sensor consists of an inbuilt diaphragm that converts the detected vibration into an audio signal.

In the proposed model, the Arduino Mega serves as the system's brain, providing the power supply to the entire system. Bluetooth is used in this concept to provide input to the LED, where a microphone sensor is used to detect the frequency of a child's pronunciation with dyslexia and check whether it matches the frequency of a normal child. The output is then displayed on the LCD screen. If the frequency matches, the LED cube display automatically moves to the next character; else it shows the same character. The resistor is connected to each LED in the cube & LCD is used to update information. The diagram below describes the implementation of the LED cube.

CONCLUSION

The proposed LED cube-based learning model, using an Arduino Mega 2560, is built to help children suffering from dyslexia improve their learning. As specified in the earlier columns of the paper, the most familiar criterion found in dyslexic children is ability to read is difficult. The difficulty in reading causes the children to lose their interest in the learning process. The requirement of a disciplined and more attractive way of learning for dyslexic children is inevitable. Many mobile game-based learning programs have been developed to assist children with special needs. But the search for physical models has never ended while helping them conceptualize 3D structures. The 5x5x5 LED cube represents the best innovative approach for this problem. The hypnotic effect of the LED cube would capture the attention of dyslexic children and make their learning process more engaging. Additionally, the proposed model helps evaluate the pronunciation of children using a microphone sensor & Bluetooth, and guides them until they're correct.

REFERENCES

[1] R. Saklani, K. Purohit, S. Vats, V. Sharma, V. Kukreja and S. P. Yadav, "Multicore Implementation of K-Means Clustering Algorithm," *2023 2nd International Conference on Applied Artificial Intelligence and Computing (ICAAIC)*, Salem, India, 2023, pp. 171-175. [http://dx.doi.org/10.1109/ICAAIC56838.2023.10140800]

[2] S. Mewada, A. Saroliya, N. Chandramouli, T. R. Rajasanthosh Kumar, M. Lakshmi, S. S. Christal Mary and M. Jayakumar, "Smart diagnostic expert system for defect in forging process by using machine learning process," *Journal of Nanomaterials*, vol. 2022, pp. 1–8, 2022. [http://dx.doi.org/10.1155/2022/2567194]

[3] M. Sowmiya, K. Ilakkiya, "LED Cube Using Arduino to Assist Dyslexic Children in Learning," *International Journal of Scientific Innovation in Engineering & Technology (IJSIET)*, vol. 2, no. 2, 2023.

[4] M. Lozano-Álvarez, S. Rodríguez-Cano, V. Delgado-Benito, & M. Á. García-Delgado, "Implementation and evaluation of a VR/AR-based assistive technology for dyslexic learners: An exploratory case study," *Societies*, vol. 15, no. 8, p. 215, 2025. [http://dx.doi.org/10.1155/2022/2567194]

[5] R.A. Alzahrani, M. Aljabri, and R.A. Mustafa Mohammad, "Ad click fraud detection using machine learning and deep learning algorithms", *IEEE Access,* vol. 13, pp. 12746-12763, 2025. [http://dx.doi.org/10.1109/ACCESS.2025.3532200]

[6] A. Iqbal, and R. Amin, "Time series forecasting and anomaly detection using deep learning", *Comput. Chem. Eng.,* vol. 182, p. 108560, 2024. [http://dx.doi.org/10.1016/j.compchemeng.2023.108560]

[7] V. Van Vlasselaer, C. Bravo, O. Caelen, T. Eliassi-Rad, L. Akoglu, M. Snoeck, and B. Baesens, "APATE: A novel approach for automated credit card transaction fraud detection using network-based extensions", *Decis. Support Syst.,* vol. 75, pp. 38-48, 2015. [http://dx.doi.org/10.1016/j.dss.2015.04.013]

[8] P. Kamuangu, "A review on financial fraud detection using AI and machine learning", *Journal of Economics, Finance and Accounting Studies,* vol. 6, no. 1, pp. 67-77, 2024. [http://dx.doi.org/10.32996/jefas.2024.6.1.7]

[9] B.N. Muthura, and A. Matheka, "A hybrid model for detecting insurance fraud using K-means and support vector machine algorithms", *Open Journal for Information Technology,* vol. 6, no. 2, pp. 143-156, 2023. [http://dx.doi.org/10.32591/coas.ojit.0602.05143m]

[10] A. Olushola, and J. Mart, "Fraud Detection using", *Mach. Learn.,* no. Jan, 2024. [http://dx.doi.org/10.14293/PR2199.000647.v1]

[11] D.K. Yaduwanshi, S. Bag, and S. Pal, "Numerical modeling and experimental investigation on plasma-assisted hybrid friction stir welding of dissimilar materials", *Mater. Des.,* vol. 92, pp. 166-183, 2016. [http://dx.doi.org/10.1016/j.matdes.2015.12.039]

[12] D. Kim et al., "Fabrication of functionally graded materials using aluminum alloys via hot extrusion," *metals*, Vol. 9, Page 210, vol. 9, no. 2, p. 210, Feb. 2019. [http://dx.doi.org/10.3390/met9020210]

[13] V. S. Putta, K. Raseena A., P. R. Keerthana, J. Prabhu, and S. Sivadharshini, "LED Cube to Assist Dyslexic Child by Measuring Speech Frequency," International Journal of Innovative Science and Research Technology, vol. 8, no. 3, pp. 1635–1637, Mar. 2023. [http://dx.doi.org/10.5281/zenodo.7793074]

[14] S. Srivastava et al., "Lung Infection and Identification using Heatmap," 2023. [http://dx.doi.org/10.1109/ICAAIC56838.2023.10140204]

[15] S. Y. S. and Y. A. Chowdhury, "IoT based solar energy monitoring system," 2021.

CHAPTER 8

Yoga Pose Detection Using Mediapipe and the Cue Method

Sankara Mahalingam M.[1,*], M. Narendra[2], Sk. Heena[3], A.L. Parvathi[3], Ch. Silpa[4], Rodelio Dela Fuente[5] and **G. Maheswara Rao[6]**

[1] *Department of Computer Science and Engineering, School of Computing, Kalasalingam Academy of Research and Education, Krishnankoil 626126, Tamil Nadu, India*

[2] *Department of MCA, QIS College of Engineering & Technology, Ongole 523272, Andhra Pradesh, India*

[3] *Department of CSE, QIS College of Engineering & Technology, Ongole 523272, Andhra Pradesh, India*

[4] *Department of IT, QIS College of Engineering & Technology, Ongole 523272, Andhra Pradesh, India*

[5] *College of Information and Communication Technology, Taguig City University, Taguig City 1630, Philippines*

[6] *Department of ECE, QIS College of Engineering & Technology, Ongole 523272, Andhra Pradesh, India*

Abstract: Popular exercises, such as yoga, have numerous positive health benefits. However, incorrectly executed yoga poses can be harmful and lessen the advantages of the practice. In recent years, yoga positions have been investigated and altered using computer vision techniques. This study presents a novel Mediapipe-located cue-located calculating fantasy method for reconstructing yoga postures. The urged method is compared to good adjustment by requesting deep knowledge algorithms to identify the ultimate main physique parts in yoga poses. The computer, therefore, instructs the consumer to adjust their posture to achieve the appropriate adjustment as soon as possible. The projected method is validated using a dataset of yoga poses, and the veracity and real-world opportunity accomplishment effects are promising. In yoga classes, especially when conducted online or in other settings, the submitted method may be employed to increase benefits, though it also poses risks of harm to practitioners.

Keywords: Cue method, Mediapipe, OpenCV, Pose correction.

[*] **Corresponding author Sankara Mahalingam M.:** Department of Computer Science and Engineering, School of Computing, Kalasalingam Academy of Research and Education, Krishnankoil 626126, Tamil Nadu, India;
E-mail: sankaramahalingam@gmail.com

D. Arul Pon Daniel, T. Rajasanthosh Kumar & Satya Prakash Yadav (Eds.)

INTRODUCTION

Yoga is a practice with its roots in ancient India, emphasizing the development of the body, mind, and spirit. Yoga is now widely acknowledged as a form of physical activity that enhances balance, flexibility, strength, and overall health [1]. To get the most out of yoga and lower the risk of injury, correct posture and technique are essential, just like with any physical activity [2]. One of the most crucial challenges in practising yoga is ensuring proper execution of the various positions, or asanas. Even seasoned practitioners can develop negative habits that are challenging to break, and beginners often struggle to get their bodies into proper position [3]. Yoga practitioners have traditionally relied on the guidance of professional instructors to refine their form and receive feedback. But, if you live in a distant place or during a pandemic when many studios are closed [4], there can be some restrictions on where you can attend in-person classes. In this case, technology is essential. Computer vision and machine learning advancements have made it possible to analyze video footage and correctly identify significant human body components [5]. Yoga practitioners can utilize this technology to enhance their posture by providing beginners with immediate feedback on their poses [6]. Real-time posture monitoring and recognition using deep learning computer vision frameworks like OpenCV and Video Pipe may modify yoga poses [7]. Experts may improve their alignment using Media Pipe and OpenCV by comparing their body alignment to the yoga posture. Aural alarms or visual overlays allow practitioners to modify [8]. With real-time input, technology may enhance yoga poses, form, and muscle memory, while improving performance and decreasing injury risk [9]. Technology makes yoga more accessible and inclusive, particularly for individuals without skilled teachers or those who are uncomfortable in conventional classes [10]. Medical professionals with either physical or mental limitations may adapt their techniques using Media Pipe and OpenCV, which provides yoga posture correction for all levels [11, 12, 15, 16]. Modern technology makes yoga more private, safe, & accessible [13, 14].

RELATED WORKS

The emerging discipline of yoga posture correction uses algorithms for learning and computer vision. Yoga poses were assessed using the motion-sensing Kinect in a 2017 Society of Sports Medicine and Science research, revealing its promise in workouts and rehabilitation. Fig. (**1**) illustrates the entire workflow of the system.

Kinect may help yoga practitioners modify posture by precisely recording the angles of joints and motion trajectories, according to the research. Wearable IMU technology was used to correct yoga posture in a 2018 Journal of Neural Science and Rehabilitation research. The IMU gadget, attached to participants' extremities, employs machine learning algorithms to correct yoga postures in real-time.

In 2020, the Journal of Healthcare Systems covered a smartphone app for yoga posture correction. Through a Media pipe, the program locates and analyzes the body's most critical anatomical characteristics, delivering instantaneous form input. A 2020 article published in the Journal of Healthcare Systems discussed a smartphone app designed to improve yoga posture. The program monitors key body aspects using MediaPipe to provide instant form input. This technology can repair improper yoga postures and enhance overall practice. While computer vision and machine learning may improve yoga safety and efficacy, further research is required to determine their strengths and weaknesses.

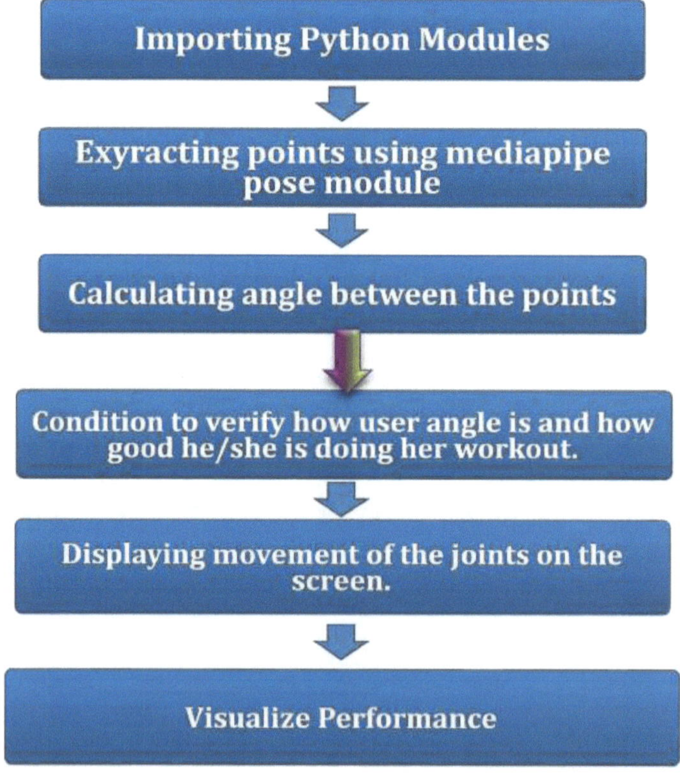

Fig. (1). The workflow of the system.

PROPOSED METHODOLOGY

Yoga positions may be difficult to perform with the perfect alignment for maximum benefit, even for experienced practitioners. Computer vision technology can be used to detect and correct improper posture in real time.

The use of computer vision for repairing yoga postures was first evaluated by Sharma *et al.* (2020), who collected datasets of photos or videos of individuals executing various yoga stances from different viewpoints. A machine learning algorithm will sort suitable and inappropriate sites using this dataset. For the model to distinguish incorrect positions in various contexts, the dataset must contain body form, clothes, lighting, and camera angles. Then, from every pose or frame of the video, the vital information can be extracted using Aggarwal *et al.'s* postural forecasting algorithm for Media Pipe (2021). Using data from the head, shoulders, elbows, wrists, hips, kneecaps, and ankles, the model can identify 33 different metrics as shown in Fig. (**2**). Furthermore, the user will find the marker's coordinates here. Learn how to find, align, and manipulate your body parts in a yoga posture with the help of these essentials. Islam *et al.* (2022) state that transferring learning, data enhancement, and hyperparameter change may increase the machine learning accuracy of models. Photo and video flipping, resizing, and rotation enhance model diversity and robustness by adding training data. Optimizing machine learning technique variables, including learning rate, normalization magnitude, and layer count, improves validation data performance. Applying a model to assess an individual's stance on yoga positions enhances model accuracy and speeds up the process.

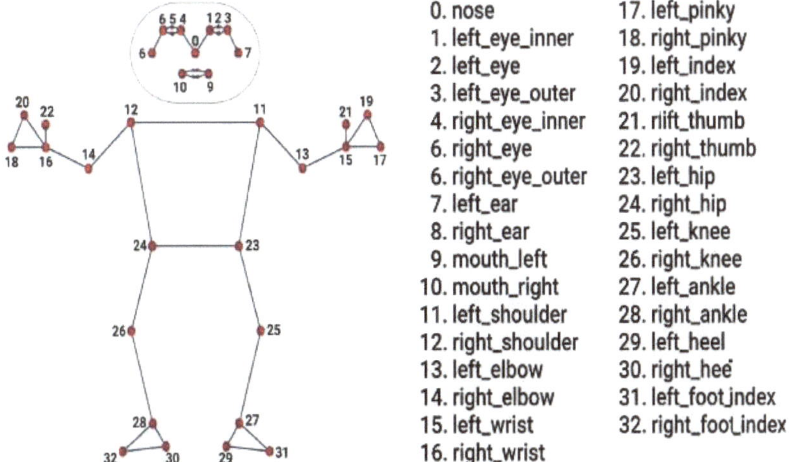

Fig. (2). Shows the landmark points.

Singh *et al.* (2019) suggest using OpenCV to fix yoga positions in real-time. The gadget employs a trained machine learning model to detect bad posture and provide tips to improve. This input could come in the visual or auditory form, as per Liu *et al.* (2020). The technology might highlight proper and inappropriate positions by layering a skeleton or shadow of the appropriate posture over a user's photo or video.

This technique aims to provide a framework that helps yogis improve their posture and practice by incorporating ideas from other authors. The system's real-time, customized input helps promote mind-body connection, bodily awareness, and injury prevention. It does this by utilizing computer vision and machine learning.

We used the OpenCV, Mediapipe, and NumPy modules/packages for our project. Starting at index 0, remove data.

A total of 33 cue points are used. (Fig. **3**) Each represents a different joint. For instance, the angle of a right-handed bicep curl exercise needs to be determined by the shoulder, elbow, and wrist joints (12, 14, and 16, respectively). To compute the angle between the joints, we must first gather the coordinates of the three joints. Then, using NumPy, the joint's slope can be calculated. The resulting angles can be transformed from their standard unit of measurement, radians, to degrees.

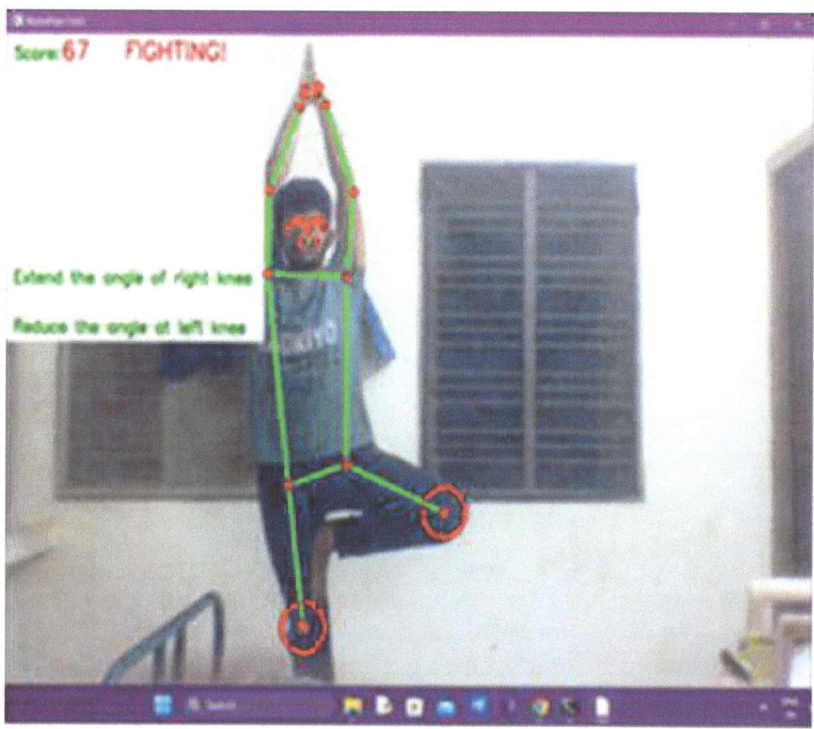

Fig. (3). shows the cue points.

SYSTEM ARCHITECTURE

The overall system architecture is depicted in Fig. (**4**).

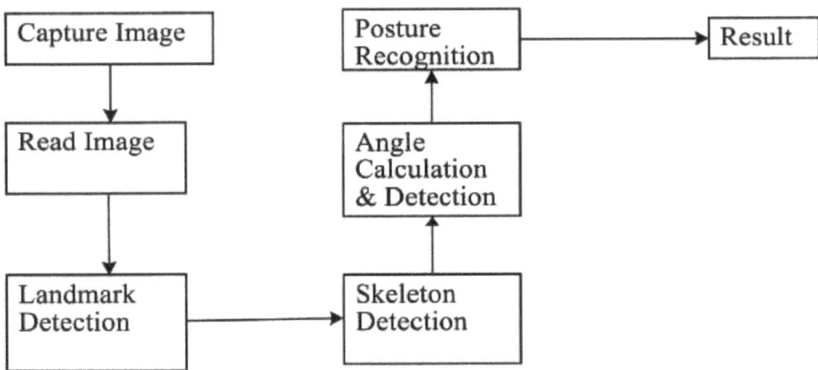

Fig. (4). System Architecture.

METHODOLOGY

Mediapipe

Google enables real-time computer vision and machine learning applications through its platforms and tools. Pose detection, which correctly locates and orients a person's body in a picture or video, is one of Mediapipe's most common applications. Mediapipe's posture detection pipeline uses machine learning to identify important joints and anatomical characteristics. These basic points may be used after calculating the body and limb locations and orientations. In AR, health monitoring, and motion capture, the Mediapipe posture detection pipeline is designed for real-time performance. Users may utilize the pipeline with phones, computers, and Google's Coral Crest TPU. Mediapipe offers a flexible platform for building custom vision and artificial intelligence applications beyond its own pipelines. Academics and developers in the fields of artificial intelligence and machine learning may utilize the framework's data preparation, model training, and deployment capabilities. Mediapipe is a robust artificial intelligence framework with prebuilt pipelines and tools for video vision and neural network applications, developed by Google. Academics and programmers require a rapid and flexible posture detection pipeline.

The fundamental types of computer vision tasks in this field include classification, detection, segmentation, image recognition, and keypoint detection.

Brief descriptions of each class follow.

- Classify an image or video into a certain category. Detection involves classifying and identifying objects or classes of interest.
- Data segmentation aims to identify the exact perimeter or diameter of a focused item or category.
- Key point detection involves identifying specified locations or landmarks.

OpenCV

The computer vision and artificial intelligence software library OpenCV, as shown in Fig. (**5**), offers a range of image and video analysis functions, including object detection, identification, tracking, and location estimation. In a picture or video, pose estimation determines the spatial location and orientation of an individual or object. SSD, YOLO, and Mask R-CNN are among the most common posture estimation methods in OpenCV. These deep learning-based methods extract features from input photos or frames using CNNs.

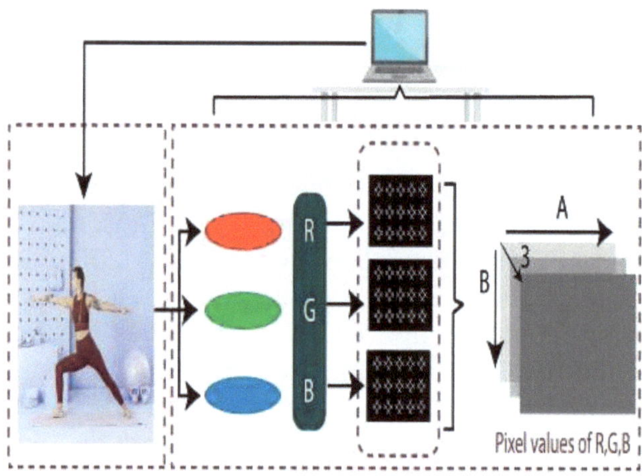

Fig. (5). object detection.

OpenCV post-inspection begins with a picture or video stream from a camera or file. After that, data will be scaled, normalized, and colour-converted. Pose estimation methods use preprocessed data to detect people and objects' connections and focus points in photos and videos.

Pose estimation models from OpenCV may be changed or trained to improve detection accuracy and resilience. Its models run on CPUs, GPUs, and smartphones, making it a flexible and widely used computer vision library.

In conclusion, vision and artificial intelligence researchers and programmers need OpenCV. It is a powerful, extensible library with several location-finding features.

The following steps describe how to fix yoga positions with MediaPipe and OpenCV (Fig. **6**):

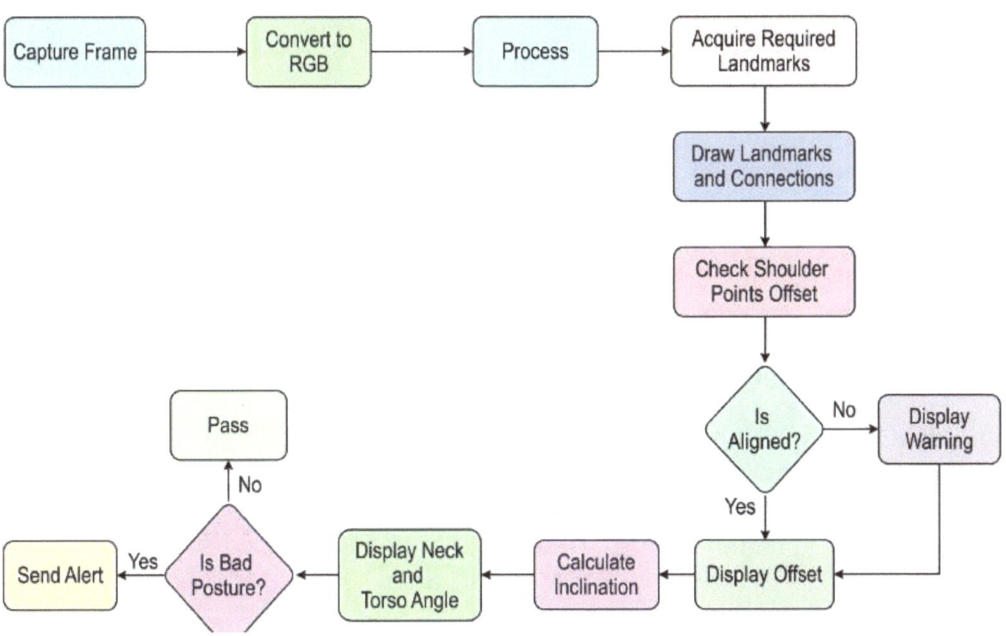

Fig. (6). Flow diagram representation.

- In your development environment, install the MediaPipe and OpenCV libraries.
- To customize a yoga stance, load a video or picture file using OpenCV.
- Use Media Pipe Posture Detection API to identify landmarks or focus areas during yoga postures.
- Identify key landmarks for yoga poses.
- Use trigonometric formulae to compute angles between critical locations.
- Compare the calculated angle to the optimal angle for the yoga position.
- Determine suitable angles and necessary adjustments.
- Optimize angles by making required changes.
- Draw arcs and triangles on a movie or picture file using OpenCV to demonstrate good yoga posture. Create new yoga posture alteration videos or images.

Installing the Necessary Libraries

Installing the Mediapipe and OpenCV libraries in your development environment should be your first step. Mediapipe is an open-source machine learning framework that includes pre-trained models for pose estimation, object tracking, and other applications, whereas OpenCV is a well-known computer vision library that offers numerous methods for image and video processing.

When loading a video or picture file, we can use OpenCV to load a video or picture file of the yoga stance you want to correct, after downloading the library. With the cv2, load a video file. Either the cv2's VideoCapture () method or an image file. A method called VideoCapture () and the read () method. The Mediapipe Pose Detection API can be used to locate focal points or landmarks on a subject while they are in a yoga pose. The API offers a collection of models that have been trained to identify significant body components, like joints and bones, in real-time movies and still images. To recognize important characteristics of a person executing yoga poses, a pre-trained model might be employed.

Contrasting the Calculated Angles with the Ideal Angles

Following the calculation of the angles, you must compare the calculated angles with the ideal angles of the yoga pose. The appropriate angles for the pose can be determined by understanding the proper alignment for the yoga practice. Following that, you may spot the angles that need to be adjusted.

Take Corrective Action

Once you've identified the incorrect angles, you need to take corrective action to replace them with the correct ones. Trigonometry and mathematical formulas can be used to change the angle. To illustrate corrected yoga positions on video or image files, you can use OpenCV to draw lines and circles.

Output

Fig. (7) illustrates the output with perfect prediction results. Our proposed model provides feedback and instructs the trainer to assume the correct pose. It will be able to perform any kind of yoga pose, irrespective of the asana. It perfectly detects whether the pose is correct or not, according to the calculation of angles between body parts. The model includes many training asanas; the model is expected to yield the best results in the future.

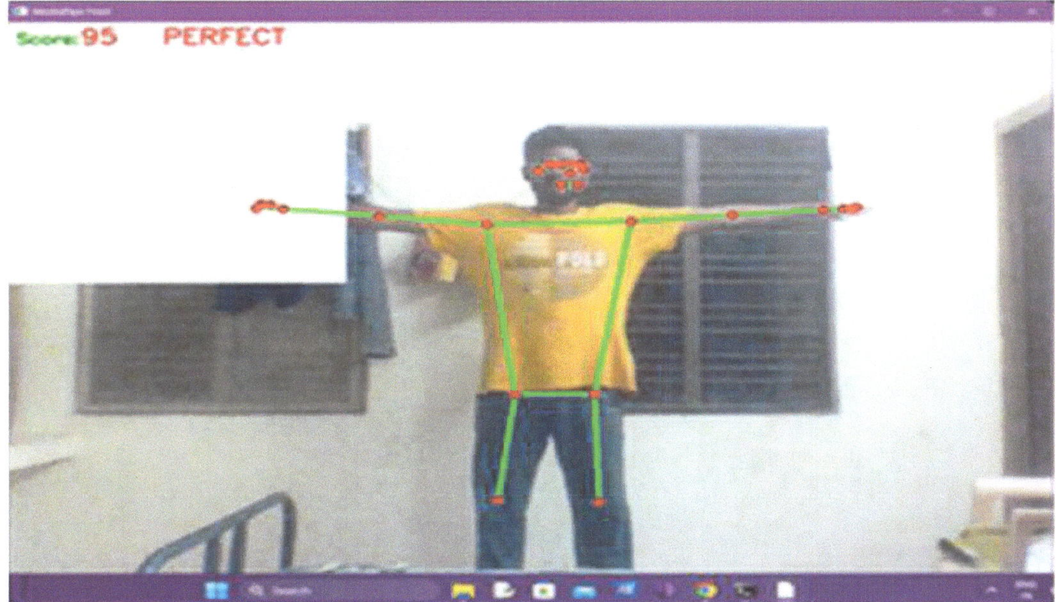

Fig. (7). Output with perfect prediction.

CONCLUSION

In recent years, technology has become increasingly prevalent in the yoga community. The yoga position can be adjusted using a combination of Mediapipe and OpenCV technology. These tools utilize computer vision and machine learning algorithms to analyze a user's movements in real-time and determine whether their posture is appropriate. Practitioners benefit from the technology's immediate response. These tests aid setup, injury avoidance, and technique development. Technology can also measure development, allowing practitioners to adjust their methods accordingly. Yoga students and instructors benefit from technology. Technology makes learning more efficient and dynamic, helping students improve and deepen their understanding of their practice. Technology can help instructors prepare lessons and provide students with more effective feedback. However, modern technology cannot replace a great yoga teacher, and teachers' guidance and assistance cannot be replaced. Overall, incorporating Mediapipe and OpenCV technologies into yoga practice may alter how practitioners approach their practice. By helping students and instructors, this technology may enhance the practice and provide new perspectives on ancient yoga traditions.

REFERENCES

[1] C Singh, S Rao, Y Mahaboobjohn *et al*.. Applied Machine Tool Data Condition to Predictive Smart Maintenance by Using Artificial Intelligence. [http://dx.doi.org/10.1007/978-3-031-07012-9_49]

[2] S. P. Pavan Kumar Gatikoppu, V. Subramanian G., Thamizh Devi C., Maruthupandi V., "*Yoga Pose Detection Using Mediapipe and the Cue Method*," *IEEE ISense*, 2024. [http://dx.doi.org/10.1109/ISENSE63713.2024.10871988]

[3] R.A. Alzahrani, M. Aljabri, and R.A. Mustafa Mohammad, "Ad click fraud detection using machine learning and deep learning algorithms", *IEEE Access,* vol. 13, pp. 12746-12763, 2025. [http://dx.doi.org/10.1109/ACCESS.2025.3532200]

[4] F.K. Alarfaj, and S. Shahzadi, "Enhancing fraud detection in banking with deep learning: Graph neural networks and autoencoders for real-time credit card fraud prevention", *IEEE Access,* 2024. [http://dx.doi.org/10.1109/ACCESS.2024.3466288]

[5] B.M. Naman, B. Mardan, and A. Mohsin Abdulazeez, "Credit card fraud detection based on machine learning classification algorithm", *Indonesian Journal of Computer Science,* vol. 13, no. 3, 2024. [http://dx.doi.org/10.33022/ijcs.v13i3.3996]

[6] I.D. Mienye, and N. Jere, "Deep learning for credit card fraud detection: A review of algorithms, challenges, and solutions", *IEEE Access,* vol. 12, pp. 96893-96910, 2024. [http://dx.doi.org/10.1109/ACCESS.2024.3426955]

[7] A. Iqbal, and R. Amin, "Time series forecasting and anomaly detection using deep learning", *Comput. Chem. Eng.,* vol. 182, p. 108560, 2024. [http://dx.doi.org/10.1016/j.compchemeng.2023.108560]

[8] H. Du, L. Lv, H. Wang, and A. Guo, "A novel method for detecting credit card fraud problems", *PLoS One,* vol. 19, no. 3, p. e0294537, 2024. [http://dx.doi.org/10.1371/journal.pone.0294537] [PMID: 38446831]

[9] C. Farkostteknik, "Credit Card Transaction Fraud Detection Using Neural Network Classifiers," 2023, Accessed: Mar. 09, 2025. [Online]. Available from: https://urn.kb.se/resolve?urn=urn:nbn:se:kth:diva-325808

[10] M. Dong, L. Yao, X. Wang, B. Benatallah, C. Huang, and X. Ning, "Opinion fraud detection via neural autoencoder decision forest", *Pattern Recognit. Lett.,* vol. 132, pp. 21-29, 2020. [http://dx.doi.org/10.1016/j.patrec.2018.07.013]

[11] J.M. Johnson, and T.M. Khoshgoftaar, "Medical provider embeddings for healthcare fraud detection", *SN Comput. Sci.,* vol. 2, no. 4, p. 276, 2021. [http://dx.doi.org/10.1007/s42979-021-00656-y]

[12] A. Kanksha, A. Bhaskar, S. Pande, R. Malik, and A. Khamparia, "An intelligent unsupervised technique for fraud detection in health care systems", *Intell. Decision Technol.,* vol. 15, no. 1, pp. 127-139, 2021. [http://dx.doi.org/10.3233/IDT-200052]

[13] V. Van Vlasselaer, C. Bravo, O. Caelen, T. Eliassi-Rad, L. Akoglu, M. Snoeck, and B. Baesens, "APATE: A novel approach for automated credit card transaction fraud detection using network-based extensions", *Decis. Support Syst.,* vol. 75, pp. 38-48, 2015. [http://dx.doi.org/10.1016/j.dss.2015.04.013]

[14] P. Kamuangu, "A review on financial fraud detection using AI and machine learning", *Journal of Economics, Finance and Accounting Studies,* vol. 6, no. 1, pp. 67-77, 2024. [http://dx.doi.org/10.32996/jefas.2024.6.1.7]

[15] T. Rajasanthosh Kumar, K. V. Sai Pavan, R. Kukati, and M. Srinivasa Reddy, "Quantitatively examines the feasibility of different configurations of the aftermarket supply chain enabling additive manufacturing," *Solid State Technology*, vol. 63, no. 5, pp. 492–507, 2020.

[16] M. Vubangsi et al, “Optimizing Moving Target Defense For Cyber Anomaly Detection,” *International Conference on Computational Intelligence, Communication Technology and Networking (CICTN)*, pp. 791-795, 2023.
[http://dx.doi.org/10.1109/CICTN57981.2023.10140835]

CHAPTER 9

Self-Checkout System using One-Time QR Code

R. Amutha[1,*], **D. Karunamma**[2], **M. Bhavya**[2], **K. Vivek**[2], **R. Shankar**[2], **Edward N. Cruz**[3] and **M. Sathya**[4]

[1] *Department of ISE, AMC Engineering College, Bengaluru 560083, Karnataka, India*

[2] *Department of CSE, QIS College of Engineering and Technology, Ongole 523272, Andhra Pradesh, India*

[3] *College of Computer Studies, University of Perpetual Help Systems DALTA Molino, City of Bacoor 4102, Cavite, Philippines*

[4] *Department of IT, Nadar Saraswathi College of Engineering and Technology, Theni 625 531, Tamil Nadu, India*

Abstract: Inventory Management System (IMS) is software that assists firms operating hardware stores to track sales and purchases. This project streamlines the process by eliminating paperwork, human errors, and manual delays. The Inventory Management System will track sales and available inventory, alerting business owners when it's time to restock. Sales, inventory, Customer Relationship Management (CRM), Human Resource Management (HRM), and account handling are just some of the business activities that the program documents. The application mainly allows a self-checkout environment supporting a takeaway system. The software is beneficial to firms that manage retail outlets and keep track of sales and purchases. In this application, the purchase and sales transactions are employed using Code Igniter, PHP, and Web Development tools to develop an inventory system. It provides a thorough corporate perspective and helps owners manage development and sales.

Keywords: Cooperation management, Company-client interaction, Employee management, Invoice management, Inventory management, Rapid application development, Self-checkout, United modelling language.

INTRODUCTION

Model-View-Controller (MVC) is a three-part architectural design [1]. Its original purpose was to create GUIs for desktop computers, but nowadays it's all about making applications for phones and the web. A robust PHP framework, CODE IGNITER follows the well-liked MVC design style [2-4]. Designed for developers looking for a lightweight framework to build feature-rich web apps, it

* **Corresponding author R. Amutha:** Department of ISE, AMC Engineering College, Bengaluru 560083, Karnataka, India; E-mail: amutha.shruthi@gmail.com

D. Arul Pon Daniel, T. Rajasanthosh Kumar & Satya Prakash Yadav (Eds.)

prioritizes minimalism. The Framework and View classes are not required; however, the Controller classes are [5], [6]. The Hierarchical Model View Controller (HMVC) allows the developers to maintain the grouping of Controller, Models, and View arranged in a directorial format, which can be directly modified by the Code Igniter framework. Records are managed across the system [7-9]. The user must enter product names as well as the rate amount. This area is an optional field for invoicing management. Meanwhile, after completing all these fields, proceed to client management. The administrator can also manage system users [10]. On the other hand, a key characteristic of this invoicing system is that it generates invoices based on sales [11]. An administrator must provide due dates, customer information, product items, quantity selections, and discount amounts [12]. Otherwise, the system will automatically add all extra amounts, such as TAX and VAT, during the calculation [13]. Based on this management, the system generates an overall invoice for each customer.

LITERATURE REVIEW

The organic merger of inventory management and information technology in the IT environment aids in setting up an information-based inventory management system. Improving inventory accounting accuracy and inventory management validity has significant practical implications.

According to the study, this assessment task manages the part of the stock administration of consumer loyalty in paper production. The data for this project's improvement will be acquired through surveys from various levels of administration in the distribution.

Furthermore, it concludes that there are two missing things: inventory control and bill eras. The article raises an alert regarding the bill's information portion, which is in PDF format so that the shopkeeper is informed about the remaining inventory.

Vendor Managed Inventory (VMI) is a cost-effective replacement strategy that allows a vendor to adapt to demand without relying on purchase decisions to do so. EDIFACT inventory news in a standard business system environment, such as SAP R/3, has been utilized in previous VMI implementations. Small and Medium Enterprises (SMEs), which often operate at the low end of the supply chain, find such deployment excessively expensive.

Consequently, the VMI concept has been largely overlooked in this domain. A cost-effective alternative to Electronic Data Interchange (EDI) is web services. This research provides an implementation plan and a VMI architecture that is built on composite Web Services.

PROPOSED WORK

More precisely, it divides the app into three logical parts: the model, the view, as well as the regulator. MVC is a popular architectural style that demonstrates these three pieces.

Its original use was in desktop graphical user interface design, but it is now more often used in the development of mobile and online apps.

The application primarily utilizes the MVC architecture, which divides the application into three parts: model, controller, and view. The main advantage of using this architecture is that it is easily modifiable.

The application requires constant updating and has to support large-scale web application usage, which is a requirement. Since it is an integrated working environment, the server cost can also be minimized. It is also an SEO-friendly platform.

We have also used CodeIgniter to implement this application. CodeIgniter is an MVC-based framework that can be comfortably migrated to different environments. For the web implementation, use HTML, CSS, JavaScript, and MySQL.

Self-checkout System Using QR Code

After successfully authenticating with a one-time QR from the shop and the customer's mobile number, the self-checkout software (Fig. **1**) allows store customers to use their mobile phones to scan the products they're interested in.

Then, once they have finished shopping, they may use the app to buy the products they want. The self-checkout retail technology solution does not require the business to invest in additional hardware.

Link with the merchants' existing back-office systems and payment gateways to a carefully curated partner network, ensuring a quick and low-cost implementation.

Self-serve requesting through Square Online provides a contactless, in-person requesting experience that enhances security and workflow productivity. Rather than perusing a paper menu and setting orders with a staff member, clients use their cell phones to scan a QR code at their table, seat, parking space, or any other location where they want to place an order. Each QR code can be linked to a specific ordering station—ideal for smaller food venues and cafés—or customers can be prompted to enter their location manually, which is better suited for large-scale events and arenas. To improve self-serve operations, explore best practices for self-serve ordering through Square Online, particularly those that support tip collection.

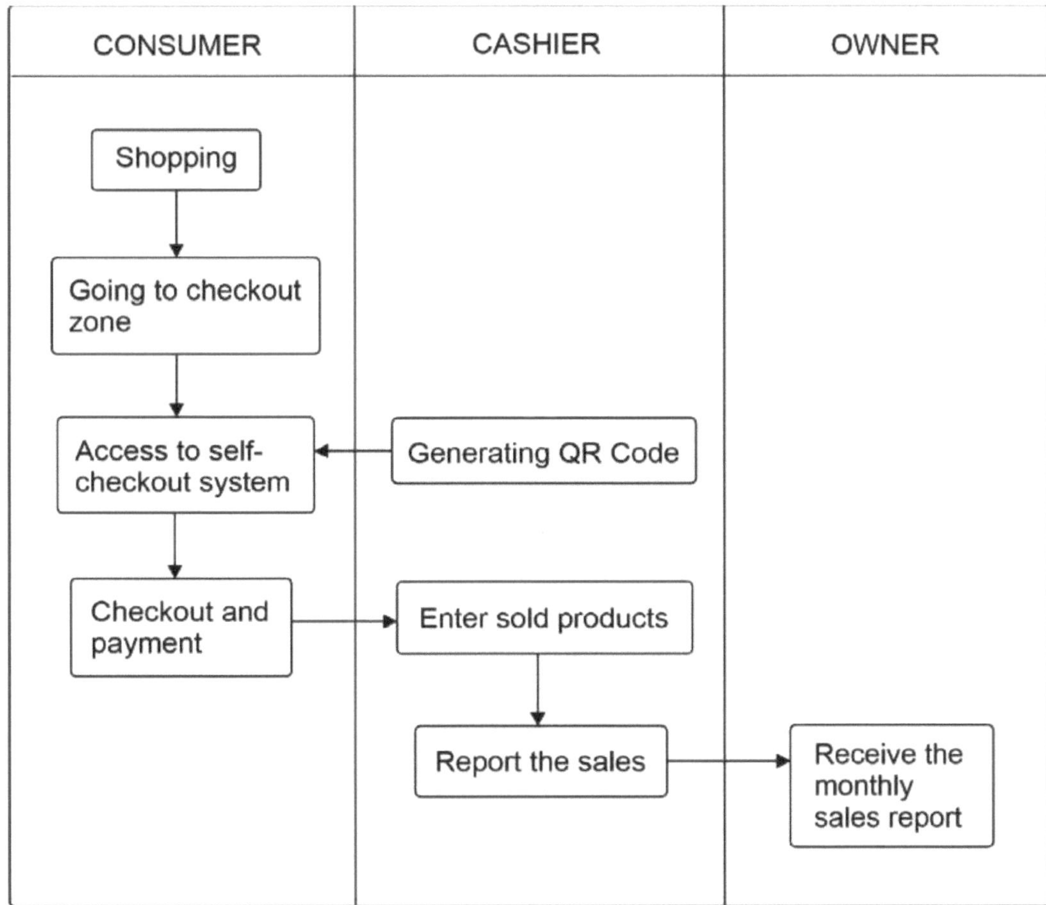

Fig. (1). self-checkout software.

STRUCTURAL DESIGN

Fig. (**2**) displays the overall structural design of the system. The front controller, index.php, prepares the fundamental resources required to execute Code Igniter. Routers examine incoming HTTP requests and determine their next steps based on their contents. The system bypasses its regular processing and instantly gives the cache file to the browser if it exists. Before loading the application controller, we check the HTTP request and any data the user provides for security issues.

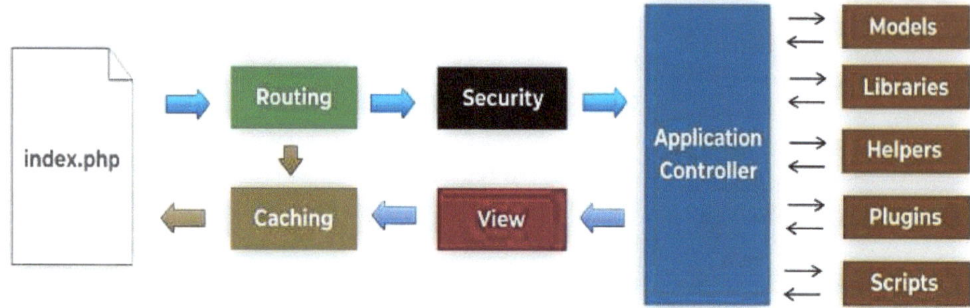

Fig. (2). Structural design.

The model, core libraries, helpers, and any other resources required to perform the individual request are loaded by the Controller. The produced View is then delivered to the web browser for viewing. If caching is enabled, the view is cached first so that it may be provided on subsequent requests.

Invoice Generation

Maintain a track of the finer points of invoice management so that we can organize information in a single table. Every one of the subtle aspects can be discovered by the company's owner in a single-view page design.

All the stock sections should be maintained in this manner so that they can be replenished as needed. The invoice design may be printed *via* the printing module. It can be easily converted into a PDF and used to create an invoice, helping clients determine the appropriate quantity of goods to purchase at any given moment.

Stock Management System

Supply chain management is the process of tracking products as they move from purchase to manufacture and ultimately to sale. It dictates how your company handles stock management (refer to Fig. (**3**), use case diagram).

Attendance Management System

Employee working hours are tracked using this module. It maintains accurate time records for employees' attendance, breaks, time off, and clock-in and clock-out times. It safeguards a record against any form of error. It improves the precision and efficiency of your attendance management.

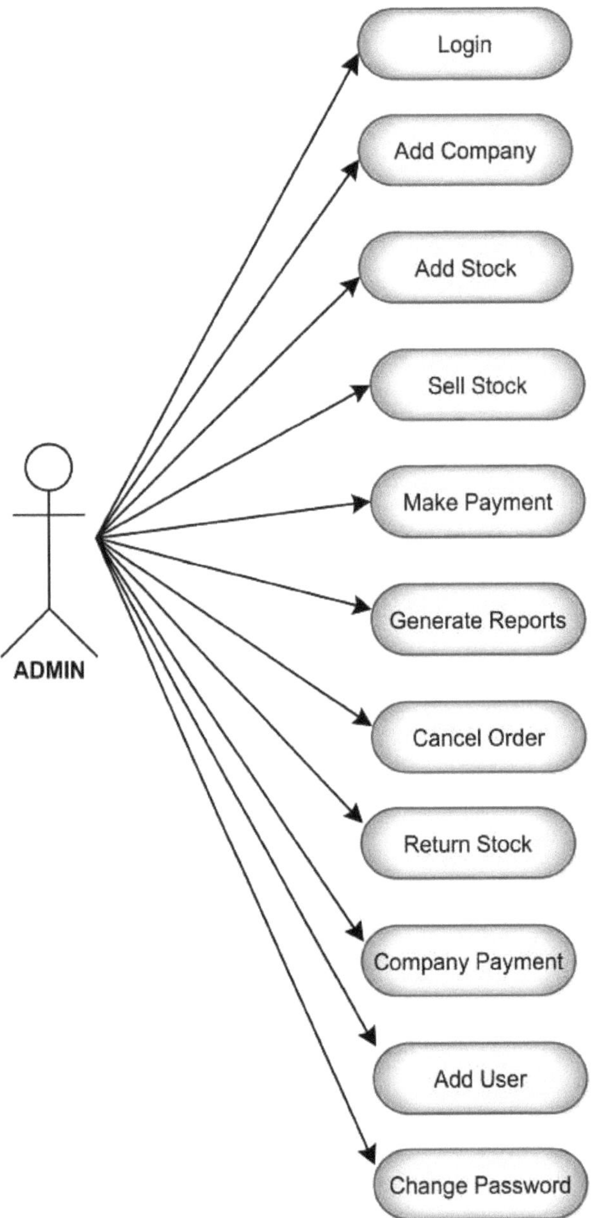

Fig. (3). Stock management system.

The smartphone app allows employees to log their time and attendance. Because the programme automates attendance management, the information should be provided in real-time to the HR department, allowing for accurate payroll and rewarding your employees for their time.

Report Module

In this, the owner of this business can see a single tab detail of all the customers who have purchased items over a day, week, or month to count the items and determine which items are required for the customer, as well as bookkeeping, so that they can evaluate markdowns and other special offers.

Stock Management Module

In this case, the business owner can view a single tab that details all stock purchases and the management of stock generation, including tax invoices based on the purchased stock.

CONCLUSION

The application takes complete management of the inventory management system and self-checkout system *via* the QR code. It is an application that can be used to minimize problems in malls and large stores caused by crowds. Then, as customers have finished shopping, they can use the app to purchase the products they want. The self-checkout retail technology solution does not require the business to invest in additional hardware. Stock changes continually. Every day, returns, deals, fresh receipts, and even theft and burglary influence the stock levels. A successful retail or discount company relies on stock management and control, which may be intimidating.

The firm grows and manages more stock, making stock management more critical. Innovation can simplify the lives of both owners and employees. Therefore, retail businesses require effective stock management systems. This guide will inform you of all that is needed to be aware of stock administration frameworks. This guide will help you understand the various frameworks available and determine which one best suits your needs. It will also outline the key elements a framework should offer to enhance productivity and overall customer satisfaction. By the end, the goal is to develop an application capable of managing inventory, sales, purchases, attendance, and more, incorporating a modern self-checkout system using QR code technology.

REFERENCES

[1] Mewada, Shivlal & Saroliya *et al.* Smart Diagnostic Expert System for Defect in Forging Process by Using Machine Learning Process. Journal of Nanomaterials. pp. 1-8, 2022.

[http://dx.doi.org/10.1155/2022/2567194]

[2] P. Moradi, K. Levy, and C. Cheyre, "Pseudo-Automation: How Labor-Offsetting Technologies Reconfigure Roles and Relationships in Frontline Retail Work," *Proc. ACM Hum.-Comput. Interact.*, vol. 9, no. 2, pp. 1–21, May 2025.
[http://dx.doi.org/10.1145/3711051]

[3] Singh, Chaitanya & Subrahmanya Srinivasa Rao, Motukuri & Mahaboobjohn, Y. & Bonthu, Kotaiah & Kumar, T. Applied Machine Tool Data Condition to Predictive Smart Maintenance by Using Artificial Intelligence. 2022.
[http://dx.doi.org/10.1007/978-3-031-07012-9_49]

[4] R. Devi, S. K. N. Kumar, and M. Ramesh, "Optimization for the human resources management strategy of the IoT industry based on analytic hierarchy process," *Wireless Personal Communications*, vol. 113, no. 2, pp. 873–891, 2020.
[http://dx.doi.org/10.1007/s11277-020-07345-1]

[5] Y. Chen, C. Zhao, Y. Xu, and C. Nie, "Year-over-year developments in financial fraud detection via deep learning: A systematic literature review," Jan. 2025, Accessed: Mar. 09, 2025.
[http://dx.doi.org/10.48550/arXiv.2502.00201]

[6] C. Huot, S. Heng, T.K. Kim, and Y. Han, "Quantum autoencoder for enhanced fraud detection in imbalanced credit card dataset", *IEEE Access,* vol. 12, pp. 169671-169682, 2024.
[http://dx.doi.org/10.1109/ACCESS.2024.3496901]

[7] A. Iqbal, and R. Amin, "Time series forecasting and anomaly detection using deep learning", *Comput. Chem. Eng.,* vol. 182, p. 108560, 2024.
[http://dx.doi.org/10.1016/j.compchemeng.2023.108560]

[8] K. S. N. V. K. Gangadhar, B. A. Kumar, Y. Vivek, and V. Ravi, "Chaotic variational auto encoder based one class classifier for insurance fraud detection," Dec. 2022, Accessed: Mar. 09, 2025.
[http://dx.doi.org/10.48550/arXiv.2212.07802]

[9] A. Kanksha, A. Bhaskar, S. Pande, R. Malik, and A. Khamparia, "An intelligent unsupervised technique for fraud detection in health care systems", *Intell. Decision Technol.,* vol. 15, no. 1, pp. 127-139, 2021.
[http://dx.doi.org/10.3233/IDT-200052]

[10] F. Louati, F.B. Ktata, and I. Amous, "Enhancing intrusion detection systems with reinforcement learning: A comprehensive survey of RL-based approaches and techniques", *SN Comput. Sci.,* vol. 5, no. 6, p. 665, 2024.
[http://dx.doi.org/10.1007/s42979-024-03001-1]

[11] D. Kim, K. Park, M. Chang, S. Joo, S. Hong, S. Cho, and H. Kwon, "Fabrication of functionally graded materials using aluminum alloys via hot extrusion", *Metals (Basel),* vol. 9, no. 2, p. 210, 2019.
[http://dx.doi.org/10.3390/met9020210]

[12] G. V. Bhau, R. G. Deshmukh, S. Chowdhury, Y. Sesharao, and Y. Abilmazhinov, "IoT based solar energy monitoring system," *Materials Today: Proceedings*, vol. 80, pp. 3697–3701, 2023.
[http://dx.doi.org/10.1016/j.matpr.2021.07.370]

[13] A. Seem, A. K. Chauhan, R. Khan, and S. P. Yadav, "Distributed Artificial Intelligence for Document Retrieval, in Distributed Artificial Intelligence: A Modern Approach", *Academic Press*, 2020, ch. 4, pp. 59–68.

CHAPTER 10

E-Commerce Website Management System

Aiman Peerzade[1,*], **H Swaraj Bharath**[2], **Renu Vij**[3] and **Monica Bhutani**[4]

[1] *Department of Management Studies, Rizvi College of Arts, Science and Commerce, Mumbai 400050, Maharashtra, India*

[2] *Department of CSE (Data Science), CMR College of Engineering & Technology, Hyderabad 501401, Telangana, India*

[3] *University School of Business, Department of AIT Management, Chandigarh University, Mohali 140413, Punjab, India*

[4] *Department of Electronics and Communication, Bharati Vidyapeeth's College of Engineering, New Delhi 110063, India*

Abstract: Popular website and e-commerce software platforms, such as CMS, are favored due to their simplicity and versatility in practice. However, website usability is one of the most significant quality elements that is difficult to quantify since it relies on various other variables. Thus, this article aims to determine which CMS is best suited for the usability and design needs of website developers. This study examines many e-commerce CMSs and outlines their characteristics that may aid with usability and design. This study uses E-commerce Total Quality Management usability. Choose Shopify, Open Cart, with the help of Magento, or WooCommerce, the most prominent e-commerce CMS. The design idea is evaluated using website design components. CMS characteristics that aid usability and design principles were found in this investigation.

Keywords: CMS, E-commerce software, E-commerce total quality management, Website usability, Website design components.

INTRODUCTION

Standard industrial practice is e-business [1]. Most successful e-commerce companies are realizing that a high-quality platform is more important than a cheap price or online presence. Due to e-commerce, several individuals universally choose to buy, transfer, sell, or provide services, and trade goods and information online. Consumer confidence drives e-commerce growth [2]. The importance of usability, which is described as "a quality characteristic that evaluates how easy interfaces are to use," should be kept in mind by software

* **Corresponding author Aiman Peerzade:** Department of Management Studies, Rizvi College of Arts, Science and Commerce, Mumbai 400050, Maharashtra, India; E-mail: peerzadeaiman83@gmail.com

D. Arul Pon Daniel, T. Rajasanthosh Kumar & Satya Prakash Yadav (Eds.)

product providers [3]. It defines usability as "the extent to which a definite set of users can use a product to realize predetermined goals in a way that is efficient, effective, and satisfying within that set of contexts" [4]. Developers must consider visitors' needs to create a successful website [5]. Many usability studies focus on end-user viewpoints, rather than developer perspectives, as a measure of website quality [6]. For designers to identify users early on and establish usability standards, usability must be prioritized.

The CMS helps manage, modify, and enhance website content [7]. The simplicity and convenience of use of these electronic programs for website and e-commerce launches are making them popular [8]. Frameworks and models enable quick design; therefore, CMS has grown [9]. CMS saves text on web pages and distributes information in databases instead of HTML pages [10]. The features included in these tools were user-focused, which helped address usability concerns and plan ideas for an e-commerce website [11].

STUDYING CONTENT MANAGEMENT SYSTEM

Details about the comparative tools can be found here. WooCommerce, OpenCart, Magento, and Shopify.

Shopify

Shopify creates sales websites for everyone. Online shopping, credit card receipts, and trade sales powered by Shopify POS are available from Shopify. Shopify's e-commerce software enables users to manage their business from a single platform. Construct their online shop, launch additional distribution systems in seconds, manage products and inventory without constraints, process orders in one phase, analyze distribution and growth patterns, and more.

OpenCart

Retailers utilize OpenCart, an open-source e-commerce platform, to sell online and can expand their business by adding new products to their e-commerce store. OpenCart's built-in SEO tool helps merchants determine page positions and keywords to boost traffic and optimize their websites.

Magento

Magento eCommerce software powers online stores for big and developing organizations. Front-end and back-end processes may be managed using the software to provide a customized and bespoke user experience. For effective online shop development, the software integrates with many other applications and provides improvements, maintenance, consultancy, and training.

WooCommerce

WooCommerce serves businesses of all sizes, from small to large online operations. WordPress eCommerce add-in WooCommerce is open-source. WordPress users may create a free basic online shop using WooCommerce (customization plug-ins and modules are paid). WooCommerce users can build or purchase pre-made plugins to enhance the functionality of their store.

CMS Functions

E-commerce CMS features should include:

- API - Facilitates fast and efficient data sharing between applications.
- Activity Dashboard - Provides managers with essential information for decision-making.
- Automatic Backup - Copy website data automatically.
- Campaign Management - Activities aligned with an action plan to achieve a business goal.
- Filter for content
- Client Segmentation — The act of categorizing clients into distinct subsets
- Personalization Options for Branding—Call and Web Bridge Personalization
- Drip Marketing - Sending scheduled emails to inform and move users to preferred intervals.
- Utilize multi-channel marketing, focusing on client-favored channels.
- Processing orders
- PCI DSS Compliant - Ensures safe credit card processing, storage, and transmission for organizations.
- Catalogue of products.
- Centralize product data available from many departments and sources.
- Ratings and Reviews may increase online and offline traffic and revenue for transparency.

These features may help fix usability concerns. Key usability objectives include effectiveness, efficiency, safety, usefulness, learnability, memorability, and other quality indicators. Several measurable construct sets connected to e-commerce services are used to measure software quality. Some e-commerce service build sets were identified in this study. These construct sets are quantifiable.

- E-S-QUAL and e-SQ reflect key online service quality. An essential measure of e-SQ is E-S-QUAL, which incorporates user satisfaction.
- Information System Success is the source of E-commerce Success Metrics (ESM). The commercial characteristics of a system are the primary emphasis.

- E-commerce Total Quality Management Framework addresses consumer and expert team facets of quality. Hierarchically measuring fundamental quality metrics, traits, and sub-attributes from both viewpoints.
- Website Quality Dimensions on Customer Satisfaction in B2C E-commerce is a revised ESCM model that identifies customer satisfaction factors.
- The term "FUX" refers to the aspects of user experience beyond usability.

ISO addresses common human characteristics that impact the delivery and perception of software development projects.

Quality is measured using E-TQMF. According to the E-TQMF study, quality is perceived from the perspectives of both consumers and quality specialists. Thus, users and quality experts compute main metrics, quality attributes, and characteristics hierarchically.

The suggested frameworks include features, shown in Fig. (**1**), such as an overall evaluation of quality, internal and external quality characteristics, quality measures, and quality sub-goals. The entire quality evaluation is represented by a percentage number, indicating the e-commerce system's quality compliance. Consumers and product specialists evaluate product quality. Multiple attributes define the quality sub-goal. Table **1** presents the E-commerce TQMF quantity tree model's metrics and characteristics, focusing on usability and plotting tool features to identify usability concerns.

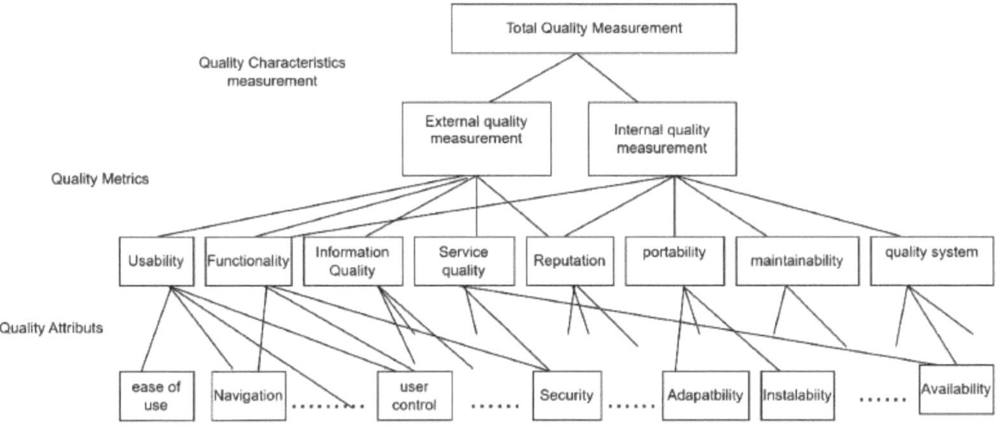

Fig. (1). Quality measurement tree for e-commerce.

Table 1. Tool features mapping, metric quality, and model attributes.

Measures of Quality	Attributes and Qualities	Characteristics	Features
Usability	Simple usage	The site is user-friendly	• Integration with Third Parties • API
	Easy to use	Easy-to-use and comprehensible website interface design	• List of Products • Templates for Emails
	Clear and uncluttered	Provide a basic framework and features	• Managing orders • Processing order
	Getting Around	Encouraging online customer engagement	• The Ability to Search
	Speed	To speed up the loading process	• API
	The capacity to learn	To simplify the software for users	• Managing Product Information
	Be consistent	For the sake of maintaining consistency	• Managing content
	Design for aesthetics	To design visually appealing websites	• Managing content
	Personalized settings	Make the page flexible.	Manage a website
	Affect performance	To provide support and paperwork	• Reviews and Ratings

RESULTS AND DISCUSSION

The 43 web developers who used e-commerce CMS technologies to design an e-commerce site, as shown in Fig. (**2**), answered a questionnaire.

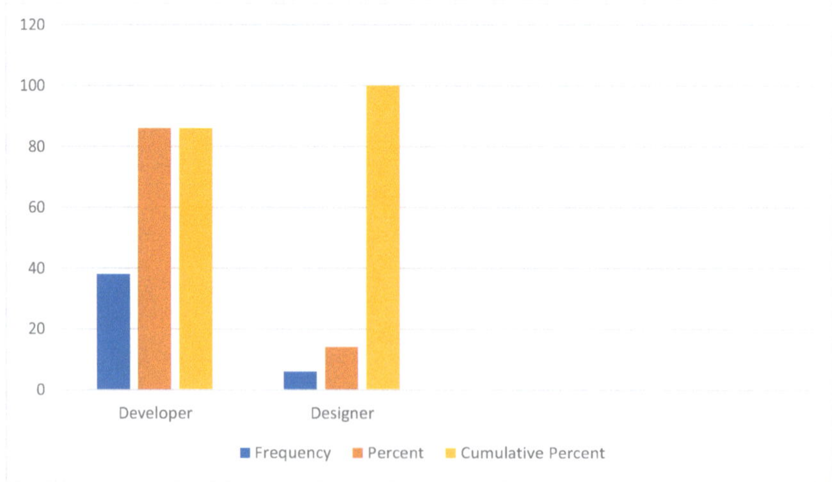

Fig. (2). Credentials of respondents.

The system usability scale findings for all four CMS programs are presented in Fig. (**3**). The systems usability scale interpret Score is below.

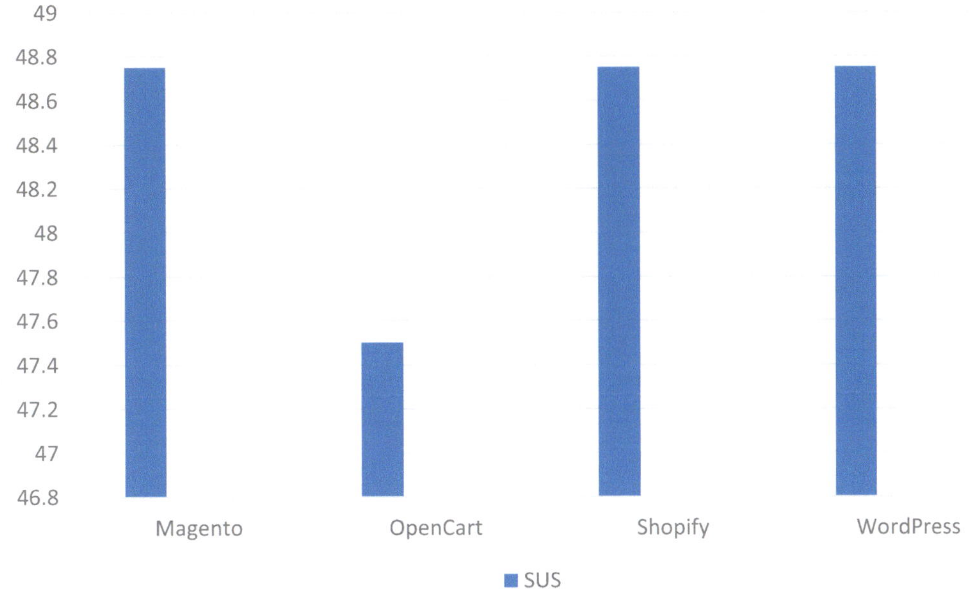

Fig. (3). Evaluation of the CMS tools' system usability.

CMS functionality, usability quality, and website design are mapped. Each property and element has several CMS characteristics, as shown in Fig. (**4**). The mapping suggests that certain CMS features are related to numerous usability characteristics. Every usability attribute has a corresponding feature. Mapping CMS features to usability quality measures may show that CMS features help e-commerce website usability. Shopify, Magento, OpenCart, and Shopify CMS have many usability features, which can help e-commerce websites address usability concerns. Except for Shopify, the Content Management Systems (CMS) for Magento, OpenCart, and Shopify all include several features focused on improving the usability of online stores' user interfaces.

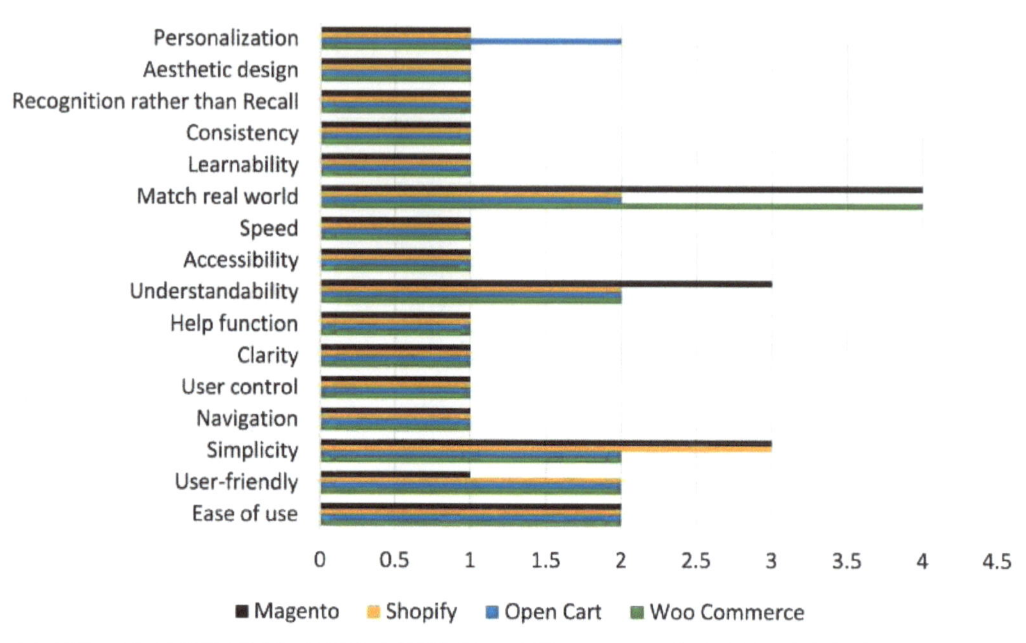

Fig. (4). Usability quality cms feature presence.

Fig. (**4**) demonstrates that the majority of these four CMS fail the Usability Quality Attributes. All four CMS only accomplish 'Match Real World', but only one or two cover the remainder of the quality.

CONCLUSION

A website's usability—clear and accurate information, no ambiguity, and required things in the right places—is one of its most significant quality aspects. Some reasons make measuring website usability challenging. E-commerce CMS capabilities were mapped to the Total Quality Management (TQM) framework, as well as usability quality and eight website design aspects, in this report. E-commerce usability measurements include 15 quality elements in the framework. Mapping 35 software comparison engine characteristics to attributes. Magento, Shopify, OpenCart, and WooCommerce are the top four Content Management Systems (CMSs) in terms of the number of features available, based on usability quality criteria and design concept aspects. Magento is the best CMS since it has the most features. Usability quality indicators may also assist in the design and development of e-commerce online content management systems.

REFERENCES

[1] Hymavathi, J., Kumar, T. R., Kavitha, S., Deepa, D., Lalar, S., & Karunakaran, P. Machine Learning: Supervised Algorithms to Determine the Defect in High-Precision Foundry Operation. *Journal of Nanomaterials*, 1, 1732441, 2022. [http://dx.doi.org/10.1155/2022/1732441]

[2] Singh Chaitanya, Subrahmanya Srinivasa Rao Motukuri, Mahaboobjohn Y., Bonthu Kotaiah, Kumar T. "Applied Machine Tool Data Condition to Predictive Smart Maintenance by Using Artificial Intelligence", 2022. [http://dx.doi.org/10.1007/978-3-031-07012-9_49]

[3] A. Iqbal, and R. Amin, "Time series forecasting and anomaly detection using deep learning", *Comput. Chem. Eng.,* vol. 182, p. 108560, 2024. [http://dx.doi.org/10.1016/j.compchemeng.2023.108560]

[4] J. L. Leevy, J. Hancock, T. M. Khoshgoftaar, and A. A. Zadeh, "One-class classification for credit card fraud detection: A detailed study with comparative insights from binary classification," Springer Series in Reliability Engineering, vol. Part F15, pp. 117–140, 2025 [http://dx.doi.org/10.1007/978-3-031-72636-1_6]

[5] A. Al-Tarawneh and M. Al-Badawi, "The Multilingual Marketplace: Translation Strategies for E-commerce Success," in From Machine Learning to Artificial Intelligence, vol. 572, A. M. A. Musleh Al-Sartawi, M. Al-Okaily, A. A. Al-Qudah, and F. Shihadeh, Eds., in Studies in Systems, Decision and Control, vol. 572. , Cham: Springer Nature Switzerland, 2025, pp. 1045–1056. [http://dx.doi.org/10.1007/978-3-031-76011-2_77]

[6] S. Rafidah, R. R. Andika, S. Sutiono, and D. O. E. Napitupulu, "Penerapan content management system untuk website e-commerce pada Afika Store," Stud. Sci. Creat. J., vol. 3, no. 2, pp. 163–173, 2025. [http://dx.doi.org/10.1186/s40537-023-00825-1]

[7] K. S. N. V. K. Gangadhar, B. A. Kumar, Y. Vivek, and V. Ravi, "Chaotic variational auto encoder based one class classifier for insurance fraud detection," Dec. 2022, Accessed: Mar. 09, 2025. [http://dx.doi.org/10.48550/arXiv.2212.07802]

[8] L. Zhang, "From labs to real-world: developing smartphone-based methodologies for enhanced phenotyping of human decision-making in clinical settings," 2023.

[9] P. Kamuangu, "A review on financial fraud detection using AI and machine learning", *Journal of Economics, Finance and Accounting Studies,* vol. 6, no. 1, pp. 67-77, 2024. [http://dx.doi.org/10.32996/jefas.2024.6.1.7]

[10] Govinda Rajulu et al, "Cloud-computed solar tracking system.," vol. 2, 2022.

[11] K. Purohit, S. Vats, R. Saklani, V. Kukreja, V. Sharma and S. P. Yadav, "Improvement in k-means clustering for information retrieval," *4th International Conference on Electronics and Sustainable Communication Systems (ICESC),* 2023, pp. 1239-1245 [http://dx.doi.org/10.1109/ICESC57686.2023.10193031]

CHAPTER 11

AIML-Based Price Negotiation in E-Commerce by Analyzing the Test and Voice-Based Chatbot

P. Sudheer[1,*], **Rupak Sharma**[2], **Alekh**[2], **A.K. Sharma**[3] and **Pramoda Patro**[4]

[1] *Department of CSE (AI&ML), CVR College of Engineering, Ibrahimpatnam 501510, Telangana, India*

[2] *Department of Computer Applications, SRM Institute of Science and Technology, NCR Campus, Modinagar, Ghaziabad 201204, Uttar Pradesh, India*

[3] *Department of CSE, School of Engineering & Technology, Career Point University, Kota 325003, Rajasthan, India*

[4] *Department of Mathematics, KLEF (Deemed to be University), Hyderabad 500045, Telangana, India*

Abstract: The popularity of buying things online has skyrocketed in recent years. During this time, most features of online buying have been refined, but others are still missing, such as the ability to negotiate prices with shop owners. To negotiate product costs, this article proposes utilizing a chatbot equipped with a voice assistant. A customer may ask the chatbot for help determining a fair price for an item. Both the buyer and the seller run the risk of having their finances squeezed when they shop online. Machine learning algorithms have been developed to aid in buying by predicting future outcomes based on past data to prevent compromise. Nevertheless, the accuracy of predicting prices might be compromised if the dataset is inappropriate or if irrelevant elements or attributes of the information are used. Because even one incorrect price forecast could result in substantial financial losses, e-commerce enterprises do not rely solely on such techniques. Furthermore, when data becomes too abundant or a characteristic is no longer available after the period used to make the model's prediction, very few models do poorly. The model proposed in this work maintains its accuracy and reliability by regulating these adjustments.

Keywords: Chatbot, E-commerce, Machine learning, Negotiate prices, Online shopping.

* **Corresponding author P. Sudheer:** Department of CSE (AI&ML), CVR College of Engineering, Ibrahimpatnam 501510, Telangana, India; E-mail: sudheerchanty7@gmail.com

D. Arul Pon Daniel, T. Rajasanthosh Kumar & Satya Prakash Yadav (Eds.)

INTRODUCTION

Modern e-commerce systems use a variety of AI methods to determine which goods are most popular, making it easier for users to search for what they need [1]. The greatest products may be expensive, however, so buyers frequently have to settle for less [2]. Additionally, problems can arise when purchasing inexpensive items. Customers might haggle over product pricing by introducing a haggling option, which would alleviate their concern [3]. Negotiation entails exploring ideas that may satisfy all parties. Within their selling range, the seller specifies a minimum price as the lower limit, while the unique item value serves as the maximum limit in the algorithm [4]. The model is implemented by integrating a chatbot into the website utilizing Flask APIs, allowing users to witness functionality in real-life circumstances [5]. The implementation method has been demonstrated in Fig. (**1**) [6].

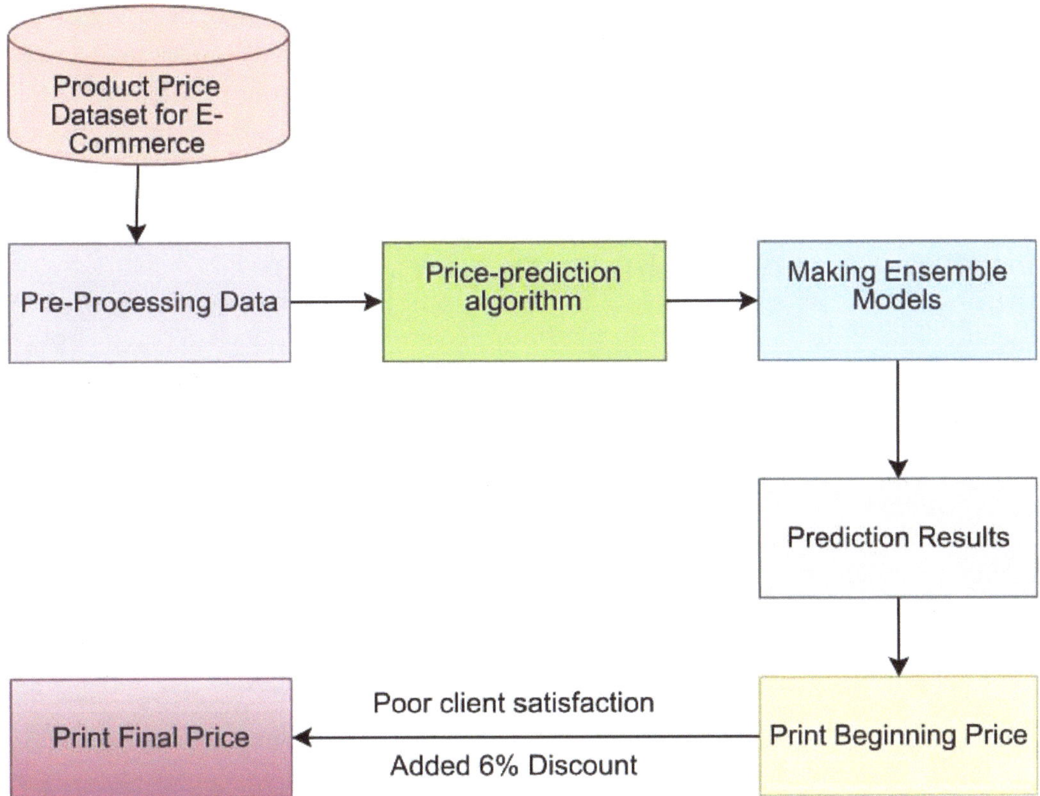

Fig. (1). Implementation method.

A chatbot is an artificial intelligence computer that converses with consumers in natural language *via* messaging, sites, mobile applications, or telephone [7]. It can manage most client concerns without human interaction. The chatbot utilizes natural language processing (NLP) techniques to comprehend user intent and provide accurate responses [8]. In addition, chatbots may automate e-commerce negotiations. With this approach, users may freely interact with the program, enter financial limits, and ask product-related inquiries for suitable replies. Chatbots in e-commerce, such as logistics and retail, may boost sales and user engagement, perhaps attracting more consumers with affordable items [9].

Conventional e-commerce platforms lack a mechanism for negotiating product costs, which is a significant drawback. The Chatbot uses machine learning techniques to enhance its replies to client requests over time, addressing this constraint. Machine learning chatbots can learn from interactions with users, grasp their intent, provide suitable replies, and adapt to different circumstances, contrasting with rule-based chatbots that employ pre-programmed responses [10]. A classification algorithm analyses input data and prospective outcomes to make predictions. Supervised learning algorithms use labeled data to predict or classify unlabeled information. The goal is to create a model that properly maps input to output variables, allowing for accurate predictions of new inputs. Typical supervised learning methods include K-nearest neighbours (KNN), support vector machines (SVM), and neural networks, as shown in Fig. (**2**). SVM is effective for dividing classes that cannot be linearly segregated by finding the optimum hyperplane in feature space. Instead, KNN predicts based on distances between new and older information facts in the training set. This non-parametric technique is frequently used for binary classification applications.

The study envisions an online purchasing app including user login, registering, chatbot negotiating, reading, order viewing, product searching, review publishing, and sentiment analysis. The chatbot collaborates with consumers to negotiate reasonable product pricing. The voice and text-based chat alternatives for selling produce cost. The research advocates for using SVM and KNN algorithms with collective learning to improve chatbot negotiating skills. The study presents a technically robust strategy that utilizes AI techniques, categorization algorithms, and chatbot-assisted negotiation in an online retail application.

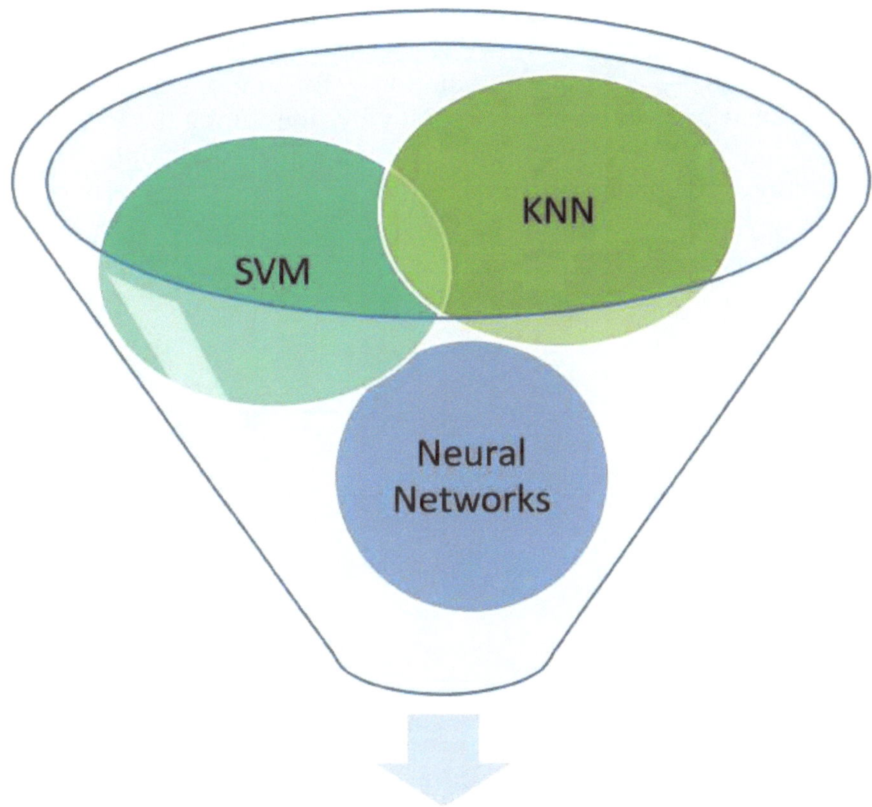

Fig. (2). Typical supervised learning methods.

METHODOLOGY

Haggling occurs using a dataset of e-commerce products, including product pricing and minimum prices. A thorough database is created using MariaDB to hold the dataset. SVM and KNN algorithms assess many dataset features, including minimum price, category, and likes, to predict pricing. Through an ensemble technique, the first agreed-upon price is calculated by analysing outcomes from both algorithms. Pre-processing is essential for the workflow since it improves the precision and performance of machine-learning procedures. The min-max scale pre-processing function from the sklearn package was used to accomplish this. Data is normalized by scaling it to a present range, generally between 0 and 1. Pre-processing is advantageous for the product price data due to its diverse range of values. Increasing the data scale facilitates comparison and analysis, resulting in more accurate conclusions. Using this technique, they divided the data into 85% training and 15% testing sets to assess model performance as depicted in Fig. (**3**). SVM and KNN algorithms were used to train an ensemble model, merging predictions for more reliable outcomes. GridSearchCV was used to improve accuracy by fine-tuning the hyperparameters of the SVM and KNN methods. This approach identified optimal parameter settings for improved model performance.

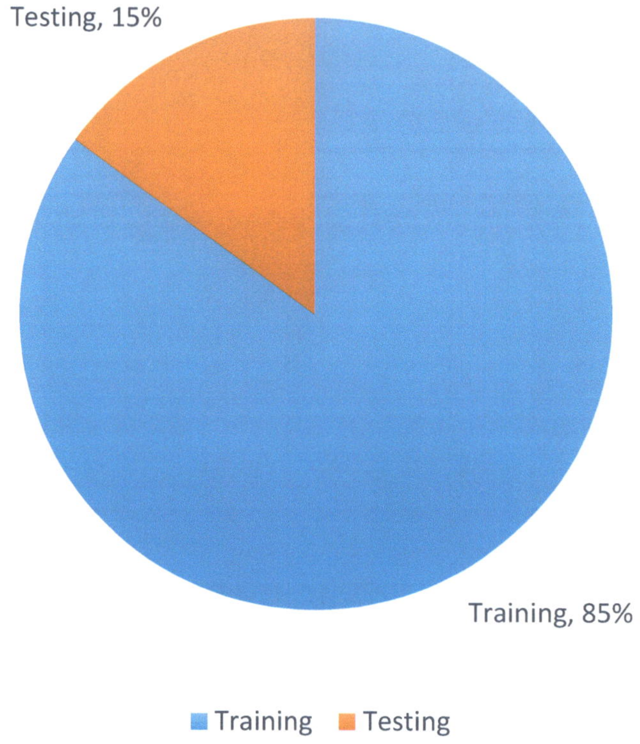

Fig. (3). Performance assessment.

Users can join and connect to the Price Negotiating Chatbot on the e-commerce website, offering both text and voice capabilities. Users may browse the item list and choose Textual or Audio mode to communicate with the chatbot after signing up and logging in. The chatbot recognizes instructions like "starting price" and "final price." The user receives the initial pricing based on an ensemble model of KNN and SVM procedures. For the final cost calculation, a 6% reduction is included. The platform may be used to examine orders, publish evaluations, and assess review sentimentality, allowing users to analyze their instructions at the agreed-upon pricing. Ensemble techniques improve model stability and predictiveness by merging different models. They developed an ensemble consisting of KNN and SVM. This method utilizes the capabilities of many machine learning models, each specializing in distinct data features.

Combining model outputs improves forecast accuracy. The ensemble balances model biases and alterations, resulting in a powerful composite forecast that surpasses individual models. This method enhances model performance and is widely used with parallel base learners.

As an instance-based or slow learning strategy, the KNN algorithm does not generalize training cases. Without depending on data assumptions, it predicts future examples by finding comparable traits and allocating them to the most applicable category among existing instances. KNN uses Euclidean distance computation to calculate the distance between points. Note that KNN may have large processing costs owing to calculating distances between all occurrences in the dataset. SVMs are suitable for regression and classification problems and are robust supervised learning algorithms. A separating hyperplane is used to define a discriminative classifier. SVM can classify new samples using labeled training data by building an optimal hyperplane. Different SVM variations address machine learning difficulties, including SVR, and improve support vector classification (SVC) capabilities. SVM utilizes margins to enhance class departure. The efficiency and speed of SVM are especially advantageous in high-dimensional settings.

Customers may choose to buy immediately or negotiate with the Chatbot. Customers may access the database using the Chatbot for simple questions. When a consumer engages in negotiation, the backend uses machine learning algorithms to predict price and begin the process. The Chatbot uses appropriate negotiation algorithms to pinpoint negotiating intentions. Customers may choose to buy at any intermediary cost or add the product to their spending basket for a reduced price after negotiation until the minimum cost is met. The vendor may adjust a product's lowest price in real-world e-commerce. Consequently, client pricing will be updated to match any changes in the cheapest rate. E-commerce websites must carefully handle offers and discounts to allow users to negotiate pricing while keeping a balance between price negotiations and other promotions.

Negotiation Algorithm

- An ensemble of models from SVM and KNN predicts the initial negotiated rate for the client.
- Adjust the price if the forecasted price is lower than the minimum price, exceeds the product price, or is significantly lower than the initial price. Calculation for

the new value: Price product - (price product – minimum value) * 0.1. This modification maintains the value close to the offered discount.

- If the pricing is acceptable, the consumer may purchase the product. Alternatively, they may negotiate further.
- In case of client disagreement with the original pricing, the maximum product discount is determined as a percentage.
- A 5% discount is applied to the prior pricing to further reduce the price. The revised pricing calculation is: Earlier price - (preceding price) * 0.05.
- Customers may continue with the transaction if they are pleased with the new pricing.
- If the consumer remains unsatisfied, the negotiating process resumes from the prior price, not the original product price. This enables iterative bargaining efforts.

Utilizing a trained model from past chatbot conversations enables the prediction of user responses. Machine learning methods like decision trees, SVMs, and neural networks improve prediction accuracy. Consider information like customer purchase history, preferences, and surfing patterns to improve forecasts. The chatbot may adjust its offer or negotiating technique based on the expected reaction, boosting sales and client happiness.

RESULTS AND DISCUSSION

The overarching area of this project is to generate an online storefront where customers may peruse product listings, communicate with a chatbot (either verbally or *via* text), and finalize their purchases. Before making a purchase, users may read all the reviews left by other users on a certain product. After interacting with the Chatbot in different ways, they can finally decide on pricing. The chatbot login pages as depicted in Fig. (**4**). There are two different kinds of voice commands that chatbots can understand: "first price" gives the consumer a decent price, and "final price" tells them to add a 6% discount before serving them. The chatbot will provide an error message if they try to use a term other than "first price" or "final price."

To initiate negotiations and purchase the product, the user must input the starting price in the aforementioned Chatbot, and to conclude negotiations and purchase the product, the user must enter the final price. In a similar vein, they may use voice or text to bargain with the Chatbot, examine product listings, and join up.

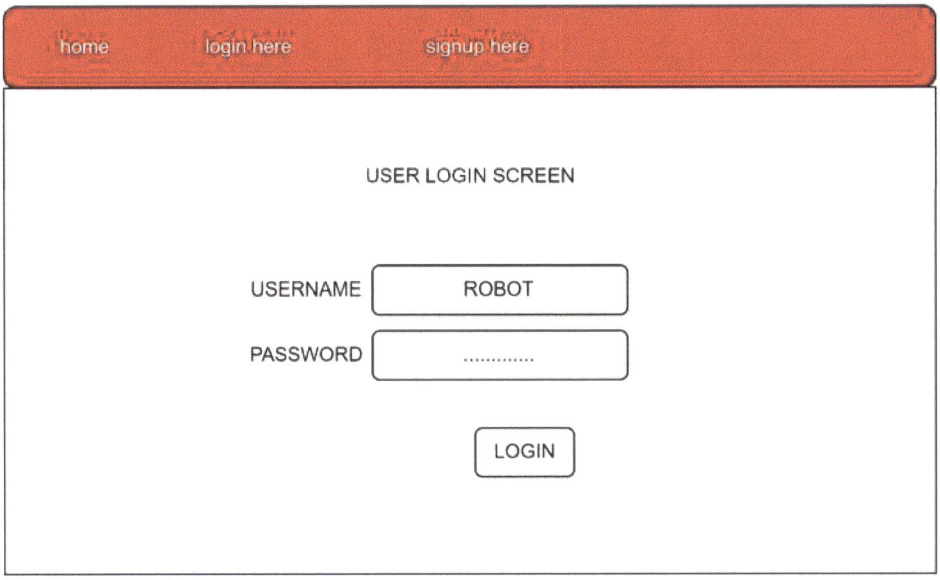

Fig. (4). Chatbot login page.

CONCLUSION

Online shopping has transformed consumer purchasing habits. Online shopping offers several advantages, such as access to a wide range of products and the freedom to purchase anytime and anywhere. Negotiating product pricing is a challenge in e-commerce systems. Customers can not negotiate prices with salesmen, unlike at traditional stores. This issue has been addressed by some companies using chatbots for consumer conversations. Electronic agents and chatbots may advise, suggest, and negotiate pricing. However, building a chatbot that negotiates pricing requires knowing customer demands. Chatbots that often charge over the minimum might cost vendors. Preventing this issue requires price prediction systems to effectively estimate product value and commence negotiations. This goal was achieved using SVM and K-Nearest Neighbour machine learning.

Understanding customer preferences and adjusting appropriately is key to negotiating. Additionally, an accurate price forecast is essential. Consumers get individualized advice and negotiate prices using KB representatives' broad knowledge. A KB agent in a chatbot may improve customer relations and customize purchases. However difficult it may be to negotiate goods prices *via* chatbots and KB assistants, these alternatives to online shopping may have some promise. Customers may have a better and more tailored shopping experience with the help of knowledge-driven agents and machine-learning techniques.

REFERENCES

[1] Mewada, S., Saroliya, A., Chandramouli, N., Kumar, T. R., Lakshmi, M., Christal Mary, S. S., & Jayakumar, M. (2021). "Smart diagnostic expert system for defect in forging process by using machine learning process." Journal of Nanomaterials, vol. 1, p. 2567194, 2022. [http://dx.doi.org/10.1155/2022/2567194]

[2] M. S. R. Y. M. B. K. T. R. K. Chaitanya Singh, " Applied machine tool data condition to predictive smart maintenance by using artificial intelligence," 2022.

[3] P. Patro, "A hybrid approach estimates the real-time health state of a bearing by accelerated degradation tests, Machine learning," 2021, Accessed: Apr. 11, 2025. [Online]. Available from: https://ieeexplore.ieee.org/abstract/document/9708591/ [http://dx.doi.org/10.1109/ICSTCEE54422.2021.9708591]

[4] H. Du, L. Lv, H. Wang, and A. Guo, "A novel method for detecting credit card fraud problems", *PLoS One,* vol. 19, no. 3, p. e0294537, 2024. [http://dx.doi.org/10.1371/journal.pone.0294537] [PMID: 38446831]

[5] B.N. Muthura, and A. Matheka, "A hybrid model for detecting insurance fraud using K-means and support vector machine algorithms", *Open Journal for Information Technology,* vol. 6, no. 2, pp. 143-156, 2023. [http://dx.doi.org/10.32591/coas.ojit.0602.05143m]

[6] Y. Supriya, N. Victor, G. Srivastava, and T.R. Gadekallu, "A hybrid federated learning model for insurance fraud detection", *IEEE International Conference on Communications Workshops: Sustainable Communications for Renaissance, ICC Workshops 2023,* pp. 1516-1522, 2023. [http://dx.doi.org/10.1109/ICCWorkshops57953.2023.10283682]

[7] A. Azadi Chegeni and P. Kapranos, "A microstructural evaluation of friction stir welded 7075 aluminum rolled plate heat treated to the semi-solid state," Metals 2018, Vol. 8, Page 41, vol. 8, no. 1, p. 41, Jan. 2018, [http://dx.doi.org/10.3390/met8010041]

[8] R.K. Verma, D. Parganiha, and M. Chopkar, "A review on fabrication and characteristics of functionally graded aluminum matrix composites fabricated by centrifugal casting method", *SN Applied Sciences,* vol. 3, no. 2, p. 227, 2021. [http://dx.doi.org/10.1007/s42452-021-04200-8]

[9] G. V. Bhau, R. G. Deshmukh, T. Rajasanthosh Kumar, S. Chowdhury, Y. Sesharao, and Y. Abilmazhinov, "IoT based solar energy monitoring system," *Materials Today: Proceedings*, vol. 80, pp. 3697–3701, 2023. [http://dx.doi.org/10.1016/j.matpr.2021.07.364]

[10] K. U. Singh, A. Kumar, G. Kumar, T. Singh, S. Kumar and S. P. Yadav, "An autonomous emotion recognition strategy employing deep learning for self-learning," *3rd International Conference on Technological Advancements in Computational Sciences (ICTACS)*, Tashkent, Uzbekistan, 2023, pp. 883-888. [http://dx.doi.org/10.1109/ICTACS59847.2023.10389867]

CHAPTER 12

AIML-Based Language-Supported Online Shopping Assistance

Rama Devi P.[1,*], **B. Amrutha Raju**[2], **M. Ravichand**[3], **Pramoda Patro**[4], **Anil Kumar N.**[5] and **M. Sandra Carmel Sophia**[1]

[1] *Department of English, KLEF (Deemed to be University), Guntur 522302, Andhra Pradesh, India*

[2] *Department of CSE (Data Science), CMR College of Engineering & Technology, Hyderabad 501401, Telangana, India*

[3] *Department of English, V. R. Siddhartha Engineering College, Siddhartha Academy of Higher Education, Vijayawada 520007, Andhra Pradesh, India*

[4] *Department of Mathematics, KLEF (Deemed to be University), Hyderabad 500045, Telangana, India*

[5] *Department of Electronics and Communication Engineering, School of Engineering, Mohan Babu University, Tirupati 517102, Andhra Pradesh, India*

Abstract: Online marketplaces offer a global platform for a diverse range of items. To make online purchasing convenient for users, our suggested system offers a variety of features. Just as when buying in a physical store, users need product and system-specific instructions when making purchases on these sites. Our e-commerce platform offers limitless talking services, and we incorporate an artificial chatting engine to provide stuff like this online. Users have the option to ask questions in the system during initialization of the e-commerce site. To acquire answers, the e-commerce system uses a pattern-matching algorithm to transmit consumer queries to the AIML Knowledge Base System. The user is then redirected to the system after receiving this response. Also, to demonstrate the chat system's multilingual capabilities, we are working on a Bangla-supported shopping assistant.

Keywords: AIML, Artificial chatting engine, E-commerce, Physical store, Shopping.

INTRODUCTION

The term "online shopping" refers to the practice of buying products and services from a seller over the Internet [1, 2, 3]. The advent of the World Wide Web

* **Corresponding author Rama Devi P.:** Department of English, KLEF (Deemed to be University), Guntur 522302, Andhra Pradesh, India; E-mail: ramadevinaresh@gmail.com

D. Arul Pon Daniel, T. Rajasanthosh Kumar & Satya Prakash Yadav (Eds.)

(WWW) has made it much easier for vendors to sell their wares online [4, 5]. Online shopping has several advantages that make it popular. Instead of spending time and energy physically searching for a product in several places, customers may locate what they are looking for by checking different internet retailers [6]. Meeting with a vendor is a great way for a buyer to learn about their goods and have their questions answered. Customers and vendors cannot meet due to time and distance constraints [7]. Human agents are sometimes enlisted to provide this service online, although they do not always deliver superior results every time [8], [9], [10]. They are irritated, confused, and unavailable at times, and may have trouble understanding what customers need. To address this issue, we created a unified platform for online purchasing that includes an AI chat feature [11]. Additionally, to facilitate multilingual capabilities, we are working on developing a Bangla conversational agent capable of chatting with users in Bangla [12].

PROPOSED SYSTEM

Chatbots have been widely used in several industries. A chatbot powered by Artificial Intelligence Machine Learning (AIML) will serve as an intelligent shopping assistant in our suggested system's interactive online store. Artificial Intelligence Markup Language (AIML) is a descendant of XML. Here, we will cover the basics of how a user can navigate the site and engage in a conversation with a smart shopping chatbot.

- An administrator (admin) and a consumer are the two main kinds of users.
- Keep the whole system running smoothly with the help of the admin. It is their job to introduce new products, revise existing ones, and remove old ones that are no longer relevant or valid. Information on customers saved in this system can be viewed and verified by them. In addition, they may see how customers rate the e-commerce site and products, which can guide the authority to make improvements.
- Customers can browse the products and their details by visiting the site. To their order list, they can add items that they want to purchase. To top it all off, they may share their thoughts about the e-commerce site and its items with the admin.
- Our e-commerce site features an artificial chatbot instead of a live customer care representative to answer questions about our products and services.
- To acquire answers to their questions, e-commerce sites submit queries to the Knowledge Base System (KBS). The files that make up the Knowledge Base System are based on AIML. Applying a pattern-matching algorithm to such files can help determine the answer to the following customer inquiry.
- After processing the user's inquiry, the result loops back to the online store.

- The user can ask more questions and generally interact more effectively in this manner.

RESULTS AND DISCUSSION

Fig. (**1**) shows the frameworks needed to build an e-commerce system: ASP.NET MVC 4 (Model View Controller) and Entity Framework 5. The product of this site is a variety of photocopying machines. In addition, this site offers a variety of solutions to meet the needs of viewers. We replace humans with an AI shopping assistant to handle online client management. Created with AIML files. The 50,000+ files that make up its category file were compiled over the course of many years, with each category sourced from a distinct site. We need to create 860 new product categories using the generic AIML files from the knowledge base system. To answer a question, each file is visited once. The number of words determines the time complexity, which is on the order of n. The location, kind, and capacity of its memory determine the space complexity. The general depiction of an AIML chatbot is shown in Fig. (**2**). There is a desktop app that works in tandem with the main online app.

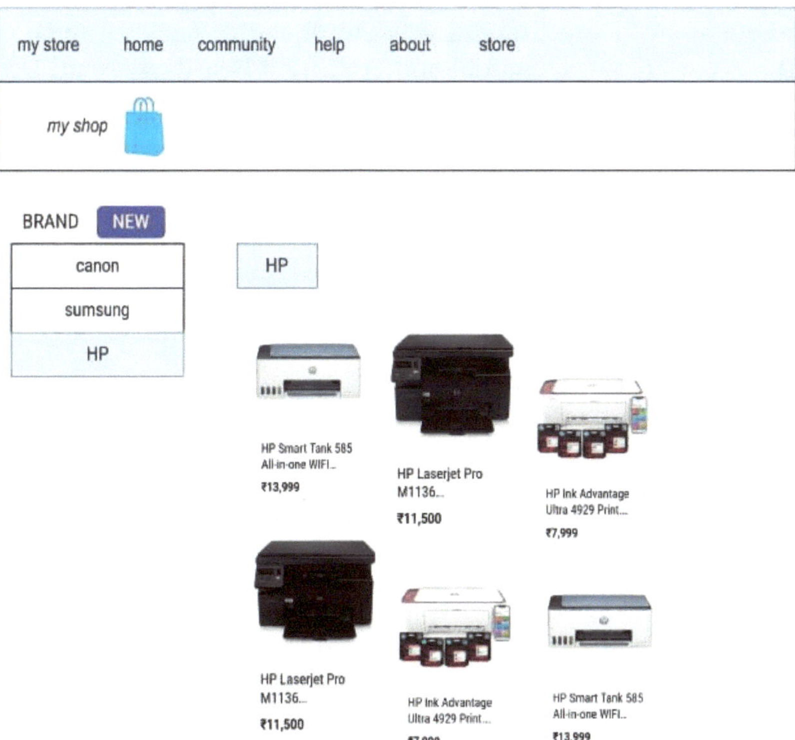

Fig. (1). Online shopping system.

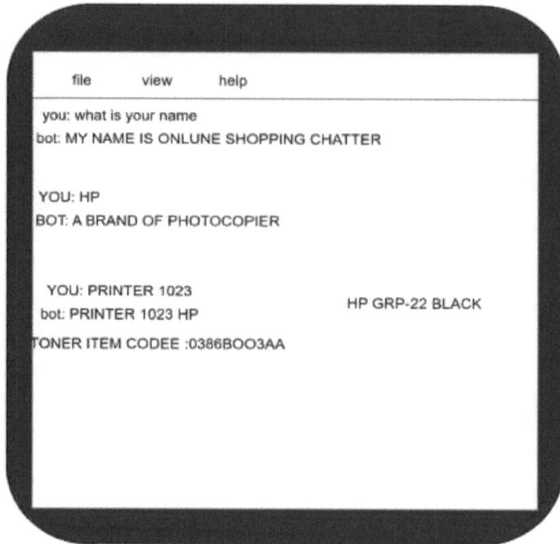

Fig. (2). Conversational AIML.

The option to support other languages makes the application even more user-friendly and engaging. Here, Bangla was employed to back up our experiment's findings. The Avro layout, Unicode, and ANSI keyboards were all supported by AIML (Figs. **3** and **4**). A translation tool was integrated into the chatbot to enable it to receive user input data.

Fig. (3). Process by an AI-powered chatbot.

Fig. (4). Promoted by an AI-powered chatbot.

CONCLUSION

This project involves creating a model of an interactive online store that offers various services to its customers, as well as constructing a trustworthy intelligent chatbot (assistant) responsible for providing consistent customer support. However, it has encountered a few constraints. In the case of one of them, the necessary mining output is missing. Furthermore, it lacks the necessary natural language features. Therefore, we aim to upgrade the chat system in the future to facilitate more engaging conversations with its users, utilizing natural language across multiple mediums.

REFERENCES

[1] J. Wang, W. Bai, & Y. Liu, "Optimization for the human resources management strategy of the IoT industry based on AHP," *Computational Intelligence and Neuroscience*, vol. 2022. [http://dx.doi.org/10.1155/2022/3514285]

[2] E. Altulaihan, M. A. Almaiah, and A. Aljughaiman, "Anomaly detection IDS for detecting DoS attacks in IoT networks based on machine learning algorithms," Sensors 2024, Vol. 24, Page 713, vol. 24, no. 2, p. 713, Jan. 2024. [http://dx.doi.org/10.3390/s24020713]

[3] Y. Yang, K. Zheng, B. Wu, Y. Yang, and X. Wang, "Network intrusion detection based on supervised adversarial variational auto-encoder with regularization", *IEEE Access,* vol. 8, pp. 42169-42184, 2020. [http://dx.doi.org/10.1109/ACCESS.2020.2977007]

[4] B.M. Naman, B. Mardan, and A. Mohsin Abdulazeez, "Credit card fraud detection based on machine

learning classification algorithm", *Indonesian Journal of Computer Science,* vol. 13, no. 3, 2024. [http://dx.doi.org/10.33022/ijcs.v13i3.3996]

[5] H. Palivela, V. Rishiwal, S. Bhushan, A. Alotaibi, U. Agarwal, P. Kumar, and M. Yadav, "Optimization of deep learning-based model for identification of credit card frauds", *IEEE Access,* vol. 12, pp. 125629-125642, 2024. [http://dx.doi.org/10.1109/ACCESS.2024.3440637]

[6] K. S. N. V. K. Gangadhar, B. A. Kumar, Y. Vivek, and V. Ravi, "Chaotic variational auto encoder based one class classifier for insurance fraud detection," Dec. 2022, Accessed: Mar. 09, 2025. [http://dx.doi.org/10.48550/arXiv.2212.07802]

[7] L. Zhang, "From labs to real-world: developing smartphone-based methodologies for enhanced phenotyping of human decision-making in clinical settings," 2023.

[8] A. Qayoom, M.A. Khuhro, K. Kumar, M. Waqas, U. Saeed, S. ur Rehman, Y. Wu, and S. Wang, "A novel approach for credit card fraud transaction detection using deep reinforcement learning scheme", *PeerJ Comput. Sci.,* vol. 10, p. e1998, 2024. [http://dx.doi.org/10.7717/peerj-cs.1998] [PMID: 38699207]

[9] C. Liu, Y. Chan, S.H. Alam Kazmi, and H. Fu, "Financial fraud detection model: Based on random forest", *Int. J. Econ. Finance,* vol. 7, no. 7, 2015. [http://dx.doi.org/10.5539/ijef.v7n7p178]

[10] K. Sanjeeviprakash, A.R. Kannan, and N.S. Shanmugam, "Additive manufacturing of metal-based functionally graded materials: overview, recent advancements and challenges", *J. Braz. Soc. Mech. Sci. Eng.,* vol. 45, no. 5, p. 241, 2023. [http://dx.doi.org/10.1007/s40430-023-04174-1]

[11] Sridhar, K. & Shinde, Govind & Chaurasia, Amrita & R, Asha. Data science: simulating and development of outcome based teaching method. 1-7, 2021. [http://dx.doi.org/10.1109/ICECONF57129.2023.10083713]

[12] A. Dhyani, A. Rawat, G. Bisht, S. Vats, V. Sharma, M. Baral, S. Yadav, "Comparative Analysis of Supervised Machine Learning Algorithms for Liver Disease Prediction with SMOTE Enhancement," 3rd Asian Conference on Innovation in Technology (ASIANCON), Ravet IN, India, pp. 1-6, 2023. [http://dx.doi.org/10.1109/ASIANCON58793.2023.10270381]

CHAPTER 13

Impact of Adopting the AI Application: Private Sector Bank Financial Performance

Gaikar Vilas B.[1,*], **M. Parameswar**[2], **Ujwal Dhokania CA**[3], **Anil Kumar N.**[4] and **Pramoda Patro**[5]

[1] *Department of Economics, Smt. CHM. College, University of Mumbai, Mumbai 421003, Maharashtra, India*

[2] *Department of CSE (Data Science), CMR College of Engineering & Technology, Hyderabad 501401, Telangana, India*

[3] *Swayam Siddhi College of Mgmt and Research, University of Mumbai, Mumbai 421003, Maharashtra, India*

[4] *Department of Electronics and Communication Engineering, School of Engineering, Mohan Babu University, Tirupati 517102, Andhra Pradesh, India*

[5] *Department of Mathematics, KLEF (Deemed to be University), Hyderabad 500045, Telangana, India*

Abstract: To increase client loyalty and satisfaction *via* digital transformation, banks are investing more in new technologies like artificial intelligence. This research uses CAMELS to examine how AI affects bank financial performance. The biggest bank in the private sector and a pioneer in AI technologies for customer experience, HDFC Bank, was chosen for the study. The authors have taken into account the four years preceding the adoption of AI (FY2013–2017), the four years following the adoption of AI (FY2019–2022), and 2018 as a transitional year for technological deployment. By comparing mean values, the research evaluates HDFC's financial performance before and after AI banking apps. Using SPSS and Excel, we tested a pair of sample t-tests on the secondary data we gathered. The results show that seven parameters—Tier 1 Capital Ratio, Business per employee, Dividend per share, Market price, Profit per employee, Cost-income ratio, and Expenses to Interest Earned Ratio—have improved noticeably. The positive effects of AI are becoming apparent, according to the authors, although major transformation may be delayed for some years.

Keywords: Adoption of AI, Financial performance, Private sector, Tier 1 capital ratio.

* **Corresponding author Gaikar Vilas B.:** Department of Economics, Smt. CHM. College, University of Mumbai, Mumbai 421003, Maharashtra, India; E-mail: gaikar_vilas@rediffmail.com

D. Arul Pon Daniel, T. Rajasanthosh Kumar & Satya Prakash Yadav (Eds.)

INTRODUCTION

Transformation and third-party ecosystems are growing in banks. Consequently, there has been a great deal of innovation in the banking industry, and banks are incorporating a lot of online features into their business operations [1]. This has led to the development of new digital solutions. Every organization, industry, and government relies on enormous data sets for productivity, efficiency, convenience, and scalability. AI improves bank efficiency, trust, and usability. Computers with artificial intelligence can work autonomously [2]. In the digital era, it helps contemporary banks compete. AI is expected to lower banking costs, enhance customer service, and automate processes [3, 4]. Digital transformation is a challenging yet lucrative path for banks to enhance their core banking services. Gartner expects that Indian banks and security firms will spend on IT systems in 2018. IT investment by banks and security organizations rose 11.8% in 2017 [5]. Financial services companies will invest more in AI and other developing technologies as digital banking grows. The largest private bank in India, by assets and market valuation, is HDFC Bank. Several use scenarios illustrate AI adoption [6]. OnChat, an AI-powered Facebook Messenger chatbot, was launched by HDFC Bank in 2017. Within a year, the Niki, an AI-developed chatbot, increased transactions by 160 percent month-over-month. According to HDFC Bank's annual audit report, over 3 lakh clients have used HDFC Bank OnChat to transact close to Rs. 250 lakhs. AI is commonly employed in customer service [7]. Eva, HDFC Bank's chatbot, has addressed over 50 lakh queries from more than one million consumers with an accuracy rate of over 86%. Eva has approximately 20,000 global customer interactions daily [8].

The bot handles bill payments, ticket bookings, and more. HDFC Bank unveiled IRA, India's first humanoid robot, serving 60 clients every day. The robot uses vision sensors to locate consumers and direct them to the closest counter. The HDFC Recruit Bot is another AI-powered operative recruiting tool [9]. This AI tool can identify candidates with the right functional and personal capabilities for large-scale recruiting. The solution reduces hiring time by 81%. Risk management, staff engagement, portfolio management, and credit scoring are HDFC Bank implementations [10]. AI assists with underwriting, credit score models, and the detection of credit payment default and fraud 11].

METHODS OF RESEARCH

Data Source

Audited HDFC Bank reports, Scopus-indexed papers, RBI reports, and other periodicals provide data and values for research.

Study Duration

According to secondary data, the bank began adopting AI tools in 2017-2018, leaving it as a gap year for AI implementation. The study considers eight years of economic data, spanning four years before and four years after AI adoption. The following logic is used to integrate AI technology with current systems, infrastructure, and data values in 2017-18:

- The 2018 study by Gartner indicates that banks invested heavily in IT. The deployment of new technology by banks is driving exponential company growth.
- According to the verified bank statement of affairs for FY 2017-18, HDFC Bank initiated applications of artificial intelligence in their job operations. Banks and other corporations are investing heavily in AI infrastructure, according to PWC Fintech Trends 2018.

Design of Research

Assuming no substantial bank changes occurred during this event that affected performance, other than the adoption of new technology, the authors analyzed the averages of the pre- and post-event periods. HDFC Bank is a pioneer in cutting-edge technology, accounting for 26% of India's banking operations. The authors limited the data to FY 2020-22; hence, the May 2023 HDFC combination with HDFC Bank was not considered.

Approach to Research

Statistics are done in SPSS and Excel. Financial performance is measured using CAMELS in this study. Financial performance changes were assessed by comparing the mean values of the CAMELS ratio. India devised this method to assess the bank's status. Mean ratios are compared before and after AI adoption. This research compares the mean values before and after AI adoption using a two-tailed paired t-test (Fig. **1**). The pre-post mean ratio difference is being tested for zero.

The CAMELS System

The CAMELS Model comprises capital, managerial efficacy, asset quality, liquidity, earning capacity, and sensitivity ratio. These six ratios help analyze bank performance. These six key indicators show the bank's financial health, operational efficiency, soundness, and regulatory compliance. In 1978, India implemented it and found it handy and effective. CAMELS evaluates bank performance using ratios.

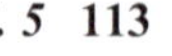

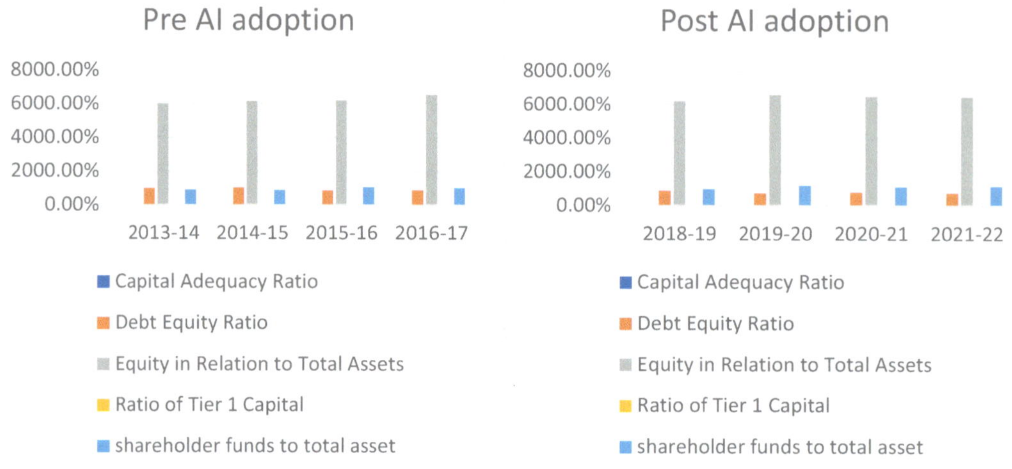

Fig. (1). HDFC pre- and post-AI capital adequacy ratios.

ANALYZE AND INTERPRET DATA

The capital adequacy ratio indicates a bank's risk and ability to absorb losses. CAR measures bank capital adequacy to risk-weighted resources. The growth in this percentage demonstrates that AI technologies enable the bank to strengthen its capital and foundation. AI applications have helped the bank reduce its debt-to-equity ratio, which is beneficial. The ratio of Tier I capital to total subjective assets is a measure of a bank's necessary capital. The bank's capacity to lend has increased owing to the implementation of new technologies, as the advances to the overall asset ratio are practically steady and have increased a bit. Shareholder funds are also increasing as the shareholder fund-to-asset ratio rises. Equity, preferred capital, reserves, and surplus are collectively referred to as shareholder funds. This growth indicates a high level of bank capital adequacy.

Bank asset quality is the second component. The research analyzes bank asset quality and financial health using the Net Interest Margin, Gross NPA, Net NPA, and Credit Deposit Ratio, as shown in (Fig. **2**). Gross and net NPA have demonstrated a consistent upward trend. The bank's primary objective is to maintain a low NPA rate to preserve profits. Gross and net NPA remain constant, with only a slight increase. The net NPA varies from 0.21% to 0.41%, with the Gross NPA ranging from 0.94% to 1.37%, indicating a consistent NPA level over the last decade. The credit deposit ratio shows loaned deposits. A higher ratio indicates proper deposit use. Over a decade, this ratio has remained steady. The interest rate minus the attention paid is called the net interest margin. During the duration, the credit payment ratio remains constant. This indicates that asset ratios remain stable and unaffected by technology or external events.

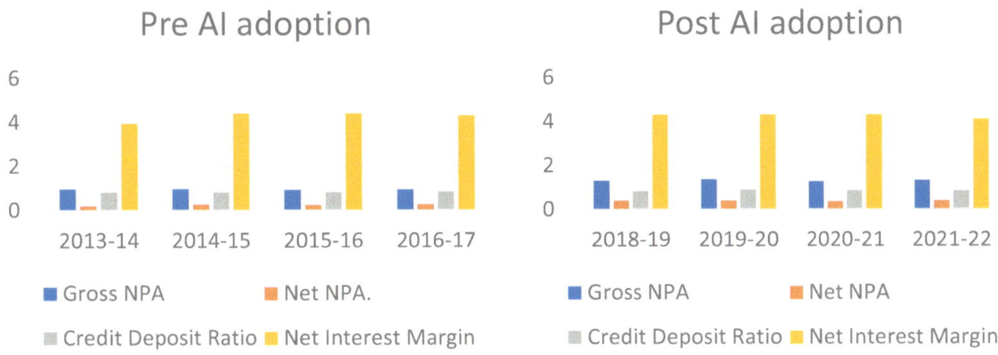

Fig. (2). HDFC bank asset quality ratios pre- and post-AI adoption.

Fig. (**3**) shows that the CAMELS Model is related to managerial efficiency, indicating profit maximization. This component is measured using four parameters. During the evaluation, the profit per employee increased, indicating that AI has improved both employee and management efficiency. Business per Employee has increased for HDFC, indicating efficiency gains *via* the use of new technology, particularly AI. The employee can now manage jobs better, improving performance. The overall expense-to-total revenue Ratio is falling, indicating that asset use might increase revenue. The falling ratio suggests that AI technologies reduce costs. Asset return has improved somewhat. Technology has not improved the return side in the near term.

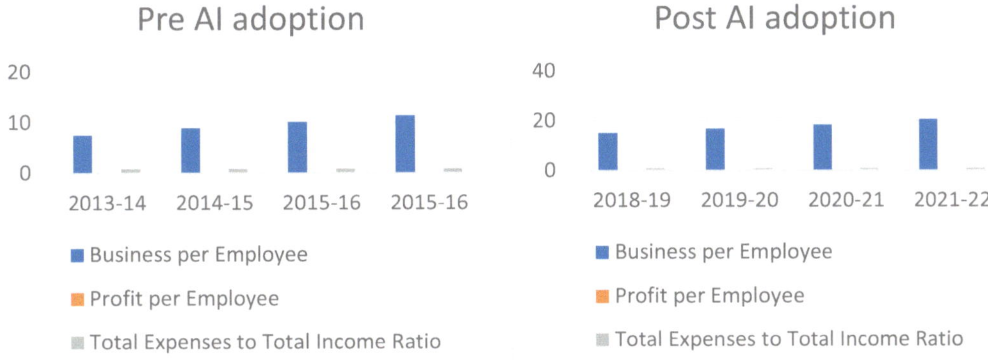

Fig. (3). HDFC bank management efficiency ratios pre- and post-AI adoption.

Bank profitability is shown by income management, the fourth component. The following four ratios (Fig. **4**) assess the bank's cost in relation to its profits. EPS and DPS show firm earnings. According to the statistics, AI usage has increased the ratio, suggesting bank profitability. Since the bank's audit report doesn't provide DPS for FY 2020-21, the lower average or lower figure of the previous two years is used for fairness. HDFC Bank has earned a competitive advantage, trust, and devoted consumers owing to its usage of cutting-edge technology, which has raised its share price. AI technologies enhance efficiency and reduce expenses, thereby lowering the cost-to-income ratio.

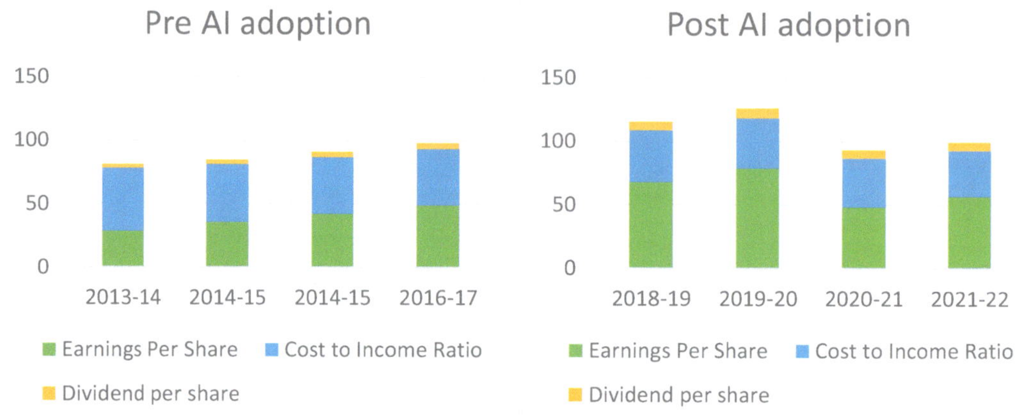

Fig. (4). HDFC Bank Pre- and Post-AI Earning Organization Ratios.

The CAMELS model's fifth component, liquidity, measures the firm's financial capacity. A large amount of liquid assets is shown by the deposit of cash percentage and the liquid assets to total assets ratios used in the research (Fig. **5**). Despite the AI installation, this percentage has remained steady, indicating stable bank liquidity. The cash-to-deposit ratio rose somewhat. Due to increasing interest rates, the interest expense-to-interest earned ratio is falling. With AI, interest costs have dropped.

Three criteria indicate the bank's performance improvement using AI technologies in the sixth component, market risk sensitivity (Fig. **6**). Price earnings ratio fluctuates but rises, indicating steady share values. Banks' long-term investment risk is indicated by the term deposit to total deposit ratio. The bank remains consistent in allocating funds for long-term investments, as noted in the ratio. The period provided shows this ratio ranging from 53.58 to 58.78. The demand-t--total deposits ratio measures a bank's risk in fulfilling depositor obligations. Due to the pandemic, HDFC's ratio has declined over the past two years as individuals have bought goods at higher costs. The price-to-earnings ratio indicates the willingness of buyers to pay for bank shares. The increase reflects bullish sentiment among banks.

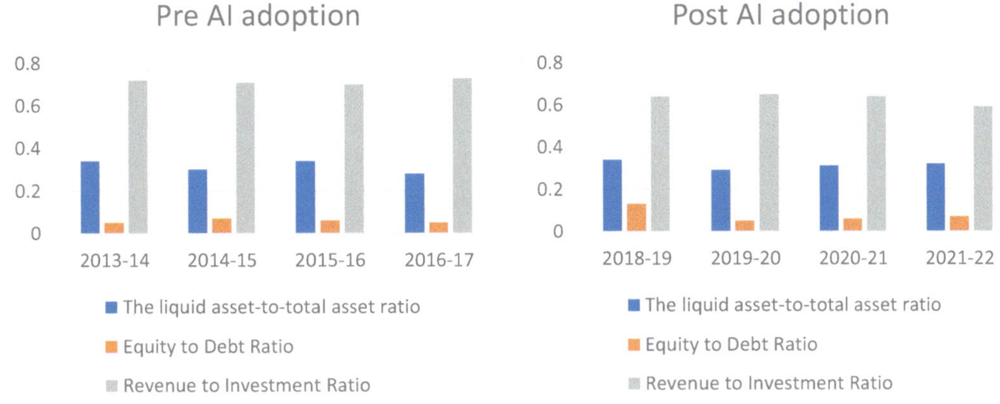

Fig. (5). HDFC bank liquidity ratios pre- and post-AI adoption.

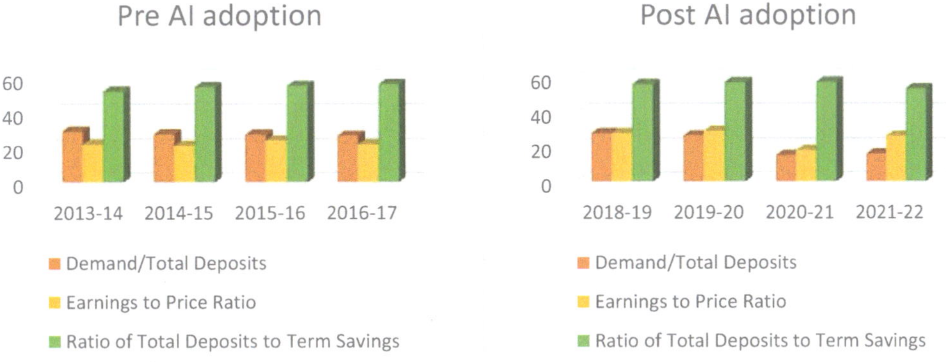

Fig. (6). HDFC Bank Pre- and Post-AI Sensitivity Ratios.

Pair sample t-test results on six CAMELS factors to examine AI's influence on HDFC Bank are shown above. The Tier 1 capital ratio has changed significantly, yet the capital adequacy ratios are improving. Progress in ratios indicates that consumers trust AI apps and have exhibited loyalty by increasing their capital/shares and selecting HDFC Bank loans owing to the deployment of cutting-edge technology. Credit deposit and net interest margins are improving, but no other ratios are changing. Gross and net NPA remain consistent, indicating that AI applications are not increasing bad loans and will likely decrease them over time. Business productivity per person and revenue per employee are changing, yet management effectiveness ratios are improving due to the adoption of AI applications. With the newest technology, employees may work more efficiently and accurately, increasing productivity and profitability.

Income ratios are all rising, indicating that AI applications will save costs and boost the bank's brand, owing to its competitive edge. The cost-to-income ratio, Market Price, and dividend payout ratio have improved significantly. Bank liquidity ratios reflect an increase in cash and liquid assets. AI applications have also improved interest expense ratio, indicating better management. The price-to-earnings ratio reflects consumer trust in banks, and the sensitivity ratio shows term deposits rising. AI applications make customers feel protected by the bank.

Most ratios are stable or improving, indicating that technologies are helping banks. Seven parameters—Profit per Employee, Business per Employee, Cost to Income Ratio, DPS, Tier 1 Capital Ratio, Market Price, and Interest Expense to Interest—differences. Bank financial performance improved significantly when AI techniques were used, such as the Earned Ratio. Over time, encouraging modifications lead to significant advances. The investigation reveals that AI tools significantly improve key performance criteria, indicating that banks should consider utilizing AI-based applications. For sustained growth and development, this industry reacts more to AI. After AI adoption, banking system efficiency metrics showed improvement.

CONCLUSION

While Indian commercial banks were initially unaware of liberalization and globalization, the government has implemented several banking reforms to enhance the efficacy of banks and promote financial well-being over the last few decades. The Indian banking system is now more sophisticated. The data explosion, cyber risks, decision delays, and increased consumer expectations are driving the use of AI. In the study article, the writers aimed to illustrate that banks had employed AI to enhance labour operations. Technology has improved operational efficiency in all areas. The research analyzes HDFC Bank's secondary data using CAMELS to evaluate AI approaches. To assess the bank's financial performance, the research calculated CAMELS' six components using multiple metrics. The findings showed that the bank's financial ratios had improved gradually when AI was introduced. The study found that AI has enhanced bank efficiency and efficacy, as evidenced by improved economic performance. AI technologies should be used and adopted by the banking sector to strengthen financial health.

REFERENCES

[1] A. Dhyani *et al*, Comparative Analysis of Supervised Machine Learning Algorithms for Liver Disease Prediction with SMOTE Enhancement," *3rd Asian Conference on Innovation in Technology (ASIANCON),* 2023, pp. 1-6. [http://dx.doi.org/10.1109/ASIANCON58793.2023.10270381]

[2] V. A. *et al*. Dhotre, "Big Data Analytics using MapReduce for Education System," 2021.

[3] Kakde, H., & Lad, K., "Impact of Artificial Intelligence and Machine Learning Adoption in Finance," Indian Journal of Computer Science, vol. 9, no. 2, 2024, pp. 8–17. [http://dx.doi.org/10.17010/ijcs/2024/v9/i2/173859]

[4] R. Parekh and O. Mitchell, "Incorporating AI into construction management: Enhancing efficiency and cost savings," *International Journal of Science and Research Archive*, vol. 13, no. 1, pp. 1049–1058, 2024. [http://dx.doi.org/10.30574/ijsra.2024.13.1.1776]

[5] Kishor, K., Agrawal, K.K., Yadav, S.P. "SPAM: An Enhanced Performance of Security and Privacy-Aware Model over Split Learning in Consumer Electronics." *Program Comput Soft 50*, 875–899 2024. [http://dx.doi.org/10.1134/S0361768824700816]

[6] F.K. Alarfaj, and S. Shahzadi, "Enhancing fraud detection in banking with deep learning: Graph neural networks and autoencoders for real-time credit card fraud prevention", *IEEE Access,* 2024. [http://dx.doi.org/10.1109/ACCESS.2024.3466288]

[7] A. Strojny-Nędza, K. Pietrzak, F. Gili, and M. Chmielewski, "FGM based on copper–alumina composites for brake disc applications", *Arch. Civ. Mech. Eng.,* vol. 20, no. 3, pp. 1-13, 2020. [http://dx.doi.org/10.1007/S43452-020-00079-1/FIGURES/18]

[8] M. Sam, R. Jojith, and N. Radhika, "Progression in manufacturing of functionally graded materials and impact of thermal treatment—A critical review", *J. Manuf. Process.,* vol. 68, pp. 1339-1377, 2021. [http://dx.doi.org/10.1016/j.jmapro.2021.06.062]

[9] A. Kumari, N. S. Punn, S. K. Sonbhadra, and S. Agarwal, "Impact of the composition of feature extraction and class sampling in medicare fraud detection," lecture notes in computer science (including subseries Lecture Notes in Artificial Intelligence and Lecture Notes in Bioinformatics), vol. 13625 LNCS, pp. 639–658, 2023. [http://dx.doi.org/10.1007/978-3-031-30111-7_54]

[10] B. Hazela, J. Hymavathi, T. Rajasanthosh Kumar, S. Kavitha, D. Deepa, S. Lalar, and P. Karunakaran, "Machine learning: Supervised algorithms to determine the defect in high-precision foundry operation," *Journal of Nanomaterials*, vol. 2022, pp. 1–9. [http://dx.doi.org/10.1155/2022/1732441]

[11] Vandana, N., Yogi, N. K. K., & Yadav, N. S. P., "Chicken diseases detection and classification based on fecal images using EfficientNetB7 model," *Joint Journal of Novel Carbon Resource Sciences & Green Asia Strategy*, Vol. 11, Issue 01, pp314-330, 2024. [http://dx.doi.org/10.5109/7172288]

CHAPTER 14

Advancements in Gender and Age Classification: Deep Learning Based Approach for Accurate Identification

Deepika Verma[1,*], **Kamal Dhanda**[1] and **Munish Kumar**[2]

[1] *Department of Computer Science and Engineering, School of Engg. & Technology, Om Sterling Global University, Hisar 125001, Haryana, India*

[2] *Department of Computer Science and Engineering, KLEF (Deemed to be University), Guntur 522302, Andhra Pradesh, India*

Abstract: Deep learning and Artificial Intelligence (AI) struggle to automatically determine gender and age from visual cues or other traits. Despite the improvements in age and gender detection algorithms resulting from large datasets and deep learning, numerous issues remain. The absence of variety in training data can lead to bias and poor performance, particularly among underrepresented groups. Deep learning for age and gender determination raises ethical considerations about discrimination and abuse. This study will evaluate precise algorithms for gender and age to address these issues. They strive to reduce prejudice and ensure fair and reliable results for everybody by stressing the diversity of training data and ethical model development. This study aims to enhance age and gender identification while promoting fairness, accuracy, and ethical practices. Our primary aim is to incorporate ethical considerations into age and gender identification model development and implementation, thereby benefiting underrepresented groups. We also seek to optimize these models for real-time marketing and security applications. This project aims to provide accurate, fair, and ethical gender and age identification systems. By emphasizing ethics, they want to design models that uphold justice, transparency, privacy, and dignity. These endeavors strive to advance technology in a manner that aligns with social ideals and benefits society.

Keywords: Computer vision, Ethical issues, Gender detection, Marketing, Seep learning.

[*] **Corresponding author Deepika Verma:** Department of Computer Science and Engineering, School of Engg. & Technology, Om Sterling Global University, Hisar 125001, Haryana, India; E-mail: deepika.ranolia15@gmail.com

D. Arul Pon Daniel, T. Rajasanthosh Kumar & Satya Prakash Yadav (Eds.)

INTRODUCTION

Research Background

Deep learning and visual computing researchers have long studied automated age and gender estimations [1]. Recent advances in deep learning and large datasets have improved age and gender classifications [2]. Traditional age and gender markers are a person's facial shape and texture. Visual data was analyzed using common classifiers [3, 4]. The diversity and complexity of these qualities made these procedures challenging. CNNs have changed deep learning thinking. These algorithms allow researchers to extract complex data properties, revolutionizing the field. CNNs significantly enhance age and gender detection by identifying complex patterns and traits that humans often overlook.

Gender and Age Recognition: CNNs and MTCNNs are novel deep-learning approaches for age and gender identification. In certain datasets, these algorithms outperform human-derived approaches [5, 6, 7]. Deep learning improves gender and age prediction, despite difficulties. Little training data might lead to bias and poor performance for underrepresented groups. The use of deep learning to forecast a person's gender and age gives rise to moral questions about potential exploitation and prejudice [8].

Deep learning is now seeing widespread usage in the field of gender and age recognition, but it also has the potential to be applied in a variety of other areas, including marketing, cybersecurity, social media, and many others. On the other hand, developers must understand the moral implications of modern technology and work to mitigate its adverse effects.

Problem Statement

A key issue that deep learning aims to address is the automated identification of a person's age and gender based solely on their appearance or other characteristics. Facial characteristics may vary over time, and different people's faces exhibit varying emotions, making it a complex process. The characteristics used in conventional approaches are often of poor quality and manually created, which limits their accuracy and adaptability [9, 10].

Objectives

- Accurate age and gender models from face characteristics or other factors are essential. This can be applied in marketing, security, and customized services.
- Data and model biases must be addressed to guarantee fairness, particularly for underrepresented populations. Datasets must be varied and representative, and

algorithms must be demographically robust.

- Considering ethics when creating and using face recognition models reduces the risk of misuse and prejudice. In model creation and implementation, openness, accountability, and permission may be required.
- In industries such as security and marketing, real-time data analysis is necessary; therefore, model optimization is essential. This demands efficient algorithms for low-resource situations.

METHODOLOGY

This chapter presents an approach to accurately determining a person's age and gender from a single facial photograph using a CNN algorithm and OpenCV libraries.

CNN

Convolutional Neural Networks (CNNs) are often utilized in Natural Language Processing (NLP) and image identification and processing since they were originally developed to provide age and gender detection for people. Often abbreviated as "ConvNet," a Convolutional Neural Network (CNN) has many convolutional hidden layers in addition to its input and output layers. CNNs have several similarities with regularized multilayer perceptrons. Fig. (**1**) depicts the three primary layers that constitute the architecture of a neural network based on convolution. This architecture comprises convolutional, pooling, and fully connected layers.

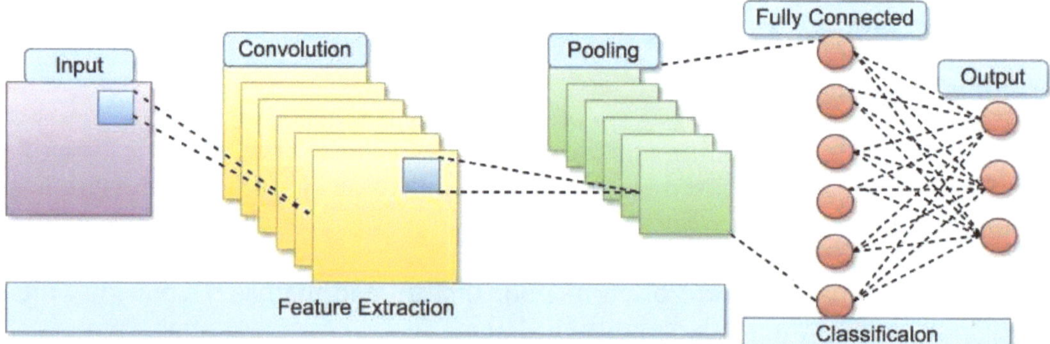

Fig. (1). Architecture of a neural network.

Layers for Convolution

Filtering the input image with a fingertip-shaped filter allows the first layer of the convolutional neural network to extract relevant features. The output is the sum of the elements from each picture, after filtering, for each sliding motion.

Layers for Pooling

Reducing the amount of trainable parameters and, by extension, the computational cost, was the primary motivation for creating this layer.

Fully Connected Layers

The output was determined by the fully connected layers, which are the final few layers. After the pooling layer flattened the output into a one-dimensional vector, it was received by the fully connected layer.

OpenCV

This article utilizes the OpenCV library to implement age and gender detection. Other names for it include Open-Source Computer Vision, which is commonly abbreviated as "OpenCV." Even the name suggests that this is a free and open-source library for ML and CV. In addition to processing images and videos in real-time, this library can do analyses.

Dataset

This paper's age and gender identification algorithm was trained using the open-source "Adience dataset" (Kaggle). As an industry benchmark, this dataset contains images of faces taken in a range of real-world contexts, including those with noise, color, stance, and appearance variations. These images are part of a collection that was made public *via* Flickr and is licensed under the Creative Commons (CC) umbrella. It has 12,250 photos of 1,300 people across eight different age groups and is about 0.6 gigabytes in size.

Furthermore, several improvements are essential to enhance the precision of gender and age detection using state-of-the-art deep learning methods, particularly CNNs. Start by extensively cleaning, normalizing, and augmenting the dataset. Try different CNN architectures with batch normalization, regularization, and depth to prevent overfitting. Adjust hyperparameters such as learning rates and batch size methodically and test alternative optimization techniques. Fine-tuning pre-trained models *via* transfer learning speeds feature acquisition.

Data augmentation and ensemble methods may combine model predictions during training. Use cross-validation and L1 or L2 regularization to more accurately assess the method's performance. Prioritize feedback-based model fine-tuning and resolution of dataset and model biases to ensure generalizability across demographic groups. By considering these characteristics, age and gender identification may be improved.

RESULTS AND DISCUSSION

The OpenCV library and the Convolutional Neural Network (CNN) approach were used to train the deep learning method, which successfully identified people's faces and estimated their ages. A "male" individual ranging in age from 45 to 50 has been detected by the system, as shown in Fig. (**2**).

Fig. (2). Male age recognition 45-50.

According to Figs. (3 and 4), the system has correctly recognized a "male" with a cap and another without, and it continues to correctly identify them as being between the ages of 20 to 25.

A "female" individual in her twenty-five to thirty-two years has been detected by the system, as seen in Fig. (**5**).

The primary motivation for this study was to identify methods that could significantly enhance the reliability of gender and age prediction based solely on facial features. The dataset was preprocessed using the OpenCV software with a Convolutional Neural Network (CNN) as the model. To enhance and prepare the face photographs for training, the team utilized OpenCV, a powerful library that provides numerous operations and tools for processing videos and images.

Fig. (3). Man without cap age recognition male 20-25.

Fig. (4). Man with cap age recognition male 20-25.

Fig. (5). Age Identification Female (25–32).

A three-layer Convolutional Neural Network (CNN) structure was used in this model. Fully linked, pooling, and convolutional layers. Convolutional layers utilize input images to generate a hierarchy of progressively more complex representations. Pooling layers reduce the spatial dimensionality of feature maps to reduce processing costs and prevent overfitting. Fully linked layers utilize pooling and layering features for efficient calls.

Their biggest issue was overcoming data and model biases. Recent revelations suggest that conventional approaches may favor specific interests and lead to unfair consequences. To remove biases from the training dataset, they applied strict selection and curation. CNN models have achieved a 94% success rate across all demographics.

Since they knew such models might have ethical ramifications, they integrated privacy settings and informed consent into their design and implementation. They authenticated and anonymized training data to protect privacy. To help buyers understand the reasoning behind certain decisions, they also ensured that the graphics were simple to comprehend and interpret.

Lastly, they intended to design models with low-resource optimization in mind, to use them in marketing and security applications that need real-time processing. By employing efficient algorithms and lightweight designs, we achieved real-time processing speeds without compromising accuracy. In situations requiring precise decision-making under time constraints, like security and surveillance, this is very crucial.

Fig. (**6**) shows the results of the testing section, which covered the normal mode and expressions on the face. All genders attained a total accuracy of 94%.

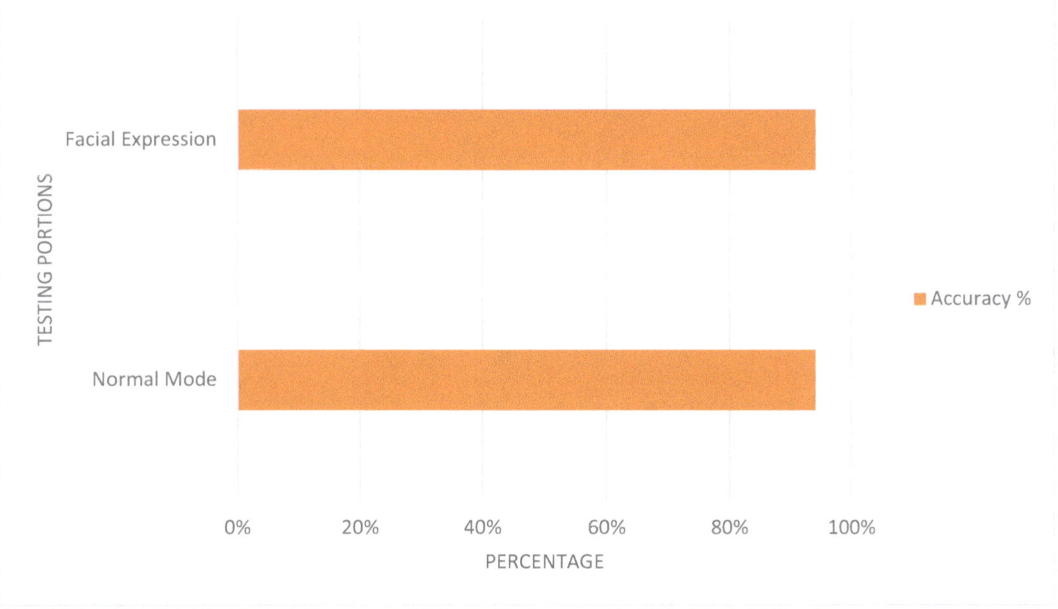

Fig. (6). Overall accuracy graph.

Fig. (**7**) shows the model's excellent performance indicators after rigorous training and assessment. The model correctly recognizes and categorizes data parts with 94% accuracy, 94% recall, and a 96% F1 score. The model's prophecies couple the dataset's labels, demonstrating its capability to label patterns and traits. For its usefulness in many tasks and domains, the model's extreme veracity, recall, and F1 score indicate that it is correctly calibrated and can produce reliable forecasts.

Overall, the experiments demonstrate that models from CNN can be utilized for various applications, provided they incorporate ethics. They believe these models can improve people's lives responsibly and ethically if prejudice and ethics are taken into consideration.

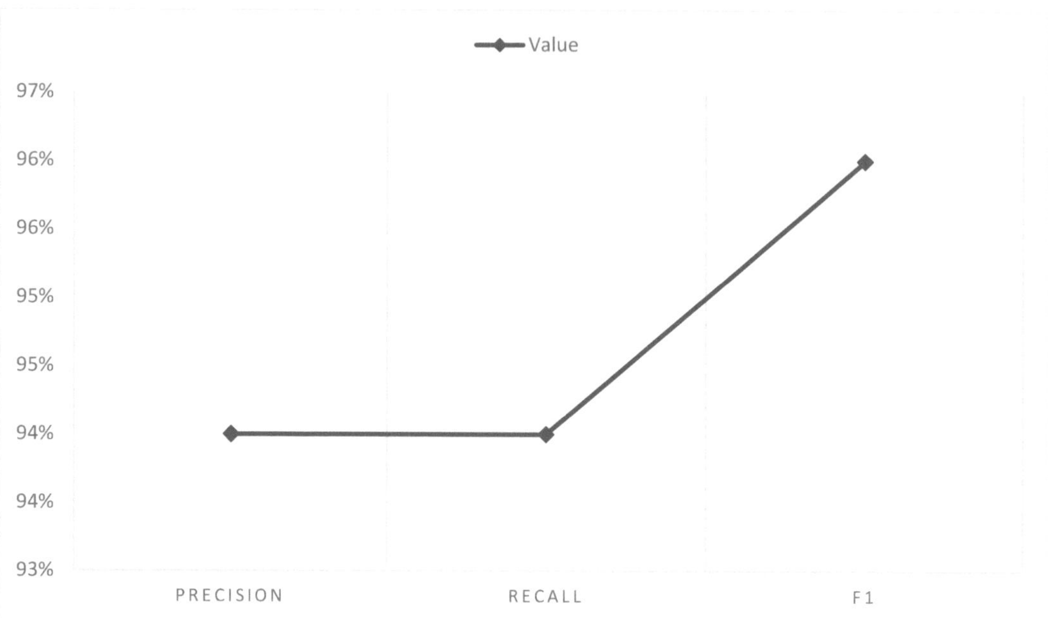

Fig. (7). Accurately trained and evaluated methods.

CONCLUSION

This research indicates that OpenCV and CNN may enhance gender and age determination using facial cues and other inputs. The study achieved a 94% success rate thanks to modern deep learning algorithms. By addressing data and model bias, these models might be used for underrepresented groups, enhancing outcomes. Ethics, including the use of data sources and anonymization, promoted transparency and fairness in the research. For specific deployment rules, researchers integrated ethical issues into model design. Efficiency in low-resource settings may lead to real-time marketing and security processing. Rapid data processing and decision-making are possible with model optimization. CNN models are flexible and ethical in various vocations, a study shows. These approaches may enhance lives responsibly by promoting ethics and fighting discrimination. This study shows the promise of justice and transparency in deep learning.

REFERENCES

[1] Vandana, Kuldeep Kumar Yogi & Satya Prakash Yadav, "Chicken diseases detection and classification based on fecal images using EfficientNetB7 model," Joint Journal of Novel Carbon Resource Sciences & Green Asia Strategy, Vol. 11, Issue 01, pp 314-330, 2024. [http://dx.doi.org/10.5109/7172288]

[2] K. U. Singh, A. Kumar, G. Kumar, T. Singh, S. Kumar and S. P. Yadav, "An Autonomous Emotion Recognition Strategy Employing Deep Learning for Self-Learning," 2023 3rd International Conference on Technological Advancements in Computational Sciences (ICTACS), Tashkent,

Uzbekistan, pp. 883-888, 2023.
[http://dx.doi.org/10.1109/ICTACS59847.2023.10389867]

[3] D. Goel, D. Singh, A. Gupta, S. Yadav and M. Sharma. “An Efficient Approach For To Predict The Quality Of Apple Through Its Appearance.” *International Conference on Computer, Electronics & Electrical Engineering & their Applications* (IC2E3): 1-6, 2023.

[4] S. Sajna, S. Mounika, R. Santhosh, Sriknath D. V, “Thermal analysis of advanced IC engine cylinder,” *International Journal of Automobile Engineering Research and Development* (IJAuERD), Vol. 6, Issue 3, 17-2, 2016. Available Online: https://ssrn.com/abstract=2838730

[5] R.A. Alzahrani, M. Aljabri, and R.A. Mustafa Mohammad, "Ad click fraud detection using machine learning and deep learning algorithms", *IEEE Access,* vol. 13, pp. 12746-12763, 2025.
[http://dx.doi.org/10.1109/ACCESS.2025.3532200]

[6] Y. Supriya, N. Victor, G. Srivastava, and T.R. Gadekallu, "A hybrid federated learning model for insurance fraud detection", *2023 IEEE International Conference on Communications Workshops: Sustainable Communications for Renaissance, ICC Workshops 2023,* pp. 1516-1522, 2023.
[http://dx.doi.org/10.1109/ICCWorkshops57953.2023.10283682]

[7] N. Cristianini, and J. Shawe-Taylor, "An introduction to support vector machines and other kernel-based learning methods", *An Introduction to Support Vector Machines and Other Kernel-based Learning Methods,* no. Mar, 2000.
[http://dx.doi.org/10.1017/CBO9780511801389]

[8] K. Sanjeeviprakash, A.R. Kannan, and N.S. Shanmugam, "Additive manufacturing of metal-based functionally graded materials: overview, recent advancements and challenges", *J. Braz. Soc. Mech. Sci. Eng.,* vol. 45, no. 5, p. 241, 2023.
[http://dx.doi.org/10.1007/s40430-023-04174-1]

[9] Singh Chaitanya, Subrahmanya Srinivasa Rao Motukuri, Mahaboobjohn Y., Bonthu Kotaiah, Kumar T, *Applied Machine Tool Data Condition to Predictive Smart Maintenance by Using Artificial Intelligence*, 2022 .

[10] S. Srivastava, N. Dhyani, V. Sharma, S. Vats, S. Yadav, V. Kukreja *et al.*, “Lung Infection and Identification using Heatmap,” *2nd International Conference on Applied Artificial Intelligence and Computing* (ICAAIC), Salem, India, pp. 1093-1098, 2023.
[http://dx.doi.org/10.1109/ICAAIC56838.2023.10140204]

CHAPTER 15

Supervision of Water Distribution Using Android and IOT

M Nirmala[1,*], **L. Bharathi**[2], **K. Sreenath**[2], **Dolores L Montesines**[3], **M. Rama**[2], **K. Ankababu**[4] and **Saurav Das**[5]

[1] *Department of Computer Science and Engineering, New Horizon College of Engineering, Marathalli, Bangalore 560103, India*

[2] *Department of IT, QIS College of Engineering & Technology, Ongole 523272, Andhra Pradesh, India*

[3] *College of Computer Studies, University of Perpetual Help Systems DALTA, City of Bacoor 4102, Cavite, Philippines*

[4] *Department of MCA, QIS College of Engineering & Technology, Ongole 523272, Andhra Pradesh, India*

[5] *Department of Mechanical Engineering, QIS College of Engineering & Technology, Ongole 523272, Andhra Pradesh, India*

Abstract: These days, the population in big cities is growing rapidly, along with the need for comfortable living, as more people move from rural to urban areas. The distribution interference with the supply, protection, utilization, and quality of water, as well as other water-related issues, has grown in importance as cities have expanded in tandem with their populations. Resolving water supply concerns requires an effective monitoring and control system. The system uses water pressure and ultrasonic wave sensors, a motorized electrical water valve, a GSM module, a Raspberry PI, and an Arduino UNO microcontroller. This article focused on IoT-based water distribution regulation and monitoring. The project aims to enhance the community's water infrastructure by utilizing a reliable and cost-effective approach. Prototypes mimicked water distribution. Pumping station monitoring and operation were done *via* a front-end web app. The prototype system makes scientific conclusions using fuzzy logic. In conclusion, the experiment met all requirements for monitoring and managing water delivery using an IoT model.

Keywords: Front-end web application, Fuzzy logic algorithm, GSM module, Internet of things, Quality of water.

* **Corresponding author M. Nirmala:** Department of Computer Science and Engineering, New Horizon College of Engineering, Marathalli, Bangalore 560103, India; E-mail: nirmal@gmail.com

D. Arul Pon Daniel, T. Rajasanthosh Kumar & Satya Prakash Yadav (Eds.)

INTRODUCTION

A recent investigation found that municipal water distribution problems were directly attributed to population expansion. Insufficient quantities of water for daily requirements are a problem for many communities [1]. A major issue arises when water distribution is not monitored and controlled, resulting in unequal supply of water [2]. Consumers in high-ground regions or those distant from pumps or water tanks may not have access to water because of issues with the delivery line, such as pipeline damage caused by high or low water pressure. These problems with water distribution have their roots in the system's antiquated, manual methods of operation and the absence of a real-time monitoring and regulating mechanism [3].

Modern urban centers are undergoing a metamorphosis as they embrace smart technology to create more environmentally friendly neighborhoods [4]. They have made water a top priority in their pursuit of economic progress and the amenities that boost their vitality. Water sustainability can only be achieved *via* collaboration across many fields. Additionally, cutting-edge machinery is necessary to streamline operations and management, particularly in gathering and analyzing data to facilitate intelligent planning, decision-making, and management [5].

Developments are ongoing in the city of Ilagan, Isabela, with the goal of raising the standard of living. It aspires to be a smart city and is both the capital and the largest town in the area, with barangays [6]. The City of Ilagan Water District (CIWaD) oversees the provision of water across the city, especially to the barangays in the Poblacion region. An important consideration in the city's ongoing growth, which includes the construction of commercial structures, residential subdivisions, and businesses, is the provision of water [7]. Meeting the community's water demands is a top priority, and CIWaD is actively working to extend its service area to meet that need. Due to its reliance on human intervention, the ineffective method for monitoring and managing water supply has become a concern for management.

IoT technology is utilized to develop an intelligent water management system for CIWaD, which monitors water tanks, pumping stations, and water pressure, a topic also explored in this article [8]. The suggested system also includes a control mechanism to prevent the tanks from being filled to the brim and pipes from leaking duc to excessive pressure. The development of a prototype allowed for tcsting and simulation. Specifically, the controlling and monitoring were carried out using Arduino micro-controllers and other Internet of Things devices. The operation's progress was tracked using a web application [9]. This article focuses only on the distribution and management of water in CIWaD. The prototype alone was used to evaluate the research [10].

ARCHITECTURE OF THE SYSTEM

The Internet of Things (IoT) model utilized to monitor and run the water distribution system in this work includes ultrasonic sensors, pressure sensors, a motorized electrical water valve, a GPS module, an Arduino microcontroller, a Raspberry Pi, and a solid-state relay switch. Systems operations and interoperability are shown in Fig. (**1**).

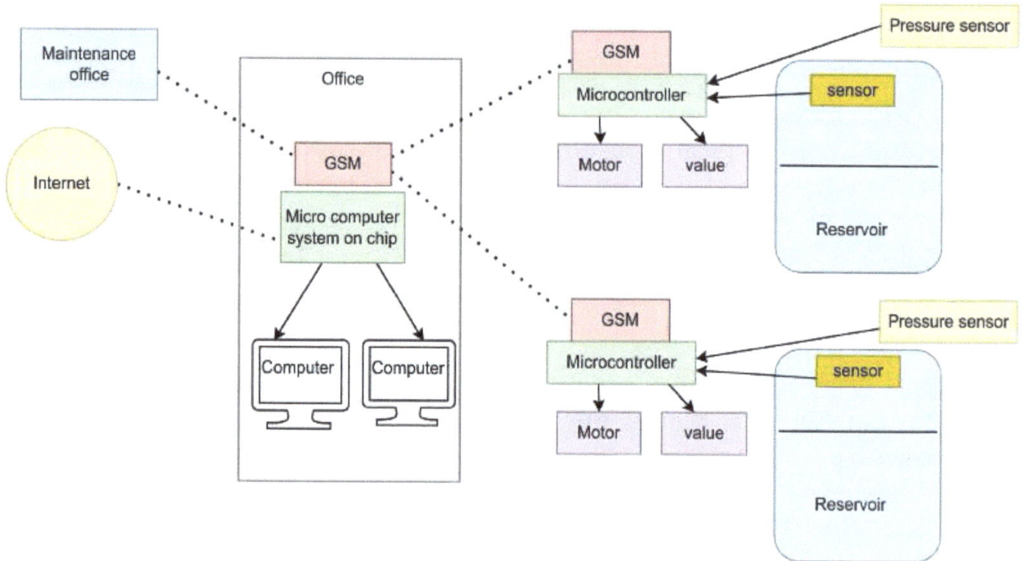

Fig. (1). System operations.

The tank's level of water is monitored by a sensor. For safety reasons, the microcontroller engages the water pump relay switch to turn it on or off when the water level reaches a set threshold, preventing the tank from overflowing or becoming empty. Water pressure is managed in the same way to avoid pipeline damage. The microprocessor can also monitor water pressure changes and rotate the motorized electric water valve to precisely regulate water flow. In this case, the microcontroller may also utilize GSM to notify the user of its actions. In order to keep the office updated on the current state of a certain reservoir of water or pumping station, an SMS is delivered *via* the GSM module. After receiving a report, the office's System-on-chip microcomputer can save the relevant information and notify the maintenance officer by SMS. The built web application enables management to monitor the status of multiple water reservoirs and pumping stations. The System-on-Chip microprocessor is also organized as a web server.

METHODOLOGY

The two circuit designs that make up the Internet of Things (IoT) model for regulating and monitoring water distribution are the web server and the control and monitoring system, which use microcontrollers and system-on-chip microcomputers, respectively.

System for Monitoring and Control

This module includes a 240VAC relay switch, a 2-way motor electric ball valve, an ultrasonic sensor, an analogue water pressure sensor, and a SIM800 GSM shield module. The prototype's monitoring system relied on an ultrasonic sensor, which could non-destructively probe the inside of the water tank. The proximity or water level in the tank may be determined by connecting the ultrasonic sensor to an Arduino UNO microcontroller, which can then read and analyze the data sent by the sensor. The uploaded code instructs the Arduino microcontroller to activate the water pump's solid-state relay switch when the tank's water level drops low enough to require replenishment. To prevent the water tank from overflowing, whether it is filled or nearing empty, the same procedure is followed as a control mechanism. The solid-state relay switch can be turned on when the water level is low and turned off by the Arduino microcontroller if the water level is already high. Additionally, a water pressure device linked to the Arduino UNO microcontroller allows for control of water pressure. The main line must be maintained at an adequate pressure in order to supply water without breaking. When the pressure drops below or rises above a certain threshold, the microcontroller triggers a solid-state relay switch, which in turn opens or closes the motorized electric valve. Additionally, the microcontroller can initiate the linked GSM module to transmit data to the server, informing it of the water reservoir's current state and the pumping station's ongoing processes. The information is sent by Short Message Service (SMS), which is considered the most efficient and cost-effective form of communication. To disable the module's built-in automated control system, the control and monitoring system may also accept SMS messages sent by the attendant located in the CIWaD office.

Web Server

The software and hardware are the two main parts of this module. The Raspberry Pi 3 Model B, 5V battery, SIM800 GSM module, LED screen, USB mouse, Class-10 Micro SD card, and keyboard are all components of the hardware package. The software package comprises the following components: Raspbian

OS, MySQL, Apache (LAMP) for web services, Python for scripting the GSM module, and PHP for web services. This project uses the Raspberry Pi as a web server to monitor and regulate CIWaD's water storage tanks and pumping stations. The built web app can parse the report messages to gather the necessary data for display in the app's user interface. A maintenance officer may be assigned to a specific water supply or pumping station, and the GSM module may also provide them with SMS reports detailing the current activities. In addition to managing the various pumps and water reservoirs, the web app allows users to send an SMS with a predefined keyword to bypass the present actions, such as turning a pumping station on or off, or opening or closing a reservoir's gate valve.

DISCUSSIONS AND RESULTS

Researchers use collected data to envision a solution to the CIWaD's issues and create a working model for further testing, assessment, and simulation. The researchers acquired all the necessary gear and equipment for developing the prototype. Researchers swiftly developed scripts, compiled them, and uploaded them into an Arduino microcontroller after creating the prototype control and monitoring system. In addition, the researchers built a web app that serves as the front-end system for managing and monitoring, and they set up and configured the Raspberry Pi to function as a web server.

Evaluation

The researchers verified the data and code submitted by testing the prototype control and monitoring system. The tank level and the amount of pressure of the water flowing through the pipeline were the inputs. Specifically, the plan called for an extra tank to serve as a makeshift reservoir for groundwater, with the water being pumped there using an electric motor pump.

The temporary reservoir of water was elevated to mimic the CIWaD water structure, increasing pipeline pressure using gravitational force to fulfill testing requirements. The water level may be easily measured using the inches labelled on the base. The constructed monitoring and regulating system was tested using the water distribution prototype layout design, as shown in Fig. (**2**) below.

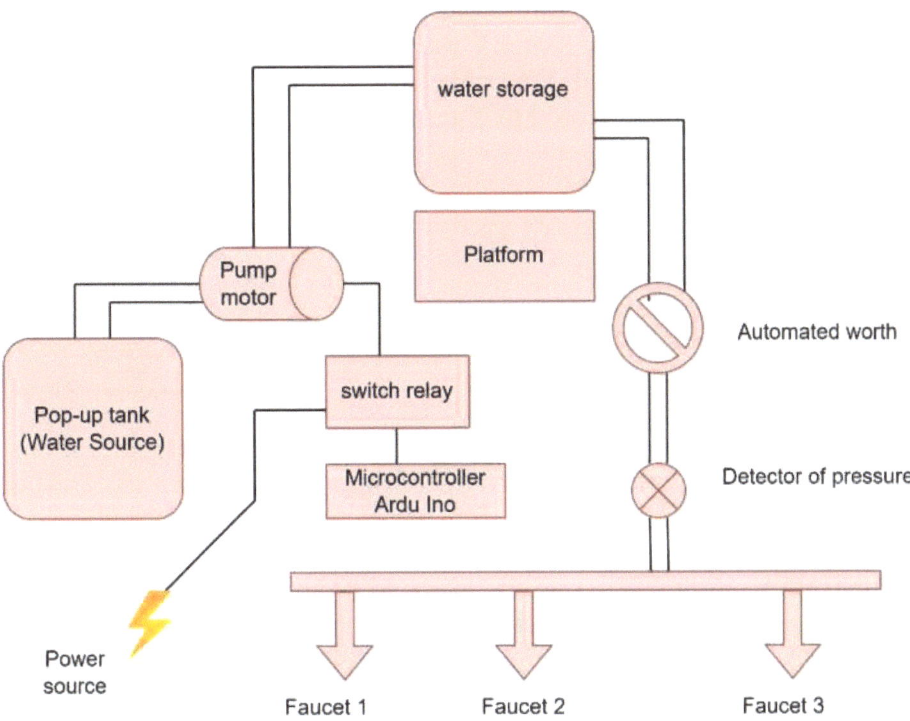

Fig. (2). prototype layout design.

Water level and pressure threshold values were defined by the researchers in the code that was submitted. The system used this to determine its next move. Several sub-parameters were used to decide when the water reservoir needed to be refilled or when the report should be sent to the server. Additionally, the microcontroller disables the motor pump upon reaching the maximum water level that has been pre-set as a safety precaution throughout the refilling process. The implementation of a fuzzy logic method enabled the transmission of water reservoir condition reports and motor pump instructions to the server *via* SMS. Water level in inches was used as the input, as stated in Table **1**. It is possible to receive an SMS report or instructions on what to do, based on the rules programmed into the microcontroller.

Table 1. Water level.

Level	Rank	Re-fill Act
21" and under	Low Level	On
22" to 36"	Usual	Off
37" to 41"	Filled	Off

The same procedure and algorithm were also used to regulate and monitor the water pressure. The pressure of water is measured in pounds per square inch (psi) here. Table **2** shows that several input characteristics recorded in PSI served as the foundation for the output generated by the fuzzy logic algorithm.

Table 2. Pressure of water.

PSI	Status	Valve Action
4 and below	Small	Exposed
5 - 7	Usual	Exposed
8 and above	Tall	Close

The web application received all of the SMS reports and uploaded them to the server side. Additionally, the registered operator's mobile phone was notified *via* a notification message about the state of a specific pump station or water tank. An override mechanism for the deployed control and monitoring system is also part of the web application. The built-in web software can manually activate or deactivate the pumps and open or close the motorized electrical water tank valve using the predefined phrases shown in Table **3** below. The web interface features a toggle button that enables users to easily turn the motorized electric valve and the pumping station motor on and off.

Table 3. pre-defined phrases.

Station Pumping Motor	Electric Motorized Valve
Turning Off PSM	Close the Valve
Turning On PSM	Open the Valve

CONCLUSION

A significant challenge for community leaders is to deliver high-quality services in a sustainable manner. The created system may be of great assistance to the CIWaD administration in resolving the current water distribution issues. It provides a way for the easy management of water delivery to the community *via* the use of low-cost smart technology. According to the requirements and intended use, the produced prototype works as expected. Based on the various input settings, it produced the intended result and passed all tests. When it comes to delivering smart communities, the ongoing development of technology, especially IoT devices, presents a wonderful opportunity for this research to enhance future ideas and concepts.

REFERENCES

[1] N.K. Velayudhan, P. Pradeep, S.N. Rao, A.R. Devidas, and M.V. Ramesh, "IoT-enabled water distribution systems—a comparative technological review", *IEEE Access,* vol. 10, pp. 101042-101070, 2022.
[http://dx.doi.org/10.1109/ACCESS.2022.3208142]

[2] A.M. Mateoiu, A. Korodi, A. Stoianovici, and R. Tira, "Supervisory monitoring and control solution on android mobile devices for the water industry 4.0", *Sustainability (Basel),* vol. 15, no. 22, p. 16022, 2023.
[http://dx.doi.org/10.3390/su152216022]

[3] K. Purohit, S. Vats, R. Saklani, V. Sharma, V. Kukreja, and S. P. Yadav, "Improvement in k-means clustering for information retrieval," *Proceedings of the 4th International Conference on Electronics and Sustainable Communication Systems (ICESC)*, Coimbatore, India, 2023, pp. 1239–1245.
[http://dx.doi.org/10.1109/ICESC57686.2023.10193031]

[4] E. Altulaihan, M. A. Almaiah, and A. Aljughaiman, "Anomaly detection ids for detecting dos attacks in IoT networks based on machine learning algorithms", Sensors 2024, Vol. 24, Page 713, vol. 24, no. 2, p. 713, Jan. 2024.
[http://dx.doi.org/10.3390/s24020713]

[5] B. Dwarakanath, P. Kalpana Devi, A. Ranjith Kumar, A.S.M. Metwally, G.A. Ashraf, and B.L. Thamineni, "Smart IoT-based water treatment with a Supervisory Control and Data Acquisition (SCADA) system process", *Water Reuse,* vol. 13, no. 3, pp. 411-431, 2023.
[http://dx.doi.org/10.2166/wrd.2023.052]

[6] S.C. Olisa, C.N. Asiegbu, J.E. Olisa, B.O. Ekengwu, A.A. Shittu, and M.C. Eze, "Smart two-tank water quality and level detection system via IoT", *Heliyon,* vol. 7, no. 8, 2021.e07651
[http://dx.doi.org/10.1016/j.heliyon.2021.e07651] [PMID: 34401568]

[7] A. Abdelmoamen Ahmed, S. Al Omari, R. Awal, A. Fares, and M. Chouikha, "A distributed system for supporting smart irrigation using Internet of Things technology", *Eng. Rep.,* vol. 3, no. 7, 2021.e12352
[http://dx.doi.org/10.1002/eng2.12352]

[8] S. Mewada, A. Saroliya, N. Chandramouli, T.R. Kumar, M. Lakshmi, S.S.C. Mary, and M. Jayakumar, "Smart diagnostic expert system for defect in forging process by using machine learning process", *J. Nanomater.,* vol. 2022, no. 1, 2022.2567194
[http://dx.doi.org/10.1155/2022/2567194]

[9] K. Kishor, K.K. Agrawal, S.P. Yadav, *et al.* "SPAM: An enhanced performance of security and privacy-aware model over split learning in consumer electronics." *Program Comput Soft* 50, 875–899, 2024.
[http://dx.doi.org/10.1134/S0361768824700816]

[10] P. Mohit, P. Roopa, S. Siddharth, V. Vipul, & K.S. Rekha. "Water level monitoring system in water dispensers using IoT." *IRJET,* 05(04), 1217-1220, 2018.

CHAPTER 16

Churn Prediction in the Telecom Sector Using Deep Learning Techniques

Jafar Ali Ibrahim Syed Masood[1], Ayain John[1,*], N.S. Kalyan Chakravarthy[2], David Asirvatham[3], Raja Kumar Murugesan[4], P. Adi Lakshmi[5] and **U. Prasad[5]**

[1] *Department of IoT, School of Computer Science and Engineering, Vellore Institute of Technology, Vellore 632014, Tamil Nadu, India*

[2] *Center for Data Science, QIS College of Engineering & Technology, Ongole 523272, Andhra Pradesh, India*

[3] *Faculty of Innovation and Technology, Taylor's University, Subang Jaya 47500, Selangor, Malaysia*

[4] *School of Computer Science, Taylor's University, Subang Jaya 47500, Selangor, Malaysia*

[5] *Department of CSE, QIS College of Engineering & Technology, Ongole 523272, Andhra Pradesh, India*

Abstract: A consumer is said to have "churned" when they no longer connect with their usual service provider. An examination of customer churn is conducted to prevent the loss of existing clients. Churn prediction is becoming increasingly important in the telecommunications industry, as it involves analyzing the behaviors of various consumers to identify those who are on the verge of terminating their membership with a service provider. It is more cost-effective to keep current customers than it is to get new ones. This study focuses on several machine learning and Neural network approaches to forecast customer churn and identify customers who are closer to leaving their service from the relevant service provider. Specifically, the methods are used to identify customers who are more likely to leave the telecommunications service. Several machine learning techniques, including Logistic Regression, Support Vector Machines, Random Forests, AdaBoost, and Artificial Neural Networks, are employed in predicting the customer turnover rate. Data is obtained from the AT&T website, and learning models are assessed using two criteria: Accuracy and Area under the Curve. The accuracy criterion is given greater weight than the Area under the Curve criterion. We assess and measure the performance of several algorithms, and the one that ends up being the most accurate throughout all of the tests wins.

Keywords: Accuracy, Customer, Machine learning, Neural network, Transfer learning.

* **Corresponding author Ayain John:** Department of IoT, School of Computer Science and Engineering, Vellore Institute of Technology, Vellore 632014, Tamil Nadu, India; E-mail: jafarali.s@vit.ac.in

D. Arul Pon Daniel, T. Rajasanthosh Kumar & Satya Prakash Yadav (Eds.)

INTRODUCTION

Maintaining relationships with existing consumers and pursuing new clientele are two of the most pressing issues faced by modern organizations [1]. Companies that have been around for a long time prioritize maintaining relationships with their current clientele, whereas startups are more concerned with expanding their consumer base [2]. Suppose we want to expand our customer base. In that case, as Gaur and Dubey stated, we need to prioritize expanding our customer base while also maintaining strong relationships with our current clientele for an extended period of time [3 - 5]. Raza says that with the widespread use of the internet, customers are now empowered and no longer stick with a single service provider, which has increased the competition between companies [6]. When competition between service providers is just a click away [7], empowered customers now mostly contribute to improving the attrition rate of services. In the current scenario [8], with the emergence of e-commerce, there is a wide scope of information available to customers, enabling them to think and switch. In addition, empowered customers now mostly contribute to reducing the attrition percentage of services [9]. Because of this risk, service providers must maintain cutting-edge, up-to-date, and efficient methods for analyzing customer feedback [10], projecting potential customer behaviors in the future, and estimating the likelihood that they will switch providers [11].

As a result, Churn Prediction entails the development of procedures that help businesses keep their lucrative customers and foresee ways in which the consumers may churn. Consequently [12], Churn Prediction is also known as customer retention. The study's overarching goal is to develop a model for the mobile telecommunications industry's pre-paid segment that is both highly effective and accurate in predicting customer churn and retaining existing customers [13 - 15]. The Meaning of the Word “Churn” Churn was initially mentioned by Berson, who said that it refers to the process of pre-paid or post-paid clients switching from one service provider to another. The Churn might take any form, such as being intentional or active, accidental or rotational, involuntary or passive, *etc.* “Service providers might minimize the susceptibility of their consumers leaving if they had enough expertise in managing client relationships, which in turn would boost their productivity and revenues. A technique needs to be developed to examine the profits generated by the qualities; hence, churn prediction can be characterized as “a mechanism that assists in predicting the majority of potential churners in advance.”

RELATED WORK

According to S. Shumaly, P. Neysaryan [30], and Y. Guo's research, "The advent of internet commerce has expanded new methods for organizations to increase new ways for companies to respond to clients' expectations by the amount of information that is now accessible." In the meantime, customers have the opportunity to gain a deeper understanding of the market's possibilities. Their expectations become higher, and as a result, they are more inclined to move to a different provider. As a direct consequence of this, the word "churn" came into being. During the 1850s, the primary emphasis was placed on productive activities, and as a result, individuals sold whatever they had earned. At the beginning of the 1900s, as a result of increased consumer agency, service providers were required to present a justification for customers to subscribe to their services to remain in business. In the mid-20th century, a significant shift occurred, causing retailers to shift their focus from trying to convince consumers to purchase whatever they were selling to creating products that customers desired. The preceding change in marketing orientations led to a move toward a focus on the consumer in the 21st century. According to the research findings, this innovative customer-oriented strategy was able to take into account each of its clients on an individual basis, based on their requirements and preferences. In general, these days, due to the availability of production, businesses are able to categorize customers based on the similarity of their preferences and tastes. As a result, they can formulate marketing strategies to cater to customers who want to be treated in a manner that is specific to their requirements and preferences. According to S. Preetha and R. Rayapeddi, "Customer Relationship Management (CRM) requires both information technology and knowledge management." Customer Relationship Management (CRM) can be viewed as a more comprehensive approach to customer service, which involves the collection and management of a substantial amount of data, enabling companies to utilize that data for customer acquisition, retention, expansion, and even customer selection.

PROPOSED METHOD

AT&T's website is used to download the dataset, which is then formatted into 7044 rows and 19 columns of labelled data with sections such as "customer ID, gender, Senior Citizen, Partner Dependents, tenure, Phone Service, Multiple Lines, Internet Service, Online Security, Online Backup, Device Protection, Tech Support, Streaming TV, Streaming Movies, Contract, Monthly Charges, Total Charges and Churn where only customer ID, Numerical or continuous values, while the remaining columns include categorical data with various keywords; this categorical data need to be translated to numerical form before we can train our dataset. Our dataset does not lack null values; rather, it includes many blank columns, even though these columns should have been filled up from the beginning to make an accurate forecast of the results. The last column, labeled "Churn" and containing the answers "yes" and "no", provides information on whether customer retention occurred (sample data), as illustrated in Fig. (**1**).

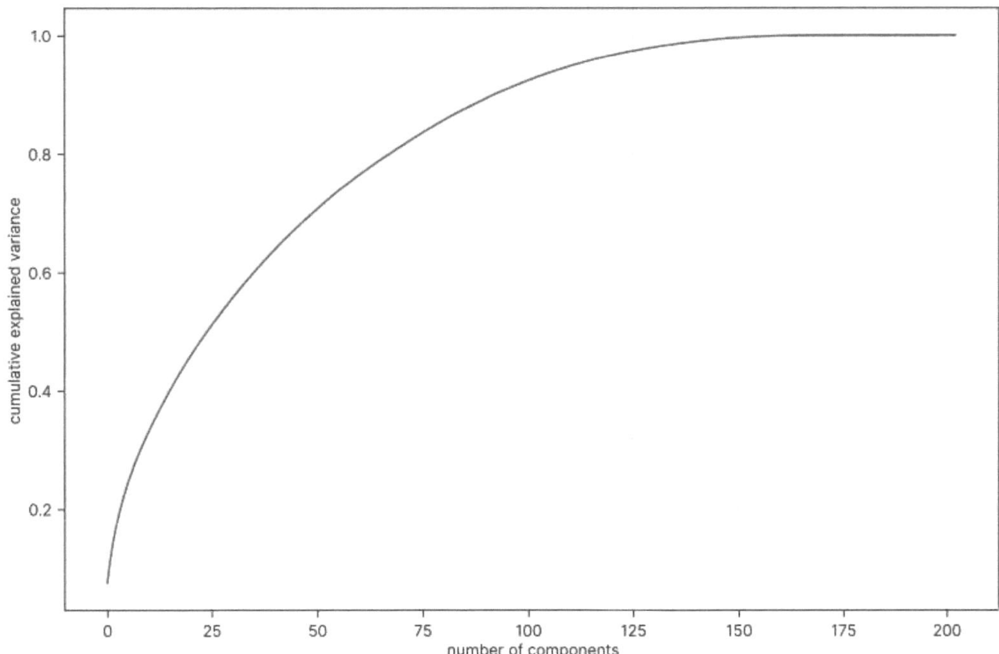

Fig. (1). Sample Data.

This part presents the suggested model on the consumer prediction of churn, which is displayed in Fig. (**2**). The proposed method contains procedures such as data preprocessing, EDA, and machine learning algorithms. Moreover, the proposed model is presented in this section. In the first stage of our data preparation, which involves importing the CSV file, converting categorical data into numerical data, deleting missing data by replacing it with null values, and verifying data correlation, we transform categorical data into numerical data.

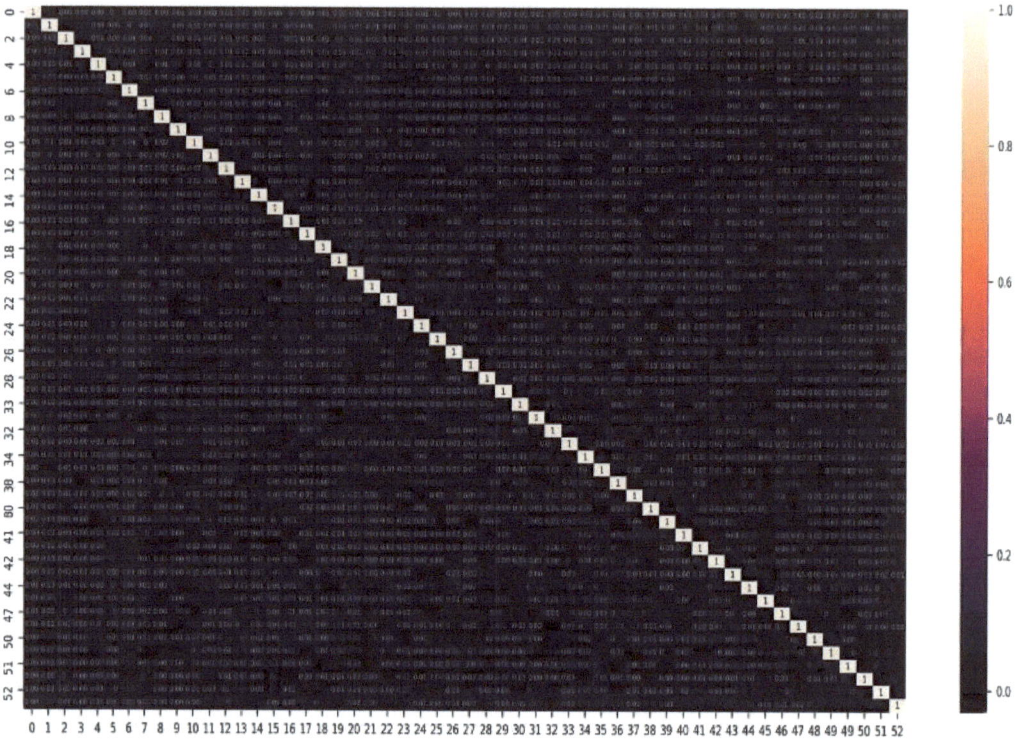

Fig. (2). Suggested Model.

In the second part of this process, the dataset is evaluated to get knowledge on demographics, customer accounts, service distributions, the link between monthly and total expenses, and churn rates depending on all parameters. The third step of our process includes the use of a variety of classification strategies, including logistic regressions, Support Vector Machines (SVM), AdaBoost, random forests, and artificial neural networks. After the day, each model is examined, and the Best Fit method is the one that is suggested.

A Preprocessing of Data

In real-world data, there is an abundance of noise, consistency concerns, and omissions. When applied to real-time data, a variety of data preparation approaches assist in the areas of data cleansing, instance reduction, and information discretization. The data are preprocessed to ensure the optimal format for training our machine learning model. When compared to tenures and two-year contracts, the data suggests that "positively connected with churns" describes the relationship between monthly contracts and the lack of solid tenure and technical assistance. It would seem that there is an inverse relationship between the data. We can observe that the facilities like "TV streaming, technical assistance, online backup, online security, *etc,* "with no internet connections, appear to be adversely related to churns." Before we dig further into identifying the variable and modeling it, we first analyze all patterns to look for the correlations mentioned above.

Data Exploration

To grasp "patterns in the data" and "potentially develop a hypothesis," first, we have to consider looking at the dispersion. If we want to understand "patterns in the dataset" and "probably develop a hypothesis," we should check the distribution of various variables and then see if there are any remarkable trends in our data.

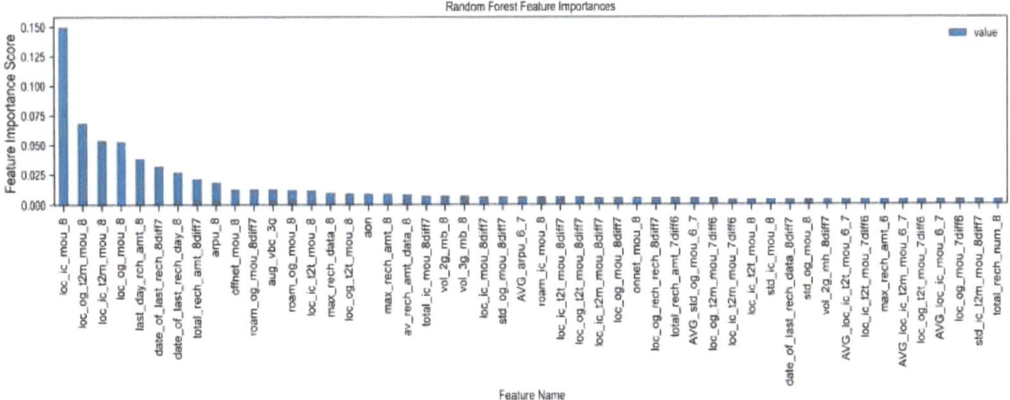

Fig. (3). Gender distribution.

This allows you to understand "patterns in the data."

1. The clients' demographics are investigated, namely their gender, age range, relationship status, and dependent status.
   a. Gender Distribution — From Fig. (**3**). Male clients make up 50.5% of the total, while female customers make up 49.5% of the total.

   b. % Senior Citizens – From Fig. (**4**), we can see that 16.2% of customers are senior citizens and 83.8% are youth; so it can be concluded that the data consists mostly of young customers.

   c. Partner and dependent status – From Fig. (**5**), we can see that 52% of customers have partners, whereas 30% of customers have no partners.

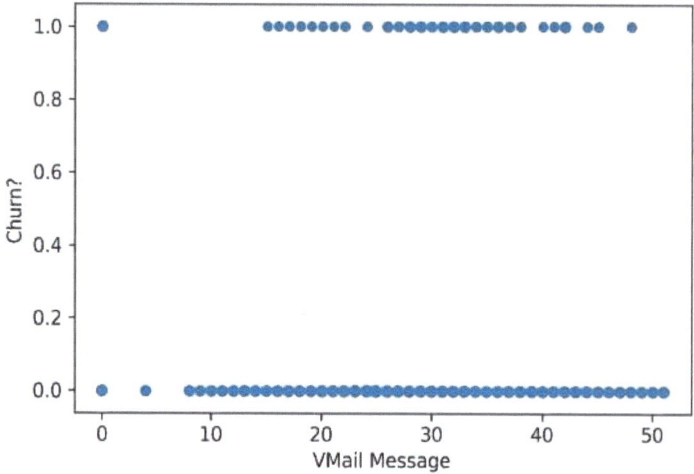

Fig. (4). % Senior citizens.

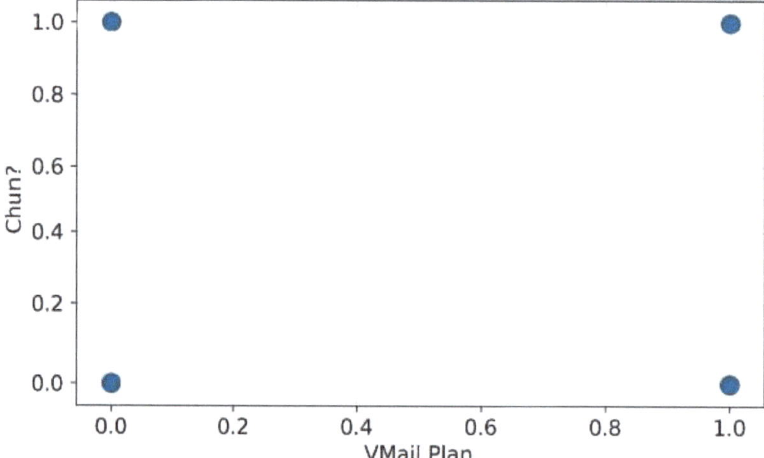

Fig. (5). Partner and dependent status.

Interestingly, among customers with partners, half have dependents, while the other half do not. From Fig. (**5**), we observe that approximately 80% of customers have neither partners nor dependents. If we examine partners who have both partners and dependents, as shown in Fig. (**6**), we observe that almost 60% of customers have partners with dependents.

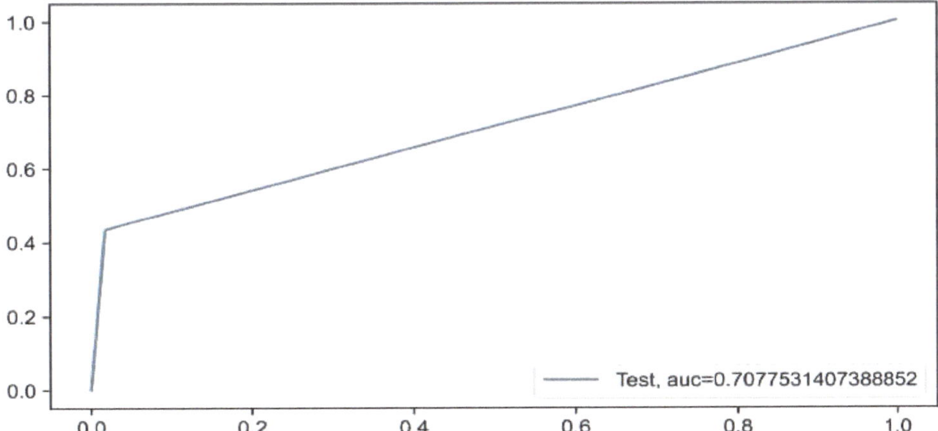

Fig. (6). % of customers with both partners and dependents.

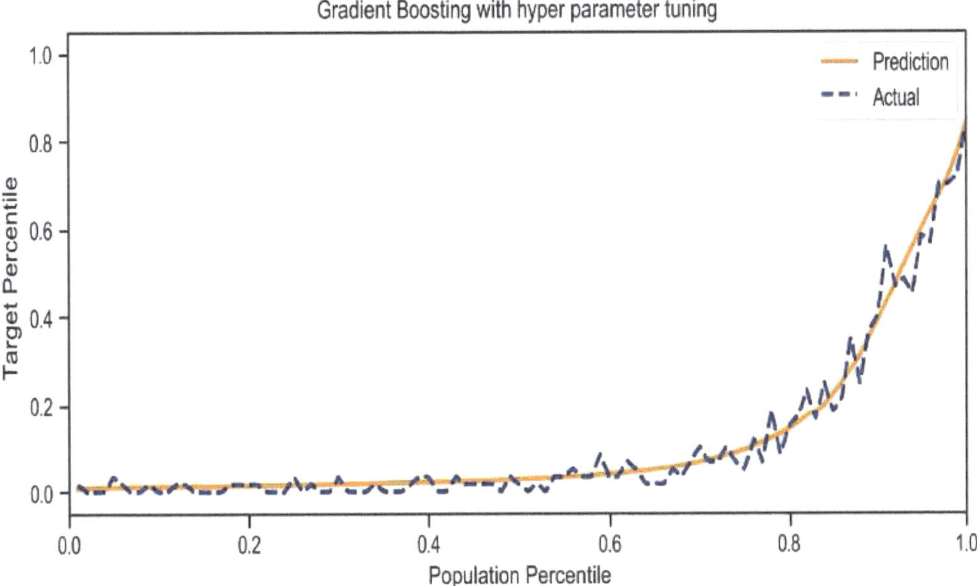

Fig. (7). Customers tenure.

2) Customer Account Information: Now let's start looking at "tenure, contract, services, charges, and churn rate correlation"

a. Tenure: In Fig. (7), the below histogram shows that "several clients were with the telecom provider for barely a month, while a few are there for nearly 72 months. As a possible explanation, "different contracts" may be to blame. Thus, "depending on the sort of agreement that they have signed to, it could be more/less easy for the clients to stay/leave the telecommunication firm".

b. Contracts: Fig. (**8**) looks into customers by contract type to understand customers' tenure. The image below shows customers with different contracts.

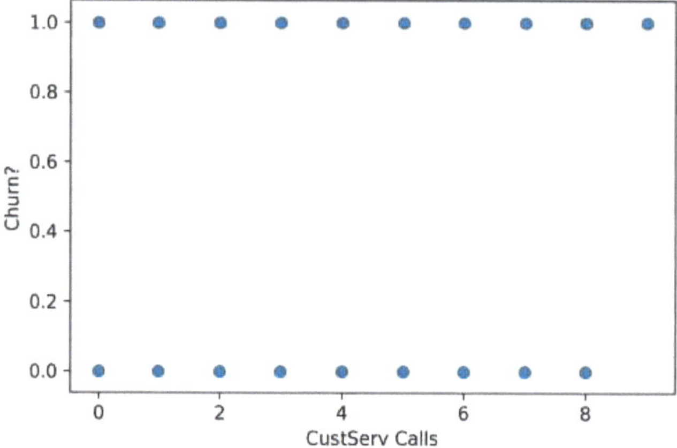

Fig. (8). Customers by contract type.

I. RESULT ANALYSIS

In Fig. (**8**), we can see that the "majority of the clients have enlisted for a month-to-month contract," but "1-year and 2-year contracts" have a similar number of customers enrolled. Here, we examine "customer tenure based on contract type."

c) In Fig. (**9**), the Churn predictor variable and its interaction with other factors, as identified in the correlation plot, are examined.

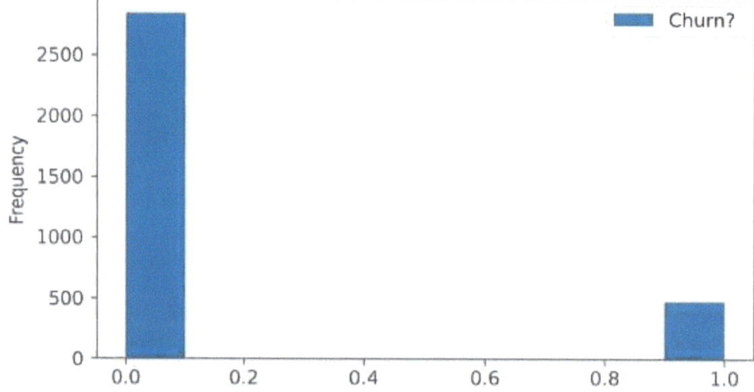

Fig. (9). Churn predictor variable analysis.

In Fig. (**9**), our analysis indicates that 74% of our clients do not leave. As expected, the data is distorted, as the vast majority of customers do leave. This skewness can lead to false negatives during model training, as the model may become biased toward the dominant class. Therefore, addressing this imbalance is a key focus during the modeling phase to improve prediction accuracy.

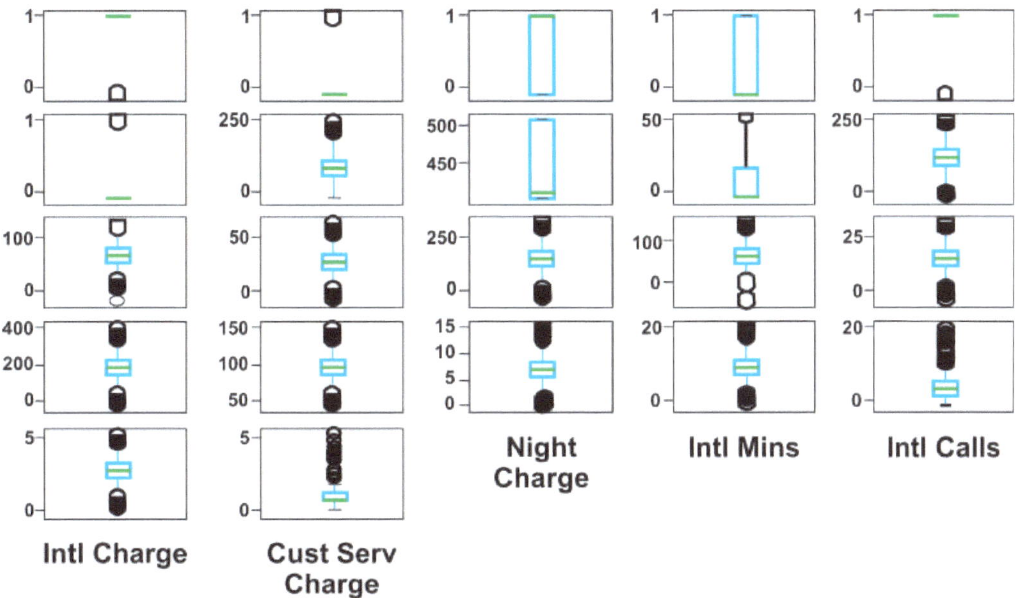

Fig. (10). Churn vs tenure.

1. In this subsection, let's start exploring how these variables affect the churn rate, look at 'tenure, seniority, contract type, monthly costs, and total charges.'
   a. Churn vs Tenure: From Fig. (**10**), we can observe that the "customers who do not churn, tend to stay for a longer tenure with the telecom company".

   b. Churn by Type of agreement: In Fig. (**11**), similar to corrplot, clients on month-to-month contracts have a high rate of churn. Let's take a closer look at the "distribution of different services used by clients" in the meantime below.
   c. Churn by Seniority: In Fig. (**12**), we can observe that "Senior Citizens have mostly doubled the churn rates than young populations". With this knowledge, now let's look at the "relations between monthly and whole charge".

   d. Churn by Monthly Charges: Fig. (**13**) shows that "a higher percentage of churning of customers occurs if the monthly charge rises".

e. Churn by Final Charges: Fig. (**14**) shows that "there is higher churn when the total charges are lower".

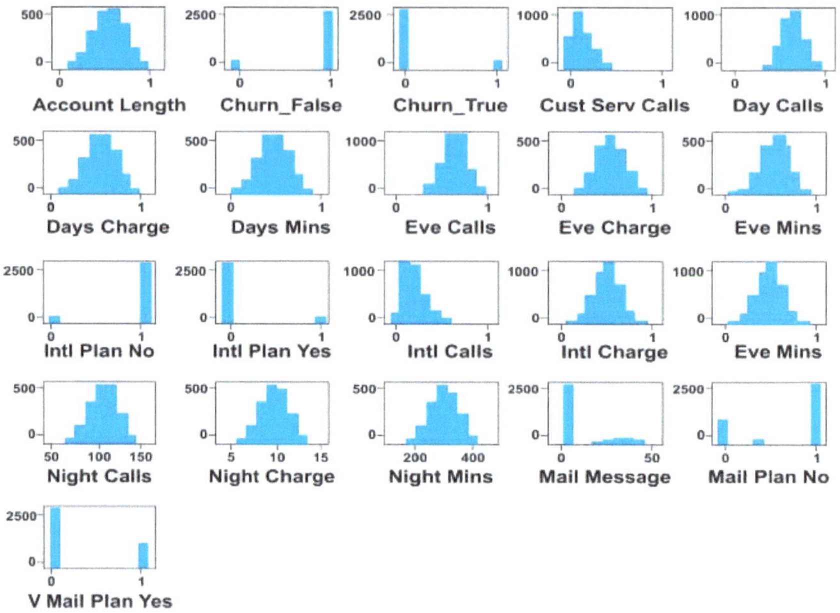

Fig. (11). Churn by contract type.

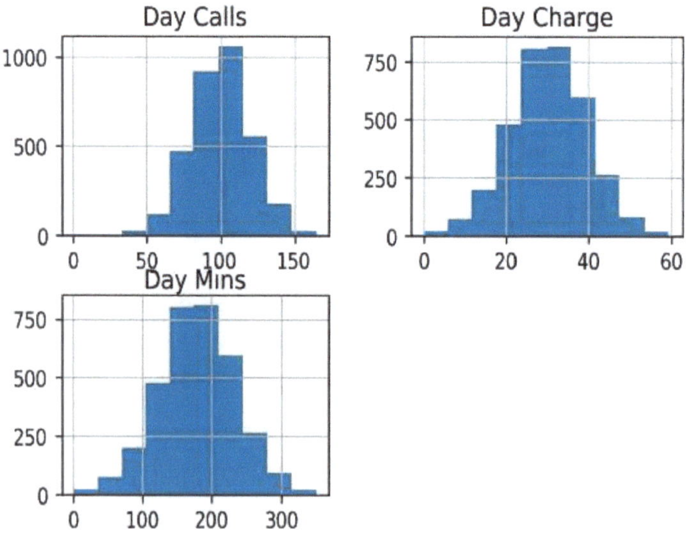

Fig. (12). Churn by seniority level.

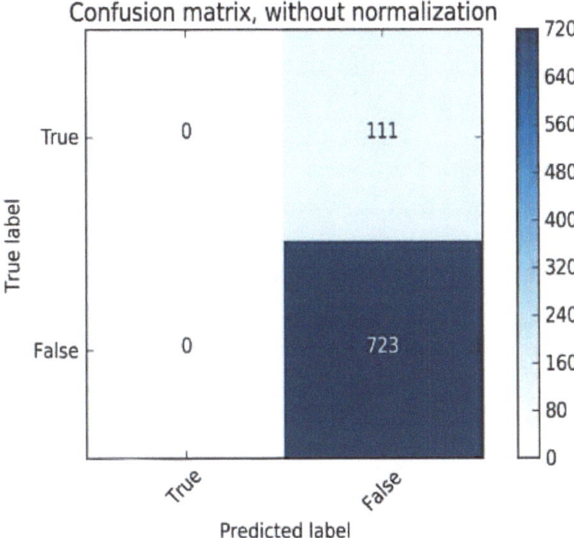

Fig. (13). Churn by monthly charges.

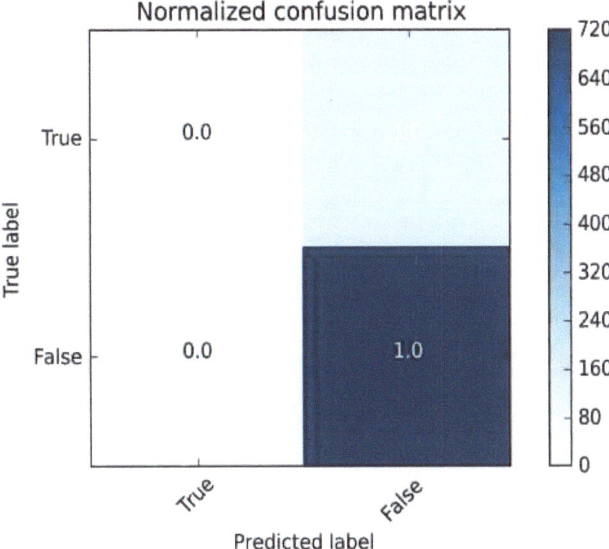

Fig. (14). Churns by final charges.

After completing all the above steps to analyze the data, we construct machine learning models for prediction and evaluate the outcomes. Logistic Regression, Support Vector Machine, Random Forest, AdaBoost, and ANN are implemented.

Customer Segmentation and Loss Forecasting Based on Churn.

It is clear from the statistics that the dataset includes two distinct categories of clients. "First, are the consumers who do not churn; they continue to be loyal to the firm and are seldom influenced by the companies that are in direct competition with them. The second category consists of repeat clients. The suggested approach seeks to identify the factors that contribute to client turnover and target those consumers specifically. Additionally, it develops retention methods to combat the issue of employees leaving to work for other companies.

In this investigation, five different machine learning strategies are employed to categorize consumer data using a labeled dataset. Our primary goal is to determine which method most accurately classifies consumers as being likely to churn or remain loyal to the company. Logistic Regression (LR), Support Vector Machine (SVM), Random Forest (RF), AdaBoost, and Artificial Neural Networks (ANN) are the methods that are used. The Library of Scikit-Learn Python is used to invoke the algorithms, and the model is trained and tested using it. Additionally, our models are assessed using a confusion matrix and a classification table, and revalidated using K-fold testing. The cross-validation approach, the outcomes of which are described in more depth below. The results are analyzed to evaluate the performance of several suggested machine learning models, and the accuracy of each model is shown in Table **1**.

Table 1. Comparison of the accuracy of proposed models.

S. No.	Model	Accuracy
1	Logistic Regression	79.9%
2	Support Vector Machine	80.96%
3	Random Forest	81.3%
4	ADA Boost	80.95%
5	Artificial Neural Network	86.63%

CONCLUSION

The telecom industry is experiencing a significant amount of loss due to the high turnover rate of its clients. The migration of a customer away from a service provider may be controlled, but the loss that comes along with it cannot be avoided. In light of recent developments in machine learning, it is necessary to construct effective models and to improve upon previously established procedures to circumvent obstacles faced by the industry. Because the Internet is so widely used, a massive quantity of data is readily accessible for data analysis and prediction. Churn prediction utilizes this data to generate revenue for the service provider. If you can prevent clients from terminating their relationship with a service provider, you have a far greater opportunity to renegotiate the contract and keep the customer. The majority of the currently available research relies on just one or two algorithms to make predictions about the outcome; nevertheless, there is a gap in our understanding of the application of many algorithms to the same issue in a comparable experimental setting with large datasets. In this study, five different machine learning algorithms are evaluated for their ability to forecast customer turnover. The goal is to determine which model is the most appropriate solution to the original issue. We observed that the accuracy gained with ANN is higher compared to other strategies, which enables us to claim unequivocally that ANN is an effective strategy for predicting customer churn. Nevertheless, there is room for development employing other techniques of Deep Neural Networks (DNN).

REFERENCES

[1] A. Gaur, and R. Dubey, "Predicting customer churn prediction in telecom sector using various machine learning techniques", *2018 International Conference on Advanced Computation and Telecommunication (ICACAT),* 2018 Bhopal, India
[http://dx.doi.org/10.1109/ICACAT.2018.8933783]

[2] I. Ullah, B. Raza, A.K. Malik, M. Imran, S.U. Islam, and S.W. Kim, "A churn prediction model using random forest: analysis of machine learning techniques for churn prediction and factor identification in telecom sector", *IEEE Access,* vol. 7, pp. 60134-60149, 2019.
[http://dx.doi.org/10.1109/ACCESS.2019.2914999]

[3] V. E, P. Ravikumar, C. S and S. K. M, "An efficient technique for feature selection to predict customer churn in the telecom industry," 2019 *1st International Conference on Advances in Information Technology (ICAIT)*, Chikmagalur, India, 2019.

[4] S. Shumaly, P. Neysaryan, and Y. Guo, "Handling class imbalance in customer churn prediction in telecom sector using sampling techniques, bagging and boosting trees", 2020 10th International Conference on Computer and Knowledge Engineering (ICCKE), Mashhad, Iran, 2020.
[http://dx.doi.org/10.1109/ICCKE50421.2020.9303698]

[5] A.S. Halibas, A. Cherian Matthew, I.G. Pillai, J. Harold Reazol, E.G. Delvo, and L. Bonachita Reazol, "Determining the intervening effects of exploratory data analysis and feature engineering in telecoms customer churn modelling", 2019 *4th MEC International Conference on Big Data and Smart City (ICBDSC)*, Muscat, Oman, 2019.
[http://dx.doi.org/10.1109/ICBDSC.2019.8645578]

[6] M. Ali, A.U. Rehman, and S. Hafeez, "Prediction of churning behavior of customers in telecom sector using supervised learning techniques", 2018 *IEEE 3rd International Conference on Computing, Communication and Security (ICS)*, Kathmandu, Nepal, 2018.

[7] M. Ali, A. Ur Rehman, S. Hafeez, and M.U. Ashraf, "Prediction of churning behavior of customers in telecom sector using supervised learning techniques", *2018 International Conference on Computer, Control, Electrical, and Electronics Engineering (ECE),* 2018 Khartoum, Sudan

[8] Dongbo Xie, *Actuators and sensors for application in agricultural robots: A review..* Machines 10.10 (2022): 913.
[http://dx.doi.org/10.3390/machines10100913]

[9] K.B. Nampalle, "Vision Through the Veil: Differential Privacy in Federated Learning for Medical

Image Classification", arXiv preprint arXiv:2306.17794 (2023). [http://dx.doi.org/10.48550/arXiv.2306.17794]

[10] L.P.L. Cavaliere, "Emotional Intelligence and Driving Change in Public Sector: The Mediating Role of Culture", *Turkish Online Journal of Qualitative Inquiry,* vol. 12, p. 7, 2021.

[11] Pavel V. Mizinov, *Parametric study of hand dorsal vein biometric recognition vulnerability to spoofing attacks.*. Journal of Computer Virology and Hacking Techniques (2023): 1-14. [http://dx.doi.org/10.1007/s11416-023-00492-z]

[12] P. Swetha, S. Usha, and S. Vijayanand, "Evaluation of Churn Rate Using Modified Random Forest Technique in Telecom Industry", 2018 3rd *IEEE International Conference on Recent Trends in Electronics, Information & Communication Technology (RTEICT)*, Bangalore, India, 2018. [http://dx.doi.org/10.1109/RTEICT42901.2018.9012251]

[13] A.S. Choudhari, and M. Potey, "Predictive to prescriptive analysis for customer churn in telecom industry using hybrid data mining techniques", *2018 Fourth International Conference on Computing Communication Control and Automation,* 2018 Pune, India [http://dx.doi.org/10.1109/ICCUBEA.2018.8697532]

[14] M. Bagri, J.K. Singh, and M.K. Abhilash, S. R.S. and S. Kumar, "Churn analysis in telecommunication industry", *2018 International Conference on Automation and Computational Engineering (ICACE),* 2018 Greater Noida, India [http://dx.doi.org/10.1109/ICACE.2018.8686852]

[15] "Efficient data preprocessing approach for imbalanced data in email classification system", *2020 International Conference on Smart Technologies in Computing, Electrical and Electronics (ICSTCEE),* 2020pp. 338-341 [http://dx.doi.org/10.1109/ICSTCEE49637.2020.9277221]

CHAPTER 17

Platform Development for Hawker and Peddlers

S Shivananda[1], **Jafar Ali Ibrahim Syed Masood**[2,*], **N.S. Kalyan Chakravarthy**[3], **Pastor R Arguelles, JR**[4], **Sk. Sheema**[5], **D. Divya Kalpana**[5] and **N. Hariharan**[6]

[1] *Department of ISE, M S Ramaiah Institute of Technology, Bangalore 560054, Karnataka, India*

[2] *Department of IoT, School of Computer Science and Engineering, Vellore Institute of Technology, Vellore 632014, Tamil Nadu, India*

[3] *Center for Data Science, School of Computer Science and Engineering, QIS College of Engineering & Technology, Ongole 523272, Andhra Pradesh, India*

[4] *College of Computer Studies, University of Perpetual Help Systems Dalta, City of Bacoor 4102, Cavite, Philippines*

[5] *Department of CSE, QIS College of Engineering & Technology, Ongole 523272, Andhra Pradesh, India*

[6] *Department of Mechanical Engineering, QIS College of Engineering & Technology, Ongole 523272, Andhra Pradesh, India*

Abstract: Developing a mobile app allows hawkers and peddlers to share their location in real-time. This could help customers easily locate hawkers in their area and get information about the products or services they offer. Overall, sharing the live location of hawkers can be a useful tool for supporting these small-scale businesses and helping them to reach new customers. It may also provide people with additional choices and boost a community's vitality and variety. Most mom-and-pop stores and other small enterprises are run by one person or a small team. Street corners, marketplaces, and retail districts are common places to find them. These types of companies offer a wide range of goods and services, including food stands, shops, barbershops, and more. The ability to respond quickly and effectively to changes in consumer tastes is a major strength of mom-and-pop stores and other types of small enterprises.

Keywords: Barbershops, Food stands, Hawkers, Marketplaces, Small-scale businesses.

INTRODUCTION

Suppliers can not conceal their products and services from app users [1]. Several options are available to ensure transparency and accessibility. One common

* **Corresponding author Jafar Ali Ibrahim Syed Masood:** Department of IoT, School of Computer Science and Engineering, Vellore Institute of Technology, Vellore 632014, Tamil Nadu, India; E-mail: jafarali.s@vit.ac.in

D. Arul Pon Daniel, T. Rajasanthosh Kumar & Satya Prakash Yadav (Eds.)

approach is to display a menu with descriptions and pricing. The menu can be organized using tabbed interfaces or scrolling lists [2]. Adding media files: Visuals would help users understand the app's products and services. Food and clothing vendors might use photos to attract consumers. If the merchant sells items via the app, it may involve placing orders. Possible steps include choosing products from a catalogue, entering payment details, and deciding whether to have them delivered or picked up [3]. Generally, for a hawker app to be successful, it must provide users with comprehensive and easy-to-understand product descriptions, enabling them to make informed purchases [4]. An aesthetically pleasing and intuitive user interface for the program can be built using an XML-rich collection of configurable widgets and tools [5]. It may include a menu or list of services or items, accompanied by pictures or videos of those items, and the ability to place an order or use a shopping cart, built withing server-side functionality, such as a database API using Java. Firebase may store and handle app purchases, orders, and customer data. APIs enable programs to retrieve and display location data. Apps use APIs to retrieve location data from the back-end server [6 - 8].

IMPLEMENTATION

Hawker's backend utilizes Java and Firebase. XML powers its front end. Commonly used by programmers, Java is ideal for creating sophisticated apps like the Hawker app. It offers a range of features and tools that make it easy to develop robust, scalable applications capable of handling large volumes of data and traffic. In the Hawker app, Java manages data storage, performs calculations, and executes complex algorithms to deliver a smooth and seamless user experience. The mobile application connects hawkers/street vendors with customers. The application consists of two parts: one for Hawker and the other for the user. Fig. (**1**) depicts the Hawker Flowchart.

Hawker/Vendor Mode

The Hawker/Vendor can share their live location, which will be visible to the customers, making it easy to access their location. - Using GPS for a long time can drain the battery of a vendor, so they have the option to lock their location (to set their location on a specific spot and switch GPS off). - A status feature that would be visible to the customers, which the vendor can update (example: will be on this location till 6 pm). - A profile section where the vendor can add photos, a menu, and a description of items they are selling, making these details visible to the customer.

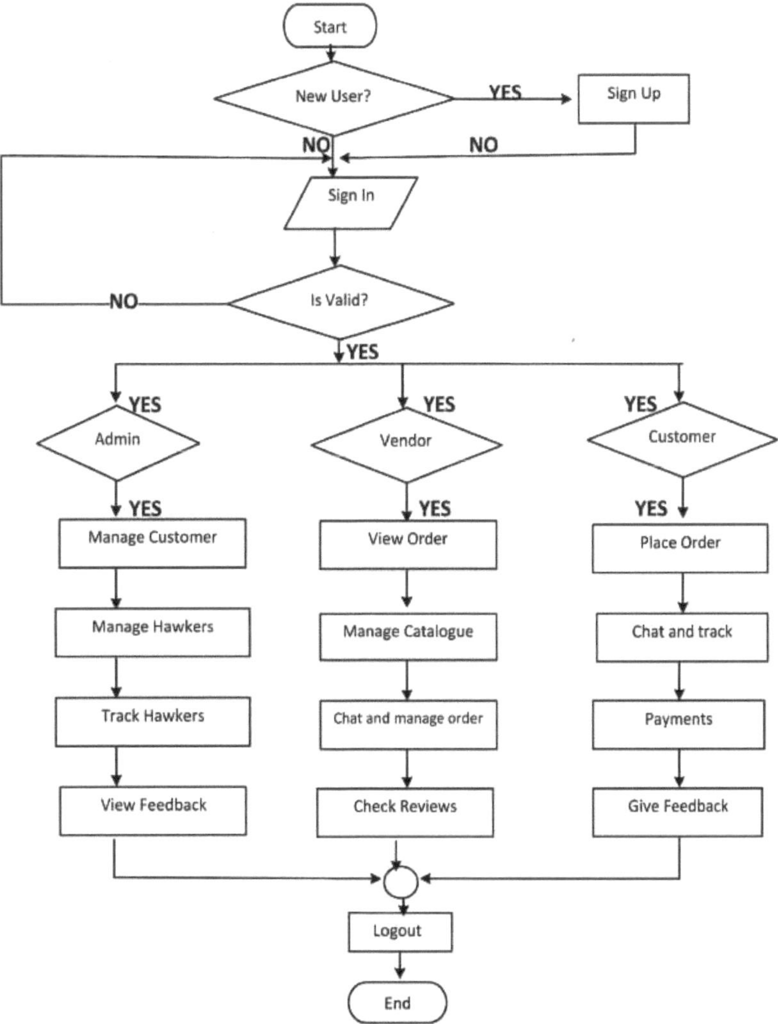

Fig. (1). Flowchart of Hawkers System.

Customer Mode

The customer would have access to all the street vendors' locations near them. The customer can view the status of the Vendor, profile, and vendor's menu. The customer can click on 'Directions,' which redirects to Google Maps to take the user to the hawker. The customers have an exclusive rating feature using which they can rate their experience with the hawker and also review them, which would reflect in the hawker's profile

ARCHITECTURE DESIGN

As shown in the system architecture design below, the components include a user, an Android device, Firebase, and a vendor. The Android device is where the user views the data, which can be fetched from the Firebase geo-location API. The vendor controls the accuracy of the location shared with the user and the catalogue. The application enables users and vendors to communicate with each other. The conceptual layout of data structures and databases is illustrated in more detail in Fig. (**2**).

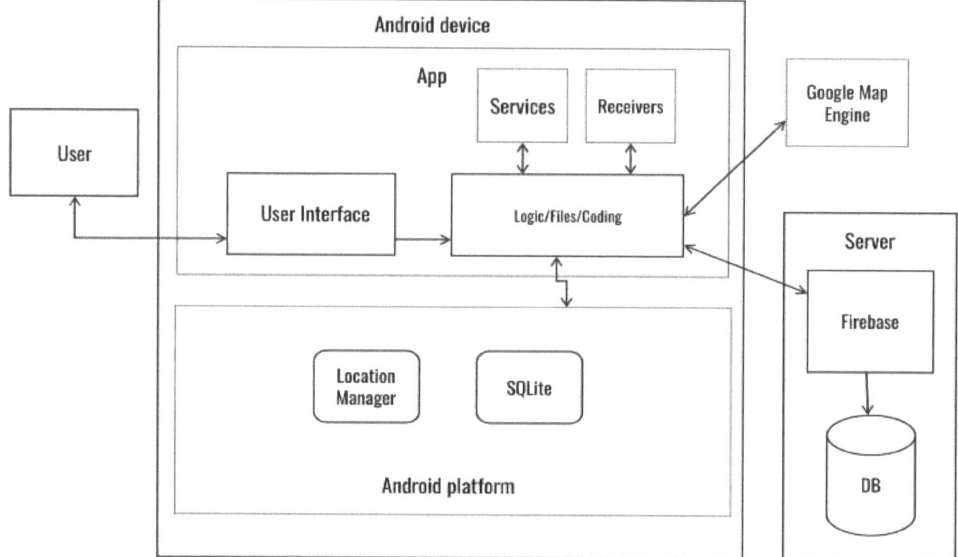

Fig. (2). System Architecture Design.

MARKET SURVEY OF VENDOR AND CUSTOMER

Vendor Survey

These findings provide valuable insights into vendors' demographic, operational, and technological preferences in the hawker and peddler industry.

Age Distribution

Most vendors fall within the 31-40 age range, indicating that this age group is actively involved in the hawker and peddler business.

Sales Focus

Approximately 33% of the vendors surveyed primarily sell food items. This suggests the food sector is a significant hawker and peddler industry segment.

Vendor Mobility

73.3% of vendors have stable sites, whereas 26.7% move about. This suggests that many suppliers choose mobility over permanent locations.

Mobile Phone Use

66.7% of vendors possess a phone. This shows that vendors surveyed use mobile technologies.

Survey Preference for alerts

Nearby prospective consumers are the most desired alerts for the majority of suppliers (66.7%). This indicates that vendors are seeking to enhance their sales and marketing opportunities by utilizing technology to receive notifications when they are near prospective clients.

Customer Survey

Distribution by Gender

Of the consumers polled, over three-quarters were men and around a quarter were women. This suggests that hawkers and peddlers mostly have male customers, with somewhat lower female involvement.

Preferences by Age

Eighty-three per cent of the people polled were in the age bracket of fifteen to twenty-five. This age group shows a significant interest in hawker and peddler services.

Grocery Shopping Habits

Among the surveyed customers, 31% indicated purchasing vegetables and fruits regularly every few days. This highlights the demand for fresh produce from hawkers and peddlers.

Preferred Shopping Method

The survey revealed that 46.5% of the customers prefer shopping through hawker and peddler platforms. This suggests that customers find this method convenient and preferable for their grocery needs.

Vendor Proximity Notification

A noteworthy finding is that most customers (exact percentage not mentioned) expressed interest in receiving notifications when a vendor is near them. This suggests that customers appreciate the convenience of being notified when a hawker or peddler vendor is nearby.

RESULT AND CONCLUSION

Sign-Up

Hawker simplifies food vendor-customer relationships. Both parties may use their email-based login functionality. Passwords may be encrypted to safeguard accounts. Fig. (**3**) displays the sign-up home page.

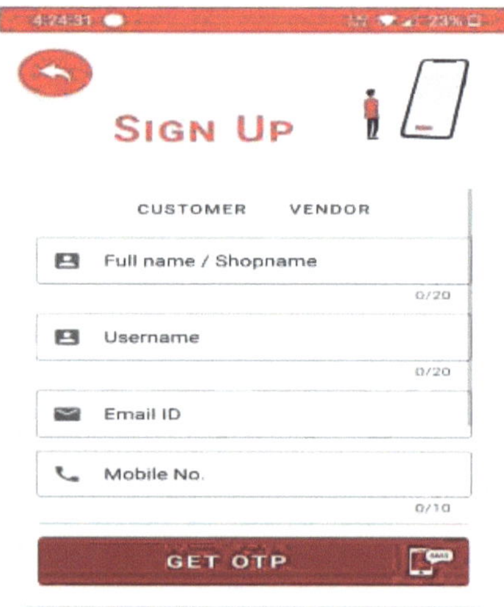

Fig. (3). Sign Up.

Login

Vendors and consumers may quickly sign up for Hawker accounts. Vendors and clients must register using their name, email, and password (Fig. **4**).

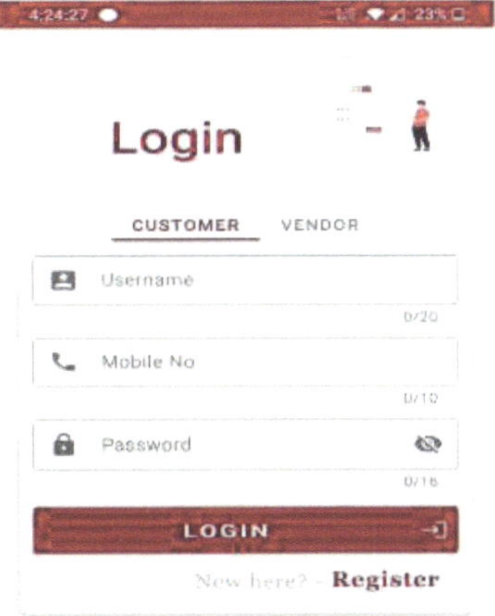

Fig. (4). Login.

5.3. Verification Page

Hawker app account verification may be needed for security and authenticity. Users may get a text or email with a verification code to verify their identity, as shown in Fig. (**5**).

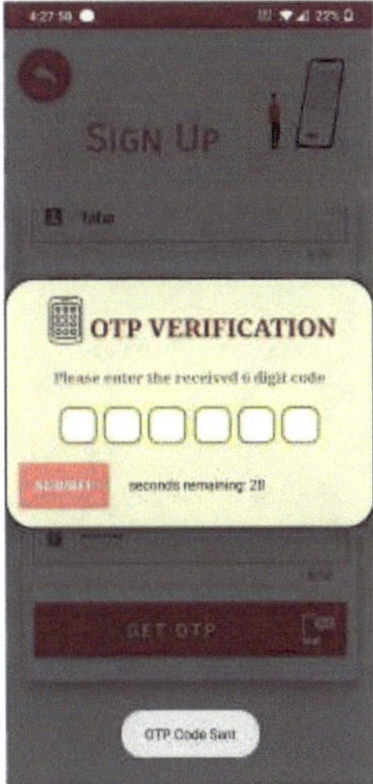

Fig. (5). Verification Page.

Home Page

Users may be asked to verify their credentials to maintain the security and validity of the Hawker app (Fig. **6**). One way to do this is to have them authenticate their identification by sending them a verification code.

Fig. (6). Home Page.

Vendor Location Page

The Hawker app displays vendors' locations on maps, enabling buyers to easily locate them. The marker indicates the vendor's location, and if the customer is within 150 meters, a circle is displayed to clarify their location, as shown in Fig. (7).

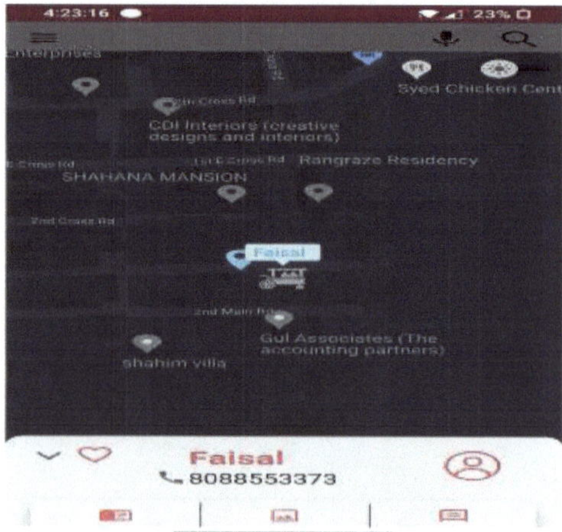

Fig. (7). Vendor Location Page.

Product Menu Page

Sellers may easily add new items to their menu using the Hawker app. Product names, descriptions, prices, and images can be added quickly by vendors, ensuring menus always display the newest products (Fig. **8**).

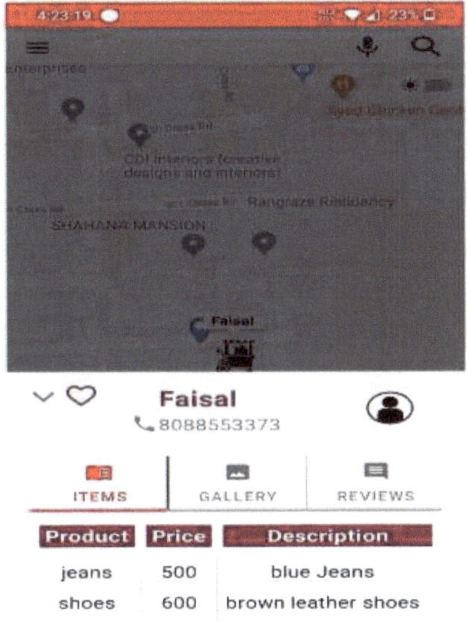

Fig. (8). Product Menu Page.

Review Page

Users can enhance transparency and help others make informed decisions by adding ratings and reviews to the Hawker app (Fig. **9**).

Fig. (9). Review Page.

Customized Location Option Page

Merchants with permanent sites will find the Hawker app's function that allows them to secure their locations while immobile. People who travel may not often benefit from this feature since it gives them more control over their platform presence and is more convenient. Fig. (**10**) displays the customized location option page.

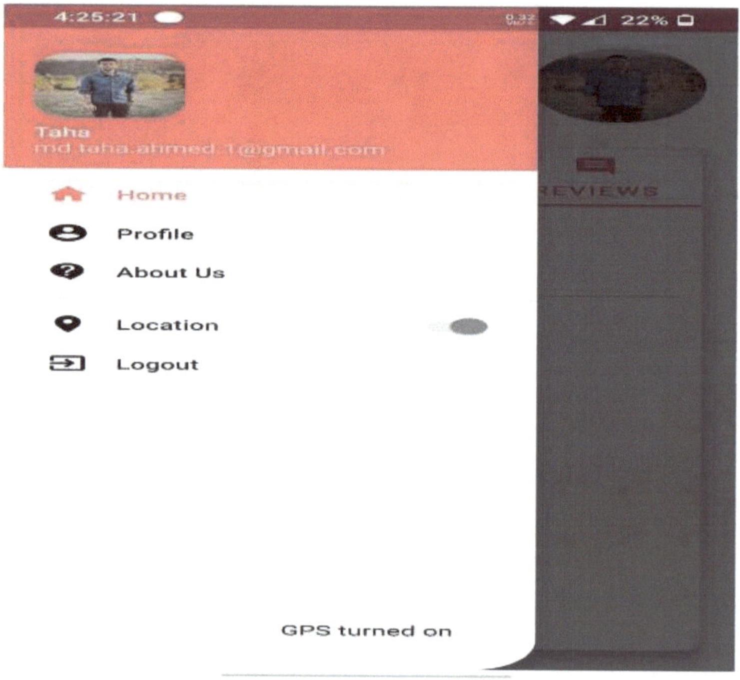

Fig. (10). Customized Location Option Page.

CONCLUSION

Both sellers and buyers can profit from the Hawker app, as eloquently summarized in the conclusion. It emphasizes how important features like location control, product management, and reviews and ratings contribute to a good user experience. It can be said that consumers gain ease and knowledge when making purchases, and suppliers gain exposure to a wider audience. In conclusion, the Hawker app offers distinctive features that differentiate it from other platforms. Furthermore, to make the app more efficient, future enhancements or feature expansions might further enhance the app's value offer for suppliers and consumers.

REFERENCES

[1] L. Kong, A. Wong, and A. Hawker, "Hawker culture and its infrastructure: Experiences and Hawker culture and its infrastructure: Experiences and contestations in everyday life contestations in everyday life Citation Citation",

[2] *Aimi Liyana Amir; Mohd Hafifi Bin Mohd Supir; Albin Lemuel Kushan; Norlindamalia Zulkifli; Mohammad Hafidz Rahmat.* Integrating Business Intelligence and Recommendation Marketplace System for Hawker Using Content Based Filtering, 2023.

[3] V. Shrivastava, H. Dhakad, S. Bajaj, and V. Divyasheesh, "GPS based city wise integration system for city vendors," *International Journal of Engineering and Computer Science*, vol. 9, no. 4, pp. 24984–24988, 2020. [http://dx.doi.org/10.18535/ijecs/v9i04.4457]

[4] A.A. Israel Dunmade, *Social Lifecycle Impact Assessment of Cocoyam Chips Hawking in Lagos.*Nigeria, 2019.

[5] D. Anna Dhotre, H. Mohammad, P. Kumar Pathak, A. Shrivastava, and Tr. Kumar, "Big Data Analytics using MapReduce for Education System," 2021, [Online]. Available: www.hivt.be

[6] K. Purohit, S. Vats, R. Saklani, V. Kukreja, V. Sharma, and S. P. Yadav, "Improvement in K-Means Clustering for Information Retrieval," *4th International Conference on Electronics and Sustainable Communication Systems (ICESC)*, pp. 1239–1245, 2023. [http://dx.doi.org/10.1109/ICESC57686.2023.10193031]

[7] R. Bandyopadhyay, "Institutionalizing informality: The hawkers' question in post-colonial Calcutta," *Modern Asian Studies*, vol. 50, no. 2, pp. 675–717, Mar. 2016. [http://dx.doi.org/10.1017/S0026749X1400064X]

[8] A. Bhattacharyya, "Hawking on the lines: Tales of the railway hawkers and their everydays," *Social Trends*, vol. 7, pp. 114–127, Mar. 2020.

CHAPTER 18

Usage of Mobile Phone Detection and Mailing System Using Deep Learning Techniques

L. Kanya Kumari[1,*], **K. Bhanu Sree**[1], **K. Sai Charitha**[1], **K. Sunila Jasmin**[1] and **B. Chaitanya**[1]

[1] *Department of IT, Andhra Loyola Institute of Engineering and Technology, Vijayawada 520008, Andhra Pradesh, India*

Abstract: A spike in email filtering due to a large number of detected emails leads to yearly losses. One way to mitigate this loss is to categorize different types of suspicious emails, such as fraudulent or promotional messages from unknown senders. The first steps in identifying message categorization were based on simple approaches, such as word filters. More complex methods, such as language modeling based on deep learning, are already being used. The text classification problem is often addressed using Recurrent Neural Networks (RNNs), with Gated Recurrent Units (GRUs) being a popular variant due to their efficiency in capturing sequential dependencies.. Since classifying phishing emails is the focus of this study, GRU techniques were used. This study's results show that, in a dropout-free environment, GRU attained a high accuracy rate. A large amount of detection mail is created worldwide from several botnets, which impacts the limited mailbox capacity. They affect the security of private mail and the loss of communication space. The time required to identify and reply to detected emails is affected by them. Identifying suspicious emails is still considered a challenging job in the modern day. Due to email detection frequency, identification can be improved. The researcher constructs a Gated Recurrent Unit- Recurrent Neural Network (GRU-RNN) to identify emails. A new method was tested with a Detecting basis dataset. The procedure is 99.8% accurate. After considerable testing, the researcher concludes that the offered technique detects emails well.

Keywords: Deep learning, Detected emails, Dropout-free, GRU-RNN, Promotional messages.

INTRODUCTION

Electronic email detection is the process of monitoring a subscriber list for the delivery of commercial or damaging emails [1]. The recipient has not consented to receive unsolicited emails [2]. The issue of detection has risen in the world of

* **Corresponding author L. Kanya Kumari:** Department of IT, Andhra Loyola Institute of Engineering and Technology, Vijayawada 520008, Andhra Pradesh, India; E-mail: kanyabtech@yahoo.com

D. Arul Pon Daniel, T. Rajasanthosh Kumar & Satya Prakash Yadav (Eds.)

the internet. Spatial, temporal, and message delivery inefficiencies are identified. Even while automated email filtering can be the greatest defense against discovery, new detection methods may easily circumvent it. Most detections that originated from specific email addresses might have been manually disabled until about a year ago. The detecting process will make use of DL methods [3]. At the end of the email filtering period, three main strategies were implemented: "content analysis, white and bans of internet addresses, and community-based procedures." As a detection and prevention strategy, text analysis of messages is often used [4]. Considerations for both servers and buyers lead to a plethora of potential solutions. In most cases, users and organizations would prefer that no critical communications go missing [5]. It is quite probable that the blacklist method was the initial one employed to detect separation. This strategy's goal is to reply to all senders, except those using local or digital email addresses [6, 7]. Ever since modern areas joined the domain name detection category, this strategy has become less effective. Emails sent to publicly registered domains and email addresses are prioritized using the white category technique, while all other emails are sent to a far lower queue [8]. Senders who agree with confirmation requests sent by a "junk mail filtering system" will find this strategy to be the most effective [9 - 11].

Problem Statement

Sending unwanted ads, messages, or viruses to huge numbers of people online is called spam. It might be difficult to eliminate dubious emails from email due to their size and effort. Fraudsters may steal company data from these emails in addition to viruses and malware. Given these conditions, all organizations should implement spam filters on their messaging systems first. Deep learning algorithms outperform classical prediction approaches in categorizing texts for both multi-class and binary classification in NLP testing and verification.

METHODOLOGY

A method for detecting emails is proposed here by the researcher. The authors selected the RNN-GRU as the primary component of the module, relying on an anomaly detector. It is in the following module that the trained model is loaded. Statistical evidence supports its effectiveness. This component determines whether a certain email is an anomaly message. Using a mail-based dataset extracted from the UCI DL repository, the proposed method is tested. For a neural network to recognize emails, there are two steps: training and testing. Fig. (**1**) shows the process used to detect and identify phishing schemes using RNN. There are three stages to the proposed models. One of these steps is feature extraction, while another is RNN-GRU using SVM.

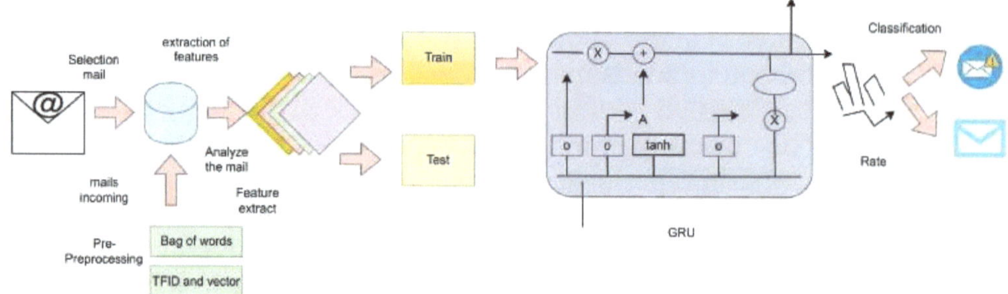

Fig. (1). Detect and identify phishing schemes process.

DESCRIPTION OF THE MODULE

The following modules are included in this system:

Preparing Datasets

The collected raw data from the website will be used to train DL models. Two columns were used to list the emails that Kaggle finally obtained. The first column, titled "type," had possible values for detection or messaging and was used to classify emails. The second column, labeled "e-mail Content," included several forms of email content.

Converting Tokens

Word tokenization is the process of converting a phrase's words into numerical indices. This process creates a word tokenizer from a predetermined set of intriguing lexical phrases. Following creation, a phrase's words are transformed into sequence information using a word tokenizer. Tokenization takes words and turns them into indexes, with the unknown phrases having their index set to 0.

Scrambling

Once the tokens have been produced, the next step is to stem them. Undoubtedly, stem is the method by which the data-derived phrases are transformed back into their original form. The underlying sentence is then stripped of any prefixes and suffixes. The stemming technique is then used to return the fundamental or stem words of both altered and misspelled words. Similarly, they have perfectly done the stemming operation for this step by using the NLTK Python Library. Words that are considered spam may be located rapidly once email content has been stopped.

Building Models

They construct spam classification models in this experiment, utilizing two deep learning algorithms, one of which incorporates GRU techniques. An enhancement of the LSTM approach, the GRU is a deep learning technique that uses reset gates and update gates to simplify the system's architecture. The amount of the hidden state sent on to the next stage is controlled by the updating gate. To establish how significant the previously hidden state data is, the reset gate is used.

Examining

Keras, a free neural network application, can build models. Keras only accepts actual data. Thus, they tokenized the most common movie review phrases before vectorizing. Blockchain-enabled words are vectorized in the following example.

Efficiency

After training the models, they evaluate their performance on the test dataset. According to the results, the accuracy levels of the model-based LSTM and GRU are comparable.

TECHNIQUE

A large dataset is processed using RNN technology to classify emails as detectable or not. Recurrent Neural Networks (RNNs) are a kind of supervised machine learning that mimics STM. A person's short-term memory is located in the frontal part of the brain. A crucial principle of RNN operation is the preservation of previously learned information (Fig. **2**). It continues by making use of this data. As an example, RNN relies on its hidden units to generate output and feed them back into the system. The RNN uses imperfect memory to process the data.

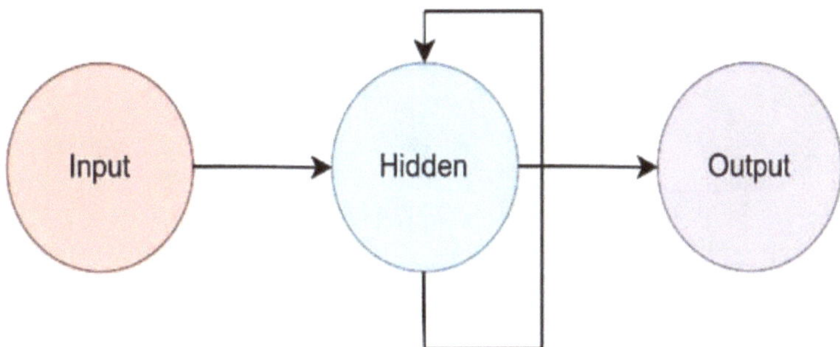

Fig. (2). RNN Operation.

The neurons link with each other throughout time. This exemplifies the concept of possessing a Short-Term Memory (STM), which is a specific sort of memory. Neurons can retrieve and remember the information they already have. The neuron acquires knowledge from previous observations and communicates it to the subsequent neurons. A Recurrent Neural Network (RNN) acquires information by leveraging the outcomes generated by preceding neurons. The time step refers to the duration required for the result to transition from one state to another in response to a change in the input. The quantity of characteristics represents the inputs. Before using the activation operation in a Recurrent Neural Network (RNN), the input values and the previous output are established. This result will be represented by the subsequent layer. Based on the data, this occurs because it can effectively address the problem of overfitting in neural networks and differs among different outputs.

K-Nearest Neighbor Method

- A supervised learning algorithm, the K-Nearest Neighbor is one of the most basic forms of deep learning.
- By clustering new instances into regions that resemble older ones, the K-NN algorithm suggests a relationship between the latest model and the older instances.
- The K-NN algorithm (Fig. **3**) organizes available data and categorizes new points based on similarity. This means that the K-NN approach can rapidly and reliably classify new data.
- Although the K-NN technique can solve regression and classification inquiries, it is mostly used for classification tasks.
- K-NN, a non-parametric technique, does not assume data validity.
- The algorithm is slow because it stores training data instead of learning immediately. Classifying data utilizes the data to perform a job.
- The KNN technique stores the dataset during training and categorizes additional data that is useful.

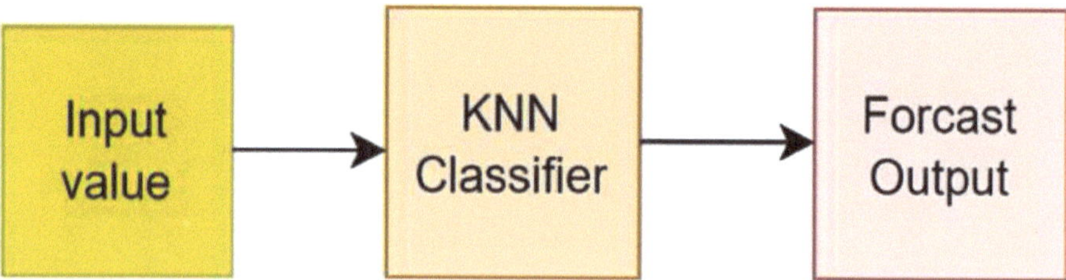

Fig. (3). K-Nearest neighbor method.

K-Nearest Neighbors Analysis

Look at the flowchart below to understand K-NN (Fig. **4**). Consider classifying new data for usage. Consider the Accuracy of the Model in the graph below (Fig. **5**).

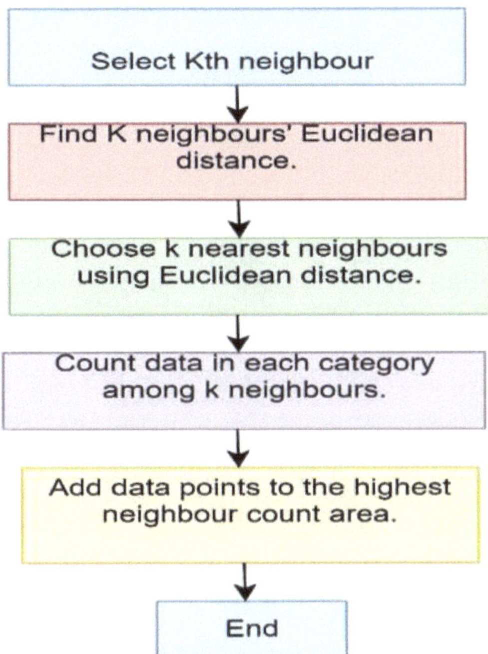

Fig. (4). Flowchart of KNN.

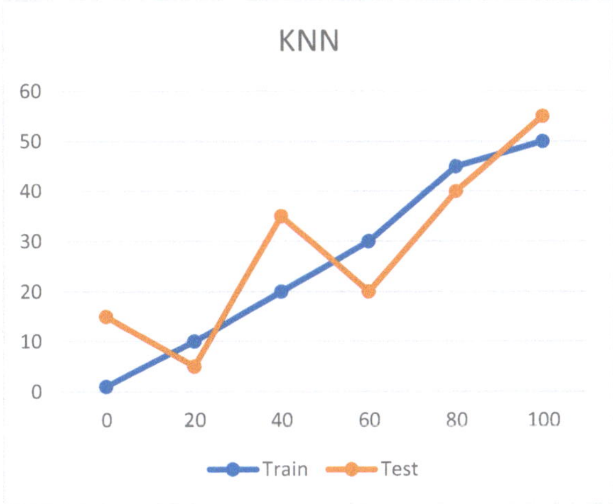

Fig. (5). Accuracy of model.

The most reasonable approach to evaluate the performance of a classification model is to compute the proportion of accurate predictions. This line of analysis was taken up to determine the Accuracy score. As a classification parameter, the accuracy range in DL contains the proportion of predictions that were properly predicted by a model. The metric is popular since it's easy to compute and understand. Additionally, it evaluates model correctness with one value.

Gated Recurrent Unit

GRU neural networks are unique variations of Recurrent Neural Networks (RNNs), which are widely used in industries and can retain longer-term data dependence. Slow convergence and poor learning still plague GRU. An optimized gated recurrent unit neural network design is suggested. The reset gate in the OGRU model enhances GRU's learning method, improving learner and prediction performance. Recurrent Neural Networks (RNNs) like the Gated Recurrent Unit (GRU) are like long-term memory. GRU works faster and uses less memory than LSTM, although LSTM is more efficient with longer sequences. GRUs also address the conventional recurrent neural network vanishing gradient issue. If grading decreases as it backward propagates, the neural network may become inefficient, and learning may suffer. RNNs may "forget" lengthy sequences when a layer fails to learn. GRUs employ updated and reset gates to fix this. Gates can be taught to remember past data and pick what data to output. Thus, it may provide crucial event chain information to improve forecasts.

Paralleling GRU networks is challenging because of their sequential training process. GRU parallelization has mostly employed data-parallel and model-parallel techniques for training. Existing methods are still performance-constrained by instruction time when sequences are quite lengthy. This study introduces a Multi-Grid Reduction In Time (MGRIT) concurrent GRU training method. MGRIT splits a sequence into several sub-sequences and trains them on separate processors simultaneously. To speed it up, the hidden layer must be hierarchically changed to enhance end-to-end communication throughout gradient descent's forward and backward propagation phases. Each movie is an image sequence, and the dataset's experimental findings reveal that the novel parallel training approach speeds up training by 6.6 times over sequential methods. The efficiency of the unique parallel GRU algorithm grows with sequence length because sequence length affects its efficacy.

For each time step, the hidden layers are calculated using the following formulas:

$$Update\ gate: zt = \sigma(w_z.[ht - 1, xt])$$

$$Reset\ gate: rt = \sigma(w_r.[ht - 1, xt])$$

$$New\ memory: ht = tanh(w.[rt * ht - 1, xt])$$

$$Final\ memory: ht = (1 - zt) * ht - 1 + zt * h \sim t$$

w is the weight vector, * is element-wise multiplication, and σ is a sigmoid function. At t, the procedure reveals the GRU's internal environment (Fig. **6**).

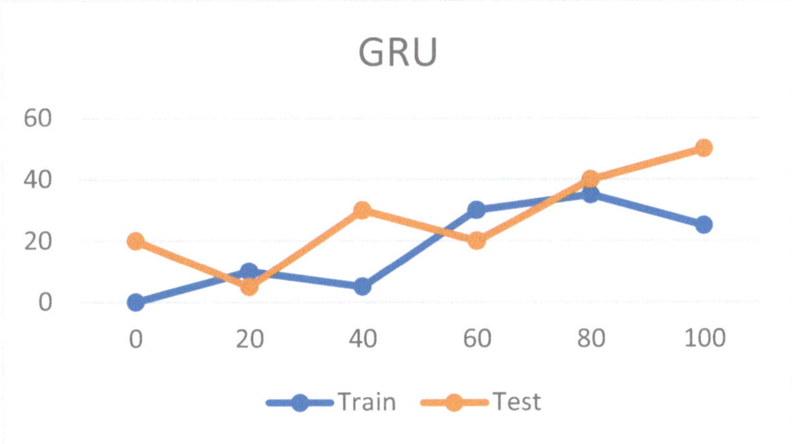

Fig. (6). GRU.

4.4. KNN Comparison to GRU Method

The aforementioned comparison graph illustrates the spectrum of differences in accuracy levels between the Gated Recurrent Unit and the K-Nearest Neighbor Algorithm (Fig. **7**). As an initial step, they studied email identification using the KNN algorithm, which yielded an accuracy rate of about 91%. This research makes use of Kaggle-collected pre-trained datasets. The dataset includes hundreds of pictures or pieces of data that are based on detecting emails and texts. The Jupiter notebook, which is used for data set training, was utilized. The following is the flowchart to apply the K-Nearest Neighbor algorithm, which is a Deep Learning algorithm (Fig. **8**).

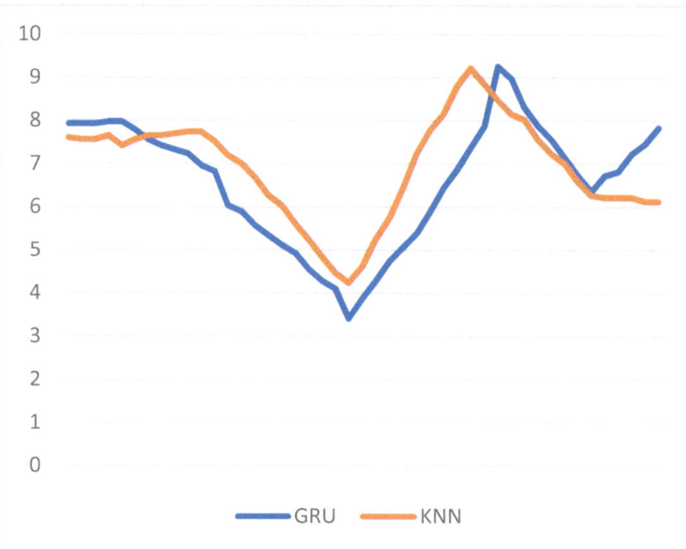

Fig. (7). Comparison of classifiers.

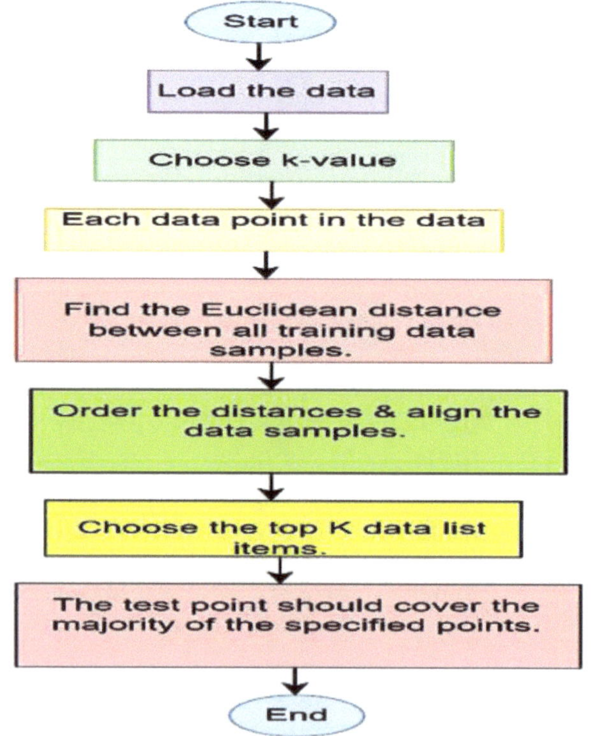

Fig. (8). Flowchart for KNN.

This work employed a confusion matrix in the KNN algorithm and a likelihood ratio test to validate KNN classification accuracy. Repetitive stages in KNN regression estimate the average K value and assign it to the indeterminate data point instead of designating the group with the most votes. However, the KNN algorithm has drawbacks.

- High storage space needs
- Finding the value of K is essential.
- Slow prediction occurs when there is a large concentration of N.
- Highly sensitive to irrelevant traits.

KNN drawbacks were addressed using a Gated Recurrent Unit. The GRU algorithm achieves an accuracy exceeding 91% in this project, utilizing Kaggle pre-trained datasets in this investigation. The dataset comprises thousands of spam-related photos and data. Data sets were trained using Jupiter Notebook. GRU is faster than KNN and has several advantages:

- Shorter GRU algorithm training time
- Fewer data points are needed to capture data attributes.

RESULTS AND ASSESSMENT OF PERFORMANCE

All selected datasets had their TPR, TNR, FPR, median validation accuracy rate, and F-Score computed. With an accuracy of about 99.66%, the deep RNN demonstrates the highest possible recognition rate and precision for the method. Additionally, with F-score rates of about 97.94%, AUC of around 98.62%, and TPR of around 98.66%, the suggested strategy is the best. Fig. (**9**), which is shown below, displays the email sent to another user in the form of text using this programme. The email verifies if it is spam and whether it contains any bullying material after it has been delivered to the user. Fig. (**10**) explains performance evaluation.

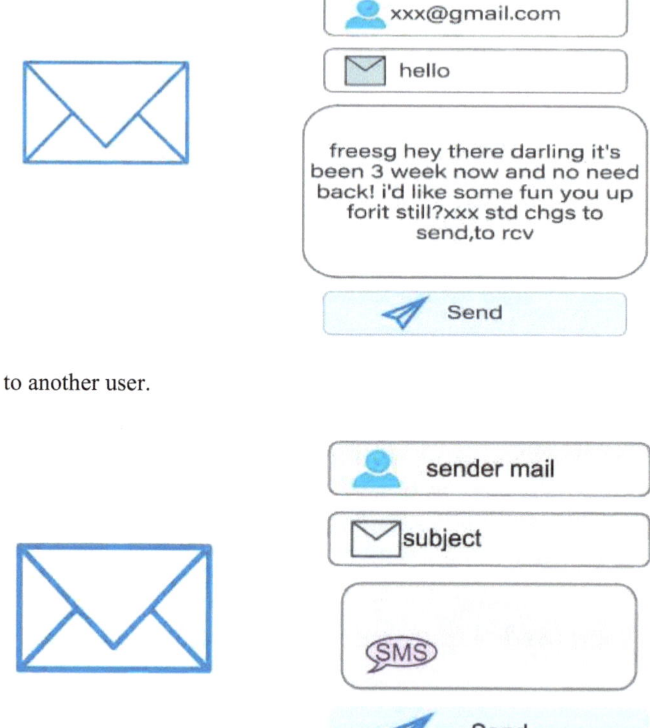

Fig. (9). Email sent to another user.

Fig. (10). Evaluation of performance.

This indicates that the GRU-RNN yields the best results; however, the class-conditional freedom limits its performance, resulting in the misclassification of certain tuples. In contrast, ensemble techniques work because they forecast classes using multiple classifications.

CONCLUSION

The approach is limited to analyzing mail using a tiny corpus, and the sheer volume of messages sent and received nowadays makes this a formidable challenge. Instead of using site URLs or other criteria, the solution that allows spam detection may filter emails according to the content of the email. Therefore, the main body of the email is now quite short. In many ways, the project might be better. Possible improvements include the following: It is possible to filter spam based on respected and verified web addresses. "The fake email categorization is especially important in identifying spam from non-spam messages and in categorizing emails." This method may help large organizations differentiate between legitimate and fake emails. An innovative technique was evaluated using a foundational dataset for detection. The accuracy of the process is 99.8%. Based on extensive testing, the researcher found that the proposed approach effectively identifies emails.

REFERENCE

[1] *Aimi Liyana Amir; Mohd Hafifi Bin Mohd Supir; Albin Lemuel Kushan; Norlindamalia Zulkifli; Mohammad Hafidz Rahmat.* Integrating Business Intelligence and Recommendation Marketplace System for Hawker Using Content Based Filtering, 2023.

[2] A. Abdelmoamen Ahmed, S. Al Omari, R. Awal, A. Fares, and M. Chouikha, "A distributed system for supporting smart irrigation using Internet of Things technology", *Eng. Rep.,* vol. 3, no. 7, 2021.e12352
[http://dx.doi.org/10.1002/eng2.12352]

[3] S.C. Olisa, C.N. Asiegbu, J.E. Olisa, B.O. Ekengwu, A.A. Shittu, and M.C. Eze, "Smart two-tank water quality and level detection system via IoT", *Heliyon,* vol. 7, no. 8, 2021.e07651
[http://dx.doi.org/10.1016/j.heliyon.2021.e07651] [PMID: 34401568]

[4] A.M. Mateoiu, A. Korodi, A. Stoianovici, and R. Tira, "Supervisory monitoring and control solution on android mobile devices for the water industry 4.0", *Sustainability (Basel),* vol. 15, no. 22, p. 16022, 2023.
[http://dx.doi.org/10.3390/su152216022]

[5] L. Zhang, D. C. Mohr, and M. N. Burns, "Improved mental health clinical practice informed by digital phenotyping," *Santé Mentale au Québec*, vol. 46, no. 1, pp. 135–136, 2021.
[http://dx.doi.org/10.7202/1076908ar]

[6] B. Xu, Y. Fan, J. Qian, and Y. Zhou, "A machine learning approach for detecting cell phone usage while driving," *IEEE Access*, vol. 7, pp. 118921–118930, 2019.
[http://dx.doi.org/10.1109/ACCESS.2019.2936825]

[7] D. Rathee and S. Mann, "Detection of e-mail phishing attacks using machine learning and deep learning," *International Journal of Computer Applications*, vol. 184, no. 42, pp. 7–11, 2022.
[http://dx.doi.org/10.5120/ijca2022921868]

[8] H. Liu and B. Lang, "Machine learning and deep learning methods for intrusion detection systems: A survey," *Applied Sciences*, vol. 9, no. 20, p. 4396, 2019.
[http://dx.doi.org/10.3390/app9204396]

[9] P. Mishra, V. Varadharajan, U. Tupakula, and E. S. Pilli, "A detailed investigation and analysis of using machine learning techniques for intrusion detection," *IEEE Communications Surveys & Tutorials*, vol. 21, no. 1, pp. 686–728, 2019.
[http://dx.doi.org/10.1109/COMST.2018.2847722]

[10] P. Patro, "A hybrid approach estimates the real-time health state of a bearing by accelerated degradation tests", *Mach. Learn.,* 2021.

[11] A. Kumar, D. Goel, S. Agarwal, P. Gupta, and Y. Singh, "An efficient approach to predict the quality of apple through its appearance," *International Journal for Research in Applied Science and Engineering Technology*, 2023.
[http://dx.doi.org/10.22214/ijraset.2023]

CHAPTER 19

Quantum ML Method Use to Predict Error in Chemistry

Yogeesh N[1,*], D.K. Girija[2], M. Rashmi[3], J. Divyashree[4], M S Ramesha[5] and **P. William[6]**

[1] *Department of Mathematics, Government First Grade College, Tumkur 572102, Karnataka, India*

[2] *Department of Computer Science, Government First Grade College, Tumkur 572102, Karnataka, India*

[3] *Faculty in Computer Science, Government First Grade College, Bangalore 560057, Karnataka, India*

[4] *Department of Chemistry, PES PU College, Bangalore 560050, Karnataka, India*

[5] *Department of Mathematics, Government College for Women, Mandya 571401, Karnataka, India*

[6] *Department of Information Technology, Sanjivani College of Engineering, Savitribai Phule Pune University, Pune 411007, Maharashtra, India*

Abstract: Optimizing work scheduling efficiency is crucial for reducing carbon footprint and wasteful expenditure in computational quantum mechanics-based materials and molecular designing campaigns, which need more high-performance computer resources. Quantum Machine Learning (QML) methods provide computational price estimates for typical chemistry quantum activities. QML method of wall times shows a consistent decrease in out-of-sample prediction error with training set size for 2D nonlinear toy frameworks, individual point of view, geometric optimisation, and transition state calculations. They provide numerical proof for millions of living molecule organisms, including transition states, open and closed equilibrium shell structures, and a toy system with two different roles and three regularly used optimizers. The MP2/6-311G(d), B3LYP/def2-TZVP, CASSCF/VDZ-F12, local CCSD(T)/VTZ-F12, as well as MRCISD+Q-F12/VDZ-F12 levels of electronic structure theory are all taken into account. After training on thousands of molecules, QML-based wall time estimates considerably increase work scheduling efficiency across the board, compared to traditional indiscriminate job treatment. Cutting CPU time overhead by 15% to 85% is the result.

Keywords: Carbon footprint, Job treatment, Numerical proof, Prediction error, Quantum machine learning.

[*] **Corresponding author Yogeesh N:** Department of Mathematics, Government First Grade College, Tumkur 572102, Karnataka, India; E-mail: yogeesh.r@gmail.com

D. Arul Pon Daniel, T. Rajasanthosh Kumar & Satya Prakash Yadav (Eds.)

INTRODUCTION

An NP-hard issue is solving Schrödinger's equation with arbitrary precision, which is a significant computational task in the field of chemistry and materials science [1]. As a result, the computing costs of doing correct quantum chemistry calculations tend to scale sharply and nonlinearly with the size of molecules, which is a restriction that affects all such computations [2]. Thus, computer hardware scarcity will continue to be a significant element in the near upcoming, regardless of how stable Moore's law is. Also, at national and local levels, academic HPCs have been seeing a significant increase in CPU time going toward chemical and materials-based computer programs. The Swiss National Supercomputing Center (CSCS) and Argonne Leadership Computing Facility used around 30% and 40% of their total capacity in 2021 for chemical and materials sciences research programs, respectively. Chemistry and materials sciences accounted for 35% of resources at the National Energy Research Scientific Computing Center in 2022 and 55% of the ARCHER supercomputing capacity in the preceding month [3]. Based on a 40% worldwide share of the top 400 supercomputers (Fig. **1**) over the past 26 years, this equates to 0.6 exaFLOPS every year. The atomistic simulation requires a significant amount of resources, particularly on the computer groups of most medium to large universities or research institutions. In the University of Basel's computer collection, at sciCORE, this percentage often approaches 55%. These infrastructures are expensive to purchase, operate, and maintain. Alternatively, increasing efficiency would lead to immediate savings [4]. HPC hardware and software are continually improved, such as NVIDIA's announcement of support for Advanced RISC Machines (ARM) CPUs at the Worldwide Supercomputing Conference, enabling energy-efficient exascale machines by year's end. Applications on large computers often use schedulers to optimize the workload of thousands of hundreds of computations. Although these schedulers are tuned to minimize the directly above, application-specific enhancements are still possible owing to user-specified run time estimations that are sometimes biased [5, 6].

Ensemble set-ups, common in molecule and material design computer campaigns, present challenges because of the diverse computing demands of individual instances. To optimize scheduling, consider using the scaling behaviour of methods to order lists by wall time and arrange computations by run time [7].

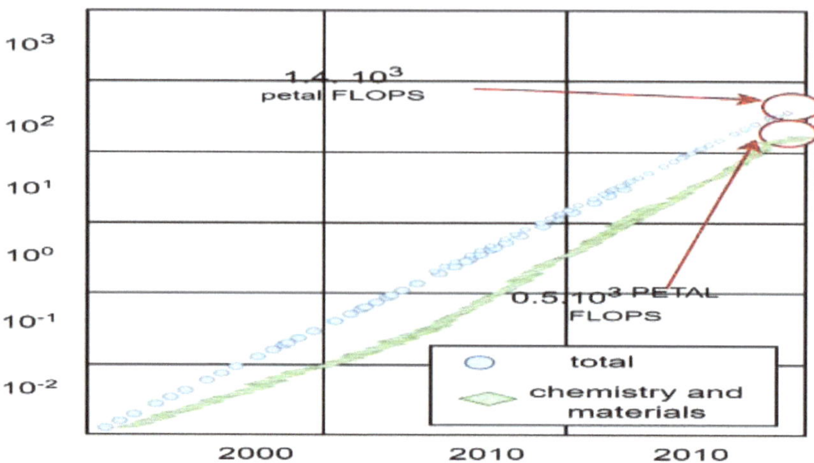

Fig. (1). 400 fastest public supercomputers' resource growth.

One common issue with MCSCF is the need to transfer the matrices of the Coulomb and other operators onto the fresh orbit base during macro-iterations. This technique scales as nm^4 when there are n full orbitals and m base functions. In a situation where n represents the number of associated filled ring roads and m represents the number of fundamental tasks, all CISD schemes based on Davidson's work scale as n^2m^4. As scaling rules and geometry optimizations vary based on the beginning geometry, a more advanced methodology was used. This paper shows how to schedule quantum-based ensemble computer campaigns more efficiently by using QML to improve run-time predictions [8].

Computer science research has focused on optimizing standard algorithms for HPC platforms, as well as predicting memory consumption and computational cost. These prediction algorithms may directly minimize the anticipated environmental effect of computation as the goal amount. ML has improved scheduling and processor work routines. Quantum chemistry applications may benefit from running time optimization of contraction tensor arrangements using predictive modeling approaches on particular hardware. In 2022, running time optimization of a Self-Consistent Field (SCF) method on several computer designs was achieved by a simple linear method based on dead instructions and cache misses. Other notable computational chemistry work includes predicting the run time of molecular dynamics codes and the success of DFT optimizations for categorizing transition metal species.

There are several QML models for quantum chemistry applications in the chemical space nowadays. Gaussian Process Regression (GPR), Kernel Ridge

Regression (KRR), and Artificial Neural Networks (ANN) are common approaches used in machine learning. Unlike pure computer science, researchers employ the same chemical representation in the QML models to estimate the running time of new molecules and simulate quantum characteristics. They consider computational price a molecular property based on quasi, which may be deduced for novel, out-of-trial particles, similar to additional quantum characteristics like atomization energy and dipole moment. Typically, quantum chemistry SCF calculations optimize molecular wave function parameters, resulting in the least in the self-consistent nonlinear equation structure. Consider a smooth computing cost for single-point quantum chemistry calculations over the chemical space. Chemical systems may be able to avoid pathological SCF convergent failures if the quantum chemistry method is used correctly for single-point calculations. Problems with progress control in Geometry Optimization (GO) and Transition State (TS) searches arise due to the potential energy surface's many points of saddle and local minimums, which are determined by the degree of independence of an atom coordinate in the molecule.

Researchers examined the efficiency of ML methods in determining the number of distinct stages in typical optimizers for minimal search for nonlinear 2D functions, which may create convergence issues for many traditional optimizers. The second phase included testing QML's ability to determine computing costs for various quantum chemistry jobs, such as SP, GO, and TS computations. They used FLOPS as a 'clean' assessment to demonstrate hardware independence of quantum chemistry computation costs.

METHODOLOGY

Quantum ML

Initially, established supervised kernel-based machine learning algorithms were applied in this work. Ridge regression involves mapping input into a characteristic space and fitting it accordingly. The optimal feature space is uncertain and computationally difficult to develop. Using the 'kernel trick', inner products of an implicit high-dimensional feature space can be found by putting on a kernel k to an exemplification space R. The Gram matrix elements $k(x_i, x_j)$ of two representations x ϵ R between two input molecules i and j are the inner products (i, j) in the feature space. For example, a typical kernel option is the Laplacian or Gaussian kernel (equation 2), where σ is the length scale hyperparameter. To exclude I/O-related runs, tasks

$$QM9^{SP}_{TZ/CC}, QM9^{SP}_{DZ/CC}, QMspin^{GO}_{CASSCF}, QMspin^{SP}_{MRCI}, QM9^{GO}_{MRCIB3LYP},$$

were removed with time for wall overheads over 4%, 6%, 11%, 31%, and 51%. Timings were averaged from the test set to create curves of learning for all seven activities, all of which had comparable MAE. Out-of-sample wall time forecasts informed the scheduling method. QML model predictions of negative wall timings were substituted with the average of all non-negative projections. QMLcode performed all QML computations. Wall timings, CPU times, and QML scripts for all seven jobs are included in the SI.

Application: Best Possible Setting Up

Work Steps as well as Array

Computational chemistry and materials design often involve evaluating similar tasks on multiple molecules or materials. Task distribution on a computer cluster comes in two forms. When employing task arrays, the scheduler queues each computation individually by assigning computer resources to it. This method leads to increased wall time and no overhead for tasks, but introduces inefficiencies for schedulers, as each job's wall time estimate must be near the extreme period. In the next technique, a scheduler receives fewer jobs, and tasks are done simultaneously as job stages. The principal method has slight work overhead but may be inefficient. The second option is inefficient since load balancing is not implemented. These two approaches often use conservative run time estimates and do not need knowledge of individual job run times.

Simulated Scheduling

Scheduling leftover computations becomes a bin-packing challenge when using QML-based projected absolute times. To solve this challenge, we employed the First Fit Decreasing (FFD) method, which sorts run-time estimations in decreasing order as well as selects the longest task that fits inside the residual computer work period. No work is selected, and resources are released early if there is no predicted gap-filling task. A simulator was created for all three work schedulers: conventional steps, traditional arrays, and our innovative QML-based scheduler, assuming idempotent uninterruptible jobs. Utilizing a simulator is advantageous since task arrays and job step durations rely on random order, necessitating repeated runs for averaging. The simulator was tested in two environments: the university cluster sciCORE, allowing single-core task submissions, as well as the Swiss national supercomputer, limiting allocation to complete 13-core nodes. They assumed a 32-second scheduler start and a 1-hour task queue in all scenarios.

DISCUSSION WITH RESULTS

Toy System

For every optimizer and function, we randomly selected 3,300 users, and we computed the projected error for various training sets with N variables. Rosen and Him's learning curves for their functions are shown in (Fig. **2**). Every function and optimizer demonstrated a well-behaved learning curve. When data is less volatile, ML models like Him-BFGS and Him-N-CG tend to yield a smaller offset. Shorter runs cause more mistakes because the function space has more non-smooth regions, which in turn causes the Rosen-Newton-CG offset.

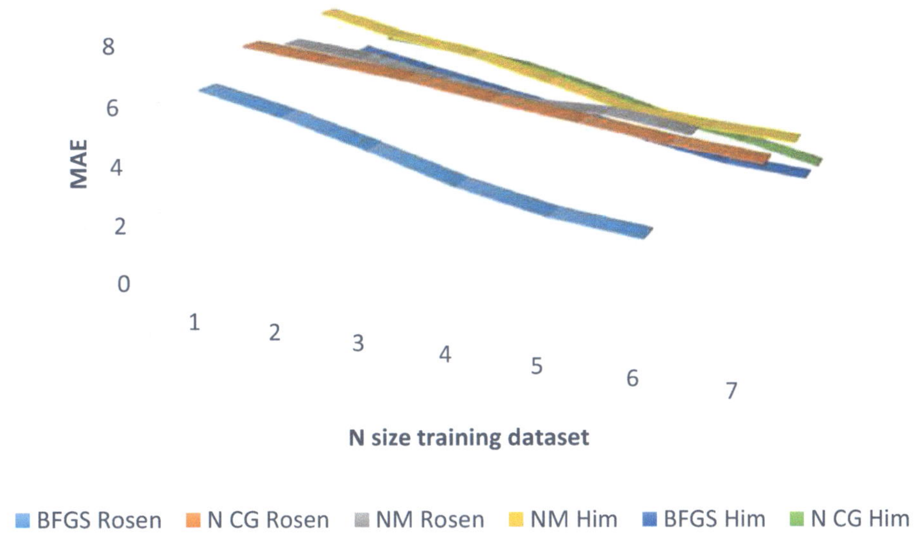

Fig. (2). Learning curves for him and rosen functions.

Machine Learning Quantum

Individual-Point Wall Timings

The article discusses knowledge wall times for several quantum chemistry jobs, as well as CPU time learning, with findings shown in the SI. The identical tasks QM9TZ/CCSP and QM9DZ/CCSP showed that learning a smaller base set was simpler, resulting in a smaller training set needed to achieve comparable prediction accuracy. Using the FCHL representation improves the learning curve offset compared to BoB, similar to physical observables. Although multi-reference calculation times are challenging to learn, BoB initially has a bigger offset than FCHL, but as training set sizes increase, their learning curves converge.

4.2.2. Go Wall Timings or Geometry Optimization

The learning GO timings are more challenging than SP timings due to the larger offset in the learning curves. Expect this since GO durations incorporate both SP computations and geometry optimization stages. The QML model must learn from the accuracy of early estimations to improve future GO results. These functions are not anticipated to be smooth in chemical space. When the original geometry is near a saddle point, even little adjustments may cause significant changes in the mapping to the target geometry, leading to various stationary spots on the possible surface of energy. A wider variation in the time required to optimize geometry is caused by the statistical learning problem, which is not as well-conditioned as single-point calculations. In contrast to SP timings, GO timings are far more difficult to master. Note that each job (including toy system applications) requires a unique QML model. Initial geometry and convergence conditions determine the GO cost. It fluctuates significantly within a data collection. The molecular structure is represented by the former, which the simulation captures. Task QMrxnMp2GO input structures are comparable because of their shared chemical skeleton. This also applies to tasks QMspinCASSCFGO andQM9B3LYPGO, which are produced from QM9 molecules. While convergence criteria remain consistent across computations within a dataset, training a computer on many datasets would make learning more challenging. The toy system demonstrated the ability to acquire the number of stages for various optimizers on various surface areas. To enhance task QMspinCASSCFGO performance, they divided the execution into GO1 and the following phases (GO2). This selection was based on the fact that the initial GO step had the largest volatility, whereas succeeding stages had far less variance. Fig. (**3**) illustrates how separating the learning curves led to a better QML model with errors below 30% at N = 850, and improved work scheduling optimization (Figs. **4a** and **4b**). It demonstrates geometry optimizations using the basic method against the QML method in terms of CPU overhead and wall time.

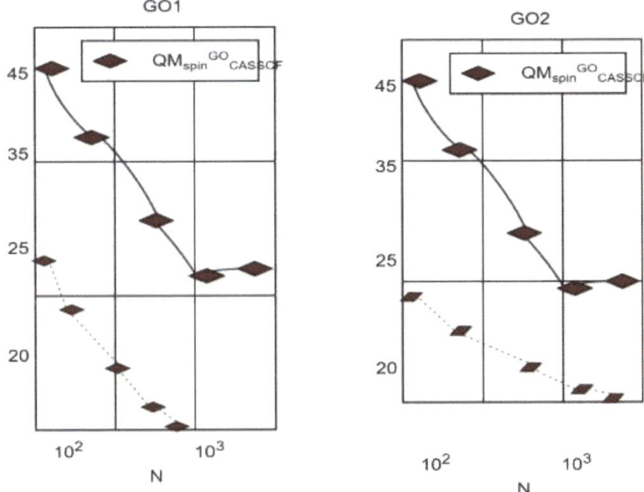

Fig. (3). Separating learning curves led to a better QML.

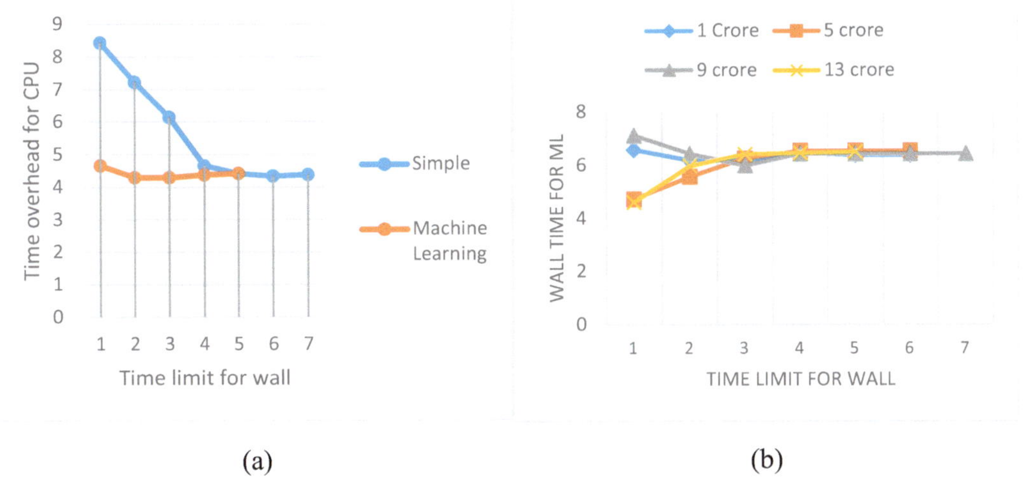

Fig. (4). Geometry optimizations using the basic method.

4.2.3. Wall Periods during Transition State

Geometry optimization times were somewhat more difficult to obtain than transition state search durations. They achieved MAEs of 33.8% and 28.1% for BoB/FCHL with larger training sets, reducing the offset by 15% relative to the GO use case learning curves. As previously mentioned, GO and TS times vary with electron count and starting structure. The scaffold was functionalized with several functional groups for transition state search. The learning curves have a lower offset than in the use case GO where original geometries were created using a semi-empirical method (PM6) for task subscripttakQMrxnMp2GO, carbenes were calculated from molecules in QM9 for task QMspinCASSCFGO, and a different basis set was used for the taskQM9B3LYPGO.

4.2.4. Single-Point FLOPs

Figs. (**5a** and (5b) show that the models applied to FLOP counts for the challenge QM9DZ/CCSP give numerical confirmation that learning wall timings are justified. FLOP count, a clean measure of cost computation, was simpler to acquire than times of the wall, with similar curves for learning. For example, the QM9DZ/CCSP model achieved ~5% MAE with 400 training samples, while wall times with BoB required ~1100 samples. The performance of FCHL is comparable, but the FLOP model has a steeper slope, indicating quicker acquisition or less noise.

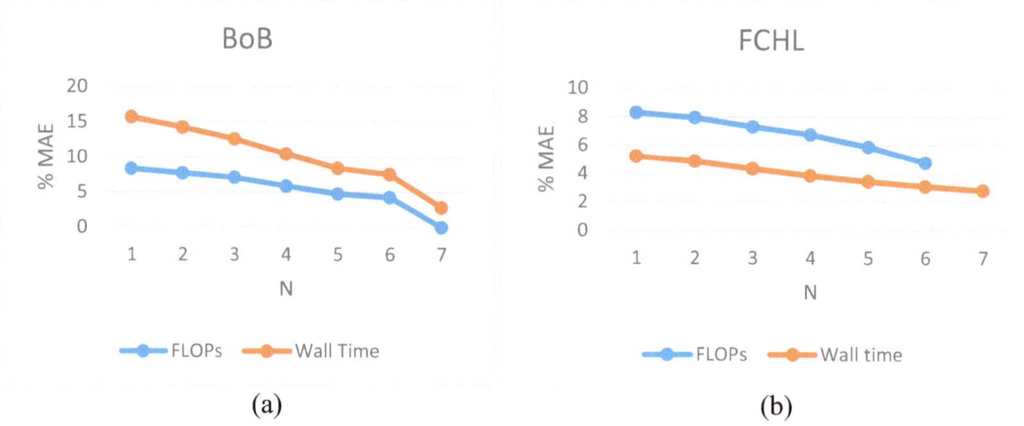

Fig. (5). BoB and FCHL models applied to FLOP counts for the challenge.

CONCLUSION

A study found that QML models can estimate the computational challenge of quantum chemistry computations throughout chemical space. They began with a 2D nonlinear toy system with challenging-to-optimize functions. With these test functions and three optimization techniques, they created the first ML method. The curve learning indicates that the number of optimized steps can be determined from the starting location. Representations focus on efficiently covering all essential dimensions in the chemical space. If QML models can learn the computational cost, it shows a smooth function over many chemical spaces. This method accurately estimates timeframes for various quantum chemistry computations, including individual-point computations, transition state searches, and geometry optimizations, across various basis sets and levels of theory. The quantum chemistry approach and the computational cost learnt influence ML performance. Prediction accuracy varies by computing approach but commonly ranges from 5% to 35% for total run time. Using QML out-of-sample predictions, they improved computer cluster efficiency by rearranging workloads instead of assuming that all computations fit within a single time frame. They lowered the CPU overhead by 15%-85%, depending on the job, without major changes in time-to-solution. This method optimizes computer resource consumption for large-scale chemical space missions. In this scenario, the community may get important code, data, and an easy-to-use interface online. The findings of this study are significant because standard QML models for physical observables may not apply to implicit variables, such as computing cost.

REFERENCES

[1] P.O. Dral, O.A. von Lilienfeld, and W. Thiel, "Machine learning of parameters for accurate semiempirical quantum chemical calculations", *J. Chem. Theory Comput.,* vol. 11, no. 5, pp. 2120-2125, 2015. [http://dx.doi.org/10.1021/acs.jctc.5b00141] [PMID: 26146493]

[2] Luis Cesar de AzevedoGabriel A. PinheiroMarcos G. QuilesJuarez L. F. Da SilvaRonaldo C. Prati, "Systematic Investigation of Error Distribution in Machine Learning Algorithms Applied to the Quantum-Chemistry QM9 Data Set Using the Bias and Variance Decomposition," vol. 61, no. 9, 2021.

[3] M. Sajjan, Quantum Machine Learning for Chemistry and Physics. Cambridge, U.K.: Cambridge University Press, 2022.

[4] R. Ramakrishnan and O. A. von Lilienfeld, "Machine learning, quantum chemistry, and chemical space," Reviews in Computational Chemistry, vol. 30, A. L. Parrill and K. B. Lipkowitz, Eds. Hoboken, NJ, USA: Wiley, pp. 225–256, 2017. [http://dx.doi.org/10.1002/9781119356059.ch5]

[5] P. O. Dral, "Quantum chemistry in the age of machine learning," *The Journal of Physical Chemistry Letters*, vol. 11, no. 6, pp. 2336–2347, 2020. [http://dx.doi.org/10.1021/acs.jpclett.9b03664]

[6] D. Goel *et al*., "An Efficient Approach to Predict the Quality of Apple Through Its Appearance," *Proceedings of the 3rd IEEE International Conference on Computing, Communication, and Intelligent Systems (ICCCIS)*, 2022.

[7] P. Patro, *A hybrid approach estimates the real-time health state of a bearing by accelerated degradation tests, Machine learning,* 2021.https://ieeexplore.ieee.org/abstract/document/9708591/ [http://dx.doi.org/10.1109/ICSTCEE54422.2021.9708591]

[8] H. Yadav *et al*., "Brain Tumor Detection with MRI Images," *2022 International Conference on Computational Intelligence and Sustainable Engineering Solutions (CISES)*, 2022. [http://dx.doi.org/10.1109/CISES54857.2022.9844387]

CHAPTER 20

Indian Banks Utilize Artificial Intelligence for Financial Management

Thiruma Valavan A[1,*], **C Barna A Naidu**[2], **Shabnam Siddiqui**[3], **Bilal Asghar**[4], **N Kirubasankar**[5] and **Ajit Prasad Mahato**[6]

[1] *Training Department, Indian Institute of Banking & Finance, Mumbai 400005, Maharashtra, India*

[2] *School of Business & Management, Christ University, Pune 412112, Maharashtra, India*

[3] *Department of Commerce and Management, Faculty of Management Studies (FMS-WISDOM), Banasthali Vidyapith, Tonk 304022, Rajasthan, India*

[4] *School of Business, Al Fayha College, Al Jubail 31961, Saudi Arabia, AL Jubail Kingdom of Saudi Arabia*

[5] *Department of Business Studies, Sri Manakula Vingayagar Engineering College, Madagadipet 605107, Puducherry, India*

[6] *Department of commerce, NERIM Commerce College, Guwahati 781022, Assam, India*

Abstract: Indian banks have used AI technology in recent years. Banks are rapidly using AI to improve customer experience by exploiting their massive datasets. Farming, AI in banking focuses on client service and interaction, such as balance inquiries, micro statements, money transfers, etc.AI can leverage the massive quantity of organized and unstructured data to eliminate inefficiencies in the banking industry. It enhances customer experience, reduces operating costs and risks, detects fraud, streamlines lending facilities, and resolves customer issues promptly. The research examined AI's effects. With a structured questionnaire, the researcher collected a substantial amount of primary data from 50 respondents and analyzed it using Logistic Regression Analysis, F-test, and Descriptive Analysis. Through this investigation, the investigator will determine the influence over time.

Keywords: AI, Detects fraud, F-test, Indian bank, Logistic regression analysis.

INTRODUCTION

Banking is crucial to technological innovation in India. Banking operations are more cost-effective, productive, and efficient thanks to technology [1]. It has

* **Corresponding author Thiruma Valavan A:** Training Department, Indian Institute of Banking & Finance, Mumbai 400005, Maharashtra, India; E-mail: thirumavalavan63744@gmail.com

D. Arul Pon Daniel, T. Rajasanthosh Kumar & Satya Prakash Yadav (Eds.)

facilitated small-value transactions, offers many options, and helps develop new markets. Customer-centric and technologically compliant banks have emerged in recent years. Technological disruptions have impacted banking, insurance, financial services, automotive, legal services, education, and healthcare analytics center [2]. To make things easier for clients, these industries adopt new trends periodically. Most developments nowadays improve the user experience. Traditional banking in India faced several issues, including lengthy wait times, a lack of security, poor client retention, and excessive bank charges, a few decades ago [3]. The banking sector has automated and modernized to enhance the customer experience through the adoption of core banking solutions, no-frills accounts, mobile banking, demat accounts, net banking, automated teller machines, electronic banking services, electronic Know-Your-Customer (e-KYC) initiatives, and other similar advancements [4]. Banking has incorporated AI, chatbots, and RPA since 2020. Several Indian and international banks have utilized robots to improve worker efficiency and service delivery. SIA, an AI-enabled digital assistant, was initially launched in India by the State Bank of India to support clients with banking chores and inquiries [5]. HDFC launched "Eva," an Electronic Virtual Assistant. Eva instantly delivers details regarding the bank's goods and services and addresses clients' questions to improve service. Moreover, ICICI Bank utilized software-assisted robotics in its business operations across various departments [6]. Bank of America developed two AI technologies, including "Erica" for smart customer solutions. "CashPro" predicts customers' cash situations using AI and ML [7]. Many financial institutions utilize AI-based solutions to streamline middle-end, front-end, and back-end processes, thereby enhancing functionality. JPMorgan Chase implemented COIN to streamline the management of complex contracts and staff IT access requests, resulting in over 360,000 man-hours saved. The bank can now do a lot more, including investigating and suggesting unrealized investment possibilities, managing large amounts of work, reducing operating expenses and error rates, and monitoring vulnerabilities [8 - 10].

RESEARCH GAP

Few studies have examined the impact of AI on primary data in Indian banking. This research examines the effect and consumer satisfaction of AI in Indian banking before and after adoption.

Goals of Research

- To assess the effect of AI on Indian banks.
- Analyze client satisfaction before and after AI installation.

HYPOTHESIS

The following Table **1** displays the hypothesis of the study:

Table 1. Hypothesis.

H10	AI does not affect Indian banking.
H1a	Indian banking is affected by AI.
H20	No change in customer satisfaction before and after AI installation.
H2a	Customer satisfaction changes before and after the deployment of AI.

PROBLEM STATEMENT

The use of IT in banking promises improved customer service and a competitive edge over competitors. It enhances proactive measures, including security, statements, and networking, for banks. This is to maintain customer contact. As consumers grow more tech-savvy and demanding, they have higher expectations than in previous years. It has both beneficial and harmful effects. This research explores the influence of technology advancements and AI adoption on the banking industry.

METHODOLOGY

The researchers utilized primary and secondary data. The researchers collected primary data from 50 clients through a structured survey and secondary data from websites, journals, and published papers. This research collected data *via* snowball sampling. Researchers analyzed and interpreted data using factor analysis, regression analysis, and the F-test.

ANALYSIS AND DISCUSSION

The 20 variables were dimensionally reduced to examine the influence of AI on Indian banking. We conducted an exploratory factor analysis for AI variables. The influence of Artificial Intelligence on the Indian banking industry, as measured by KMO, yielded the value of .860, suggesting a sufficient sample size. Bartlett's Test of Sphericity ($p < 0.000$) indicates that the variables are significant. The number of elements evaluated via factor analysis revealed three converging factors. Together, they explained 78.324% of the effect of AI on Indian banking (Tables **2** and **3**).

Table 2. Displaying KMO/Bartlett's Test.

Bartlett's Test /KMO		
Kaiser-Meyer-Olkin Sample Valuation.		.860
Bartlett's Sphericity Assessment	Approx. Chi-Square	1076.475
	DF	172
	Sig.	.001

Table 3. A regression analysis of the impression level on indian banking.

The independent variable	Artificial Intelligence and Indian Banking
The Self-determining Adjustable	Efficacy, scalability, low-cost, high-performance computation, secure storage, administration, and sustainability
The Walden tests	52.26%
The Hit relation	78.08
The R2 Value	65.36
The Substantial value	.02

Factors explaining different dimensions or components are shown in the rotating component matrix. A careful investigation of the items is conducted to comprehend the dimensions mentioned in the factor analysis (Table **4**). According to Wald's test, all variables in the Table appear to be significant. The hit ratio of 78.08 indicates model validity. A hit ratio of 78.08% (above 75%) indicates a very satisfactory average prediction accuracy. In addition, the model has a high R value (0.653 > 0.6) and a significant p-value of 0.02. Academics reject the null hypothesis and adopt the substitute hypothesis.

Table 4. Rejecting the null hypothesis and accepting the substitute hypothesis.

H0	AI does not affect Indian banking.	Rejected
Ha	Indian banking is affected by AI.	Accepted

F-TEST

The researcher employed an F-test to examine variations in Indian banking customer satisfaction. The table displays the normal market value of real estate in different Chennai locations. The researcher employed an F-test to analyze consumer satisfaction in the Indian banking industry before and after the installation of AI. F value = 1.376506752≤ F Critical one-tail charge 6.388232910. The investigator accepts the alternative hypothesis and rejects the null hypothesis (Table **5**).

Table 5. Presentation F test two sample adjustments.

Two-Sample F-Test for Adjustments		
	Adjustable	Adjustable 2
Callous	9741.2	8663.4
Modification	7668999.8	5643996.9
Explanations	11	11
df	9	9
F	1.376506752	
P(F<=f) one-tail	0.382172638	
F Serious one-tail	6.388232910	

RESEARCH RESULTS

Regression Analysis identifies AI's influence on Indian banking as the dependent adjustable, while effectiveness, scalability, high-level computation, low-cost, secure storage, and sustainability are the independent variables. In addition, the model's R-squared value is high (0.653 > 0.6) and significant at p = 0.02. They reject the null hypothesis and accept the alternative hypothesis: AI has an impact on Indian banking, as evidenced by the variance analysis from the F-test. F Critical one-tail value is 6.388232910, whereas the F value is 1.376506752. After rejecting the null hypothesis, the researcher adopts the alternative. Before and after the adoption of AI, consumer happiness differs (Table **6**).

Table 6. AI adoption affects customer happiness.

No change in customer satisfaction before and after AI installation.	Disallowed
Customer satisfaction changes before and after the deployment of AI.	Acknowledged

CONCLUSION

Research strongly recommends AI-based technology. AI-based technology solutions should be adopted by all Indian banks to deliver personalized services and products to consumers and facilitate transaction monitoring. If a typical person can complete a mental work with less than one additional thought, we can systematize it using AI either now or soon,' claims HBR. However, startups are renowned for taking risks and continuously improving their AI systems. Due to their data aggregation capabilities, newer challenger banks can utilize technology and data to offer customers a superior banking experience and increase market share.

REFERENCES

[1] S. Pahari, A. Polisetty, S. Sharma, R. Jha, and D. Chakraborty, "Adoption of AI in the Banking Industry : A Case Study on Indian Banks", *Indian Journal of Marketing,* vol. 53, no. 3, pp. 26-41, 2023.
[http://dx.doi.org/10.17010/ijom/2023/v53/i3/172654]

[2] Munish Sabharwal, "The use of Artificial Intelligence (AI) based technological applications by Indian Banks." International Journal of Artificial Intelligence and Agent Technology, *Vol 2, issue 1, Feb*, 2014.

[3] N. Pathak and T. Singh, "Emerging role of artificial intelligence in Indian banking sector," *Journal of Critical Reviews*, vol. 7, no. 16, pp. 1370–1373, Jun. 2020.

[4] A. B. Malali and S. Gopalakrishnan, "Application of artificial intelligence and its powered technologies in the Indian banking and financial industry: An Overview," *IOSR Journal of Humanities and Social Science (IOSR-JHSS)*, vol. 25, no. 4, pp. 55–60, Apr. 2020.
[http://dx.doi.org/10.9790/0837-2504065560]

[5] S. Joseph, "Generative AI in Financial Fraud Detection", *SSRN Electronic Journal* 2024.

[6] P. Kamuangu, "A Review on Financial Fraud Detection using AI and Machine Learning", *Journal of Economics, Finance and Accounting Studies,* vol. 6, no. 1, pp. 67-77, 2024.
[http://dx.doi.org/10.32996/jefas.2024.6.1.7]

[7] C. Liu, Y. Chan, S.H. Alam Kazmi, and H. Fu, "Financial Fraud Detection Model: Based on Random Forest", *Int. J. Econ. Finance,* vol. 7, no. 7, 2015.
[http://dx.doi.org/10.5539/ijef.v7n7p178]

[8] G.V. Bhau, R.G. Deshmukh, T.R. kumar, S. Chowdhury, Y. Sesharao, and Y. Abilmazhinov, "IoT based solar energy monitoring system", *Mater. Today Proc.,* vol. 80, pp. 3697-3701, 2023.
[http://dx.doi.org/10.1016/j.matpr.2021.07.364]

[9] K. P. Saklani and S. Purohit, "Multicore implementation of K-means clustering algorithm," *International Journal of Computer Applications*, vol. 185, no. 32, pp. 1–6, 2023.

[10] S. Goel, D. K. Raut, M. Kumar, and M. Sharma, "How Indian banks are adopting artificial intelligence?," *RBI Bulletin*, Oct. 2024. Available online: https://www.researchgate.net/publication/385328737

CHAPTER 21

Enhancement of a Cloud-Based Decision-Support System for Human Resource File Information

Vikas Roshan[1,*], **Rashi**[2], **Sanjay Sharma**[1], **Vijay Singh Thakur**[3], **Abhishek Jain**[4] and **Arpit Jain**[5]

[1] *Department of Applied Sciences and Humanities, Ajay Kumar Garg Engineering College, Ghaziabad 201009, Uttar Pradesh, India*

[2] *GL Bajaj Institute of Management and Research. PGDM Institute, Greater Noida 201310, Uttar Pradesh, India*

[3] *Department of Computer Science and Engineering, Hindustan College of Science and Technology, Mathura 281122, Uttar Pradesh, India*

[4] *Department of Computer Science and Engineering, Uttaranchal University, Dehradun 248007, Uttarakhand, India*

[5] *Department of Computer Science Engineering, KLEF (Deemed to be University), Guntur 522302, Andhra Pradesh, India*

Abstract: In today's fast-paced, technologically-driven world, managers need a way to collect massive amounts of high-quality data, and data mining is the way to go. A human resource archival information Decision Support System (DSS) is built for management and decision-making using cloud computing's scalability, stability, flexibility, and extensibility. The seven levels that make up this system are as follows: system application, data standards conversion, network support, cloud computing support, data collecting, and decision support layers. It examines the benefits of resource sharing and integration in cloud computing. The working mode is also discussed. The solution addresses shortcomings of conventional archive administration, including limited data resources, difficulty in achieving isomorphism, and insufficient standardization of processing data from diverse sources.

Keywords: Decision support, DSS, Network support, System application, System layer.

INTRODUCTION

Human and intellectual resources are vital to firms as science and technology improve, and their value indicates competitiveness. During the early stages of

* **Corresponding author Vikas Roshan:** Department of Applied Sciences and Humanities, Ajay Kumar Garg Engineering College, Ghaziabad 201009, Uttar Pradesh, India; E-mail: vikasroshan1@gmail.com

D. Arul Pon Daniel, T. Rajasanthosh Kumar & Satya Prakash Yadav (Eds.)

computer information technology, huge organizations relied on manual calculations, which resulted in mistakes, waste of people, materials, time, and excessive costs [1]. A human resource management information technology system was created to address this issue. Advancements in information technology have led to the unification of human resource organization information system databases and linked data, creating an integrated material source [2] with a particular UI. For enterprise management, human resource information management collects, reports, and analyzes data in an automated and smart manner [3, 4]. HR management practices vary when HRM systems are studied and developed. HR efficiency affects the system. Traditional HR file management has limitations, including restricted resource sharing and an imbalance of information. Limited heterogeneous information sharing hinders meeting diverse human resource supply and demand patterns. Sharing information and resource information is crucial for solving this issue [5].

The authors investigate the design and application of a human resource archive material DSS using "cloud computing." Cloud computing refers to the on-demand purchasing of IT infrastructure resources over the network, allowing for easy expansion [6, 7]. Essentially, cloud computing involves on-demand, readily extendable service delivery and consumption across the network [8]. Software, information technology, the Internet, and other services may fall under this category. Desktop, distributed, centralized, and grid computing are all modeled after it [9, 10]. Cloud computing has more advantages than grid computing.

PLATFORM FOR HUMAN RESOURCE ARCHIVE DECISION SUPPORT CLOUD COMPUTING INFORMATION

Construction of Systems

Human resource management data is heterogeneous, making the development of a unified system challenging. Cloud computing can build an effective, scientific, and uniform management platform. Fig. (**1**) shows a cloud-based HR archive data decision support platform. In Fig. (**1**), the platform comprises 7 levels. The Dialectic data collection layer displays system element connections, causality, and mutual constraints. Archive data mining relies on data collecting as its raw material. To provide sufficient "quality" and "quantity" for future decision support, this layer ultimately imports traditional text data together with current images, audio, and other data in the necessary format. Inputting current graphics, photographs, music, and other data in the required format, together with traditional text data, is the objective of this layer, which will aid in future decision-making. Data transmission *via* network settings, developing hybrid convergence points for information collection, and establishing adaptive

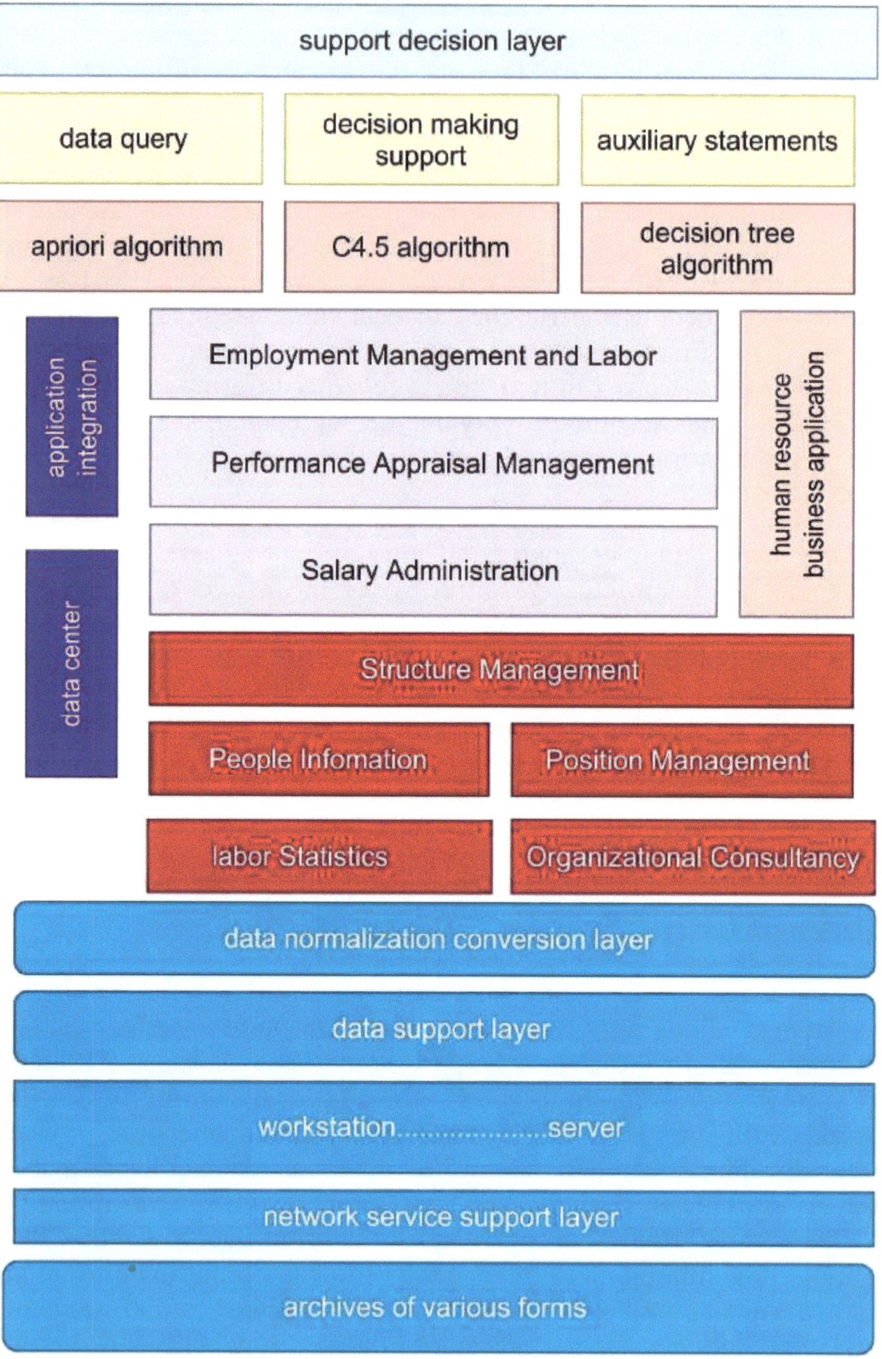

Fig. (1). HR file information DSS architecture.

and self-organizing communication systems are all responsibilities of the network service support layer. Data may be sent from the network service support layer to the raincloud *via* the cloud computing support layer, enabling processing and capital exchange. To guarantee uniform data handling, the data transformation layer standardizes cloud data, unifies access to all components of the integrated data middleware system, and paints a single image of various human resource archives. The system application layer uses B/S and C/S computer technologies to deliver user services, such as maintaining human resource files and permissions. Using B/S and C/S computer technologies, the system service layer provides a variety of services, including file referral and information resource integration. The decision-support layer may integrate data from all nodes and conduct data mining and analysis using "cloud computing" as its basis. Using technology to aid user decision-making, this layer enhances search engine HRM. Medium data for marketing, production, and recruitment is gathered *via* the data-gathering layer. Technical translation into the communication support layer will be performed on these structured and unstructured datasets. For the system to accomplish its purpose of integrating and modifying interdependent components as needed, the data collection layer must provide enough resources, in terms of both quantity and quality. After the data collection layer collects information, the communication support layer transmits it to the cloud. With the help of hardware and software, this layer makes it possible for networks to communicate in a way that is both adaptable and self-organizing. Due to the unpredictable nature of cloud data, achieving high-level "standardization" in data transit requires uniformity throughout this layer. This layer provides middleware that allows access to integrated data across the system. In the system application layer, you'll find systems like human resources, compensation, and recruiting. Functions at the management level are horizontally combined on the information platform. On the platform, management businesses may be grouped according to their functions. This layer provides managers with a variety of information levels, frequencies, and precisions through system services, expert advice, and report prototypes from the next tier. By integrating data from all layers and nodes, the decision support layer enables users to make informed decisions.

Designing DSS

With the use of cloud computing and big data, the DSS platform for HR management facilitates decision-making *via* data mining, processing, and analysis. Decision information resource pools, analytics platforms, and service implementations are all parts of the system that may improve managers' abilities, decision-making accuracy, and efficiency. Inform action on decisions, the resource pool is the whole system's data source and determines the effectiveness of decision support information. Data quality and reaction speed drastically impact the system, including computing, storage, and the complexity of data and resource pools. The computing resource pool, managed by servers, workstations, and PCs, manages the system's computing function. Storage resource pools serve as a unified storage method by connecting and virtualizing many disk arrays, drives, and other devices. Amorphized and mined heterogeneous data from the cloud is part of the data resource pool. The decision analysis platform is comprised of three functional modules: (1) data classification and indexing; (2) data processing, which involves rearranging, organizing, and integrating data after classification; and (3) decision interpretation, which involves providing a unified, combined, and shared standard environment to aid in human resource management decision-making. To sort and categorize the collected data, the decision examination platform employs a human-machine collaborative investigation. To establish assessment objectives and compensation schedules, it employs analytical methods and mathematical models to generate a decision program.

RESULTS

Implementing File Management

After logging in, files may be added, viewed, reviewed, and deleted using the File Management tool located on the left side of the menu bar. Details such as ID, cell phone number, email, department, job title, pay range, and other relevant information are included in employee profiles. The system's ArchiveAdd.jsp page requires the personnel expert to update employee file information for recruits. Pressing the "Submit" button after completing the form triggers the checkForm technique in ArchiveAdd.js. To locate the add Archive() function for data storage, use the human archive action that corresponds to the element. Adding file information is now finished. The payroll and human resources management system is also accessible to users. Use the left-hand menu item "Pay Management" after logging in to see personal pay, set compensation criteria, review salary reports, and study salary reports. On the left side of the page, when users check in, they'll see Recruitment Management. From there, they can add, edit, delete, screen, prepare exams, screen interviews, and review resumes.

Improved Information Calculation Optimization

Additionally, this research improves attribute value traversal. Optimizing the sorting and searching process, as well as identifying the local and segmentation thresholds, reduces the time required for discretizing continuous data. Existing limitations include the necessity for traversal for most characteristics. This study evaluates the use and efficacy of the improved method by comparing four datasets stored in the UCI machine learning repository. Collect statistical data and conduct evaluations of the C4.5 method and its improved version. For a visual representation of the impact of the two algorithms on the three indicators, refer to Fig. (**2**). Using the C4.5 algorithm as its foundation, the traversal attribute process optimization approach may decrease time complexity without sacrificing classification accuracy or decision tree size.

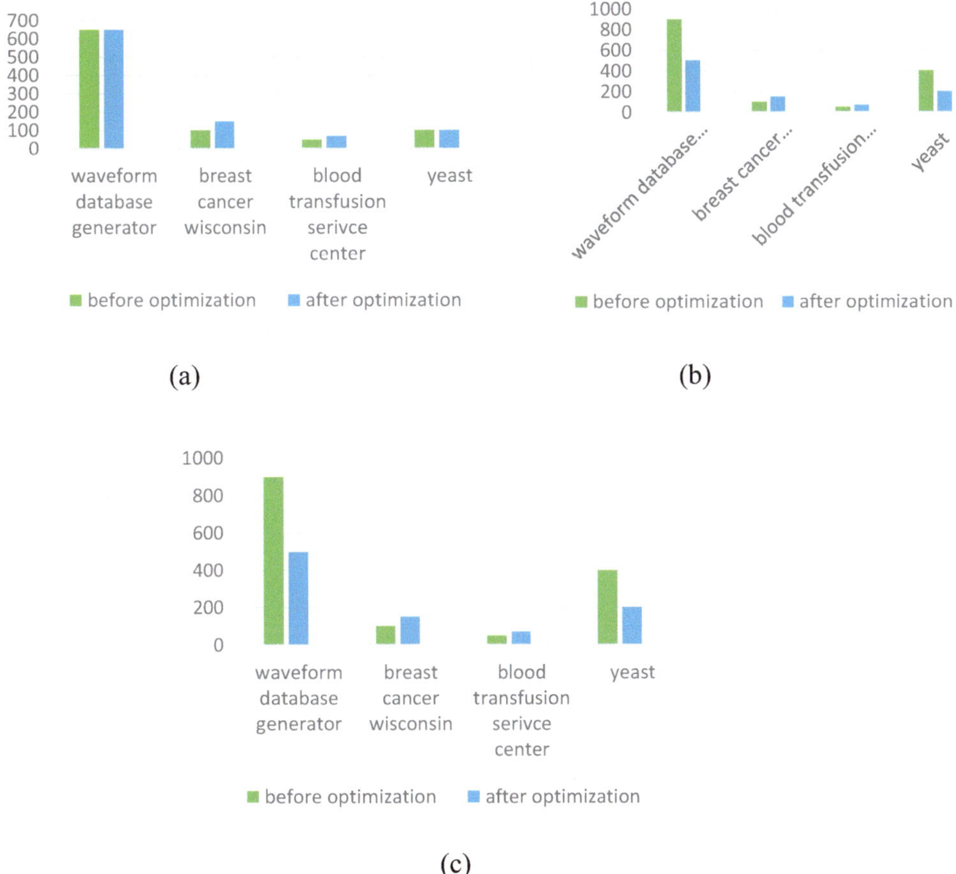

Fig. (2). Decision tree size, calculation time, and organization accuracy: attribute value traversal optimization.

HR Change Analysis System

Due to rapid information technology development, business volume, and type growth, enterprise departments experience rapid growth and personnel turnover, making it challenging for technical departments to manage personnel. Scientific planning of future human resources work is necessary, with supply and demand forecasts guiding present analysis and management planning. This work tries to provide a quantitative basis for analyzing human resource transformation. A transfer probability matrix and statistical technology can predict future changes in human resources, analyse staff inflow and outflow, and guide future development. Using a company as an example, Fig. (**3**) displays staff changes in 2019. The flow and outflow likelihood of each position is expressed as a percentage, using a one-year statistical timeframe. A–G indicate 10 places. Turnover likelihood for all 10 positions from A to G is below 30%, while individual job turnover is below zero. HR may use several management styles to enhance the internal structure of the organization based on the flow of roles among departments. Beginning with the 2019 personnel distribution, the number of workers in each job and overall outflow may be computed using the beginning time data and personnel change matrix. Organizational positions accounted for 4% of new hires, sales for 12%, technical for 65%, and work for 20%, according to previous recruitment procedures. Expectations for demand for each position are 40, 114, 323, and 109. For every position in past years, you may see the total number of entries, transfers, and resignations. The firm may improve its ability to forecast the present and prepare for the future by establishing a dynamic decision support system for the supply and demand of human resources. Improving decision accuracy and assisting corporate HR information management are the goals of the author's study into the dynamic decision-making strategy for human resource supply and request. This technique integrates several approaches.

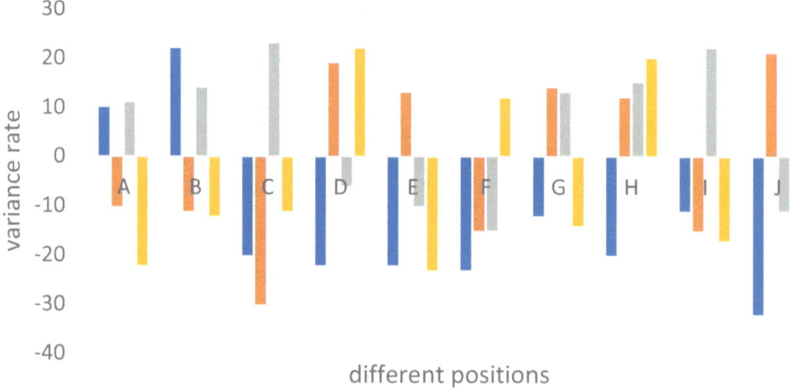

Fig. (3). The ratio of employees entering and leaving employment within an organization.

CONCLUSION

With the rise of big data, it is crucial to prioritize the administration of personnel archives, expedite their digitalization, and fully utilize their functions. Taking advantage of cloud computing's scalability, reliability, flexibility, and expansibility, this project builds a decision-support system for HR archival information. Data collection, system service support, cloud computing, data calibration, system application, system layer, and decision support layers all work toward the same goal: integrating and sharing resources *via* the use of "cloud computing" benefits. The chapter goes into the structures and functions of each layer structure, in addition to describing how DSS works. The system addresses certain shortcomings of conventional archives administration, including limited data resources, difficulty in achieving isomorphism, and insufficient standardization of data processing across numerous sources. One example of interdisciplinary technology in HRM is the "cloud computing" decision-support system for HR data storage. By using this approach, we have been able to overcome the shortcomings of traditional archive management, break down barriers between companies and information sources, and share a great deal of data resources. To facilitate multisource data mining and meet the decision-making needs of managers at various levels, this strategy utilizes "cloud computing" for resource integration, collaborative management, and distributed computing. Accurately predicting future trends in personnel file management can lead to improved matching, performance assessment, and talent team stability, optimizing human resource management. Big data and information technology can aid in this process.

REFERENCES

[1] S. Karthi, and S. Prabu, "A review on challenges of storage and retrieval for spatial applications of GIS and cloud computing", *International Journal of Control Theory and Applications,* vol. 9, no. 26, 2016.

[2] C. Cai, and C. Chen, "Optimization of human resource file information decision support system based on cloud computing", *Complexity,* vol. 2021, no. 1, 2021.8919625 [http://dx.doi.org/10.1155/2021/8919625]

[3] P. Zhang, X. Shi, S. U. Khan, B. Ferreira, B. Portela, T. Oliveira, G. Borges, H. Domingos, J. Leitão, I. P. Mohottige, H. H. Gharakheili, T. Moors, V. Sivaraman, N. Najari, S. Berlemont, G. Lefebvre, S. Duffner, C. Garcia, A. Parmentier and H. Shan, "IEEE draft standard for spectrum characterization and occupancy sensing," *IEEE Access*, vol. 9, no. 2, pp. 1-6, 2019. [http://dx.doi.org/10.1109/ACCESS.2019]

[4] V.B. Sandra, *Jardim, "The Electronic Health Record and its Contribution to Healthcare Information Systems Interoperability.* vol. Vol. 9. Procedia Technology, 2013.

[5] A. Romero-Lopez, "Market research about agriso mobile application for farmers", *Sustainability,* vol. 12, no. 1, 2020.

[6] A. Holm, M. Krause, M. Herkel, P. Schossig, C. Schweigler and N. Henze, "Solares Bauen – klimagerechtes Bauen in anderen Klimaten," *Proc. ForschungsVerbund Erneuerbare Energien (FVEE) Jahrestagung*, Berlin, Germany, 2009.

[7] V. Tramontin, C. Loggia, and M. Basciu, "Passive design and building renovation in the mediterranean area: New sensitive approach for sustainability", *Journal of Civil Engineering and Architecture,* vol. 4, no. 36, 2010.

[8] J.A. Laub, "Assessing the servant organization; Development of the organizational leadership assessment (OLA) model. Dissertation abstracts international", *Procedia Soc. Behav. Sci.,* vol. 1, no. 2, 1999.

[9] P. Patro, R. Azhagumurugan, R. Sathya, K. Kumar, T. R. Kumar and M. V. S. Babu, "A Hybrid Approach Estimates the Real-Time Health State of a Bearing by Accelerated Degradation Tests," Proc. 2021 Second International Conference on Smart Technologies in Computing, Electrical and Electronics (ICSTCEE), Bengaluru, India, pp. 1–9, 2021. [http://dx.doi.org/10.1109/ICSTCEE54422.2021.9708591]

[10] S. Mewada, A. Saroliya, N. Chandramouli, T. Rajasanthosh Kumar, M. Lakshmi, S. Suma Christal Mary and M. Jayakumar, "Smart Diagnostic Expert System for Defect in Forging Process by Using Machine Learning Process," *Journal of Nanomaterials*, vol. 2022. [http://dx.doi.org/10.1155/2022/2567194]

CHAPTER 22

Monitoring and Web-Based Maintenance of Machines on the Shop Floor

B. Lakshmi[1,*], **J Siva Ram Prasad**[2], **K Parish Venkata Kumar**[3], **Suresh Babu Chandolu**[4], **T. Suresh**[3], **U. Sireesha**[3] and **K. Guru Surya Bharat Kumar**[3]

[1] *Department of Computer Applications, Velagapudi RamaKrishna Siddhartha Engineering College, Siddhartha Academy of Higher Education (Deemed to be University), Vijayawada 520007, Andhra Pradesh, India*

[2] *Department of Mathematics, Velagapudi RamaKrishna Siddhartha Engineering College, Siddhartha Academy of Higher Education (Deemed to be University), Vijayawada 520007, Andhra Pradesh, India*

[3] *Department of Computer Applications, Velagapudi RamaKrishna Siddhartha Engineering College, Siddhartha Academy of Higher Education (Deemed to be University), Vijayawada 520007, Andhra Pradesh, India*

[4] *Department of CSE (AI & ML), Dhanekula Institute of Engineering and Technology, Vijayawada 521139, Andhra Pradesh, India*

Abstract: Production management has traditionally focused on maintenance and expenses, as unexpected breakdowns reduce system dependability and asset return. Innovative maintenance methods that gather and handle shop-floor data may save costs and boost business sustainability. A machine monitor framework with condition-based preventative maintenance is presented in this study. To assist condition-based preventative maintenance, the latter analyzes shop-floor machine tool data *via* information fusion. The technique is implemented as a Cloud-based software service. The service determines component life based on machine tool and equipment operating data, such as process time and time spent machining per tool. Additionally, it notifies machine tool users and maintenance departments and allows mobile communication. A machining SME case study is used to demonstrate the application of the framework.

Keywords: Cloud-based software, Information fusion, Production management, Shop-floor data, SME.

* **Corresponding author B. Lakshmi:** Department of Computer Applications, Velagapudi RamaKrishna Siddhartha Engineering College, Siddhartha Academy of Higher Education (Deemed to be University), Vijayawada 520007, Andhra Pradesh, India; E-mail: itslakshmi.h@gmail.com

D. Arul Pon Daniel, T. Rajasanthosh Kumar & Satya Prakash Yadav (Eds.)

INTRODUCTION

The manufacturing lifecycle relies on maintenance, which accounts for 61–71% of its expenditures [1]. Industrial studies show that repairing worn-out components may account for 71% of maintenance costs. Existing maintenance solutions are utilized without addressing the true state of machine tools and equipment, notwithstanding their high cost [2]. Due to interconnected production systems, machine tool failures may cause supply bottlenecks in the company's and customers' value-added operations [3]. Advanced manufacturing systems utilize monitoring to assess equipment status and predict breakdowns. But there is still no connection between monitoring methods and maintenance solutions [4, 5].

Condition-based maintenance may result from real-time monitoring, visualization, and data analysis of machines, tools, and equipment [6]. Additionally, condition-based maintenance schedules maintenance without disrupting machine operations using condition measurements [7, 8]. Sensor readings assist Condition–Based Preventative Maintenance (CBPM). Mobile technologies and communication allow IT tool cooperation [9]. Production systems are increasingly seen as social structures with personnel acting as social machines to analyze data and distribute it between IT tools [10]. This research presents a real-time shop floor monitoring-based system for condition-based preventive maintenance of machines and cutting tools, improving teamwork between the maintenance department and machine tool workers through the use of cloud and mobile technology [11, 12].

CURRENT STATE

Customer pleasure is tied to a manufacturer's product quality. However, the condition of the equipment greatly affects quality. Thus, their upkeep is crucial to maintaining “like new” performance. Industry has not fully adopted modern maintenance methods that boost production system sustainability. Avoiding equipment breakdown is the goal of preventive maintenance. Degradation of equipment defines the requirement for preventative maintenance; hence, a machine learning maintenance planning framework has been developed. Taylor's tool life model is used for tool deterioration. Mean Time Between Failures is another preventative maintenance factor. MTBF is defined as the inverse of component failure rate λ and is considered a reliability criterion. Maintenance-free operating duration is a new reliability criterion.

Research emphasizes the importance of real-time machine tool monitoring in maintenance planning. Multiple monitoring methods have been used to assess tool wear and machine availability. Vibration, sound, and temperature sensors are utilized for monitoring. Installing current transducers as sensors is easy and provides accurate machine status information. Information fusion algorithms have been employed to provide meaningful system information as diverse data sources proliferate. Sensor, feature, and decision-level information fusion methods exist. The Dempster-Shafer theory of data (DS) dominates decision-level fusion.

Web technologies improve data processing and automate maintenance in production. E-maintenance has been prevalent in maintenance research since the early 2000s. Product-service monitoring that sends email reminders for preventative remote maintenance. An improved framework uses the open and royalty-free industrial procedure for communication, MTConnect, to communicate with the machine controller. E-maintenance, which combines web-based services and agent technologies, may also provide intelligent industrial system features. Manufacturing requires collective intellect and dynamic adaptation. The e-maintenance strategy introduced by Cloud technology in manufacturing will enable data sharing across IT tools and provide universal access to information for different users and IT tools. Cloud technology enhances manufacturing by scaling to meet corporate size and demands, and providing ubiquitous network connectivity, according to another study.

Advanced maintenance systems have near-real-time monitoring capabilities, but the information is not completely used for predictive maintenance operations, according to the literature assessment. The advantages of Cloud and mobile monitoring and maintenance have not been fully realized. This research proposes a CBPM architecture using real-time monitoring service data. The monitoring service uses Dempster-Shafer evidence fusion to calculate the machine tool and equipment's total working hours. Mobile communication channels keep machine tool operators and maintenance specialists informed. With Infrastructure-as-a-Service (IaaS), the system is built on the Cloud.

PROPOSED FRAMEWORK ARCHITECTURE AND DESIGN

A machine tracking framework using CBPM is proposed in this article (Fig. **1**). This framework uses the multi-sensory systems and operator input to collect machine tool data. The hardware in the sensory system monitors all motor drive currents and spindle head RPMs. Mobile devices enable operators to submit machine tool status, job status, cutting tool availability, and any failures, and to calculate machine tool and cutting tool machining times based on operator and sensory system input. After data gathering, the data is analyzed to estimate the machine tool's rotation and the cutting tool's machining time. Information fusion is used to determine the state of the machine tool and machining time from monitoring data.

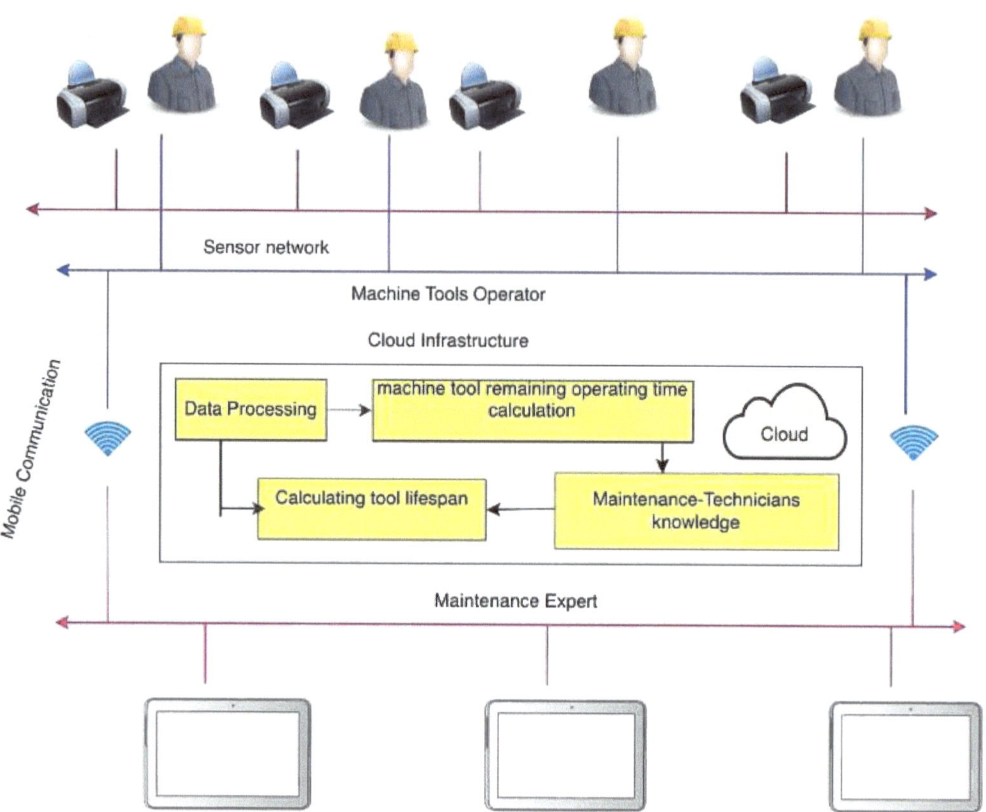

Fig. (1). Structure of the suggested framework.

To determine spindle and axis status, the information fusion approach uses the DS hypothesis as evidence. Second, the machine tool status is identified. According to the source type and environment, weights represent the machine tool's status, depending on the source's capabilities. The fusion of two spindle sensors affects the machining time of cutting tools. High-level fusion also affects machine tool maintenance and machining time. The Cloud framework calculates machine tool and equipment life and remaining life. After obtaining the feed rate, cutting speed, and tool physical and workpiece attributes from the procedure plan and data, the extended Taylor's equation calculates the cutting tool's residual life. Machine tool MTBF depends on specs and the maintenance department's expertise.

The suggested system calculates the time until the next service job using maintenance department data and machine tool specifications. Remaining Operating Time (ROT) is calculated by subtracting actual machining time from machine tool MTBF (Eq.1).

$$ROT = MTBF - AMT \quad (1)$$

The suggested maintenance technique may detect machine tool and cutting tool problems. The maintenance department is aware of the shop-floor condition based on machine tool running time and failure frequency. The maintenance crew can then quickly and efficiently maintain machine tools. The suggested framework also notifies the worker and maintenance department of production failures. Fig. (**2**): The operator and maintenance sections are informed of the total machining time and remaining operational time for the cutting tools. Mobile technology allows operator-maintenance department communication. Tele-maintenance services report minor failures from operators to maintenance professionals. In the event of fresh machine tool failures, the system's database stores all failure occurrences and offers remedies for easy reuse.

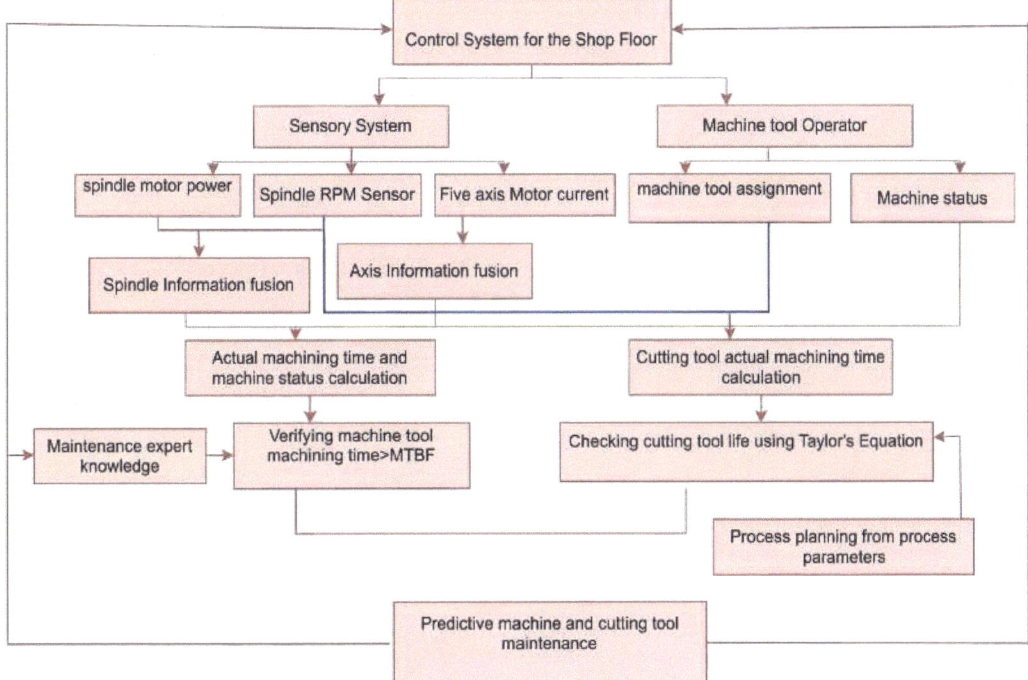

Fig. (2). Framework process details.

CREATING SOFTWARE

Modern manufacturing systems in the cloud utilize a new business model that leverages the Internet of Things and mobile computing to manage data growth. To complete the requested job, a Cloud-based system is created. Web Applications built on Cloud Services implement the framework. This application uses the REST architectural paradigm, based on HTTP. An IaaS virtual machine consecutively hosts Linux, the cloud-based platform, which comprises an Apache Web server, a Ruby on Rails structure, and a MongoDB database. GUIS are also created for data input and result display.

The platform lets machine tool operators and maintenance departments discuss problems. The maintenance department can help the operator immediately *via* mobile communication since it is informed of machine tool failure frequency and kind (Fig. **3**). By improving system efficiency and flexibility, the maintenance department encourages operators to handle minor equipment problems. Security is a major issue with cloud-based monitoring solutions. The shop floor, online application, and cloud-based operating scheme layers make up the monitoring service's security. The most important protective measures against threats are data transfer encryption, client identification using Transport Layer Security/Secure Sockets Layer (TLS/SSL) procedure in conjunction with a protected database authorization system, and Virtual Private Network technology.

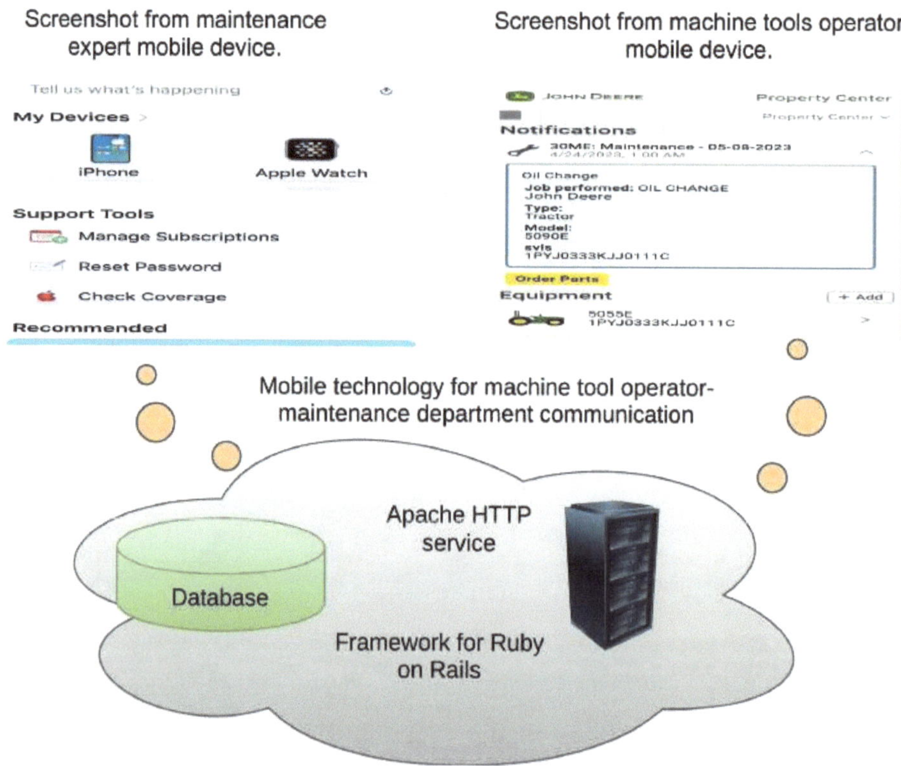

Fig. (3). Framework architecture and screenshots.

RESULTS AND CASE STUDY

The consumer asks for help from the maintenance department *via* the system when the engine tools malfunction. The maintenance staff only learns about machine tool issues after they occur. Production-related machine tool failures are common in most sectors, especially mold-making. Mold-makers verify the suggested monitoring and maintenance approach. Using machine specs and maintenance department information, five milling machines on the shop floor were examined for MTBF and MTTR values, as shown in Fig. (**4**). Due to a sensor board and gateway, these five milling machines' monitoring systems send sensor data to the Cloud. The suggested structure determines the ROT in accordance with Eq. 1 and notifies the maintenance department of the machine tools' present state based on data input after the maintenance section and monitoring system machining time. Machine tool status and remaining working time are sent to the service department *via* the monitoring system. Machine tool operators also get cutting tool machining time. With this information, the maintenance staff may plan work based on equipment wear rather than predetermined intervals.

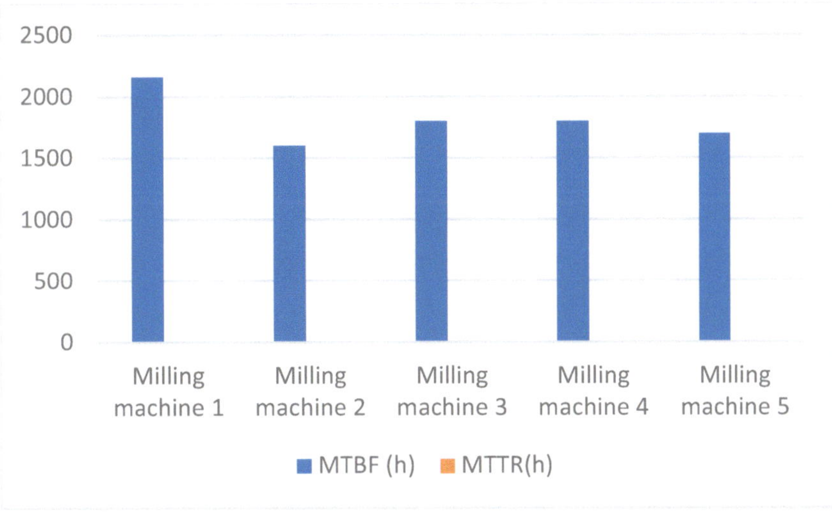

Fig. (4). Real-world machine tool MTBF and MTTR numbers from specs and maintenance.

In section 4, the proposed framework focuses on mobile device communication between machine tool operators and maintenance departments. The machine tools users reported 21 minor issues to the maintenance specialists in one month after being issued mobile devices. The maintenance staff estimated that fixing these issues would take over 11man-hours. Machine tool faults were rectified in 5 man-hours using data from the mobile communication and monitoring system. In case of minimal failures, the mould-making sector received over 51% of maintenance time. This research helps machine tool users and maintenance specialists communicate directly. The monitoring system delivers near-real-time information on machine tools' remaining working time, enabling a maintenance approach that saves time and money for industry.

CONCLUSION

This study presents a monitoring-based machine tool and equipment maintenance method. The maintenance team and operators get real-time machine tool and cutting tool condition data from this technique. Machine tool failures are reported in near real time to the maintenance department, which can respond directly and support operators without being on the shop floor, reducing maintenance time and increasing shop-floor production. This maintenance solution uses sophisticated monitoring techniques to assess machine tool condition and operating time in near real time. The mobile technology-based framework improves department coordination and gives shop-floor workers and maintenance professionals a quick overview of maintenance analysis findings. Subsequent research will validate the suggested system, extending functionality related to cutting tool life. Monitoring system-based shop-floor maintenance planning will enrich this research.

REFERENCES

[1] M.S.A. Wasule, and P.M.S. Panse, "A telemedicine monitor based On labview web services", *Int. J. Eng. Res. Appl.,* vol. 3, no. 1, 2013.

[2] M. Saracostti, X. de Toro, A. Rossi, L. Lara, and M.B. Sotomayor, "Implementation of a web-based system to measure, monitor, and promote school engagement strategies. A Chilean experience", *Front. Psychol.,* vol. 13, 2022.980902
[http://dx.doi.org/10.3389/fpsyg.2022.980902] [PMID: 36204741]

[3] M.B. Smith, A. Albanese-O'Neill, Y. Yao, D.J. Wilkie, M.J. Haller, and G.M. Keenan, "Feasibility of the web-based intervention designed to educate and improve adherence through learning to use continuous glucose monitor (IDEAL CGM) training and follow-up support intervention: Randomized controlled pilot study", *JMIR Diabetes,* vol. 6, no. 1, 2021.e15410
[http://dx.doi.org/10.2196/15410] [PMID: 33560234]

[4] L. Haverman, M.A.J. van Rossum, M. van Veenendaal, J.M. van den Berg, K.M. Dolman, J. Swart, T.W. Kuijpers, and M.A. Grootenhuis, "Effectiveness of a web-based application to monitor health-related quality of life", *Pediatrics,* vol. 131, no. 2, pp. e533-e543, 2013.
[http://dx.doi.org/10.1542/peds.2012-0958] [PMID: 23296436]

[5] G.D. Chen, C.Y. Wang, and K.L. Ou, "Using group communication to monitor web-based group learning", *J. Comput. Assist. Learn.,* vol. 19, no. 4, pp. 401-415, 2003.
[http://dx.doi.org/10.1046/j.0266-4909.2003.00045.x]

[6] H. Mehrens, R. Douglas, M. Gronberg, K. Nealon, J. Zhang, and L. Court, "Statistical process control to monitor use of a web-based autoplanning tool", *J. Appl. Clin. Med. Phys.,* vol. 23, no. 12, 2022.e13803
[http://dx.doi.org/10.1002/acm2.13803] [PMID: 36300872]

[7] S. Doan, Q. Hung-Ngo, A. Kawazoe, and N. Collier, "Global health monitor - A web-based system for detecting and mapping infectious diseases", *Proceedings of the Conference,* 2008

[8] J. Halvorsen, S.K. Ertesvåg, and P. Roland, "Teachers' participation in evaluating a web-based tool to monitor intervention fidelity", *Educ. Res.,* vol. 65, no. 3, pp. 357-374, 2023. [http://dx.doi.org/10.1080/00131881.2023.2223594]

[9] J. Peirce, K. Dundas, R. Hirst, N. Agafonov, and A. Pitiot, "Linearisation of a monitor for web-based experiments", *J. Vis.,* vol. 23, no. 9, p. 5427, 2023. [http://dx.doi.org/10.1167/jov.23.9.5427]

[10] S.M. Slootmaker, M.J.M. Chin A Paw, A.J. Schuit, J.C. Seidell, and W. van Mechelen, "Promoting physical activity using an activity monitor and a tailored web-based advice: design of a randomized controlled trial [ISRCTN93896459]", *BMC Public Health,* vol. 5, no. 1, p. 134, 2005. [http://dx.doi.org/10.1186/1471-2458-5-134] [PMID: 16356182]

[11] G. V. Bhau, R. G Deshmukh, T. R. Kumar, S. Chowdhury, Y. Sesharao, and Y. Abilmazhinov, "IoT based solar energy monitoring system," *Materials Today: Proceedings*, vol. 80, pp. 3697–3701, 2023. [http://dx.doi.org/10.1016/j.matpr.2021.07.364]

[12] S. S. Chauhan, S. P. Yadav, S. Awashthi, and M. S. Naruka, "Sentimental analysis using cloud dictionary and machine learning approach," in Cloud□Based Intelligent Informative Engineering for Society 5.0, K. Kishor, N. Saxena, and D. Pandey, Eds. Boca Raton, FL, USA: Chapman & Hall/CRC, 2023, pp. 157–170. [http://dx.doi.org/10.1201/9781003213895-9]

CHAPTER 23

Implementing the Microservice Framework by Integrating the IoT-Based

Aditya Sai Srinivas[1,*], Vishwa Priya V[2], R. Senthamil Selvan[3], Basi Reddy A.[4] and J. Rameshkumar[5]

[1] *Department of AIML, Jayaprakash Narayan College of Engineering, Mahabubnagar 509001, Telangana, India*

[2] *Department of computer science, Vels Institute of science, technology and advanced studies, Chennai 600117, Tamil Nadu, India*

[3] *Department of Electronics and Communication Engineering, Annamacharya Institute of Technology and Sciences, Tirupati 517520, Andhra Pradesh, India*

[4] *Department of Computer Science and Engineering, School of Computing, Mohan Babu University, Tirupati 517102, Andhra Pradesh, India*

[5] *Department of Electronics and Communication Engineering, K.S.R. College of Engineering, Namakkal 637215, Tamil Nadu, India*

Abstract: Modern Supply Chain Management (SCM) systems use several services to use IoT and cloud technology across delivery, distribution, and manufacturing. This article performs post-processing tasks such as supply chain tracking, item location analysis, and expected delays. It does this by presenting a comprehensive microservice design and implementation that consumes and semantically annotates feeds of information from online systems. The technique is evaluated *via* a set of deployment scenarios, and suitable application code is also inserted using easy workflow-programming-based structures.

Keywords: Cloud, Internet of things, Online systems, SCM, Supply chain.

INTRODUCTION

New possibilities for the real-time tracking, administration, and improvement of supply chains and the distribution of commodities have arisen with the introduction of the IoT [1]. Cloud services, software as a service product management scheme, and other new capabilities allow for the definition of conditioned rules that alert stakeholders when certain events occur, as well as the enforcement of product monitoring of Things through embedded smart devices

* **Corresponding author Aditya Sai Srinivas:** Department of AIML, Jayaprakash Narayan College of Engineering, Mahabubnagar 509001, Telangana, India; E-mail: taditya@jpnce.ac.in

D. Arul Pon Daniel, T. Rajasanthosh Kumar & Satya Prakash Yadav (Eds.)

that can be scanned to provide information like humidity, location, and temperature [2]. For commercial and agricultural use cases, the status of sensitive items may be monitored, and problems with distribution can be addressed using mixtures of technologies such as smart sensing, communications, and central, cloud-based analysis [3]. One of the most important features is data centricity [4]. By using these technologies, businesses may improve their supply chain management strategies and risk assessments by gaining a better understanding of their intricate supply networks. From a more pragmatic standpoint, however, these combinations present significant challenges due to the heterogeneity of the relevant IT systems and the current state of technological capabilities or data merging and effective semantic reasoning [5]. The rivalry among suppliers has intensified thanks to globalization, which should lead to improved supply conditions for businesses. However, the difficulty, adaption requirements, and danger involved with maintaining an international supply chain might make these advantages disappear [6]. One of the most important factors in improving supply chain management is achieving agility *via* integrating processes and information [7]. Other important factors include adapting to the demands and procedures of the manufacturing and incorporating new technology [8].

In Section 2, the AffectUs framework is introduced as a microservice-based system design and implementation that aims to integrate and deploy different essential components of a system for supply chain management, described in Section 3, with ease. External IoT platforms provide baseline information feeds; semantic services, which are decoupled from the end user but enhanced with specialized ontologies, annotate received data; and Artificial Intelligence (AI) devices detect abnormalities in the annotated feeds. Section 4 details the operational metrics, and Section 5 concludes the work.

DESIGN AND MODEL OF THE SYSTEM

Fig. (**1**) shows the system architecture. There are three primary parts to it: the front end, which implements the user interface and the modules for coordination and adaptation; the back end, which implements subsystems like the Semantic service & data storage and the artificial intelligence subsystem; and finally, the Node-RED middleware. RabbitMQ, a messaging layer for non-REST-based interactions, including asynchronous alerts to monitoring users for infractions, data feeds, *etc.*, links all system pieces vertically.

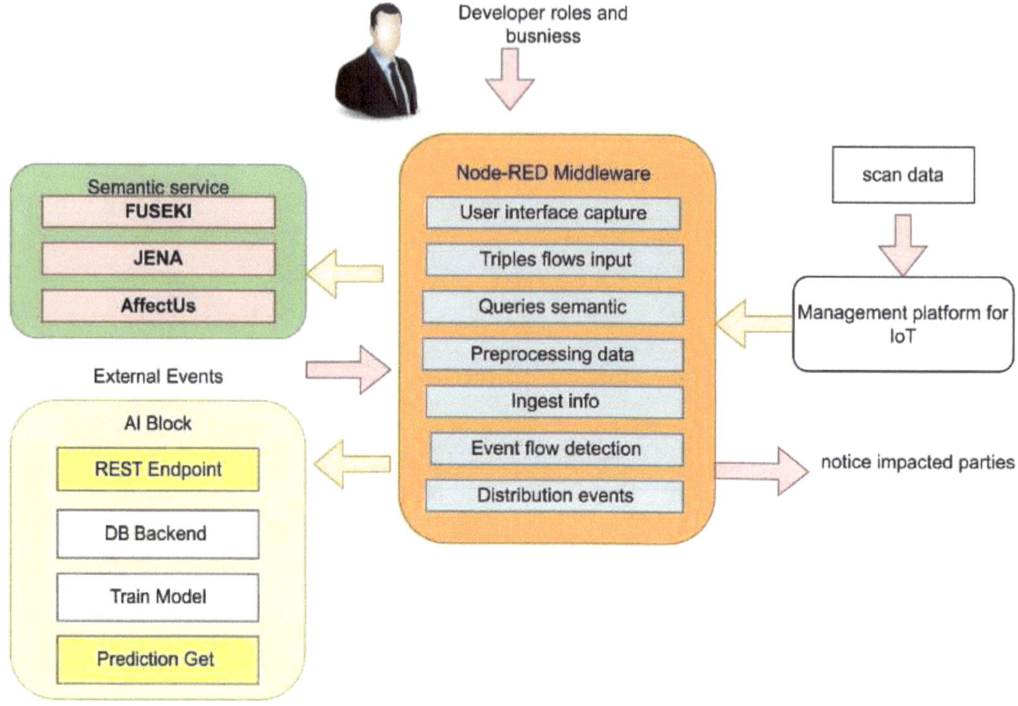

Fig. (1). System blocks and architecture.

Layer for Node-RED

Node-RED allows flow development of adaptability, net services, UIs, and middleware logic. It serves these objectives in AffectUs:

- As a UI application layer with graphic interfaces, actors may specify product consumption, dependencies, and supply chain features like locations and phases. They also provide API keys for connection to other IoT systems.
- As a plugin to current IoT management systems to broadcast product and notification feeds based on smart sensor scan data.
- The middleware and connection layer enable data source adjustments and adaptations, as well as the implementation of application-specific logic, within a user-friendly software design approach. It utilizes the Semantic service to improve supply chain annotations to incoming data streams and transfer them to the data management blocks for AI processing.

Service Block Semantics

Service semantics is the second important component. With the AffectUs ontology, supply chain concepts such as stages, locations, and actor connections are linked. These linkages may relate product data streams to supply chain semantics and detect dependencies from additional parties or items. The AffectUs Ontology structure is explained in the semantic framework's three parts: SPARQL 1.1 queries and integration with Node-RED programmatic rules and custom Jena reasoner rules in the Knowledge Base, which utilizes the OWL domain for implication and reasoning. Since the planning is service-oriented, the KB is an SWS. To transmit knowledge in RDF form, the Apache Jena Fuseki Server delivers RDF data *via* HTTP using SPARQL.

The Neural Network Blocks

An Artificial Intelligence and Data Storage service in the third main block infers stage metrics and detects abnormalities from annotated historical data. It maintains transmitted annotated data feeds on product entrance and exit in chain phases. From the enhanced input data, prediction models for supply chain stage transition times may be derived using previous data. This model must forecast how long an instance or batch should remain in a chain step. Real-time data may then be used to spot deviations from usual behavior and notify concerned parties. External alerts like social media, Large Crowd Concentration events, transportation, and weather data may also be used to improve prediction parameters. Python 3 powers the TensorFlow-based AffectUs AI system.

SYSTEM SETUP

All system components are Docker images, providing for simple administration, updates, and deployment. Docker containers may be deployed individually or as a service. Since it allows one-click deployment after Docker compose file creation, the latter is better. This file defines all services' virtual networks, virtual IPs, ports, start order (if dependencies exist), startup instructions, and installation details, as well as the number of desired instances, *etc*. Service deployment nodes were load-balanced using Docker Swarm, a cluster management solution. Node-RED provides User Interfaces for interfacing to other sites like EVRYTHNG and choosing items. Creating triples for the Ontological KB from these user-friendly declarations is a major feature of the framework. The interface retrieves this data from the user, links to the system to collect product attributes, and creates all the required triples to define the features internally. The end user is fully disconnected from semantic complexity with this method. An example Node-RED flow is shown in Fig. (**2**). A connector sub-flow enables searching and processing of the KB to establish semantic communication between every flow and the Semantic web service for triple presence. No Node-RED node is available to do that. Present SPARQL nodes can perform static SELECT queries. Send a query template and active parameters to make the query dynamic. JSON is used to formulate and evaluate these queries using SPARQL.js. The HTTP query and response are handled.

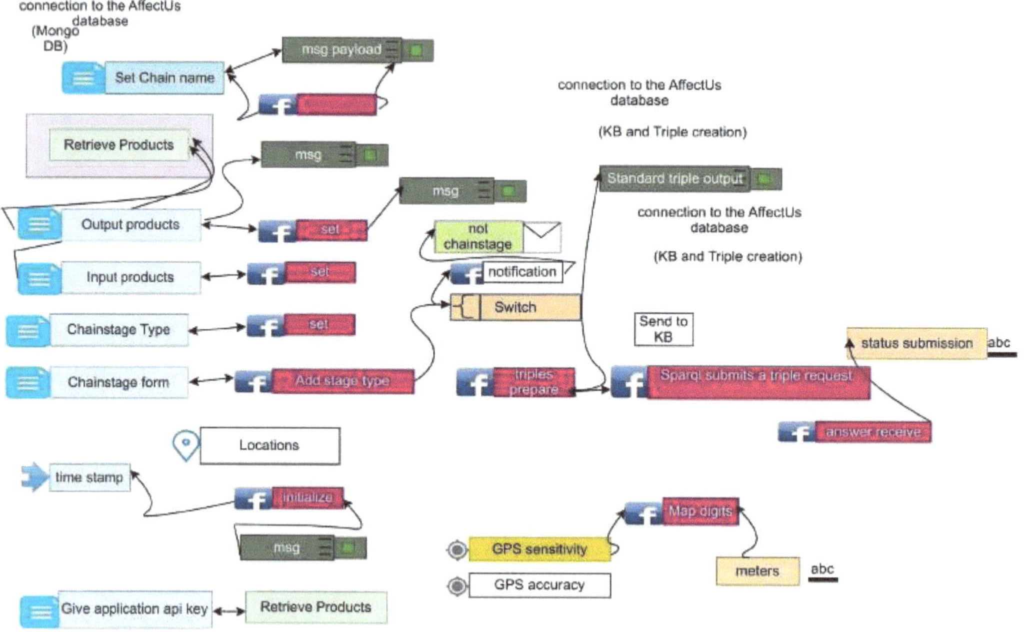

Fig. (2). Program logic to convert entered data to semantic triples in UI Node-RED.

SYSTEM TESTING AND DEPLOYMENT

The Docker compose file must be launched once to deploy the system. Service pieces are deployed and made accessible in Docker Swarm nodes. The Docker service cluster spin-up time must be evaluated first. This relates to service steadiness and/or packaged solution systems management. The container state and uptime statistics document the container's start time, but one must also account for the time required for launching users inside the package and until the endpoints are receptive in order to gauge this period delay. Because of this, Docker's "Health check" functionality is used to directly control how Docker verifies that the container's application is executing.

The launch timestamp and ongoing sampling until all service components are healthy are used to measure the startup process. To get more accurate findings, the procedure is done 100 times. Since RabbitMQ was always the last to start and the distribution is not overlapping with any other scenario, the entire spin-up duration of 42 seconds is reliant on it. Fig. (**3**)'s higher and narrower PDFs show that Python, MongoDB, and Jena containers are the most stable. At 19 and 22 seconds, Node-RED has two concentrations.

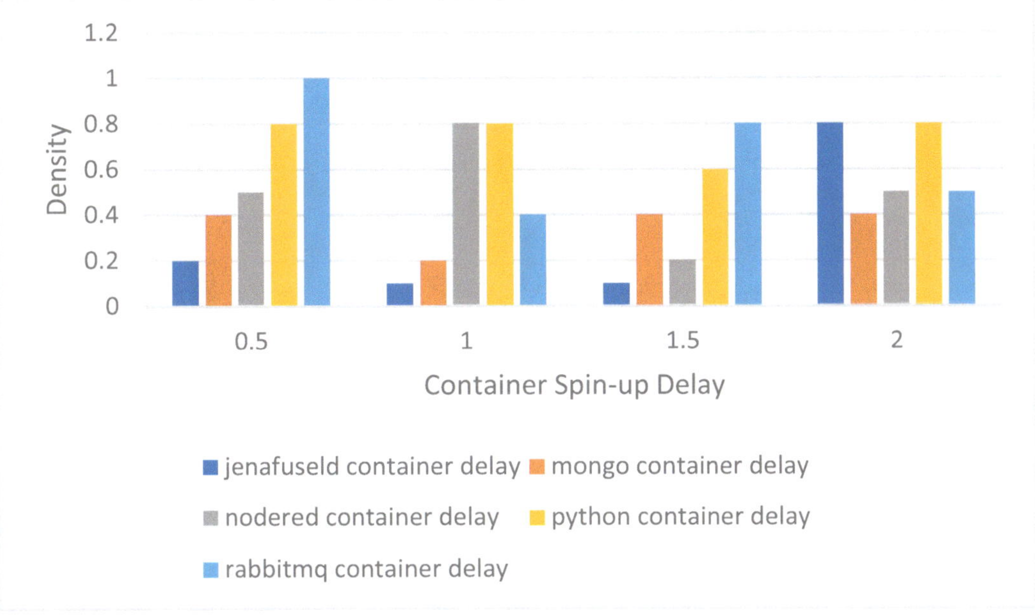

Fig. (3). Start-up times for containers.

CONCLUSION

Combining semantics, integration approaches, AI, and IoT management stages can be challenging but useful for increasing supply chain situational awareness and dependencies. Node-RED has integrated various and complicated systems, allowing information adaption and workflow design to accomplish action s equences. Lastly, the service's dock erization allowed for the automated connection, discovery, and configuration of all elements, as well as their rapid deployment. The platform's extended focus on UI inputs may lead to easier usage and declarations, completely unravelling the end user from the semantic descriptions in the outline.

REFERENCES

[1] S. Fosso Wamba, "ExperTwin: An Alter Ego in Cyberspace for Knowledge Workers", *Proceedings - IEEE 2018 International Congress on Cybermatics: 2018 IEEE Conferences on Internet of Things, Green Computing and Communications, Cyber, Physical and Social Computing, Smart Data, Blockchain, Computer and Information Technology, iThings/Gree,* vol. 8, no. 1, 2019.

[2] E. Yankson, *The ILA study group on the Role of Cities in International Law City Report.* International Law Associatiion: Arusha, 2021.

[3] D.H. Tullah, "Latform youtube sebagai alternatif media informasi pada era digital DI REL-TV.COM", *Front. Neurosci.,* vol. 14, no. 1, 2021.

[4] A. Quaadgras, "(12) Patent Application Publication (10) Pub. No.: US 2011 / 0141115A1", *Journal of Engineering Geology,* vol. 1, no. 2, 2014.

[5] A. Macías, E. Navarro, and P. González, "A microservice□based framework for developing Internet of Things and people applications," *Proc. 13th Int. Conf. Ubiquitous Computing and Ambient Intelligence (UCAmI)*, Toledo, Spain, Dec. 2019, pp. 85, Proceedings, vol. 31, no. 1, MDPI, 2019. [http://dx.doi.org/10.3390/proceedings2019031085]

[6] C. Serôdio, P. Mestre, J. Cabral, M. Gomes, and F. Branco, "Software and architecture orchestration for process control in industry 4.0 enabled by cyber-physical systems technologies", *Appl. Sci. (Basel),* vol. 14, no. 5, p. 2160, 2024. [http://dx.doi.org/10.3390/app14052160]

[7] S. Mewada, A. Saroliya, N. Chandramouli, T. Rajasanthosh Kumar, M. Lakshmi, S. S. Christal Mary, and M. Jayakumar, "Smart diagnostic expert system for defect in forging process by using machine learning process," *Journal of Nanomaterials*, vol. 2022, 8 pp., Jan. 2022. [http://dx.doi.org/10.1155/2022/2567194]

[8] S. Srivastava, "Lung Infection and Identification using Heatmap", 2023. [http://dx.doi.org/10.1109/ICAAIC56838.2023.10140204]

CHAPTER 24

Detection of Cervical Diseases Using CNN Algorithm with Digital Colposcopy Images

L. Kanya Kumari[1,*], **Lakshmi Prasad**[1], **K.Om Sathvik**[1], **K. Satya Sai Bhuvanesh**[1] and **Y. Yaswanth Kalyan**[1]

[1] *Department of IT, Andhra Loyola Institute of Engineering and Technology, Vijayawada 520008, Andhra Pradesh, India*

Abstract: The accuracy of traditional cervical cancer screening methods is low since they rely heavily on the pathologist's subjective experience. Preventing cervical cancer requires regular colposcopy screenings. Over the last half-century, colposcopy has been an important part of the effort to reduce cervical cancer incidence and death rates, in addition to pre-cancer screening and therapy. Unfortunately, visual screening leads to increased effort, which in turn promotes poor diagnostic efficiency and increases the likelihood of misdiagnosis. When it comes to deep learning for medical image processing, the Convolutional Neural Network (CNN) method is better for cervical cancer. The CYENET and VGG19-TL methods represent two deep-learning CNN architectures suggested in this research for detecting cervical cancer utilizing colposcopy pictures. For the research, VGG19 is used as a transfer learning in the CNN structural design. To automatically categorize cervical malignancies using colposcopy pictures, an original method called the Colposcopy Ensemble Network (CYENET) was created. The constructed model is evaluated for its specificity, accuracy, and sensitivity. For classification, VGG19 achieved a score of 74.4%. The findings for VGG19 (TL) are deemed satisfactory. The VGG19 model seems to fall into the intermediate categorization group based on its kappa score. The suggested CYENET demonstrated excellent performance in the experiments, with a sensitivity of 93.5%, a specificity of 97.3%, and a kappa value of 89%. The CYENET method outperforms the VGG19 (TL) model by 10% in terms of classification accuracy, achieving 93.4%.

Keywords: Cervical cancer, CNN architecture, Colposcopy, CYENET, VGG 19.

INTRODUCTION

Medical professionals consider cervical cancer the second most common cause of cancer-related deaths among women, following breast cancer [1]. Unfortunately, the disease is sometimes thought to be incurable, especially in its advanced stages

* **Corresponding author L. Kanya Kumari:** Department of IT, Andhra Loyola Institute of Engineering and Technology, Vijayawada 520008, Andhra Pradesh, India; E-mail: kanyabtech@yahoo.com

D. Arul Pon Daniel, T. Rajasanthosh Kumar & Satya Prakash Yadav (Eds.)

[2]. There have been a lot of recent developments in the field of image-based illness identification [3, 4]. Cervical cancer accounts for 8.6% of all female cancer fatalities, ranking it as the fourth most common malignancy worldwide, according to statistics published by the World Health Organization [5, 6]. The early detection of cervical cancer may save lives since the disease is responsible for around 86% of cervical cancer-related fatalities in lower and intermediate-income countries each year. An estimated 6% of females with cervical cancer are associated with HIV, and the risk of cervical cancer is six times greater in positive HIV compared to negative HIV [7]. Screening efficacy is influenced by factors such as equipment access, test uniformity, monitoring, treatment, and identification of discovered lesions [8, 9]. Although scientific and medical advances have been made, this condition remains incurable, especially if identified in a developing stage. Smear PAP and HPV checks are expensive and have poor sensitivity. However, colposcopy is often utilized in poor nations. Colposcopy screening addresses limitations in smear Pap imaging and HPV testing. Early treatment is favored for cervical and extra-cervical cancers, although the absence of symptoms limits early detection 10].

Successful cervical cancer screening programmes may reduce illness and mortality [11]. In countries with low or middle incomes, cervical cancer screening facilities are few due to workforce shortages and inadequate funding for screening programmes [12].

Colposcopy is a common cervical cancer prevention surgery. Classification and Early detection of this type of cancer might help develop patient treatment. Different methods have been employed to extract information from digital colposcopy images. The primary goal of this research is to offer healthcare providers tools for colposcopy examinations, regardless of their expertise. Studies have used computer-aided systems for diagnosis, including quality image improvement, regional splitting up, identifying pictures, unstable region identification, zone transition classification type, and classification of cancer risk. CAD devices enhance cervical colposcopy images, highlighting areas of concern and irregularities. These strategies aid physicians in diagnosis, but they need sufficient experience and competence for accuratc diagnosis. Pathological lesions may indicate neoplasms, making colposcopy analysis essential for their detection. Abnormal regions include act white, vascularization, mosaic, and punctures. The majority of literature assessments suggest identifying irregular regions in traditional colposcopy pictures. Typical efforts include zone segmentation, cervix segmentation, act white field division, mosaic area detection, vasculature and puncturing, and classification.

The vision of computers, forecasting, Natural Language Processing (NLP), and battery fitness monitoring are just a few of the many areas where deep learning has produced impressive results. Classification, identification, segmentation, and registration are all aspects of medical image processing that are crucial in the diagnosis of diseases. The bulk of the picture data handled is related to medical imaging, including Magnetic Resonance Imaging (MRI), Computed Tomography (CT), blood smear images, and ultrasound. Traditional medical CAD systems are known to have problems, but deep learning's multi-layered neural network's perception mechanism can understand more abstract picture attributes. Having a large database to support the deep learning methods is crucial, particularly for positive examples. Several methods for resolving this problem have been covered in prior research, including transfer learning and collaborative learning. In a smart city's effective Computer-Aided Diagnostic (CAD) architecture, Convolutional Neural Networks (CNNs) detect MI signals. To identify arrhythmia and increase performance by utilizing numerous tiers, a unique feature extraction procedure is suggested, which is then followed by a genetic algorithm. Here is the paper structure: The second section explores the details of the CYENET architecture in the context of cervical screening. The following section presents an analysis of the implementation results. Finally, Section 4 offers conclusions and discusses the future implications of the study.

METHODS AND MATERIALS

Colposcopy images are very helpful for early cancer diagnosis. Using the results of a Transition Zone colposcopic examination (TZ), doctors may determine if patients with irregular cytology need further treatment or screening. Another crucial component of this research is the TZ's title. It has been found that there is a fair amount of intra- and interobserver variability in how different people perceive different properties during colposcopy. However, there is much less research on how different people evaluate the visibility of TZ forms and Squamous Column Junctions (SCJs), and how to quantitatively calculate the similarities and intra-observer variability in TZ contour tracing. Due to the absence of any endocervical part, a TZ has been classified as type 1. The endocervical space remains a transitional zone between Types 2 and 3. Once the latest SCJ became completely apparent in TZ, it was categorized as category 2. Type 3 new SCJs were not completely apparent even when utilizing external equipment. Although not conclusive, it is useful for evaluating patients undergoing pathological cytology. The same colposcopy or different colposcopies might provide different results. The level of competence and experience of the treating physician is the most significant limitation of colposcopy as a diagnostic tool. The accuracy and sensitivity of colposcopy in diagnosing invasive and preinvasive cervical lesions were shown to be poor in several investigations. The Hyperspectral Image (HSI) is classified using a collaborative representation classification method, and an automated hepatocellular carcinoma detection system is implemented utilising a collaborative learning method *via* seven stacked ML algorithms. Fig. (**1**) shows the flow diagram of the automated system that has been suggested for the early detection of cervical cancer. According to colposcopic descriptions, the TZ is the zone that is between the new and old SCJ. Recognizing the TZ is crucial knowledge that is required for every colposcopy. Finding the new border between squamous and columnar epithelium is the next step in TZ-type identification. Fig. (**2**) shows several sample images from the dataset that have been classified as types 1, 2, and 3. To make the cervical region more visible, the green light was sent through the system, producing the centre green picture.

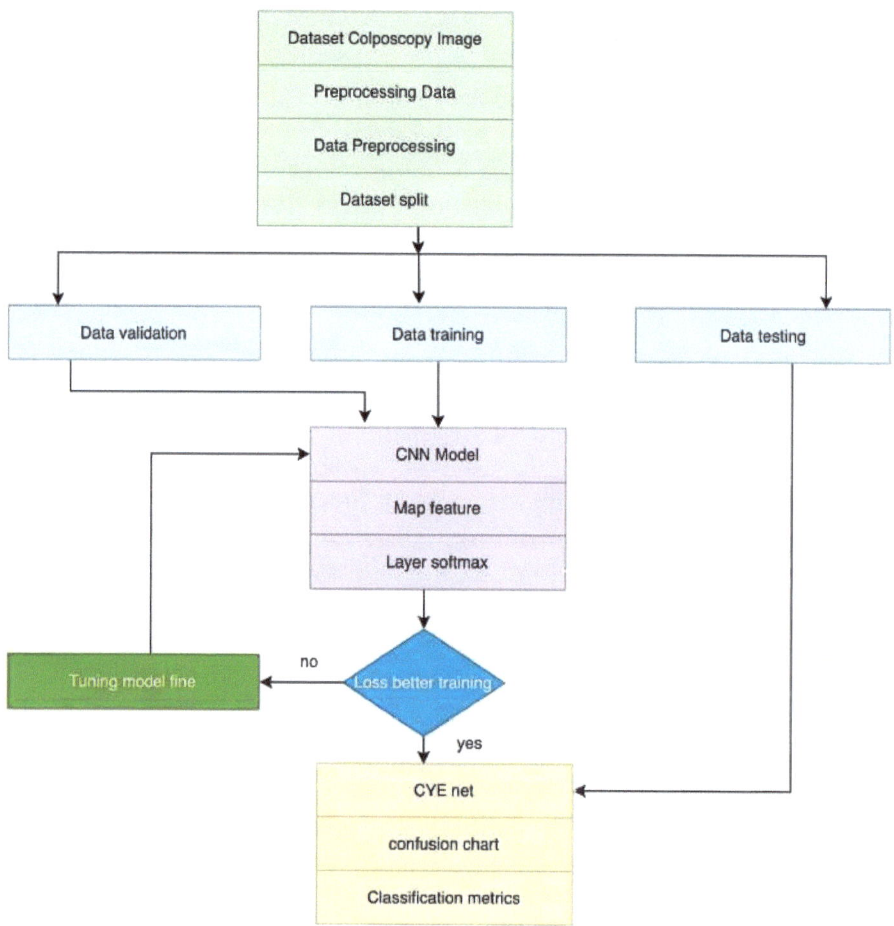

Fig. (1). Flow Diagram of the Automated System.

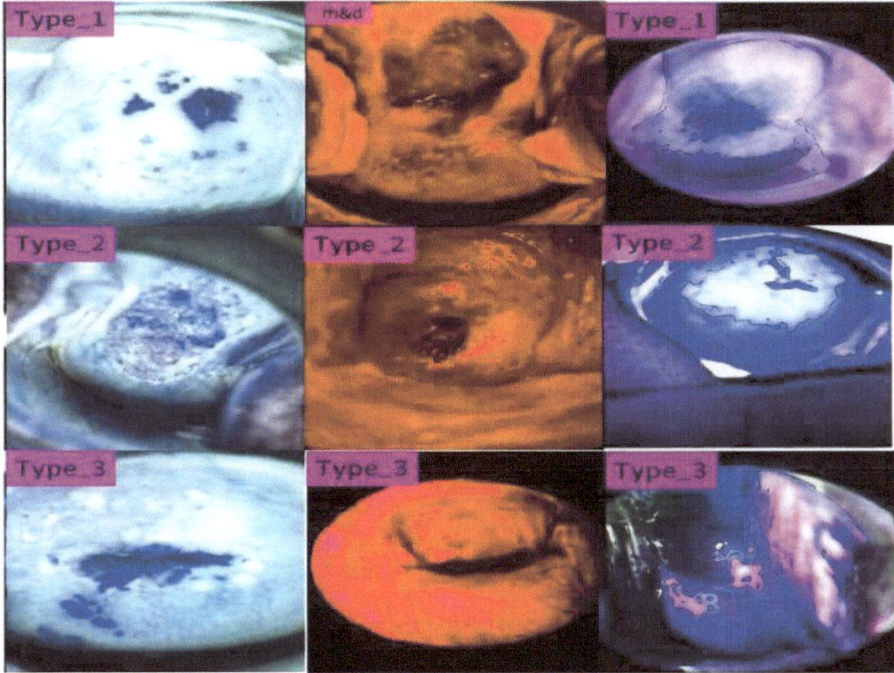

Fig. (2). Several Sample Images from the dataset.

Deep CNN

Many image processing applications, such as medical image analysis, have utilized CNN models. One glaring issue with computer vision is the detection of cervical cancer in colposcopy pictures. Integrating deep learning with traditional characteristics allows the neural network, and the convolution net in particular, to differentiate among type 1, type 2, and type 3 instances. Deeper convolution neural networks for cervical lesion diagnosis are being evaluated at a modest level. After fine-tuning the VGG 19-TL method with the cervical imaging dataset, examine its capacity to identify three different kinds of cervical cancer by freezing the topmost layers. They introduced a CYENET structure that integrates the advantages of depths and paralleled convolution filters to improve the removal of specific cervical cancer features from colposcopy images. The suggested method makes use of a pair of convolutional layers: one to filter out irrelevant features from an input, and another to extract multiple characteristics from the same input using a sequence of typical convolutional layers. To lessen the impact of overfitting, they use a series of convolutional filters to eliminate the biased components. First, the data is pre-processed. Second, the CNN method is trained. Finally, the classification results are shown. The CYENET method comprises five maximum pooling layers, four cross-channel normalization layers, fifteen convolutional layers, and twelve activation layers. The trained model is fed the test data, and then the parameters that emerge from it are measured.

Pre-Processing and Dataset

The cervical screening information collected by Smartphones and Intel ODT comprises 5780 colposcopy pictures. The diagnostic study's unique image is used to categorize the data, taking the transition zone into account. The dataset has already been processed to remove any ethical information from the instances. As a first step, diagnostic records classify the data as either type 1, type 2, or type 3. Due to the limited expertise in using MATLAB image labelling software, a pre-trained dataset is used to determine the ROI of the cervical pictures. An ROI area known as the hospital's Transition Zone (TZ) is where the lesion is located in the centre. It all starts with obtaining the original image, complete with annotations, markings, and ROI.

Parameters Model

In this study, cervical lesions are diagnosed using colposcopy pictures and a two-deep learning model. The suggested solution utilizes a VGG-19 transferred learning model that has been fine-tuned, whereas the CYENET architecture is brand new. The input data size may range from 1×1 to 5×5, and the conventional neural network design employs a single CNN filter. After feeding the input data into the filter, the output data is a discriminatory feature map that is identical to the original data. Incorporating several convolutional filters to extract multilayer features based on discrimination is the primary rationale behind the construction of multilayer convolutional filters.

A neural network's activation functions are the mathematical equations that determine the network's functionality. The network's neurons are equipped with the functionality that decides whether or not to activate them, or “fire,” in response to inputs that are relevant to the model's prediction. A piecewise linear function, ReLU returns zero as an output unless the input is positive. The rapid convergence and lack of saturation that the ReLU activation offers make it a popular choice. It solves the issue that logistical regression and the tangent hyperbolic function encounter, which is that they can't produce values greater than 1. Across all the hidden layers, the ReLU function is used for activation.

RESULTS AND DISCUSSION

A workstation PC with an Intel i9 CPU and a 24 GB Quadro NVIDIA RTX 6000 graphics card is used to experiment with MATLAB 2020b. The Kaggle dataset is used for these experiments. There is a training set of 70%, a validation set of 15%, and a testing set of 15% for colposcopy cervical cancer. Approximately 7,500 photos are used for training, whereas 1,885 images are employed for validation. Based on the results of the Bayesian optimization, they determine the layer depth, starting rate of learning, momentum price, optimizer, and L2 regularization rate. To train the model, the number of epochs is set at 50. The method is trained using 64-GPU batch dimensions, a starting learning rate of 0.0001, and a multi-GPU environment. Section 3 explains that the same picture dataset is used to train both VGG 19 and CYENET with tuning, but their parameters are fixed. It is possible to evaluate the deep learning model by examining its sensitivity, specificity, precision, and Cohen's kappa score. Since the confusion matrix addresses a problem with multiclass classification, it is also used to evaluate the models. Results are shown from the Fig. (**3**) classification model, VGG_19's training accuracy, and the CYENET performance on the dataset for training at 50 epochs are all examined using the confusion matrix.

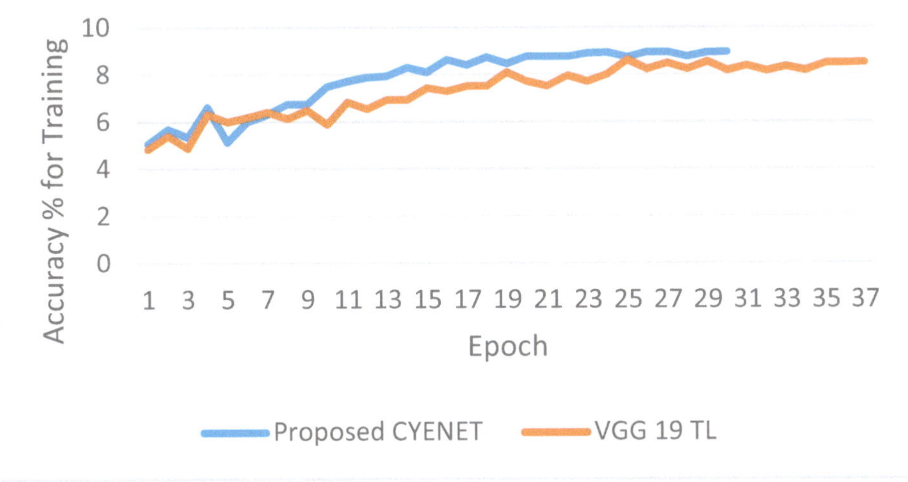

Fig. (3). Classification model evaluation results.

The CYENET method's accuracy training attained 98.2% while the VGG_19 (TL) model's training accuracy reached 88% as the epoch count rose. The suggested CYENET model's confusion matrix with test data indicates the total number of pictures projected with correct label correlation to the expected label data. Actual negative results, false negative results, actual positive results, and false positive results comprise the CYENET confusion matrix. The parameters used for assessment include accuracy, sensitivity, specificity, PPV, and NPV. When evaluating the comprehensiveness of a classifier using medical image confusion matrices, the most reliable metrics are sensitivity and specificity.

$$Accuracy = \frac{TP + FN}{TP + TN + FP + FN} \quad (5)$$

$$Sensitivity = \frac{TP}{TP + FN} \quad (6)$$

$$Specificity = \frac{TN}{TN + FN} \quad (7)$$

$$PPV = \frac{TP}{TP + FP} \quad (8)$$

$$NPV = \frac{TP}{TP + FP} \quad (9)$$

The comparison of systems model performance metrics is shown graphically in Fig. (**4**). The suggested technique for screening cervical cancer *via* colposcopy may be compromised because of the presence of several distractions, including genital hair, intrauterine devices, even human components, and the speculum. Another problem with the suggested method is that it will have worse prediction accuracy if the pictures taken are blurry.

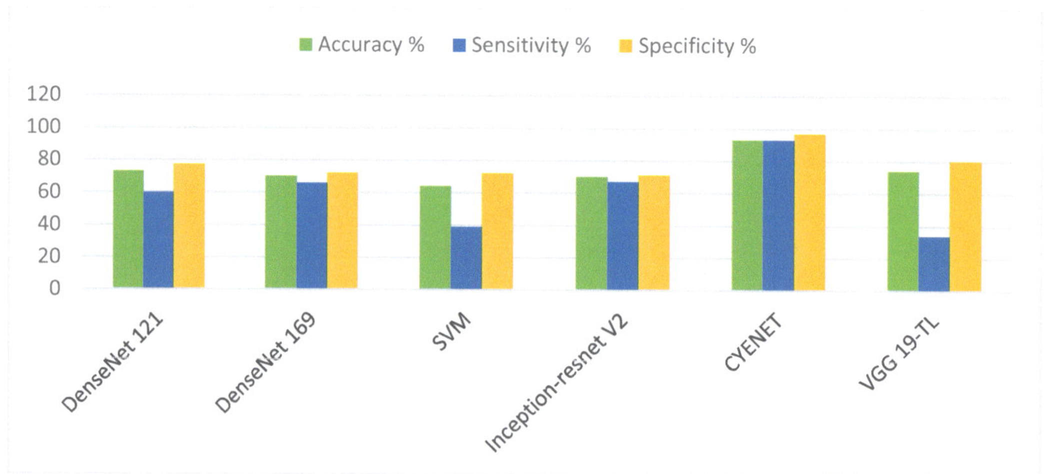

Fig. (4). Comparison of systems model performance metrics.

As shown in Fig. (**5**), the CYENET, as well as the VGG-19 models' negative and positive expected values (PPV), are displayed. Fig. (**5b**) shows that the CYENET model achieves a sensitivity of 93.41% and a specificity of 97.21% for varying infection probabilities, with the possibility of infection fixed at 0.05. In contrast, the VGG 19-TL method attains a sensitivity of 34.1% and a specificity of 80.1% for varying infection probabilities, as shown in Fig. (**5a**). Medical professionals may better categorize populations at risk of cervical cancer diagnosis using the incidence graph.

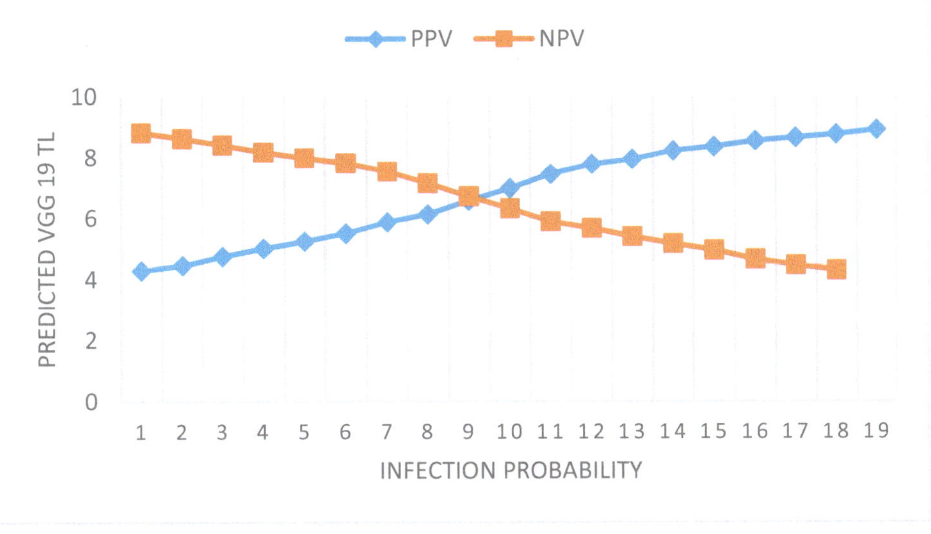

(a)

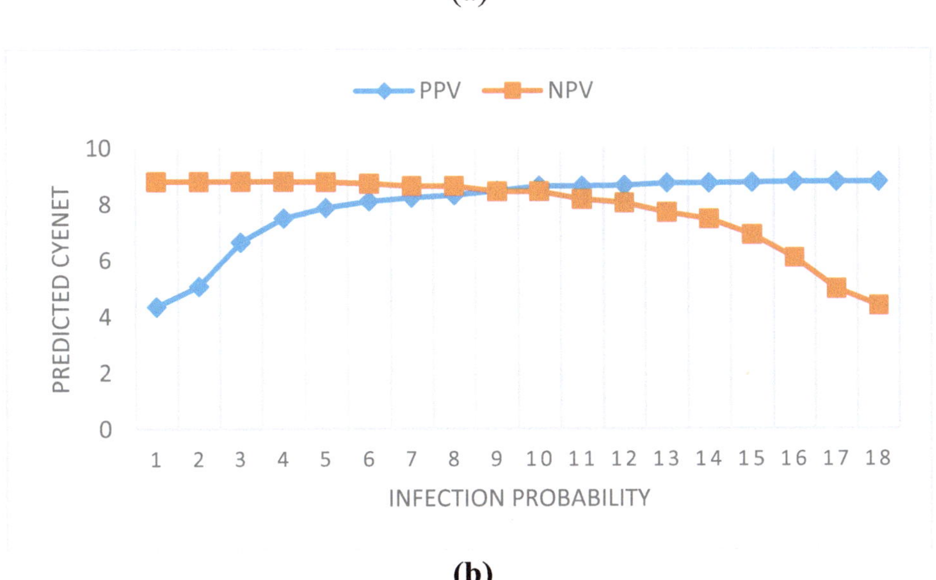

(b)

Fig. (5). (a) PPV as well as NPV curves of VGG_19-TL and (b) CYENET.

Occlusion Viewing Sensitivity Map

Using occlusion sensitivity maps, they identified the optimal aspects of colposcopy images for the classification of CYENET in this experiment. Occlusion sensitivity is a straightforward method for selecting a deep neural network that utilizes visual information for classification. In particular, occlusion sensitivity uses a grey square to regularly exclude portions of the input picture, comparing the probability score for a class depending on the mask location. Compared to other characteristics, colposcopy photos strongly contribute to cervical cancer ratings, according to occlusion sensitivity maps. The occlusion maps demonstrate that CYENET can identify areas with different opacities using a speculum. Visualization findings indicate the natural and interpretable nature of occlusion sensitivity maps compared to Grad-CAM.

CONCLUSION

A novel CYENET, deep learning architecture, is suggested to identify cervical cancer types using colposcopic pictures. The picture collection is balanced by oversampling to enhance classification outcomes. Two methods are given in this work. A transfer learning technique using the VGG19 design is one option. A novel approach, CYENET, uses ODT colposcopy images to classify cervical cancer types. Both models are assessed for sensitivity, accuracy, classification, Cohen's Kappa score, specificity, and F1-measure. The VGG19 (TL) method yields a 54.6% Cohen's Kappa score, with sensitivities of 34% and 80% and specificities of 34% and 80%, respectively. VGG19 has a classification accuracy of 74.4%. VGG (TL) yields satisfactory results. Based on the VGG19 model's kappa value, it is classified as moderate. Similarly, the suggested CYENET achieved high sensitivities (93.5%), specificities (97.3%), and kappa scores (89%). The CYENET model achieves 93.4% classification accuracy, which is 20% greater than that of the VGG19 (TL) model. Comparing CYENET findings to past research, it has the potential to serve as a diagnostic aid for clinicians. The suggested cervical cancer categorization has the potential to assist a community without intrusive intervention. The CYENET enhances categorization efficiency, improving cervical cancer diagnosis through colposcopy screening for medical professionals and healthcare practitioners. Future datasets will be used to evaluate the theorised deep learning method. An improved cervical precancerous diagnostic system might be created by integrating state-of-the-art image processing methods with Convolutional Neural Network (CNN) algorithms.

REFERENCES

[1] T.C. Wright Jr, M.H. Stoler, V. Parvu, K. Yanson, C. Cooper, and J. Andrews, "Risk detection for high-grade cervical disease using Onclarity HPV extended genotyping in women, ≥21 years of age, with ASC-US or LSIL cytology", *Gynecol. Oncol.*, vol. 154, no. 2, pp. 360-367, 2019.

[http://dx.doi.org/10.1016/j.ygyno.2019.05.012] [PMID: 31160073]

[2] M.H. Stoler, T.C. Wright Jr, V. Parvu, K. Yanson, C.K. Cooper, and J. Andrews, "Stratified risk of high-grade cervical disease using onclarity HPV extended genotyping in women, ≥25 years of age, with NILM cytology", *Gynecol. Oncol.,* vol. 153, no. 1, pp. 26-33, 2019. [http://dx.doi.org/10.1016/j.ygyno.2018.12.024] [PMID: 30638767]

[3] N. Youneszade, M. Marjani, and S.K. Ray, "A predictive model to detect cervical diseases using convolutional neural network algorithms and digital colposcopy images", *IEEE Access,* vol. 11, pp. 59882-59898, 2023. [http://dx.doi.org/10.1109/ACCESS.2023.3285409]

[4] C. Zhang, Y. Fu, F. Deng, B. Wei, and X. Wu, "Methane gas density monitoring and predicting based on RFID sensor tag and CNN algorithm", *Electronics (Basel),* vol. 7, no. 5, p. 69, 2018. [http://dx.doi.org/10.3390/electronics7050069]

[5] Z. Fan, K. Bai, and X. Zheng, "Hybrid GA and Improved CNN Algorithm for Power Plant Transformer Condition Monitoring Model", *IEEE Access,* vol. 12, pp. 60255-60263, 2024. [http://dx.doi.org/10.1109/ACCESS.2023.3316251]

[6] D. Cheng, Z. Wang, and J. Li, "Research on the application of CNN algorithm based on chaotic recursive diagonal model in medical image processing", *Applied Mathematics and Nonlinear Sciences,* vol. 9, no. 1, 2024.20231424 [http://dx.doi.org/10.2478/amns.2023.2.01424]

[7] M. Diqi, "Waste Classification using CNN Algorithm", *International Conference on Information Science and Technology Innovation (ICoSTEC),* vol. vol. 1, 2022 [http://dx.doi.org/10.35842/icostec.v1i1.17]

[8] C. Yan, X. Wang, X. Liu, W. Liu, and J. Liu, "Research on the UBI car insurance rate determination model based on the CNN-HVSVM algorithm", *IEEE Access,* vol. 8, pp. 160762-160773, 2020. [http://dx.doi.org/10.1109/ACCESS.2020.3021062]

[9] S. Kiptoo, L. Nderu, and L. Mutanu, "Automated detection of cervical pre□cancerous lesions using regional□based convolutional neural network," *Computers in Biology and Medicine*, vol. 144, p. 105379, 2022. [http://dx.doi.org/10.1016/j.compbiomed.2022.105379]

[10] H. D. Vargas□Cardona, "Artificial intelligence for cervical cancer screening: Scoping review, 2009–2022," *International Journal of Gynecology & Obstetrics*, 2024. [http://dx.doi.org/10.1002/ijgo.15179]

[11] K. B. Sai Sanjana, K. Sai Mounika, T. Raja, S. Kumar, and D. V. Srikanth, "Thermal analysis of advanced IC engine cylinder," *International Journal of Applied and Universal Engineering Research and Development (IJAuERD)*, SSRN, 2016. Available From: http://ssrn.com/abstract=2838730

[12] A. Seem, A. K. Chauhan, R. Khan, and S. P. Yadav, "Distributed artificial intelligence for document retrieval," *Cloud-Based Intelligent Informative Engineering for Society 5.0*, K. Kishor, N. Saxena, and D. Pandey, Eds. Boca Raton, FL, USA: CRC Press, 2021, pp. 35–50. [http://dx.doi.org/10.1201/9781003038467□4]

CHAPTER 25

Determining Lung Cancer Using Convolutional Neural Networks

Md. Imran[1,*], **R. Deepika**[1], **E. Pradeepthi**[1], **K. Sahithi**[1] and **Kuchikar Aneeque Ahmed**[1]

[1] *Department of IT, Andhra Loyola Institute of Engineering and Technology, Vijayawada 520008, Andhra Pradesh, India*

Abstract: This study investigates the effectiveness of Convolutional Neural Network (CNN) architectures in lung cancer classification. By applying deep learning techniques, it evaluates various CNN models for the accurate identification of pleural cancer using medical imaging representations of healthy tissue. Through extensive experimentation and confirmation, the effectiveness of CNNs in accurately diagnosing pleural cancer and revealing their potential as healthy textures for medical image recognition in oncology is demonstrated. Today, lung cancer remains the leading cause of cancer-related deaths globally. As urbanization and industrialization advance, air pollution continues to rise, contributing significantly to the disease's prevalence. Early detection is crucial, as treatment for lung cancer is far more effective in its initial stages. However, early lung cancer stages generally lack symptoms and are difficult to detect. This work classified lung nodules using SPIE AAPM-Lung CT imaging data. Deep Learning (DL) has been a prominent categorization method in recent years. DL methods, such as Transfer Learning (TL), reduce training costs and enable deep learning with less data. Researchers are experimenting with deep learning approaches to enhance the efficiency of CAD in lung cancer screening using computed tomography. Neural network models, including AlexNet, ResNet18, GoogleNet, and ResNet50, are used in this research for training purposes. The networks are employed for training and categorising CT images. By utilizing Convolutional Neural Networks (CNNs) and Transfer Learning (TL), we can achieve accurate and efficient detection of lung cancer on CT images. The method used to test the model includes the confusion matrix, recall, accuracy, specificity, and F1-score.

Keywords: CAD, Convolutional neural network, Deep learning, Transfer learning.

---

* **Corresponding author Md. Imran:** Department of IT, Andhra Loyola Institute of Engineering and Technology, Vijayawada 520008, Andhra Pradesh, India; E-mail: imran02.md@gmail.com

D. Arul Pon Daniel, T. Rajasanthosh Kumar & Satya Prakash Yadav (Eds.)

INTRODUCTION

Image recognition and deep learning have made significant progress in recent years, particularly with the development of convolutional neural networks [1]. Initially, it outperformed standard machine learning algorithms and won the ImageNet large-scale picture identification competition, drastically decreasing error rates [2]. Unfortunately, deep learning algorithms are mostly used in natural picture identification and have limited applicability in medical image diagnostics [3, 4]. Deep learning technology may enhance the diagnosis of lung cancer using CT imaging. By reducing diagnostic time for doctors and improving hospital efficiency, early diagnosis and treatment may address medical resource shortages, ultimately saving lives [5, 6]. Deep learning can be applied to medical image identification in two ways: by utilizing medical images or by developing models of convolutional neural networks from scratch. Second, transfer learning extracts features using a convolutional neural network that has been trained with the model and weight parameters [7, 8]. This work suggests and performs trials on a transfer learning technique for the diagnosis of lung cancer using CT images. Experiments confirm that the transfer learning strategy yields happy outcomes [9, 10]. By learning, the model picks accurate characteristics from training data to make proper conclusions when testing fresh data. Therefore, deep learning is vital for medical image processing. Deep learning has advanced significantly in recent years, driven by increased processing power, enhanced data availability, and the development of improved models and algorithms. Numerous convolutional Neural Network topologies have emerged to address previous issues [11]. The suggested CNN architectures in this study are AlexNet, ResNet-18, GoogleNet, and ResNet-50.

METHODOLOGY

Dataset

Lung cancer diagnosis involves the use of clinical databases. The LIDC-IDR dataset is the most widely used dataset for this purpose. The dataset includes screening and CT scans. Additionally, it organizes contests to enhance the accuracy of categorization. The SPIE-AAPM Lung Challenge dataset, supported by the American Academy of Physicists in Medicine (AAPM) and the National Cancer Institute (NCI), is a subset of the medical imaging session at SPIE. To accurately detect benign or malignant pulmonary nodules, a standard dataset is suggested for testing competition. Using the SPIE-AAPM dataset in this study. The collection contains 70 patient CTs. Ten of these examples were utilized for training, while the rest 60 were tested. In this case, the augmentation approach was employed to create hundreds of CT images from a limited dataset. Fig. (**1**) provides dataset examples.

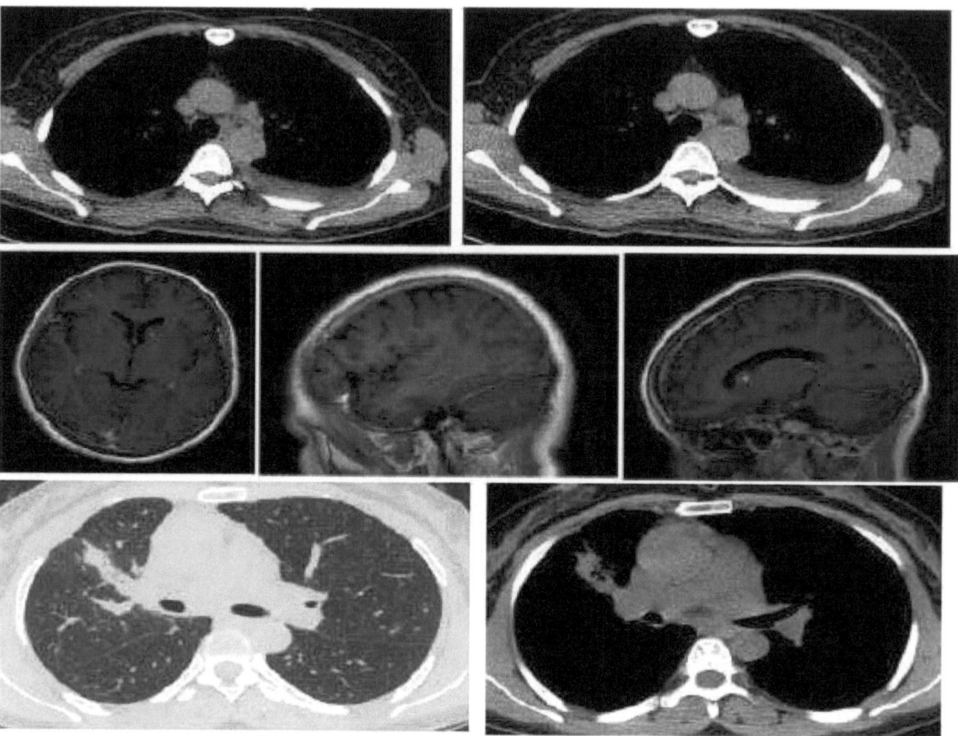

Fig. (1). Cases of lung cancer and healthy controls.

CNN/Transfer Learning Architectures

Transfer learning is a popular approach in computer vision due to its ability to create accurate models in less time. Starting with transfer learning is wrong. Consider starting from a learnt model for addressing issues instead of starting from scratch. This enables us to build upon past learning outcomes instead of starting from scratch. The current study uses deep CNNs. They provide innovative solutions to aid with categorization issues. Limited training data is a common problem for deep CNN models, which require a substantial amount of data for optimal performance. However, collecting a large dataset is a time-consuming and ongoing process. The transfer learning technique is often used to address inadequate data collecting. Transfer learning involves training CNN models on large datasets and fine-tuning them for a smaller dataset. Transfer learning involves modifying a pre-trained system, such as AlexNet, ResNet18, GoogleNet, and ResNet50, to adapt to new applications by refining the network design. See

Fig. (**2**) for the method of employing pre-trained models. Examples of pre-trained models are ResNet18, AlexNet, Googlenet, and ResNet50. The study proposes an organized categorization approach. All models in this investigation adjusted the final three layers to adapt to the new picture categorization, and made modifications to each model as follows:

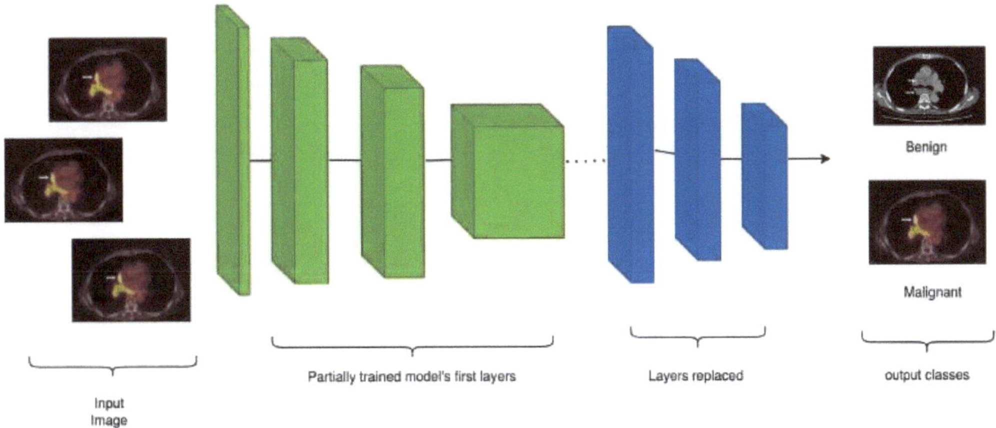

Fig. (2). Procedure for Transfer Learning using Pre-Trained Models.

- The last three layers of AlexNet—FC, softmax, and output—are altered to classify images into the relevant groups.
- The network components (fc1000, prob, and ClassificationLayer_predictions) were swapped out with fully connected, softmax, and classification output layers in ResNet18. Ultimately, the last transferable layer (pool5) is linked to the newly added layers.
- The user's text consists of a single bullet point. Furthermore, the last three levels of GoogleNet have been modified. Fully connected, softmax, and classification output layers are used to alter the loss3-classifier, prob, and output layers for classification. Subsequently, the ultimate transferable layer (pool5_drop7x7_s1) is connected to the newly added layers.
- ResNet50 substitutes the early layers of the network (fc1000, fc1000_softmax, and ClassificationLayer_fc1000) with completely linked softmax and classification output layers. Subsequently, the preceding layer that was moved (avg_pool) is linked to the newly added layers.

Augmenting Data

Deep learning excels at image processing. The Medical image application has reduced the demand for superior labeled pictures. A medical picture collection is expensive and requires specialized labeling. Learning by transfer and data augmentation were used to resolve this issue. The Data Augmentation technique enhances training data sets by generating similar data from limited data. This method effectively addresses the problem of insufficient training data and prevents overfitting. Avoid overfitting by addressing the shortage of training data. This research used image processing techniques, including rotation, to improve training data. Fig. (**3**) illustrates the rotation process for various angles in two details. Firstly, clinicians analyzed lung cancer histological pictures from various viewpoints without affecting the diagnosis. Thus, data augmentation by rotation enhances the dataset. Secondly, the rotation approach increased the dataset size without affecting picture quality.

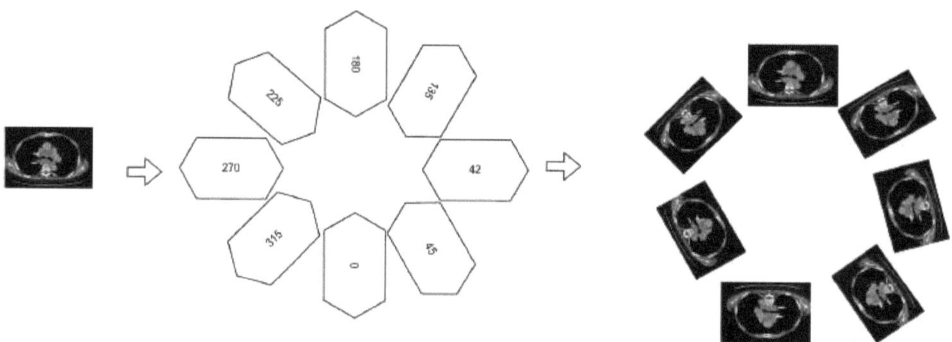

Fig. (3). Process of Rotation from Various Angles.

Evaluating Matrix

- Several matrices were utilized to evaluate the classification process, including the confusion matrix for accuracy, recall for sensitivity, precision, and specificity. Equations for Equ4 and F1-score Equ5 were used. The confusion matrix is the most direct method to test model correctness. The parameters and equations are specified below.
- In True Positive (TP), a complementing class is predicted as a positive number. TN predicts a negative class as a hostile number.
- A False Positive (FP) occurs when a negative class is predicted as a positive one. Predict the complementing class as a hostile class number using False Negative (FN).

$$Accuracy = \frac{TN + TN}{TN + TP + FP + FN} \tag{1}$$

$$Recall\ (\ sensitivity) = \frac{tp}{tp + fp} \tag{2}$$

$$precison = \frac{tp}{tp + fp} \tag{3}$$

$$specificity = \frac{TN}{TN + FP} \tag{4}$$

THE RESULTS AND DISCUSSION

The research utilized the SPIE-AAPM dataset, which comprises 22,489 lung CT images that accurately identify malignant and non-malignant tumors based on patient characteristics and tumor location. Data enhancement is used in deep learning to artificially increase the amount of labeled data, as a substantial quantity of data is necessary for precise training. Transfer learning may reduce the amount of time and data needed for training in Deep Learning. The dataset used in this phase consists of two categories of lung infections, with 70% of the data used for learning and 30% used for testing. The last three layers of the four models that had been trained (AlexNet, ResNet18, GoogleNet, and ResNet50) have been altered to match the number of classes in the final output layer. The evaluation of these pre-trained models is based on several metrics, including accuracy, precision, recall, and F1-score. Table **1** illustrates that AlexNet outperformed other topologies in overall performance, while GoogleNet exhibited subpar performance. The study analyzed pre-trained networks, such as AlexNet, ResNet18, GoogleNet, and ResNet50, to detect lung cancer infections using CT images. Additionally, it conducts a comparison of Convolutional Neural Networks, evaluating their accuracy, recall, precision, and F1-score through the process of fine-tuning. The comparison results are shown in Table **1**.

Table 1. Comparison results for pre-trained networks

Measures performance	**Alexie**	**Resnet18**	**googlenet**	**Resnet50**
accuracy	98.53	98.98	95.11	98.06
recall	99.55	99.55	95.10	99.53
precision	99.42	98.11	95.11	96.71
specificity	99.63	98.05	95.10	96.58
F1-score	98.63	98.98	95.11	98.10
time	68	193	210	526

All the models performed similarly and statistically significantly. AlexNet came out on top with 99.53% accuracy, followed by Resnet18, GoogleNet, and Resnet50 with 98.98%, 95.11%, and 98.06%, respectively. The accuracy matrix results show that AlexNet has the highest percentage at 98.48%, followed by

GoogleNet at 95.11%, Resnet18 at 98.11%, and Resnet50 at 96.70%. The F1-score, specificity, and sensitivity evaluations showed poor performance for GoogleNet, with scores of 95.11%, 95.10%, and 95.11%, respectively. In contrast, AlexNet scored the highest in the assessment matrix, with 99.55%, 98.42%, and 99.636%, respectively. Additionally, AlexNet had the fastest processing time among CNN architectures, at 68 minutes, followed by ResNet18 at 193 minutes, and GoogLeNet and ResNet50 at 210 and 526 minutes, respectively. Furthermore, Figs. (**4-7**) display the confusion matrices of the pre-trained models, with AlexNet being the most effective based on performance indicators. We visually analyzed the performance of the classifier and identified the classes highlighted by the Alexnet model's neurons based on the findings. Columns are present in the real class, but rows are in the output class.

Fig. (4). Confusion matrix for AlexNet.

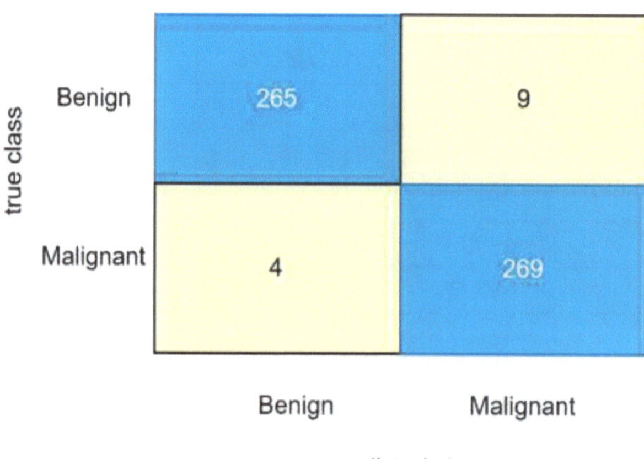

Fig. (5). A confusion matrix for Resnet18.

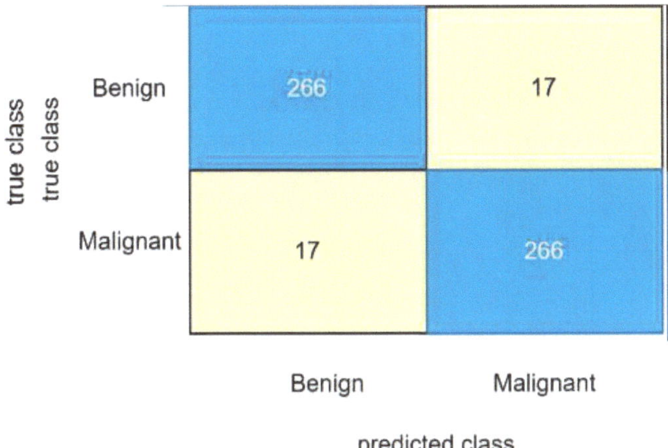

Fig. (6). Matrix of Google Net Confusion.

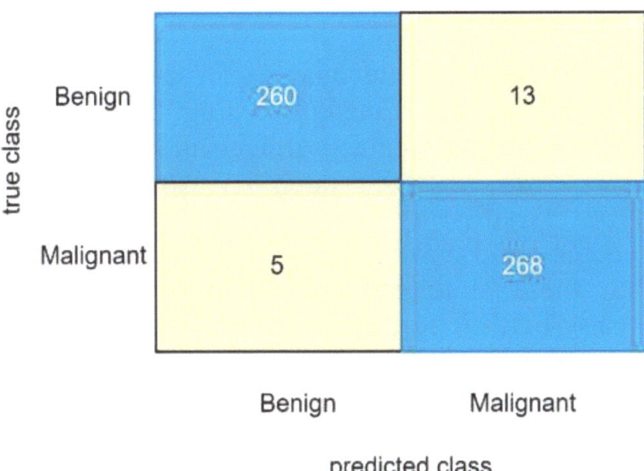

Fig. (7). A confusion matrix for Resnet50.

The learning curve is a common diagnostic tool in deep learning, which involves incremental learning from training datasets. The model may be tested on both training and persistence validation data sets after each update, and a graph of the observed performance can be generated to display the learning curve. CNN-pretrained models (Fig. **8**): AlexNet, ResNet18, GoogleNet, and ResNet50) employ learning curves and loss functions, which forecast model performance faults. In Figure 8, the loss curve approaches zero at each epoch.

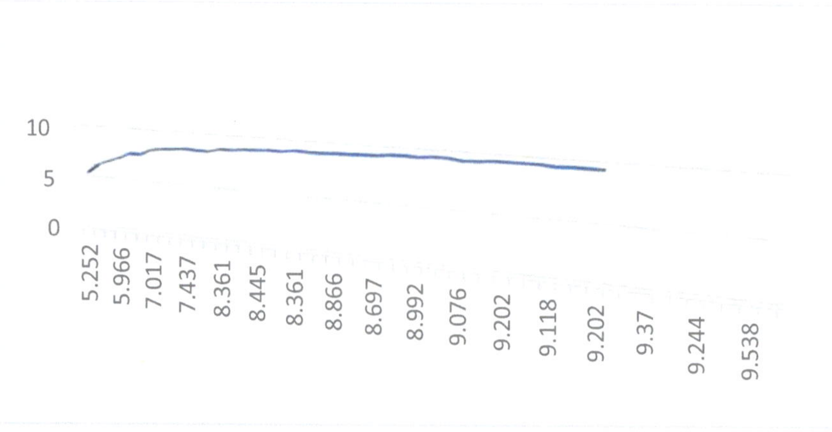

Fig. (8). Curve of the Alexnet network.

CONCLUSION

Deep learning requires a significant quantity of data for model training. The study's initial approach utilizes transfer learning. Secondly, we utilized data augmentation to address training data shortages and prevent overfitting without requiring a complete retraining from scratch. By using fine-tuning methods, lung cancer data may be classified as benign or malignant. The 20-epoch model achieved good accuracy and a well-fitted learning curve with enough training time. By applying these strategies and achieving strong model evaluation performance, the early detection of lung cancer was made possible, contributing to the prevention of patient fatalities. Future plans include enhancing the dataset and comparing the proposed model with other approaches to further improve accuracy and reliability.

REFERENCES

[1] C.J. Lin, and Y.C. Li, "Lung nodule classification using taguchi-based convolutional neural networks for computer tomography images", *Electronics (Basel),* vol. 9, no. 7, p. 1066, 2020. [http://dx.doi.org/10.3390/electronics9071066]

[2] P. Divya, and P. Yamini, "Employing U-NET and rotational based convolutional neural network to build an automatic lung cancer segmentation and classification system", *Middle East Journal of Applied Science & Technology,* vol. 06, no. 02, 2023. [http://dx.doi.org/10.46431/MEJAST.2023.6207]

[3] R. Sharma, R. Sharma, Y.B. Prabha, S. Rema Devi, P. Saxena, and T. Rajasanthosh kumar, "Iot monitoring lathe machine performance", *Mater. Today Proc.,* vol. 80, pp. 3570-3574, 2023. [http://dx.doi.org/10.1016/j.matpr.2021.07.300]

[4] B.K. Hatuwal, and H.C. Thapa, "Lung cancer detection using convolutional neural network on histopathological images", *Int. J. Comput. Trends Tech.,* vol. 68, no. 10, pp. 21-24, 2020. [http://dx.doi.org/10.14445/22312803/IJCTT-V68I10P104]

[5] S. Luo, "Lung cancer classification using reinforcement learning-based ensemble learning", *Int. J. Adv. Comput. Sci. Appl.,* vol. 14, no. 8, 2023.

[http://dx.doi.org/10.14569/IJACSA.2023.01408120]

[6] N. Papandrianos, E. Papageorgiou, A. Anagnostis, and K. Papageorgiou, "Efficient bone metastasis diagnosis in bone scintigraphy using a fast convolutional neural network architecture", *Diagnostics (Basel),* vol. 10, no. 8, p. 532, 2020. [http://dx.doi.org/10.3390/diagnostics10080532] [PMID: 32751433]

[7] W. Rahman, M.G.G. Faruque, K. Roksana, A.H.M.S. Sadi, M.M. Rahman, and M.M. Azad, "Multiclass blood cancer classification using deep CNN with optimized features", *Array,* vol. 18, 2023.100292 [http://dx.doi.org/10.1016/j.array.2023.100292]

[8] H.J. Park, N. Park, J.H. Lee, M.G. Choi, J.S. Ryu, M. Song, and C.M. Choi, "Automated extraction of information of lung cancer staging from unstructured reports of PET-CT interpretation: natural language processing with deep-learning", *BMC Med. Inform. Decis. Mak.,* vol. 22, no. 1, p. 229, 2022. [http://dx.doi.org/10.1186/s12911-022-01975-7] [PMID: 36050674]

[9] H. Zhang, Y. Peng, and Y. Guo, "Pulmonary nodules detection based on multi-scale attention networks", *Sci. Rep.,* vol. 12, no. 1, p. 1466, 2022. [http://dx.doi.org/10.1038/s41598-022-05372-y] [PMID: 35087078]

[10] L. Sibille, R. Seifert, N. Avramovic, T. Vehren, B. Spottiswoode, S. Zuehlsdorff, and M. Schäfers, "18F-FDG PET/CT uptake classification in lymphoma and lung cancer by using deep convolutional neural networks", *Radiology,* vol. 294, no. 2, pp. 445-452, 2020. [http://dx.doi.org/10.1148/radiol.2019191114] [PMID: 31821122]

[11] H. Yadav, S. Singh, K.K. Mishra, S. Srivastava, M.S. Narka, and S.P. Yadav, Brain Tumor Detection with MRI Images. *2022 International Conference on Computational Intelligence and Sustainable Engineering Solutions* (CISES), Greater Noida, India, pp. 519-527, 2022. [http://dx.doi.org/10.1109/CISES54857.2022.9844387]

CHAPTER 26

Utilizing Deep Neural Networks for Image Noise Reduction

KVJ. Bhargav[1,*], **Thanapal Pandi**[2], **Janardhana Rao**[3], **P. Narendra**[4], **Y. Kalyana Krishna**[5] and **Boppudi Lingarao**[6]

[1] *Department of ECE, QIS College of Engineering & Technology, Ongole 523272, Andhra Pradesh, India*

[2] *School of Computer Science and Engineering and Information Systems, Vellore Institute of Technology, Vellore 632007, Tamil Nadu, India*

[3] *Department of MBA, QIS College of Engineering & Technology, Ongole 523272, Andhra Pradesh, India*

[4] *Department of EEE, QIS College of Engineering & Technology, Ongole 523272, Andhra Pradesh, India*

[5] *Department of ME, QIS College of Engineering & Technology, Ongole 523272, Andhra Pradesh, India*

[6] *Department of S&H, QIS College of Engineering & Technology, Ongole 523272, Andhra Pradesh, India*

Abstract: Image denoising is an area where deep learning algorithms have shown promise, but researchers have also identified significant differences between various methods. Discriminative learning, particularly effective against Gaussian noise, and deep learning-based optimization enable real-world noise estimation. However, the diversity of methods has hindered research comparing deep learning in image denoising. By classifying photos into four categories based on the type of Convolutional Neural Network (CNN) used, this research evaluates several deep image-denoising algorithms. The CNNs in question include those trained on incremental white noise, real noise, blind wavelet transform, and composite noisy images. It compares state-of-the-art methods by analyzing common aims and principles and by doing quantitative and qualitative evaluations on denoised datasets that are publically accessible. The study concludes by outlining the obstacles identified and providing recommendations for future research.

Keywords: CNN, Deep learning, Image denoising, MATLAB software.

* **Corresponding author KVJ. Bhargav:** Department of ECE, QIS College of Engineering & Technology, Ongole 523272, Andhra Pradesh, India; E-mail: bhargav.k@qiscet.edu.in

D. Arul Pon Daniel, T. Rajasanthosh Kumar & Satya Prakash Yadav (Eds.)

INTRODUCTION

Image use has increased in recent years, yet noise often infiltrates photos during capture, compression, and transmission [1]. Noise, which distorts images, is caused by a variety of factors, including transmission irregularities, environmental factors, and others [2]. Unpredictable signal strength makes it difficult to extract colours and brightness from captured images. Its presence could impede image analysis, video synthesis, and segmentation [3]. Denoising images is crucial for understanding image processing [4].

Noise interference during the recording, processing, and transmission of images has grown in tandem with the proliferation of image use [5]. Environmental factors and the intricacy of transmission mechanisms skew visual data. Signal oscillations produce picture noise, which hinders the ability to extract colours and brightness from visual input [6]. More than only eyesight is affected by noise invasion [7]. Diagnoses are thrown off, and picture analysis becomes a nightmare due to noise interference [8]. Video segmentation and synthesis are crucial to analysis, but noise may hinder them. Essential picture denoising is a result of the disruptive effects it has on these processes [9].

Picture denoising reduces noise, improving image processing. Specific algorithms and methodologies remove noise to restore image fidelity in denoising. These approaches maintain visual elements and minimize noise. Their goal is to reduce noise and increase visual data quality. Denoising images is fundamental to app-wide image processing. Image-based medical diagnosis and industrial operations need noise reduction. Denoising enhances visuals and analysis across disciplines [10].

As companies and sectors seek high-quality visual data, image denoising methods become increasingly important. These denoising algorithms must evolve and be refined to combat noise and improve image processing. Picture denoising enhances image processing understanding and is crucial for accurate, dependable, and relevant visual data analysis 11].

Due to the improvement in low-light digital image capturing, image-denoising methods have become crucial to computer-aided studies. This situation makes the extraction of clean data from noisy images crucial. Denoising methods can enhance picture details while also removing noise. Distinguishing between noise and edges, as well as textures, during picture denoising is challenging for their high-frequency components [12].

Discussions about the various forms of visual noise frequently occur within the academic community. For example, AWGN, impulse, quantization, Poisson, and speckle noise all fall within this category. Analogue circuitry is the source of AWGN, while manufacturing flaws, intrinsic data mistakes, inadequate photon levels, and speckle/impulse/Poisson noise are the usual culprits.

Picture denoising techniques are essential in computer-aided analysis due to the growing use of digital imagery, particularly in low-light conditions. Visual data analysis precision depends on extracting correct and unaltered data from noisy pictures. Denoising enhances and refines picture information for thorough analysis and interpretation, beyond noise reduction.

The intricacy of picture denoising resides in both removing noise and distinguishing it from crucial components like edges and textures. To identify these elements, advanced algorithms and methods are needed due to their common high-frequency components.

Many forms of picture cacophony have been well-discussed in academic literature. One common, somewhat cacophony that may be encountered while achieving and transmitting concepts is AWGN, which is created from analogue circuits. However, skills are a variety of determinants that enable the production of impulsive sound, dotted sound, Poisson sound, and quantization sound. These contain manufacturing mistakes, dossier errors, and photon-level shortfalls, among other issues. Denoising algorithms face singular obstacles in each of these beginnings of a crash, calling for distinguished methods to reduce their influence on picture integrity and value. Essentially, countenance-denoising algorithms are an essential part of the computational study because they improve the quality and stability of representation. Denoising methods must be developed and refined as digital metaphors become increasingly prevalent in various areas and disciplines. In addition to reconstructing the optical content, the ability to extract a clean dossier from noisy pictures ensures the authenticity and effectiveness of studies conducted in various contexts. The development of photo-denoising methods is crucial to achieving improvement. In healthcare and modern decision-making, accurate and up-to-date imaging is crucial. The honour and stability of visual dossier study in a digital and representation-compelled atmosphere depend on learning picture-denoising algorithms. Image denoising is being used in medical, military, law enforcement, farming, transportation, and similar applications. In biological depiction and interpretation, denoising plans are essential. These methods are essential for removing dot, Rician, and nanoscale healing noise in demonstrative images. Reducing noise artifacts helps improve the quality of interpreters and imaging results. Remote belief requests utilize denoising algorithms to reduce certain forms of noise. The "Salt and pepper" commotion—isolated dark and bright pixels—challenges detached belief in photography. Effective denoising methods are needed to maintain remote sensing data from additional silver Gaussian noise, which is a typical interference during picture capture and transmission. The versatile function of countenance denoising in growing visual datasets features reliability and interpretability, which is emphasized by its far-reaching applications in numerous fields. As technology advances, denoising algorithms must be developed and revised to address new challenges in various applications. As companies continue to utilize visual data for decision-making, picture-denoising methods are crucial for ensuring data quality and accuracy.

LITERATURE SURVEY

A thorough comparison of several deep image-denoising algorithms was the goal of this study. To start, we divided CNNs that use deep learning into four groups: those that process pictures with pure white noise, those that process images with actual noise, those that use blind denoising, and those that process hybrid noisy images with fuzziness, low-resolution parts, and noise all mixed together.

In recent years, the use of images has surged significantly, introducing noise during data collection, compression, and transmission. Noise reduction remains a critical area of study in lower vision, constituting a well-established yet indispensable practice across real-world applications. Generally, it is assumed that 'v' represents Additive White Gaussian Noise (AWGN) characterized by a specific variance. Bayesian image denoising relies on the effective image before modeling, following the calculation of the likelihood.

The effects of HAR-specific test results have been little investigated, in contrast to the numerous studies that have examined the benefits of HAR-related activities. This methodology is evaluated using two widely recognized HAR benchmark datasets, demonstrating superior performance compared to 2D approaches using Convolutional Neural Networks (CNNs) alone and other cutting-edge techniques. Although investigations have primarily focused on the potential impacts of prospective activities associated with HAR, the approach demonstrates its superiority over the 2D CNN method and other state-of-the-art techniques on these established HAR datasets.

METHODOLOGY

Matlab

The suggested technique is both implemented and referenced in the latest version of MATLAB. With their corresponding values, provide the simulation findings below. The experiment utilizes MATLAB to replicate the code, incorporating a variety of CT and MRI images of the body. The MATLAB Quick Access logo can be activated on Windows computers by MATI AB after they log in to their account. Upon launching MATLAB, you will encounter a distinct interface known as the desktop, comprising several windows. Key components of the primary desktop interface include:

1. The Command Window
2. Command History
3. Workspace
4. Current Directory
5. Help Browser
6. Start Menu"

Deep Learning

The application of deep learning methods has significantly addressed numerous practical challenges encountered in photogrammetry. In particular, the efficacy of deep learning stands out as it surpasses non-learning-based filters and traditional denoising algorithms, positioning itself as a preferred approach in this domain. One key advantage lies in the demonstrated capability of deep learning to outperform its counterparts in various scenarios, showcasing its robustness and adaptability. Moreover, deep learning methods exhibit reduced susceptibility to the nonlinear properties inherent in noise generation processes, enhancing their effectiveness in handling complex noise patterns.

Image denoising using Multilayer Perceptrons (MLPs) is a key field of machine learning research and practice. Advanced computer graphics processing, particularly in image processing, has transformed the environment. MLPs have been replaced by CNNs due to their superior image-related performance.

Deep learning changed photogrammetry. Academics and practitioners use neural networks to minimize photogrammetric noise. Deep learning algorithms surpass denoising and non-learning filters in terms of quality and reliability of photogrammetric outputs. Deep learning can interpret complicated data patterns and properties, making it useful in photogrammetry. Adaptable deep learning systems can detect complex noise patterns from essential image portions. The photogrammetric reconstructions are sharper and more accurate using deep learning-based denoising.

Machine learning advancements in picture denoising have been spearheaded by Multilayer Perceptrons (MLPs). Their first recommendation was for learning complex data correlations using their multilayered, connected neuron architecture. MLPs have shown potential in denoising applications after learning to identify and eliminate image noise. With the advancement of computing power, Convolutional Neural Networks have completely transformed the field of image processing, particularly in denoising.

The strengths of CNN architectures prompted a paradigm shift away from MLPs and toward CNNs in picture denoising. CNNs are great for handling various noise sources while preserving image information because they can detect regional patterns and spatial connections in photos. Due to the fast analysis and extraction of hierarchical information from images by convolutional layers, CNNs outperform MLP-based approaches in noise reduction.

MLPs denoise images less effectively than CNNs. CNNs convolve input pictures with learnable filters to collect and analyze spatial information. CNNs can reduce noise significantly while preserving important image properties due to this capacity. MLPs to CNNs was a major leap in photogrammetry picture denoising. CNN-based methods utilize convolutional networks to reduce noise in photogrammetric images, marking a significant advancement in this field. Deep learning approaches, particularly CNN frameworks, are continually being refined and improved, promising to overcome obstacles and enhance photogrammetric outputs.

Convolutional Neural Network

The use of cascaded feedforward operations and supervised learning techniques characterizes CNNs as a foundational kind of artificial neural network. Convolution, a basic multidimensional process, is the architectural backbone of CNNs. Input, activation function, and feature map layers are the standard building blocks of a convolutional network; these layers perform different but complementary functions and process data in their unique ways.

Sparse representations, where sparse values predominate, local connections, which allow targeted and local interactions, and shared weights, which facilitate parameter efficiency, are the three basic notions upon which the key design principles of Convolutional Neural Networks (CNNs) rest.

Beyond picture denoising, CNNs have a lot of other uses. They can handle tasks like blind denoising, which involves processing images with noise. Despite the abundance of literature on CNN-based image-denoising algorithms, very few reviews have been conducted. With its comprehensive overview of CNN methods for image denoising, this tutorial is a valuable tool for pinpointing the origins of noise. CNNs are used for more than picture denoising. CNNs' adaptability is shown via blind denoising, which removes noise from pictures without knowing their features. CNNs can distinguish and eradicate noise across multiple kinds, even when the noise properties are unknown.

Many academics study CNN-based picture-denoising techniques. The integration of these separate efforts into a complete assessment is restricted. This shortage emphasizes the need for references like these, which unify and classify CNN approaches for image denoising.

This resource categorizes picture data noise, making it valuable. This overview organizes noise types from additive white Gaussian noise to impulsive noise and beyond to help grasp the complex issues of picture noise.

This resource provides an overview of various CNN image-denoising algorithms, focusing on reducing noise and maintaining image quality. It is useful for image-processing academics, practitioners, and hobbyists. The study unifies various CNN approaches, categorizing noise in picture data, and promotes systematic examination, marking a significant milestone in image denoising. It is invaluable as image processing continues to develop, leading to better understanding, progress, and discoveries in the quest for noise-free visual data.

DnCNN

DnCNN (Denoising Convolutional Neural Network) extracts residual pictures from colour image luminance. Luminance, which measures pixel brightness, correlates with the blue, red, and green colour information. Colour disparities may be observed in the brightness channels of an image, specifically in the blue, red, and green pixel counts. DnCNN only trains in the luminance channel because humans perceive intensity changes more than colour changes.

DnCNNs primarily function by analyzing the residual picture to identify and highlight the differences or inconsistencies between the actual image and its perfect, denoised replacement. Through the use of this residual method, the network is trained to detect and eliminate visual noise while maintaining important information.

In DnCNN training, the luminance channel is used since the human visual system is sensitive to intensity variations. Image luminosity brightness or lightness is important to human perception.

IMPLEMENTATION

An organized strategy is required for denoising an image, network loading, image preparation, and demonstrating the results when using denoising techniques. This methodical approach ensures consistency and reproducibility for both colour and grayscale image denoising. By using the same procedures in both cases, we can achieve overall efficiency and uniformity across image types.

Image Preparation

The first steps of implementation are to gather, load, and analyze images. The foundation for subsequent actions is laid at the image preparation stage. Fig. (**1**) illustrates the data collection, integrity testing, and preprocessing steps. To prepare photos for processing, this step may entail resizing, normalizing, or transforming them. Clean and prepared picture data greatly affects the denoising phases.

Fig. (1). Image Noising.

Network Loading

The system loads the previously trained denoising network after preprocessing the picture. At this stage, a neural network system that has been trained on denoising tasks before is introduced to reduce noise efficiently. The pre-trained network stores all the learned representations and parameters. Before performing denoising, it is necessary to load the pre-trained network to make its architecture and parameters accessible for use in image processing jobs.

Image Denoising

Denoising the noisy picture in Fig. (**2**) is done by running it through the pre-trained network. In this step, the noisy picture is fed into the previously trained network, which uses its learned transforms and operations to clean up the picture. Utilizing its taught knowledge, the network's denoising skills produce a denoised image based on the input picture by identifying patterns of noise. The goal of denoising is to minimize the impact of noise on an image without compromising its fundamental characteristics or details.

Fig. (2). Denoising Image.

Result Presentation

Presenting the denoised picture concludes implementation. The noise-free picture is acquired after denoising. The denoised picture is shown for visual examination and analysis in this step. The image's presentation allows for a qualitative evaluation of denoising effectiveness. To test the denoising technique, the noisy picture, the denoised image, and maybe additional reference images may be compared visually.

Uniformity Across Grayscale and Color Images

The researchers verified that the procedures for implementation apply to both colour and grayscale image denoising. Regardless of the image format or colour space, the processes remain the same. Applying the same implementation techniques ensures a uniform denoising process for all image formats.

Importance of Standardized Workflow

Reliability and repeatability in denoising processes can only be achieved with a controlled implementation methodology. Practitioners may methodically handle varied photos, consistently use denoising methods, and analyze the outcomes in a controlled way by following a defined series of procedures. Denoising in both color and grayscale images is consistent, which streamlines the process and enables the effective handling of various image datasets without modifying the fundamental methods.

The implementation technique for denoising colour and grayscale images primarily consists of a systematic workflow that includes image setup, network load, image denoising, and result presentation. Denoising processes are guaranteed to be consistent, reproducible, and efficient when they conform to a systematic approach. Efficiently denoising various picture collections and producing aesthetically pleasing results is possible with the use of standardized processes.

Fig. (**3**) illustrates the flow chart of the proposed method.

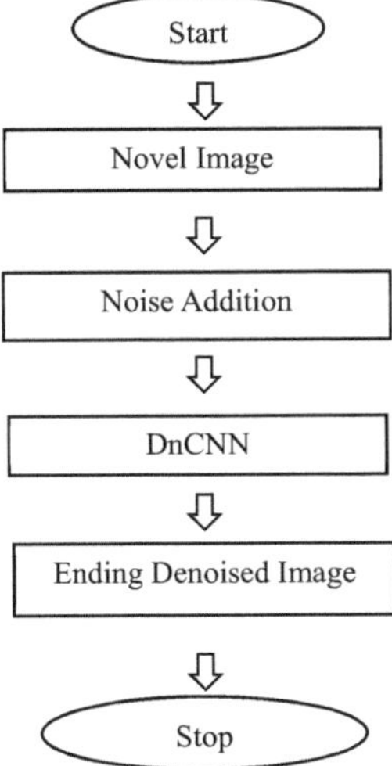

Fig. (3). Proposed method Flowchart.

RESULTS

The results of the proposed method are illustrated in Figs. (**4** and **5**).

Original Image Noisy Image Denoised Image

Fig. (4). Colour image denoising Results.

Original Image Noisy Image Denoised Image

Fig. (5). Grayscale image denoising results.

CONCLUSION

This section explores various CNN-based image-denoising techniques, offering a comprehensive overview of key concepts and strategies to enhance readers' understanding of current advancements. While several CNN denoising methods exist, some challenges persist, such as the need for an improved understanding of CNN and the complexity of unproven denoising tasks. Notably, only a limited number of CNN methods have been applied to human body images, warranting the exploration of additional CNN approaches for medical image denoising. Moreover, efforts to access relevant code and software yielded no results, highlighting the potential benefits of expanding available RAM resources to further enhance CNN-based work.

REFERENCES

[1] F.M. Muller, J. Maebe, C. Vanhove, and S. Vandenberghe, "Dose reduction and image enhancement in micro-CT using deep learning", *Med. Phys.,* vol. 50, no. 9, pp. 5643-5656, 2023. [http://dx.doi.org/10.1002/mp.16385] [PMID: 36994779]

[2] Y. Tachibana, Y. Otsuka, H. Nozaki, K. Kamagata, S. Mori, Y. Saito, and S. Aoki, "Noise reduction by multiple path neural network using Attention mechanisms with an emphasis on robustness against Errors: A pilot study on brain Diffusion-Weighted images", *Phys. Med.,* vol. 116, 2023.103176 [http://dx.doi.org/10.1016/j.ejmp.2023.103176] [PMID: 37989043]

[3] S.P. Taş, S. Barın, and G.E. Güraksın, "Detection of retinal diseases from ophthalmological images based on convolutional neural network architecture", *Acta Sci. Technol.,* vol. 44, 2022.e61181 [http://dx.doi.org/10.4025/actascitechnol.v44i1.61181]

[4] K. Xiong, G. Zhao, Y. Wang, and G. Shi, "SAR imaging and despeckling based on sparse, Low-rank, and deep CNN priors", *IEEE Geosci. Remote Sens. Lett.,* vol. 19, pp. 1-5, 2022. [http://dx.doi.org/10.1109/LGRS.2021.3131201]

[5] N. Chamundeshwari, N. Biradar, and Udaykumar, "Adaptive despeckling and heart disease diagnosis by echocardiogram using optimized deep learning model", *Comput. Methods Biomech. Biomed. Eng. Imaging Vis.,* vol. 11, no. 1, pp. 1-17, 2023. [http://dx.doi.org/10.1080/21681163.2022.2032361]

[6] M.M. Rahman, M.A.H. Wadud, and M.M. Hasan, "Computerized classification of gastrointestinal polyps using stacking ensemble of convolutional neural network", *Inform. Med. Unlocked,* vol. 24, 2021.100603 [http://dx.doi.org/10.1016/j.imu.2021.100603]

[7] A. Gupta, D. Gupta, M. Husain, M.N. Ahmed, A. Ali, and P. Badoni, "A PSO-CNN-based approach for enhancing precision in plant leaf disease detection and classification", *Informatica (Vilnius),* vol. 47, no. 9, 2023. [http://dx.doi.org/10.31449/inf.v47i9.5188]

[8] E. Pintelas, I.E. Livieris, S. Kotsiantis, and P. Pintelas, "A multi-view-CNN framework for deep representation learning in image classification", *Comput. Vis. Image Underst.,* vol. 232, 2023.103687 [http://dx.doi.org/10.1016/j.cviu.2023.103687]

[9] E. Sadeghi Pour, M. Esmaeili, and M. Romoozi, "Employing atrous pyramid convolutional deep learning approach for detection to diagnose breast cancer tumors", *Comput. Intell. Neurosci.,* vol. 2023, no. 1, 2023.7201479 [http://dx.doi.org/10.1155/2023/7201479] [PMID: 38025486]

[10] C. Arndt, F. Güttler, A. Heinrich, F. Bürckenmeyer, I. Diamantis, and U. Teichgräber, *Deep Learning CT Image Reconstruction in Clinical Practice, .* [http://dx.doi.org/10.1055/a-1248-2556]

[11] G. Govinda Rajulu, M. Jamuna Rani, D. Deepa, U. Mamodiya, R. G. Deshmukh, and T. Rajasanthosh Kumar, "Cloud□Computed Solar Tracking System," Proc. 5th Int. Conf. ICICC 2021: Computer Communication, Networking and IoT, vol. 2, Singapore: Springer Nature Singapore, pp. 75–85, 2022.

[12] R. Saklani, K. Purohit, S. Vats, V. Sharma, V. Kukreja, and S. P. Yadav, "Multicore Implementation of K□Means Clustering Algorithm," Proc. 2023 2nd Int. Conf. Applied Artificial Intelligence and Computing (ICAAIC), Salem, India, pp. 171–175, 2023. [http://dx.doi.org/10.1109/ICAAIC56838.2023.10140800]

CHAPTER 27

Detecting Malicious URLs Using Machine Learning

Md. Imran[1,*], **Uppada Bhaskar**[1], **Kodavalla Jeevan Krishna**[1], **Mulugu Prudhvi Sriram**[1] and **Mohammad Shukur**[1]

[1] *Department of IT, Andhra Loyola Institute of Engineering and Technology, Vijayawada 520008, Andhra Pradesh, India*

Abstract: In recent years, one of the major risks has been web-based attacks. Criminals posing a threat often trick consumers into visiting malicious websites to conduct attacks. To identify harmful URLs, various methods have been implemented, including blacklisting. Along with these untrustworthy methods arose the tedious task of keeping a database of blacklist URLs up to date. In recent years, there has been an exploration into using machine learning algorithms to identify dangerous URLs. To train a prediction model, this technique examines several aspects of URLs and utilizes a dataset comprising both normal and malicious URLs. To reliably identify harmful URLs, this study proposes a MUD (Malicious URL Detection) model that utilizes three supervised machine learning classifiers: logistic regression, support vector machine, and one additional classifier. Preliminary findings show that the algorithm exceeded the comparison group.

Keywords: Algorithm, Harmful URL, Machine learning, Malicious URL logistic regression.

INTRODUCTION

Research suggests that nearly half of the world's population is online [1]. People using computers at home are susceptible to external harm and danger due to a lack of education and protection [2]. These individuals struggle to distinguish between legitimate and dangerous websites due to their similar content [3]. Threat actors use their creativity to generate hazardous online content and lure customers into accessing these URLs. Raising user awareness and identifying dangerous URLs may help prevent malicious website attacks [4]. Researchers have proposed many methods for identifying rogue URLs. Machine learning algorithms are effective in

* **Corresponding author Md. Imran:** Department of IT, Andhra Loyola Institute of Engineering and Technology, Vijayawada 520008, Andhra Pradesh, India; E-mail: imran02.md@gmail.com

D. Arul Pon Daniel, T. Rajasanthosh Kumar & Satya Prakash Yadav (Eds.)

detecting bogus URLs. The efficacy of algorithms based on machine learning in detecting dangerous URLs has been studied [5].

The MUD (Malicious URL Detection) model outlines the steps to identify malicious URLs and compares the performance of three distinct machine learning methods [6]. It tests several algorithms and builds a prototype that may identify harmful URLs by looking for specific characteristics associated with such URLs [7]. Due to their inability to identify newly dangerous URLs, earlier attempts to detect harmful URLs *via* blacklisting or algorithms were found to be unreliable [8 - 10].

The following is an outline of the article's structure: The suggested Malicious URL Detection (MUD) model is defined in depth in Section 2 [11]. In Section 3, the outcomes of the experiments are presented, showing how various classifiers performed. In Section 4, the paper presents its main points and provides suggestions for further studies in this field [12].

METHODOLOGY

Suggested Malicious URL Detection (MUD) System

Created based on the characteristics of known malicious URLs, the suggested model utilizes machine learning to identify new malicious URLs. A total of fifteen characteristics are chosen for each given URL and then classified as lexical, host-based, or content-based. For this project, the classifiers were trained on the dataset and then utilized to determine whether a URL is dangerous or not. The following procedures were followed to construct and train the suggested MUD system (Fig. **1**) to identify harmful URLs: (a) information collection; (b) information preparation; (c) categorization; (d) testing and training; and (e) assessment.

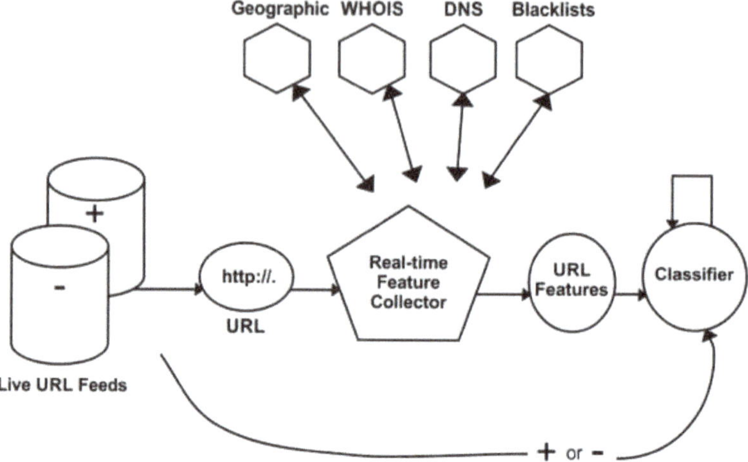

Fig. (1). The MUD model categorizes URLs.

Data Gathering

Before beginning to work with URLs, it is important to have a thorough understanding of what an internet address is and how it is generated (Fig. **2**). A Universal Resource Locator (URL) is the web address displayed in a web browser's address bar. URLs often include a protocol. HTTP, which makes it smooth to guide along route, often over water websites, HTTPS, which provides a supplementary coating of freedom to HTTP, File Transfer Protocol, which permits the transmission of the data betwixt calculations and admits for the giving of files, and Domain Name System (DNS), which is administrative of registering rule names, are few of ultimate conspicuous obligations that are used contemporary. Malicious cyberattacks often target URLs that have been hacked. To start the process of gathering URLs, you need to first survey websites that hold links to both injurious and good URLs.

Fig. (2). URL Mechanisms.

Data Preprocessing

To create a clean dataset, this process is utilized to convert raw data. The data quality has an important impact on the proposed copy's ability to train, making it a crucial component of machine learning. Data cleaning is performed during this process, including the replacement or removal of null values and rescaling. To utilize the dataset with various machine learning methods, data preparation is crucial. Data reprocessing includes feature extraction, which is a critical phase.

Feature Extraction

It is possible to extract and apply several characteristics for URL classification. Lexical features include things like URL length, character count, and special characters ("//", ".", "@"). To find the host's location, IP address, and domain registration dctails in the host properties of URLs, which are used to obtain host-based features. These qualities are crucial for identifying harmful URLs since fresh IPs are hard to come by. Downloading the content of a URL yields characteristics that are content-based. Prediction relies on it, as it aids in detecting harmful code that threat actors could insert into HTML. The detection may also benefit from other variables, such as page rank, which is related to the frequency of URL visits.

Dataset Used

A pre-processed dataset, comprising 11,055 URLs (both malicious and benign), was utilized for the study, and 30 characteristics were extracted. The dataset was obtained from the UCI Machine Learning Repository. They extract around 15 characteristics from the cleaned dataset that meet the requirements. According to computational resource needs and classification accuracy, the selected three of the top five attributes from the list describe various aspects of URLs that may help decide whether a URL is harmful or not. Features such as these were utilized:

1. IP Address: Verifies whether the URL is connected with a specific IP address
2. Length of URL: Verifies the character count. Sometimes, bad actors will utilise this function to mask the harmful portions of a URL.
3. An @ symbol: When using this symbol, the web browser will ignore everything before it and only display the actual URL after it.
4. Using a double slash '//': Referring to another website is implied when '//' is included in the URL path. The standard location for the '//' in URLs is the position for HTTPS and the position for HTTP, with the former taking precedence.

5. Tags for links: Reputable websites make use of tag elements to provide information about the HTML text.
6. Consuming a sub-domain: An existing website may be divided into many smaller sites by using sub-domains, which aid with both organisation and navigation.
7. Domain Age: The WHOIS database is a good place to get this information. The majority of malicious websites with fraudulent purposes have a limited duration on the domain.
8. Domain Name System record: It contains the information about the Web resource's registration. Researchers have discovered a correlation between the availability or lack of this data within the DNS WHOIS records and malicious activity.
9. Token of HTTPS: The following reduces the possibility that malicious information may be published on HTTPS-enabled websites.
10. Page Rank: This function attempts to determine how significant a website is about others on the web. Approximately 95% of fraudulent websites do not have a page rank, according to the information used for this research.
11. Index of Google: It checks to see if Google has indexed a website. Google seldom indexes hacking websites, as they are typically only available for a short time.
12. Iframe: Iframe is the use of the HTML element to download harmful JavaScript risk factors is well-known.
13. Redirect: Malicious activities seem to happen when URLs are redirected. If the URL is redirected, the functionality will detect it.
14. A pop-up window: Ads and exploits are common uses for the JavaScript Window Open () pop-up.
15. Favicon: This image is linked to a certain webpage. The web page probably contains malicious information if the picture appears through another website than the one visible in the URL bar.

Classification

The field of study known as "machine learning" enables computers to interact with one another, learn new tasks, adapt to new environments, and even converse with each other with little to no human input. To determine whether a URL is harmful or not, machine learning methods train a model using a collection of URLs and then utilize the model's statistical features. It is common practice for classification models, sometimes referred to as machine learning techniques, to provide multiple answers to classification issues. Among the most well-known detectors are decision trees, k-nearest Neighbours, support vector machines, Bayesian networks, and random forests. Three classifiers, a Bayesian network, a logistic regression model, and a support vector machine, are used in the article.

Support Vector Machine: When it comes to classification and regression issues, one of the strong supervised learning approaches is the Support Vector Machine (SVM). Its typical use is in two-group categorization issues. Starting with a series of training samples that are individually labeled as fitting one of the two groups, SVM, a non-probabilistic binary direct classifier, moves forward. To reduce the SVM classifier's generalization error, Support Vector Machines (SVMs) divide instances into classes by locating a hyperplane with the greatest distance to the nearest data point of each class.

Naïve Bayes: The organization technique known as Naïve Bayes is named thus because it operates on the assumption that each characteristic of the input variable is unrelated to any other feature. This classifier is based on probabilities. The model calculates the likelihood of each occurrence in the dataset and uses that information to predict or classify subsequent instances.

Regression of Logistic: Since it primarily handles binary classification issues, this technique can be used to classify malicious URLs, as it often yields a well-calibrated probability. Finding the optimal model that describes the connection between the result and the independent variables is its main objective.

Training and Testing

Here, split the dataset in half to use for training and testing purposes. It is common practice to allocate 70% of a dataset to training and utilize the remaining 30% for testing. By analyzing the training data, the classification model gains knowledge. To assess the model's efficacy, the testing set was utilized, which should be completely separate from the training set. The model's ability to execute an action on fresh data depends on how well it was trained.

Evaluation

The next step involves evaluating the performance of the classifier. This is achieved using the confusion matrix, along with evaluation metrics such as F1-score, accuracy, precision, and recall, which provide a comprehensive assessment of the models' effectiveness.

F1 Score: It is determined by averaging the two metrics, recall and accuracy.

$$F1\ \text{Score} = 2 \times \frac{\text{Precision} \times \text{Recall}}{\text{Precision} + \text{Recall}}$$

Accuracy: This is the general percentage of times the URL prediction method was correct.

$$\text{Accuracy} = \frac{\text{TP} + \text{TN}}{\text{TP} + \text{TN} + \text{FP} + \text{FN}}$$

Recall: Here is the proportion of successfully categorized positive forecasts of URLs.

$$\text{Recall} = \frac{\text{TP}}{\text{TP} + \text{FN}}$$

TP: The total amount of harmful URLs that were accurately identified as having malicious intent. TN: Number of safe URLs that were appropriately identified as true negatives. FP: The total amount of incorrectly identified URLs as harmful, including both benign and malicious ones. False negatives: The total number of harmful URLs that were mistakenly classed as benign.

RESULTS AND DISCUSSION

The recommended MUD model was thoroughly tested by three different machine learning classifiers, each of which was evaluated in terms of its accuracy, memory usage, and precision. To assess the outcomes of each learning classifier, exactness, recall, F1-score, and precision were used. This analysis is performed using the machine learning dataset that is stored in the UCI repository. In the workplace, a classifier is responsible for comparing and contrasting different patterns, as well as identifying differences between old patterns and new patterns.

To compare the three classifiers identified and labeled as dangerous and benign URLs, we consulted the confusion matrix (Table **1**). Naive Bayes achieved a maximum accuracy rating of 100%, while SVM achieved 98%, with logistic regression earning 96%, as shown in Table **2**. When logistic regression's recall rate is low compared to its precision and accuracy, the model may falsely label harmful URLs as benign, leading to a greater number of URLs being undetected. The classifier will incorrectly label good URLs as bad when the precision parameters are low. Fig. (**3**) illustrates the confusion matrix, a graphical representation of the evaluation tool that considers each classifier's correctness, F1 score, precision, and memory usage. The classifiers tested were able to get an accuracy and precision level of over 90%. Compared to logistic regression and Naive Bayes, SVM performed worse in URL classification. The effectiveness of the classifiers was significantly enhanced by the incorporation of lexical, host, and content-based URL information. To determine how well the prediction model using logistic regression classifies URLs, it was tested with several URLs, including both dangerous and benign ones, from Phish Tank. The model achieved an accuracy rate of 96%.

Table 1. Misperception Atmosphere for Estimation of the MUD Model.

		Predicted outcome	
		Positive	Negative
Actual value	Positive	True Positive	False Negative
	Negative	False Positive	True Negative

Table 2. Classifiers Evaluation in MUD Model.

Classifier	Accuracy (%)	F1 Score (%)	Precision (%)	Recall (%)
Support vector machine	98	9	98	95
Naive Bayes	100	100	100	100
Logistic regression	96	93	97	90

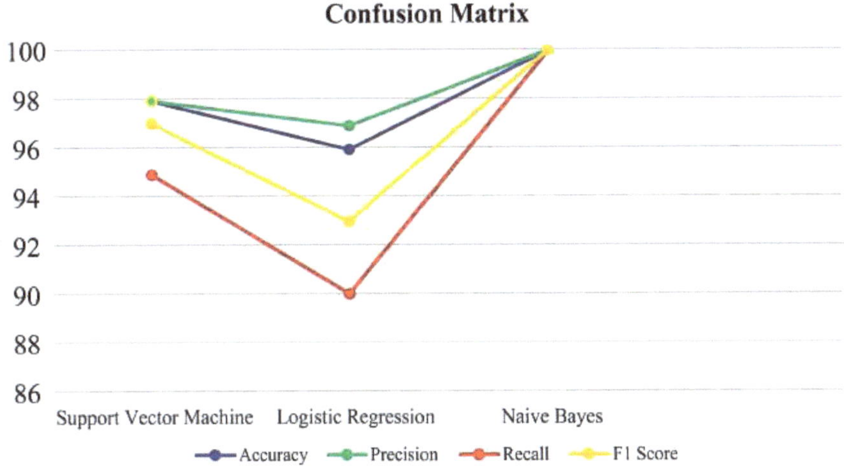

Fig. (3). Matrix of Confusion.

CONCLUSION

This chapter addresses a common cybersecurity concern: the exploitation of URLs to initiate various types of malicious attacks on unsuspecting individuals. The chapter suggests using machine learning techniques to identify harmful URLs as a solution to this problem. Three alternative mechanisms knowledge classifiers, including support vector machine, logistic regression, and Naïve Bayes, are used to train the suggested MUD (Malicious URL Detection) model. The dataset comprises 11,055 URLs, each with fifteen distinct attributes. The algorithms were tested and trained, and the results showed that the Naïve Bayes classifier had the best accuracy.

The researchers aim to evaluate the performance of the suggested model in this area in the future by assigning varying weights to different URL characteristic components. Another goal for the suggested model's online deployment is to function as a browser extension that can detect and block potentially dangerous websites in real-time. Analyze the characteristics of every URL that is clicked or inputted to identify dangerous ones. It will temporarily block the URL until the user decides to continue navigating to it, and a pop-up will notify them of the potential hazard if it is deemed harmful or suspected to be malicious. In addition to using additional classifiers, such as decision trees and random forests, future studies will validate the suggested approach against more current and varied datasets.

REFERENCES

[1] N. M. Thang, L. Q. Anh, H. S. Toàn, and N. Q. Trung, "A novel method for detecting URLs phishing using hybrid machine learning algorithm", Journal of Science and Technology on Information security, vol. 2, no. 19, 2023. [http://dx.doi.org/10.54654/isj.v2i19.978]

[2] O.V. Lee, A. Heryanto, M.F. Ab Razak, A.F.M. Raffei, D.N. Eh Phon, S. Kasim, and T. Sutikno, "A malicious URLs detection system using optimization and machine learning classifiers", *Indonesian Journal of Electrical Engineering and Computer Science,* vol. 17, no. 3, p. 1210, 2020. [http://dx.doi.org/10.11591/ijeecs.v17.i3.pp1210-1214]

[3] J. Ispahany, and R. Islam, "Detecting malicious COVID-19 URLs using machine learning techniques", *2021 IEEE International Conference on Pervasive Computing and Communications Workshops and other Affiliated Events, PerCom Workshops 2021,* 2021 [http://dx.doi.org/10.1109/PerComWorkshops51409.2021.9431064]

[4] S.S. Roy, A.I. Awad, L.A. Amare, M.T. Erkihun, and M. Anas, "Multimodel phishing URL detection using LSTM, bidirectional LSTM, and GRU models", *Future Internet,* vol. 14, no. 11, p. 340, 2022. [http://dx.doi.org/10.3390/fi14110340]

[5] R.A.M. Alsaidi, W.M.S. Yafooz, H. Alolofi, G.A.M. Taufiq-Hail, A.H.M. Emara, and A. Abdel-Wahab, "Ransomware detection using machine and deep learning approaches", *Int. J. Adv. Comput. Sci. Appl.,* vol. 13, no. 11, 2022. [http://dx.doi.org/10.14569/IJACSA.2022.0131112]

[6] F. Vanhoenshoven, G. Napoles, R. Falcon, K. Vanhoof, and M. Koppen, "Detecting malicious URLs using machine learning techniques", *2016 IEEE Symposium Series on Computational Intelligence, SSCI 2016,* 2017 [http://dx.doi.org/10.1109/SSCI.2016.7850079]

[7] S.M. Nair, "Detecting malicious URL using machine learning: A survey", *Int. J. Res. Appl. Sci. Eng. Technol.,* vol. 8, no. 5, pp. 2670-2677, 2020. [http://dx.doi.org/10.22214/ijraset.2020.5447]

[8] M. Aljabri, F. Alhaidari, R.M.A. Mohammad, Samiha Mirza, D.H. Alhamed, H.S. Altamimi, and S.M.B. Chrouf, "An assessment of lexical, network, and content-based features for detecting malicious

URLs using machine learning and deep learning models", *Comput. Intell. Neurosci.,* vol. 2022, pp. 1-14, 2022.
[http://dx.doi.org/10.1155/2022/3241216] [PMID: 36059391]

[9] M. Aljabri, H.S. Altamimi, S.A. Albelali, M. Al-Harbi, H.T. Alhuraib, N.K. Alotaibi, A.A. Alahmadi, F. Alhaidari, R.M.A. Mohammad, and K. Salah, "Detecting malicious URLs using machine learning techniques: Review and research directions", *IEEE Access,* vol. 10, pp. 121395-121417, 2022.
[http://dx.doi.org/10.1109/ACCESS.2022.3222307]

[10] F.M. Muller, J. Maebe, C. Vanhove, and S. Vandenberghe, "Dose reduction and image enhancement in micro-CT using deep learning", *Med. Phys.,* vol. 50, no. 9, pp. 5643-5656, 2023.
[http://dx.doi.org/10.1002/mp.16385] [PMID: 36994779]

[11] S. Sampath Kumar, T. Somasekhar, and P. Naresh Kumar Reddy, and T. Rajasanthosh kumar, "WITHDRAWN: Duplex stainless steel welding microstructures have been engineered for thermal welding cycles & Nitrogen (N) gas protection," Mater Today Proc, 2021.
[http://dx.doi.org/10.1016/j.matpr.2020.11.091]

[12] S.S Chauhan, and S.P. Yadav, Awashthi. S & Naruka. M.S, "Sentimental analysis using cloud dictionary and machine learning approach," *Cloud-based Intelligent Informative Engineering for Society 5.0*, Eds: K. Kishor, N. Saxena, D.. Pandey, 2023.

CHAPTER 28

Deep Facial Depth Map Learning for Obstructive Sleep Apnea Prediction

G. Durvasi[1,*], **D. Joseph Reethika**[1], **T. Nikitha**[1], **B. Sravani**[1] and **K. Gideon**[1]

[1] *Department of IT, Andhra Loyola Institute of Engineering and Technology, Vijayawada 520008, Andhra Pradesh, India*

Abstract: The condition known as Obstructive Sleep Apnea (OSA) occurs when the airway becomes frequently blocked during sleep due to the relaxation of the airway muscles and tongue. Snoring, disturbed sleep (from choking or gasping for breath), and lack of energy upon awakening are common symptoms of Obstructive Sleep Apnea (OSA). Diagnosing OSA is time-consuming and expensive. Many people go undiagnosed or misdiagnosed for this reason. The correlation between OSA and face shape has been shown in earlier studies. Using a depth map of scanned faces, this study explored the potential of deep learning for medical diagnosis. Deep maps provide a wealth of additional information on face morphology when contrasted with the more simplistic 2-D colour picture. They can obtain around 69% validation accuracy by using transfer learning, even when working with a small sample size. They are making predictions for people who have either above moderate OSA (>16) or below moderate OSA (≤ 16). In conclusion, the results of the simulations showed that the suggested VGG 19 outperformed the current method.

Keywords: Deep learning, Disturbed sleep, Face morphology, Obstructive sleep apnea, VGG 19.

INTRODUCTION

Lack of sleep has a major impact on personal and social activity [1]. There are several forms of sleep problems, and each one has its own unique cost [2]. OSA is the leading cause of all sleep disorders. When humans sleep, the muscles that line the throat relax just enough to keep the airway open [3 - 5]. However, with OSA, the airway may get repeatedly blocked for various reasons; each blockage lasts longer than 10 seconds; this deprives the lungs of oxygen, prompts the individual to wake up, and eventually restores the airway. It is possible to diagnose OSA if

* **Corresponding author G. Durvasi:** Department of IT, Andhra Loyola Institute of Engineering and Technology, Vijayawada 520008, Andhra Pradesh, India; E-mail: Kiran.durvasi@gmail.com

D. Arul Pon Daniel, T. Rajasanthosh Kumar & Satya Prakash Yadav (Eds.)

there are more than 16 apneas [6, 7]. To diagnose OSA, diagnostic imaging, a Polysomnography (PSG) test, a physical examination, and a patient history are used. As far as diagnostic tests go, the PSG test is crucial. This kind of sleep therapy requires the patient to remain in a hospital bed while sensors monitor their vitals, including their breathing, heart rate, and movement [8]. While there are technologies that may assist patients in completing these tests at home, their accuracy and reliability are still debated compared to PSG. The evaluation is completed by calculating the Apnea-Hypopnea Index (AHI). Sleep apnea is classified according to its severity using these criteria [9]. Many people with Obstructive Sleep Apnea (OSA) get misdiagnosed until they have serious symptoms because of the time and money needed to do the PSG, the intrusiveness of the procedure, the generalizability of OSA symptoms, and the scarcity of sleep clinics. In the past, there have been several efforts to use questionnaires as a predictor of OSA [10]. Some risk assessments utilize indicators such as snoring, fatigue, body mass index, and Blood Pressure (BP) to make predictions, while others, like the Epworth Sleepiness Scale, measure drowsiness in various contexts throughout the day [11, 12]. They have limitations in correctly identifying afflicted persons when administered self-administered and are expensive [13, 14].

METHODOLOGY AND DATASET

Genesis Sleep Care patients who attend for various sleep disorders and who participate in home or laboratory sleep tests have their sleep data and 3D images taken. The ECU Human Research Ethics Committee granted permission for the research, and to date, forty men and thirty-one women have participated.

Data Sets

Two categories, like "Abnormal and normal," are present in the dataset. Both the normal and abnormal categories include 111 photos, with the former offering 100. Genesis Sleep Care patients who visit for various sleep disorders and who undergo in-home or in-lab sleep testing provided the information and 3D scans used in this study. So far, the project, which has received approval from the ECU Researchers Ethics Committee, has included a total of forty male and thirty-one female participants. Fig. (**1**) shows an outline of the stages in all of the processes. Artec Eva takes the 3D scans with the help of Artec Studio. The changes in posture and added artefacts are the result of these scans being captured by separate groups at different locations. Examples of 3D raw photos from the dataset as depicted in Fig. (**2**).

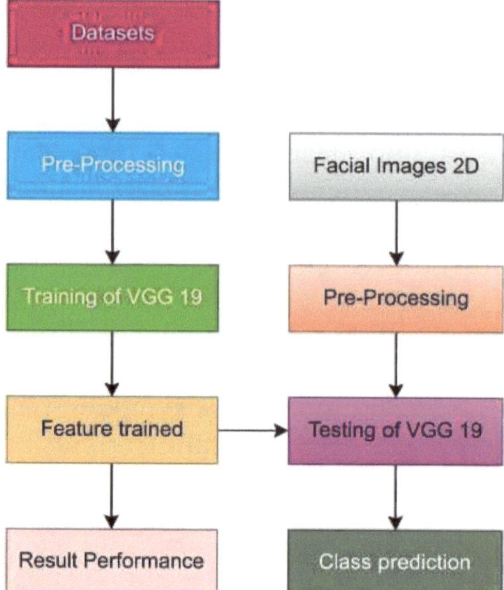

Fig. (1). Outline of the Stages (Process).

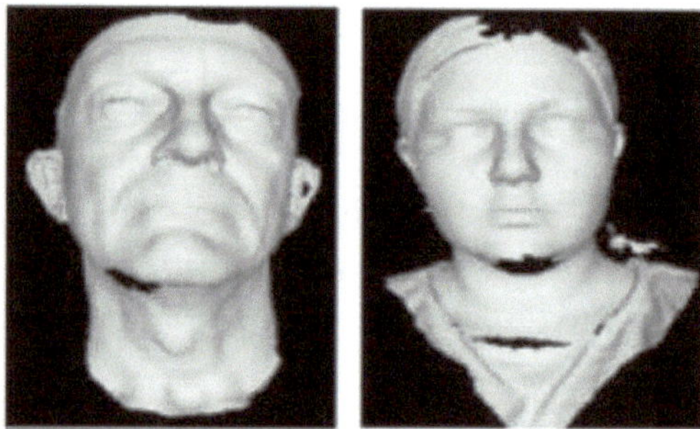

Fig. (2). Examples of 3D raw photos from the dataset.

Reducing these undesired differences is the objective while transforming these 3D images into frontal 2D depth maps. Every one of the 3D scans had its flaws fixed using Artec Studio. Sample raw and pre-processed pictures from Fig. (**2**) as demonstrated in Fig. (**3**).

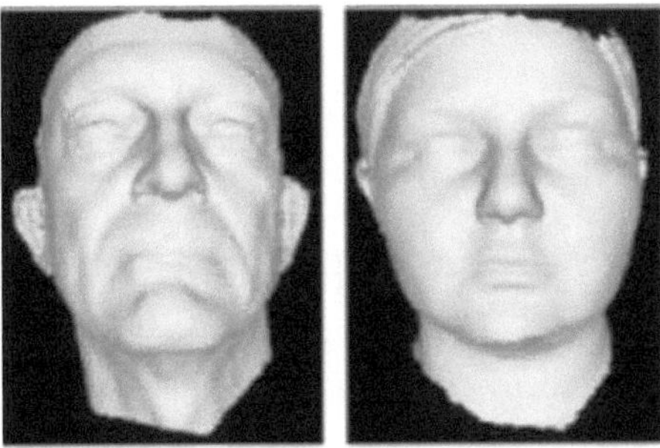

Fig. (3). Sample raw and pre-processed pictures from Fig. 2.

As illustrated in Fig. (**4**) (two-dimensional facial depth maps), the highest and lowest scales are selected to get a greater resolution across all depth values. This is done after they have made adjustments to the default postures and other criteria.

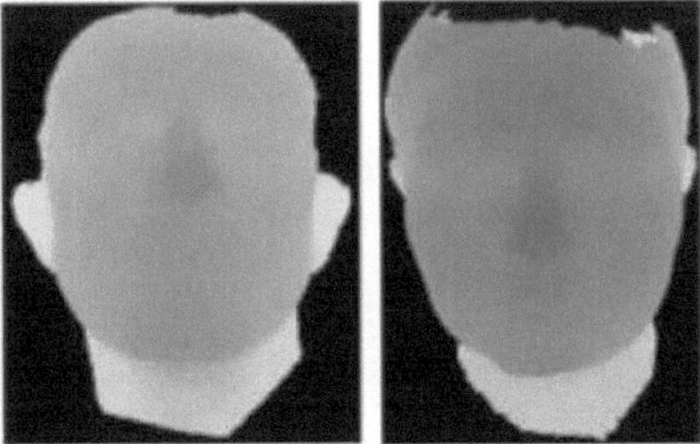

Fig. (4). Two-dimensional facial depth maps.

Preliminary Processing

The term "digital image processing" refers to the process of modifying digital photographs using mathematical methods. Digital image processing, a branch of DSP, offers several benefits over its analogue counterpart. To optimize the image information (features) used by the AI-computer vision models, digital image processing aims to suppress undesirable distortions and/or enhance some important features. This paves the way for a much wider range of methods to be utilized for the input data.

Images must be the same size as the network's input to train the net and use it to generate predictions on fresh data. Resizing an image to fit the network specifications is as simple as cropping it.

Image Resize

This stage involves creating two image display functions: one for one picture and another for two images. This will help each of us identify the change. The next step is to create a processing function that takes the photos as an argument and does nothing else. During the pre-processing step, they need to resize the photographs. Since the sizes of the images acquired by the camera and input into the artificial intelligence system may vary, it is essential to establish a standard size for all images.

VGG 19

There is not nearly enough data to train a Convolutional Neural Network (CNN) from the start. For this reason, the team utilized three separate networks that had already been trained for facial recognition. To transfer learning with the dataset, they opted for VGG Face Pose-Aware CNN Models (PAMs) for facial identification. Picking networks that have been trained on faces before, without focusing on depth maps for faces, gives them a good head start when learning. These tests also show that using face depth maps to fine-tune facial recognition is beneficial. VGG-Face achieved an impressive 98.96% accuracy after being trained on millions of photos. The architecture of this net is based on VGG-Ver--Deep-16 CNN. The researcher supplied two facial recognition networks that were previously trained: one using AlexNet and the other using a 19-layer VGGNet. Each network type is transformed to achieve bi-class classification by replacing its final fully connected layer with a new fully connected layer and a softmax layer. The block diagrams of the three networks, once the final layers are added, are shown below (Fig. **5**).

Fig. (5). Three Networks' Block Diagrams.

Background

VGG is a successor to AlexNet, which was released in 2012 and built upon traditional Convolutional Neural Networks; however, it was established by a separate group at Oxford University called the Visual Geometry Group, hence the name VGG. VGG incorporates and builds upon ideas from AlexNet and its predecessors, employing deep Convolutional neural layers to enhance accuracy.

The purpose of this study is to examine VGG19 in comparison to previous iterations of the VGG framework and to identify its practical and valuable uses. Examining ImageNet and gaining a foundational understanding of CNN will prepare us to explore the VGG19 Architecture. VGG is a deep network of Convolutional Neural Networks (CNN) that can identify pictures.

Architecture

- The square matrix has the dimensions (224, 224, 3) since the net was fed an RGB picture with a fixed dimension of (224 × 224).
- The only step in the pre-processing was to remove the average RGB value from all pixels in the training set.
- They covered the whole picture by using kernels of size (3 × 3), with a stride measurement of 1 pixel.
- To retain the image's spatial resolution, spatial padding was used.
- Maximum pooling was performed using side 2 on 2×2-pixel blocks.
- The Rectified Linear Unit (ReLU) was then employed to enhance the model's classification accuracy and reduce computing time. Compared to prior models that relied on tanh or sigmoid functions, this one performed far better.
- The three completely linked layers were as follows: a 4096-size initial layer, a 1000-channel layer for a softmax function, and a 1000-way ILSVRC classification for the final layer.

Fundamentals of CNN

The convolution layer learns the characteristics of a picture by analyzing small blocks of source data and preserves the connection between pixels; it is the principal layer for feature extraction from source images. This mathematical function takes two parameters, one of which is the source picture, and returns the spatial coordinates of the image, or the number of columns and rows. The size of the input picture and a filter or kernel that is proportional to it are represented by and, respectively, as are the image dimensions (in this case, since the original image is RGB).

The ReLU layer

A Rectified Linear Unit (ReLU) network uses the rectifier's operation for its hidden layers. If the input value is larger than zero, the simple calculation known as the ReLU function returns the input value directly. Otherwise, it returns zero. Mathematically, this may be expressed as follows, using the input and the set defined by the function:

$$g(x) = Max\{0, x\}$$

2.4.2. Maximum Pooling Layer

This layer reduces the number of parameters needed for bigger photos. Subsampling, also known as downsampling, reduces the dimensionality of each feature map while preserving the crucial data. The maximum element from the corrected feature map is considered in the max pooling operation.

2.4.3. Classifier Softmax

In this case, X is the input to all the models, Y is the output, and the hidden layers sandwiched between X and Y constitute the data pipeline. The goal is to predict which of the ten classifications the input belongs to. In this case, they assign a specific projected output to each class. This indicates that the class forecast is based on its greatest likelihood out of ten possible outputs, each representing a distinct class. The softmax classifier block diagram is shown in Fig. (**6**).

RESULTS AND DISCUSSION

In the next part, a comprehensive examination of the simulation results that were implemented utilizing the "Python environment" is presented. An additional comparison is made between the performance of the proposed approach and that of current methods by using the same dataset.

3.1. The Modules

In this module, Fig. (**7**) depicts the predicted OSA dataset results, and Fig. (**8**) displays the accuracy performance comparison.

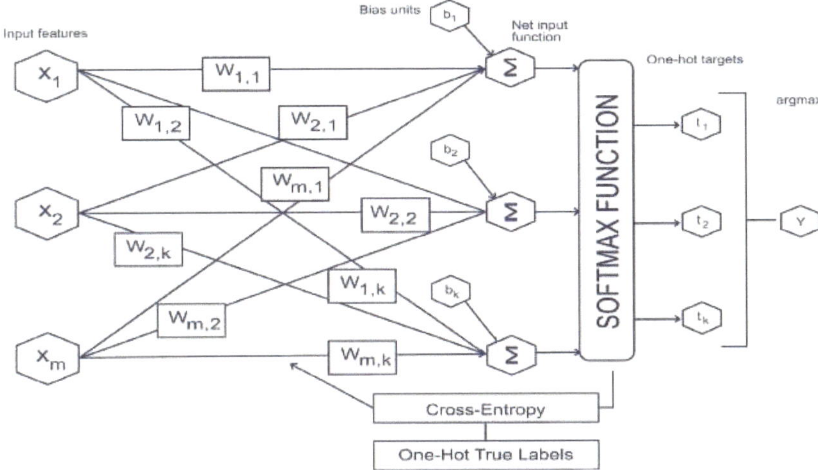

Fig. (6). Softmax Classifier Block Diagram.

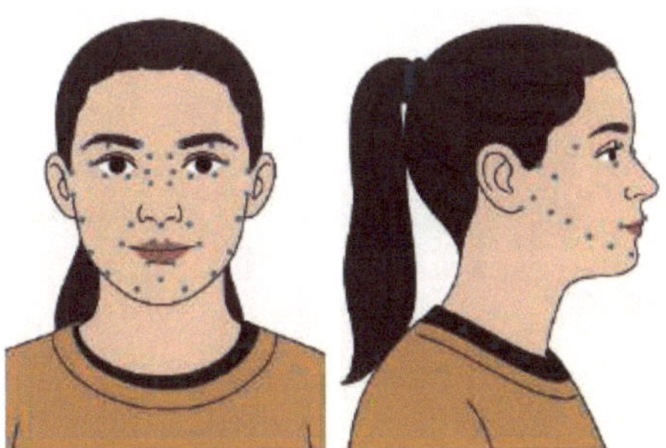

Fig. (7). Predicted OSA Dataset Results.

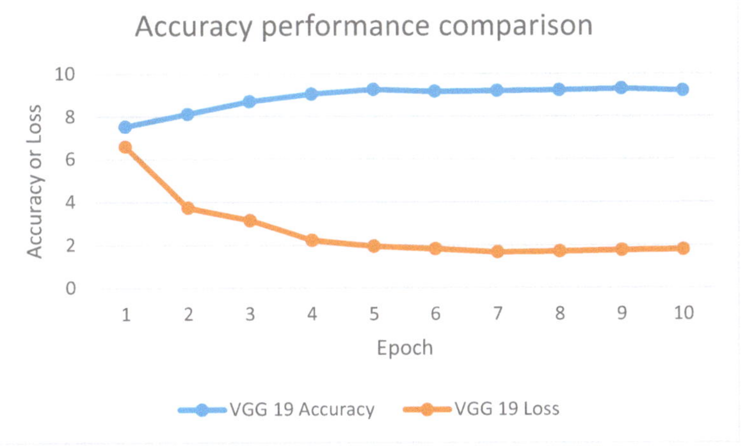

Fig. (8). Accuracy Performance Comparison.

- Obtain the OSA Faces Dataset: This section is where we will place the dataset that the software requires.
- Pre-process Dataset: This module will be used to read all photos, scale them to the same size, and then normalize their pixel values.
- Construct a VGG-19 Model: The VGG-19 algorithm will be trained using the processed pictures.
- Upload Test Information & Predict OSA: This module is used to upload fresh test images and then use the VGG19-trained model to determine whether the images are normal or if they include OSA illness.
- Graph for Comparing Accuracy: This module will be used to create a graph for comparing the accuracy and loss of VGG19 training (Fig. **8**).

CONCLUSION

The disease known as Obstructive Sleep Apnea occurs when the tongue relaxes and the airway muscles obstruct the airway many times while a person sleeps. Snoring, trouble sleeping due to gasping for air or choking, and feeling fatigued upon waking up are common symptoms. Many instances go unrecognized or misdiagnosed since diagnosing OSA may be a costly and time-consuming procedure. A link between OSA and facial features has been shown in earlier research. The purpose of this research was to investigate the feasibility of utilizing depth maps of scanned faces to support medical diagnosis using deep learning methods. When compared to standard 2-D colour photographs, depth maps provide much more information on facial morphology. The research validated the model with an accuracy of around 69% using transfer learning methods on a limited sample set. The categorization of patients with above-or below-moderate OSA (>16) was the main focus of the predictions. The results of the simulations demonstrated that the proposed approach, utilizing the VGG-19 architecture, was more effective in diagnosing OSA than the current methods. This indicates that deep learning and depth map analysis have significant potential as techniques to enhance OSA diagnosis, potentially leading to earlier diagnosis and more effective treatment. A 3D morphable model will one day address the challenge of posture correction. An automated process will generate depth maps with holes filled. Diagnostic performance can be further enhanced by incorporating additional 3D scans of individuals both with and without OSA, especially considering that this study achieved excellent results despite using a limited dataset.

REFERENCES

[1] V. Molnár, L. Kunos, L. Tamás, and Z. Lakner, "Evaluation of the applicability of artificial intelligence for the prediction of obstructive sleep apnoea", *Appl. Sci. (Basel),* vol. 13, no. 7, p. 4231, 2023.

[http://dx.doi.org/10.3390/app13074231]

[2] H. Nasifoglu, and O. Erogul, "Obstructive sleep apnea prediction from electrocardiogram scalograms and spectrograms using convolutional neural networks", *Physiol. Meas.,* vol. 42, no. 6, p. 065010, 2021.
[http://dx.doi.org/10.1088/1361-6579/ac0a9c] [PMID: 34116519]

[3] R.W.W. Lee, P. Petocz, T. Prvan, A.S.L. Chan, R.R. Grunstein, and P.A. Cistulli, "Prediction of obstructive sleep apnea with craniofacial photographic analysis", *Sleep,* vol. 32, no. 1, pp. 46-52, 2009.
[http://dx.doi.org/10.5665/sleep/32.1.46] [PMID: 19189778]

[4] H. Uppal, A. Sepas-Moghaddam, M. Greenspan, and A. Etemad, "Depth as attention for face representation learning", *IEEE Trans. Inf. Forensics Security,* vol. 16, pp. 2461-2476, 2021.
[http://dx.doi.org/10.1109/TIFS.2021.3053458]

[5] F. Khan, W. Shariff, M.A. Farooq, S. Basak, and P. Corcoran, "A robust light-weight fused-feature encoder-decoder model for monocular facial depth estimation from single images trained on synthetic data", *IEEE Access,* vol. 11, pp. 41480-41491, 2023.
[http://dx.doi.org/10.1109/ACCESS.2023.3267970]

[6] W. Wu, Y. Yin, X. Wang, and D. Xu, "Face detection with different scales based on faster R-CNN", *IEEE Trans. Cybern.,* vol. 49, no. 11, pp. 4017-4028, 2019.
[http://dx.doi.org/10.1109/TCYB.2018.2859482] [PMID: 30113907]

[7] L. Nanni, S. Brahnam, A. Lumini, and A. Loreggia, "Coupling retinaFace and depth information to filter false positives", *Appl. Sci. (Basel),* vol. 13, no. 5, p. 2987, 2023.
[http://dx.doi.org/10.3390/app13052987]

[8] M. Behzad, N. Vo, X. Li, and G. Zhao, "Towards reading beyond faces for sparsity-aware 3D/4D affect recognition", *Neurocomputing,* vol. 458, pp. 297-307, 2021.
[http://dx.doi.org/10.1016/j.neucom.2021.06.023]

[9] Y. Yan, C. Han, J. Qin, H. Chen, and T. Guo, "Facial depth descend: A generation paradigm for facial depth map", *Neurocomputing,* vol. 466, pp. 298-310, 2021.
[http://dx.doi.org/10.1016/j.neucom.2021.09.010]

[10] O. K. Oyedotun, G. Demisse, A. El Rahman Shabayek, D. Aouada, and B. Ottersten, "Facial expression recognition via joint deep learning of RGB-Depth map latent representations," in Proceedings - 2017 IEEE International Conference on Computer Vision Workshops, ICCVW 2017, 2017.
[http://dx.doi.org/10.1109/ICCVW.2017.374]

[11] S. Umirzakova, S. Ahmad, S. Mardieva, S. Muksimova, and T.K. Whangbo, "Deep learning-driven diagnosis: A multi-task approach for segmenting stroke and Bell's palsy", *Pattern Recognit.,* vol. 144, p. 109866, 2023.
[http://dx.doi.org/10.1016/j.patcog.2023.109866]

[12] X. Jin, Z. Lai, W. Sun, and Z. Jin, "Facial expression recognition based on depth fusion and discriminative association learning", *Neural Process. Lett.,* vol. 54, no. 3, pp. 2025-2047, 2022.
[http://dx.doi.org/10.1007/s11063-021-10717-1]

[13] P. Patro, "A hybrid approach estimates the real-time health state of a bearing by accelerated degradation tests," *Machine Learning*, vol. 110, no. 9, pp. 2307–2330, 2021.
[http://dx.doi.org/10.1007/s10994-021-06065-7]

[14] A. Seem, A. K. Chauhan, R. Khan, and S. P. Yadav, "Distributed artificial intelligence for document retrieval," in Distributed Artificial Intelligence: A Modern Approach", S. P. Yadav, D. P. Mahato, and N. T. D. Linh, Eds., Boca Raton, FL, USA: CRC Press, Taylor & Francis Group, 2020, pp. 59–68.
[http://dx.doi.org/10.1201/9781003038467□4]

SUBJECT INDEX

D. Arul Pon Daniel, T. Rajasanthosh Kumar & Satya Prakash Yadav (Eds.)

D

E

F

G

H

I

K

L

M

N

O

P

Q

R

S

T

U

V

W

Y

www.ingramcontent.com/pod-product-compliance
Lightning Source LLC
LaVergne TN
LVHW070116110826
845147LV00002B/133

* 9 7 8 9 8 1 5 3 2 4 9 8 3 *